STUDIES IN VICTORIAN
LIFE AND LITERATURE

Portrait of Anne Thackeray Ritchie by Richard Frederic Watts, 1862. From Winifred Gérin, *Anne Thackeray Ritchie: A Biography* (1981). By courtesy of Oxford University Press.

Anne Thackeray Ritchie
Journals and Letters

Biographical Commentary and Notes by Lillian F. Shankman
Edited by Abigail Burnham Bloom and John Maynard

Ohio State University Press
Columbus

Copyright © 1994 by the Ohio State University Press.
All rights reserved.

Publication of this book has been aided by a grant from the Abraham and Rebecca Stein Faculty Publication Fund of New York University, Department of English.

Library of Congress Cataloging-in-Publication Data
Ritchie, Anne Thackeray, 1837–1919.
[Selections. 1994]
Anne Thackeray Ritchie : journals and letters / biographical commentary and notes by Lillian F. Shankman ; edited by Abigail Burnham Bloom and John Maynard.
p. cm. — (Studies in Victorian life and literature)
Includes bibliographical references and index.
ISBN 0 8142–0638–7. — ISBN 0–8142–0639–5 (pbk.)
1. Ritchie, Anne Thackeray, 1837–1919—Diaries. 2. Ritchie, Anne Thackeray, 1837–1919—Correspondence. 3. Women novelists, English—19th century—Correspondence. 4. Women novelists, English—19th century—Diaries. I. Shankman, Lillian F., 1922–1987.
II. Bloom, Abigail Burnham. III. Maynard, John, 1941–
IV. Title. V. Series.
PR5227.R7Z476 1994
828'.803—dc20
[B]   94-15018
                                                                          CIP

Text design by Jim Mennick.
Jacket design by Hunter graphics.
Type set in Bembo by Tseng Information Systems, Inc., Durham, North Carolina.
Printed by Bookcrafters, Inc., Chelsea, Michigan.

The paper in this book meets the guidelines for permanence and durability of the Committee on Production Guidelines for Book Longevity of the Council on Library Resources. ∞

For my husband, Leonard I. Shankman

Contents

Preface *ix*
Acknowledgments *xv*
Editors' Note *xvii*
Genealogy of Anne Thackeray Ritchie *xx*
Chronology *xxi*

1. 1840–1851   *1*
   Letters *1–11*   *11*
2. 1852–1858   *27*
   Letters *12–26*   *37*
3. 1859–1863   *59*
   Letters *27–40*   *71*
4. 1864–1865   *98*
   Journal   *119*
   Letters *41–50*   *141*
5. 1866–1877   *154*
   Letters *51–65*   *173*
6. 1878   *187*
   Journal   *197*
7. 1879–1900   *213*
   Letters *66–98*   *229*
8. 1901–1919   *258*
   Letters *99–115*   *272*

Appendix: Chronological Summary of Letters, 1846–1919   *285*
Abbreviations   *293*
Notes   *295*
Works by Anne Thackeray Ritchie, 1860–1920   *357*
Index   *365*

Preface

ANNE Isabella Thackeray was born in 1837, the year of Victoria's ascendancy to the throne. The young Anny remembered and later recorded in her journals a nightmare journey in a coach to Paris that she made in 1840; as an old woman she stoically vacated her London home after it was bombed by a German plane during the First World War. Like the world around her, her life was full of extraordinary events and her writing reflects this changing world. Although Anny never ceased to be William Makepeace Thackeray's daughter, she merits study in her own right. She not only inherited many of her father's attributes, but she was also a unique person and writer.

The particular circumstances of the Thackeray family, brought about by the insanity of Isabella Thackeray, Anny's mother, contributed to the close relationship between father and daughter. Being motherless left its mark on Anny, but Thackeray helped to enlarge her world in a way that would not have been possible had Isabella been present. From the age of fourteen she was his amanuensis, writing from his dictation large sections of *Henry Esmond* and his later works. The man and his precepts loom large over her own writing. He taught her honesty, independence, and disdain of humbug; his was the greatest influence in her life. Anny was a complex woman who enjoyed a full and active life. Overcoming tragedy, she lived with enthusiasm and joy, while inwardly bedeviled by traumatic events which haunted her. She became Lady Ritchie, but she was always that intriguing phenomenon: a Victorian lady. Raised by Thackeray, and with his imprint always upon her, she nonetheless developed a flair for living that was uniquely her own.

Like her father, Anny was much admired by her friends; and although her prose does not generally suggest the range of her father's vision nor his classic polish of language, she was also a thoroughly distinguished person of letters. William Makepeace Thackeray asserted in 1846 that his nine-year-old daughter Anne Isabella was "going to be a man of genius."[1] Because of her originality Anny has always been difficult to categorize. The appellation "genius" followed her throughout her life, expressing the esteem with which she was regarded by so many persons and suggesting her extraordinary qualities. Matthew Arnold,[2] George Smith,[3] Leslie Stephen,[4] Algernon Swinburne,[5] Henry James,[6] and later Virginia Woolf[7] all recognized that she was a unique "personage."[8] Edward FitzGerald named Anne "a chip of the old Block."[9] Among other Victorians who admired her work were Robert Browning, who dedicated a book to her,[10] Robert Louis Stevenson, who wrote a poem to her,[11] and George Eliot, who claimed that Anne Thackeray was the only contemporary novelist (apart from a little of Anthony Trollope) she read. Trollope too admired Anny's writing, although with some qualifications.[12] After her father's death, Anny retained the esteem she had earned among her father's friends and literary contemporaries. She also acquired new friends who admired her both for her inherited genius and for her individuality.

Anne Thackeray's connection with Virginia Woolf is of major importance. When Leslie Stephen remarried after the death of his first wife (Anny's sister, Minny Thackeray), Anne Thackeray became Aunt Anny to Virginia and the other Duckworth-Stephen children. Aunt Anny was the model of a female writer for the young Virginia Stephen; later Virginia used her aunt as the basis for her characterization of Mrs. Hilbery in *Night and Day*.

Although not an activist, Anny espoused the feminist point of view before it had a name. Contemporary critics are starting to find Anny a genial subject, and yet much more work needs to be done. The recent biography by Winifred Gérin, and many recent articles as well, give Anny the prominence she deserves. Through the work of Gérin and others it is no longer true, as it was for a long period in this century, that Anny is mentioned only rarely and then in passing. This addition to the published body of Anny's writing was prepared in the hope that it will encourage further interest in her and her works.

Any discussion of Anne Thackeray Ritchie must consider both the woman and her work. She was a woman of great warmth, imagination, and sensitivity. Above all, she was a writer. She wrote letters, journals, introductions, essays, reminiscences, short stories, and novels. She began at a very early age, and she wrote until she died: on scraps of paper, in notebooks, on anything that would hold her words. She published twenty-one books, but her books represent only a portion of her creativity.

In the late 1800s and the early 1900s most of Anny's books went into several printings and were published in Europe and in the United States as well as in London. Her introductions to Thackeray's works provided much needed biographical material about him, and set a pattern for personal introductions. Among her five novels, *Old Kensington*, the best known, describes her life with Thackeray during the years when he wrote *Vanity Fair*, *Pendennis*, and *Henry Esmond*. Because she was Thackeray's daughter and social companion, she knew intimately the men and women of literary and artistic London. Years later, when she wrote about them, her reminiscences were evocative but uncluttered. She had known them as her father's friends and they had responded to her without the distancing of a public persona.

Of her writings, those that most illuminate the woman and her great gift for life and also demonstrate her ability as a writer are her letters and journals. This book offers the reader an ample selection of Anny's most interesting letters, her complete journals written in 1864–65 and 1878, and a number of significant letters written to her. As we learn about Anny through her writings, we also learn about Thackeray, the mainspring around which she built her life, and about the Victorian literary world in which she played a major role.

What I originally perceived as an addendum to Thackeray scholarship—an intimate look at him through his daughter's eyes—soon took on a life of its own. With the discovery of more and more letters, my knowledge of Anny grew, and so did my sense of her inheritance of genius. Because she was both a writer and a Victorian, her correspondence was prodigious. Through the letters selected here I have tried to account for Anny's character as well as her career. From the beginning Anny's correspondence was incisive and revelatory. Her ease with words, her joy in writing, and her humor manifest themselves in her earliest letters and provide corroborating evidence of her growth as a writer. Anny's early writing was nurtured and encouraged by Thackeray. Overshadowed by her father, Anny was content to be Thackeray's daughter. It was not until after he died that her talent expanded in the freedom that his death afforded.

Anny's writing, as illustrated by her letters and journals, is a worthy legacy to the modern reader. The 1864–65 journal and the 1878 journal bear detailed discussion. Started shortly after Thackeray's death, the 1864–65 journal is an eloquent and evocative statement of a daughter's love for her father written within an elegant hard-bound journal with a brass clasp lock. Disclosing intimate details of their life together, the picture of Thackeray which emerges substantiates Gordon Ray's positive conception of him in *Thackeray: The Age of Wisdom*. With some additions the 1878 journal goes over much the same ground as the earlier one, but demonstrates Anny's changed outlook on life. Fourteen years older and married, she recounts for her niece the episodes that bear retelling for a child. Although the journal is polished and charming, and reflects her own happiness, it nevertheless reveals her fears and insecurities. The journals, particularly the 1864–65 journal, are documents that stand on their own literary merit. Because they deal so fully with both Anny and her father, they are doubly important.

The largest portion of the manuscripts and letters presented here come from the major Anne Thackeray Ritchie collection of the late Gordon N. Ray, now in The Pierpont Morgan Library in New York. These letters and journals have been supplemented by additional letters written by Anny, located in collections both in England and in the United States, as well as letters from Anny's intimates and friends located in the Ray collection and in other repositories. This book neither exhausts the Ray collection nor the wealth of Anny's correspondence in other repositories; rather, it presents enough of Anny's nonfictional prose to suggest her interest as a person and importance as a writer and literary figure.[13] The greater part of Anny's two journals, as well as the letters from the Ray collection, have not been previously published: in the case of the journals, less than a third. Anny herself used the journals as source material for the introductions to her father's works. Because she was the author of the phrases borrowed, she had the privilege of editing, but not of changing content. This she never did. However, Anny's daughter, Hester Ritchie Fuller, not only corrupted the text but used it without footnotes or attribution in her books *Thackeray and His Daughter* and *Thackeray's Daughter*. She borrowed phrases and entire sentences, attributing them to "Family History," transposing them, and silently editing not only the style but the content. More recently, Ray accurately transcribed and attributed small portions of the journals and five of the letters in his works: *Thackeray: The Uses of Adversity, The Age of Wisdom,* and *The Buried Life*. Gérin also used extracts from the journals in her recent biography. By publishing the journals in their entirety and within a context created by the letters it is hoped that a much fuller and coherent picture of Anne Thackeray Ritchie will be formed than has previously been available.

Of all the dilemmas encountered, the one I have most wrestled with concerns her name. From childhood she was "Anny." As was then the custom, her first writings in periodicals were unsigned, but her first book was attributed to "Miss Thackeray." After her marriage she signed her letters "Anne Ritchie"; her books still bore the name "Miss Thackeray" and in parentheses "Mrs. Richmond Ritchie." When her husband was knighted, she signed herself "Lady Ritchie" in her published work. To call her "Anny" as a child seemed natural. When I discussed her adult work, it became a problem. To call her "Thackeray" before she was married led to confusion. To switch to "Ritchie" once she was married, led to further havoc, particularly in the chapter in which her husband Richmond Ritchie becomes crucial. And so, with few exceptions, she remained "Anny," as she did to her friends.

Acknowledgments

I am indebted to many people for this book. The late Professor Gordon N. Ray graciously gave me the use of his collection of manuscripts and guided me through the long and circuitous route I took. Not only his professionalism, his erudition, and his scholarship but his understanding and patience through my difficulties enabled me to finish this work. I am most deeply grateful to him.

I would like to thank other members of the English Department of New York University, particularly Professors William E. Buckler, John Maynard, and Edwin H. Miller.

I would also like to acknowledge my thanks to the authorities of the following institutions for granting me permission to use manuscripts found in their libraries: Armstrong Browning Library, Baylor University; British Library; Maude Morrison Frank Papers, Rare Book and Manuscript Library, Columbia University; Houghton Library, Harvard University; Huntington Library, San Marino, California; India Office Library and Records; Pierpont Morgan Library, New York; Henry W. and Albert A. Berg Collection, New York Public Library; Fales Library, New York University; Morris L. Parrish Collection, Princeton University Libraries; University of London Library; Beinecke Rare Book and Manuscript Library, Yale University.

To my family and friends, particularly my husband, Leonard I. Shankman, and Roseann and Richard Shankman; Marjorie Lederer Lee and Professor Mervyn J. Meggitt; Doctors Carmel Cohen, Frederick King, and Charles Winkelstein, I acknowledge my debt of gratitude. Their encouragement and belief in the possibility of this work made it inconceivable for me to give up. Gratefully, I am delighted and amply rewarded for becoming better acquainted with Thackeray and for getting to know his remarkable daughter Anne Thackeray Ritchie—Anny.

Lillian F. Shankman

Editors' Note

ALTHOUGH contemporary practice, with which we generally agree, is to use last names of female as well as male writers, we have left Dr. Shankman's more familiar use of "Anny" throughout for her voice as editor. Her many years of working with these intimate records created quite naturally a friend, with whom she, if not we, had a right to be on a first-name basis.

Dr. Lillian Shankman wrote in her introduction to this work, "My intention is to present the letters as close to their original state as possible." The editors decided, following Dr. Shankman, to preserve the casual and spontaneous quality of the original letters and journals. No silent emendations have been made, except as indicated in the following principles, which have been developed to assure the consistency and readability of the letters and journals presented here.

1. It has often been difficult to distinguish between the author's formation of capital and lower case letters. Unless the author's intention is clear, we have let logic dictate.
2. Anne Thackeray Ritchie frequently used her own symbol "∝" for the word "and"; this has been printed as the more common symbol "&."
3. Ritchie's dashes, sometimes longer and shorter in her hand, have been regularized.
4. Words not satisfactorily ascertained have been followed by a question mark placed within brackets. An attempt had been made to indicate, within brackets, the number of illegible words.
5. "[*Sic*]" has been used to indicate misspellings and other errors in the manuscript where the reader might otherwise be confused; we have not marked normal variations in informal spelling or other punctuation, which occur frequently, especially in children's writing. We have not attempted to point out Ritchie's errors in foreign languages, but have provided a translation where helpful.

6. Ritchie did not consistently indent paragraphs. If a line stops short and a new sentence begins on the left margin, this intentional lacuna is indicated in the text by an indented paragraph.

7. Inserts that seem to have been made at the time of writing by Ritchie have been included in their intended place without comment. Words that have been crossed out have been given in a footnote if they are of interest. All words added at a later time by her or by a different hand are indicated as such in a footnote.

8. Dates have been consistently placed on the right, where they are almost always found. Postmarks are clearly marked as such, and placed within brackets. Dates established through direct references in the text are given in brackets; dates established through other references or our guesswork are given in brackets followed by a footnote. Letters without a firm date are placed at their earliest possible date. Addresses are provided only when they occur in the letters.

9. Dr. Shankman attempted to present the complete text of each letter and each journal. When any portion of a letter is missing, this has been noted. This most frequently occurs when the signature has been cut off, most likely for autograph seekers.

10. Through the generosity of Ohio State University Press, we have provided reproductions of Ritchie's sketches on letters whenever we have been able to obtain suitable copies, which was possible in the vast majority of cases. They show another inherited genius, for inspired doodles. They are placed where they occur in the flow of text unless otherwise noted.

We wish to thank Richard D. Altick, for most helpful suggestions; John W. Bicknell; Betty Coley; Leon Edel; Carol Hanbery MacKay; Helen Young of the University of London Library. Alex Holzman and the staff of the Ohio State University Press have been most accommodating in every stage of our work.

We would not have been able to undertake this project without Leonard Shankman's warm support and encouragement. We are especially grateful to Dr. Lillian F. Shankman, who introduced us both to Anne Thackeray Ritchie studies, but who died before completing this work for publication. We have not noted the editors' contributions separately when we have merely added to Dr. Shankman's notes. We are pleased to have helped in making these letters—most not previously published—and above all Ritchie's important and most interesting journals, available in the attractive and useful form developed by Dr. Shankman.

Letters, journals, and other materials from Ritchie and the Thackeray family are here published by kind permission of Mrs. Belinda Norman-Butler. Letters by Robert Browning, Henry James, and Leslie Stephen are published by courtesy of John Murray, Alexander James, and Quentin Bell, the respective copyright owners.

A.B.B.
J.M.

Genealogy of Anne Thackeray Ritchie

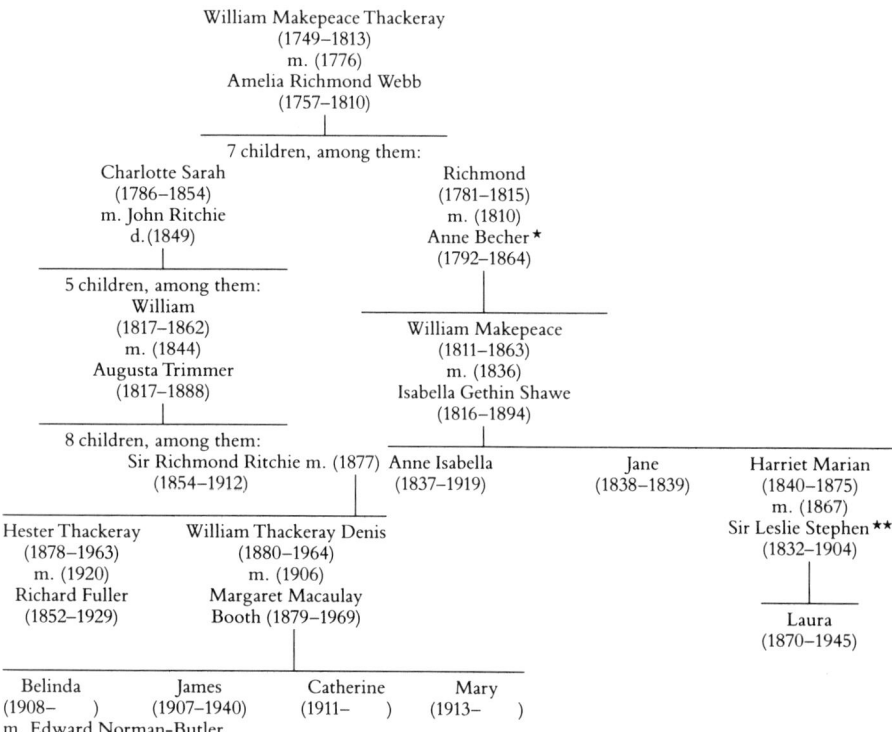

* In 1817 Mrs. Thackeray remarried, her second husband being Captain Henry Carmichael-Smyth.
** In 1878 Stephen remarried, his second wife being Mrs. Julia Duckworth. Among their children were Vanessa (Stephen) Bell and Virginia (Stephen) Woolf.

Chronology

1811
William Makepeace Thackeray born, Calcutta — 18 July

1816[1]
Isabella Gethin Shawe born, India — 5 December

1836
Thackeray marries Isabella, Paris — 20 August

1837
Anne Isabella Thackeray (Anny) born, London — 9 June

1838
Jane Thackeray born — 9 July

1839
Jane dies — 14 March

1840
Harriet Marian Thackeray (Minny) born — 27 May[2]
Isabella attempts suicide — Sept.
Thackeray brings Anny and Minny to Paris to live with Carmichael-Smyths — October–November

1845
Thackeray brings Isabella to live in Camberwell with companion — October

1846
Anny and Minny return to London to live with Thackeray at 13, Young Street, Kensington — Late September

1847

Vanity Fair in monthly numbers — January 1847–June 1848

1849

Anny and Minny with Carmichael-Smyths in Wales — July–October
Thackeray ill in London with cholera — 17 September–December

1851

Thackeray, Anny, and Minny in Paris — 8 January–7 February
Thackerays travel on Continent — 10 July–22 August

1852

Thackerays tour Europe — June
Carmichael-Smyths, Anny, and Minny tour Germany, Switzerland, France — June–July
Carmichael-Smyths, Anny, and Minny in Mennecy; Thackeray leaves for America — August–October
Anny and Minny in Paris (19 Rue d'Angoulême) with Carmichael-Smyths — November 1852–2 May 1853

1853

Thackeray arrives in Paris from America — 2 May
Thackerays travel in Germany, Switzerland — 24 June–30 August
Thackerays live in Rome — 27 November 1853–8 February 1854
Thackeray ill, malaria (Roman fever) — 3 December 1853–8 February 1854

1854

Thackerays in Naples — 9 February–30 March
Thackerays travel to Paris — 30 March–21 April
Thackerays move to 36, Onslow Square, Brompton — 18 May
Thackerays and Carmichael-Smyths in Boulogne, Chateau Bréquerecque — 26 June–10 September

Richmond Thackeray Ritchie born, Calcutta | 6 August
Amy Crowe comes to live with the Thackerays | December

1855

Thackerays in Paris | January
Thackerays in Paris, Germany | 16 June–27 July
Thackeray's second trip to America; Anny and
  Minny live in Paris | 13 October 1855–
  | 8 May 1856

1856

Thackerays travel on the Continent | 14 August–
  | 4 September
Anny and Minny in Paris | September–October

1857

Thackeray defeated in election for MP from Oxford | 21 July
Thackerays travel in Germany | September

1859

Thackerays travel: France, Italy, Switzerland | 15 September–
  | 16 October

1860

Thackeray buys house at 2, Palace Green,
  Kensington | 8 March
Anny's first publication: "Little Scholars," *Cornhill*
  Magazine | May
Thackerays travel in Holland | 11–25 September

1861

"Toilers and Spinsters," *Cornhill Magazine* | March
Major Carmichael-Smyth dies | 9 September

1862

"To Esther," *Cornhill Magazine* | January
Thackeray's *The Wolves and the Lamb* performed at
  "WMT House" | 24–25 March
Thackerays move into 2, Palace Green | 31 March

Anny visits Isle of Wight | November
"The Story of Elizabeth," *Cornhill Magazine* | September 1862–January 1863

1863

Thackerays visit Mentmore, Yorkshire, Fryston, Blendworth | January–July
Thackerays travel in Europe | 17–27 August
"Out of the World," *Cornhill Magazine* | September–October
Thackeray dies | 24 December
Thackeray buried, Kensal Green Cemetery | 29 December

1864

Anny begins 1864–65 journal | 28 January
Anny and Minny travel: Isle of Wight, Henbury, Putney, Warnford, London | January–July
"The End of a Long Day's Work," *Cornhill Magazine* | August
Mrs. Carmichael-Smyth, Anny, and Minny in Arromanches, Brittany | August–September
Anny and Minny move into 16, Onslow Gardens | 29 September
Mrs. Carmichael-Smyth dies | 18 December

1865

Amy Crowe Thackeray dies in India | 24 August
Margie and Anny Thackeray come to live with Anny | 2 October

1866

"The Village on the Cliff," *Cornhill Magazine* | July 1866–February 1867
Minny engaged to Leslie Stephen | 4 December

1867

Minny marries Leslie Stephen | 19 June

1868

Five Old Friends and a Young Prince
Anny travels to Rome with Lady Rothschild | April

1869

To Esther and Other Sketches

1870

Anny travels to Scotland
Laura Stephen born   7 December

1872

"Old Kensington," *Cornhill Magazine*   April 1872–April 1873

Anny in Normandy   August

1873

Anny and the Stephens move to 8, Southwell Gardens   March

1874

Toilers and Spinsters and Other Essays
Bluebeard's Keys and Other Stories

1875

"Miss Angel," *Cornhill Magazine*   January–June
Minny dies   28 November

1876

Anny and Leslie Stephen move to 11, Hyde Park Gate South   Late Summer
Richmond Ritchie visits Anny regularly from Cambridge   Winter

1877

Anny and Richmond engaged   May[3]
Anny and Richmond married   2 August
From an Island and Some Essays

1878

Anny begins 1878 journal
Ritchies move into 27, Young Street, Kensington   May
Hester Helen Thackeray Ritchie born   1 June

1879

"Susanna: An Introduction," *Cornhill Magazine*
(*Mrs. Dymond*, part I)   May

1880

Da Capo and Other Tales
William Thackeray Denis Ritchie born[4]   March

1881

Miss Williamson's Divagations
Life of Madame de Sévigné

1883

A Book of Sibyls

1884

Miss Angel and Fulham Lawn
Ritchies build 36a, Rosary Gardens
Anny ill

1885

"Mrs. Dymond," *Macmillan's Magazine*   March–December
Anny ill

1886

Ritchies move in with Mrs. Ritchie, Sr., Southmead,
    Wimbledon
Seeking cure, Anny travels to Ramsgate, Aix-les-
    Bains   August–September

1888

Ritchies return to London

1890

"Chapters from an Unwritten Memoir," *Macmillan's
Magazine*   July 1890–
                                                                   October 1894

1892
Records of Tennyson, Ruskin, and Browning

1894
Isabella Thackeray dies
Ritchies build End House, Wimbledon
Lord Amherst and the British Advance Eastwards to Burma
  (with Richardson Evans)
Chapters from Some Memoirs

1896
Biographical Introductions   1896–98

1898
Anny ill   June–October

1899
Anny undergoes throat operations   May 1899–(?)1900

1900
"Blackstick Papers," *Cornhill Magazine*   December 1900–
                                                    June 1907

1901
Ritchies return to London, 109, St. George's Square

1906
William Ritchie and Margaret Macaulay Booth
  married

1907
Richmond knighted   June

1908
Blackstick Papers

1910
Centenary introductions   1910–11

1911
Elected fellow Royal Literature Society
Thackeray's Centenary; Anny hosts celebration   18 July

1912
Richmond Ritchie dies   12 October
Anny and Hester move to 9, St. Leonard's Terrace, Chelsea

1913
From the Porch

1914
Sargent draws Anny's portrait   July

1916
Anny retires to The Porch, Freshwater

1919
Anny dies at The Porch   26 February
Anny buried at Hampstead next to Richmond
From Friend to Friend, posthumously

1

1840–1851

INTRODUCTION

I do not know why but when I saw your letter on the table I felt ashamed and thought that you ought to have seen the same but though I tryed ever so much I could not (Letter 4)

ON 20 August 1836 in the British Embassy in Paris, William Makepeace Thackeray, aged twenty-five, and Isabella Creagh Gethin Shawe, aged twenty, were married.[1] From the beginning it was a love match. Petite and red-haired, Isabella played the piano and sang charmingly, and eventually evinced enough courage to leave her mother and marry. Like Thackeray, Isabella was born in India. Again like him, she left India after the death of her father, Lieutenant Colonel Matthew Shawe. Innocent and insulated from the world, Isabella became Thackeray's child bride, calling to mind Dora in *David Copperfield*.

Although there are superficial similarities in the backgrounds of Thackeray and his wife, there are greater differences. Thackeray arrived in England at the age of five, the heir to a sizable fortune inherited from his father. After attending Charterhouse, Thackeray entered Trinity College, Cambridge, which he left after three terms. For two years he traveled on the Grand Tour of the Continent. Returning to London and the Middle Temple, he read law for a year. At this time, 1833, owing to the failure of a bank in India, he lost the bulk of his inheritance. After trying his hand at journalism, he left for Paris to study art.

I

When he met Isabella in 1835 in Paris, he was a gentleman by birth, education, and lost fortune. He had traveled, mingled in the bohemian societies of the artists of Paris and the journalists of London, while retaining his public school and university ties. Because of the circumstances of his childhood, he remained all his life a man divided. The family life from which he was uprooted in India took on an exaggerated glow of goodness and warmth, and the stimulating outside world he had met in his youthful wandering challenged him intellectually and artistically.

In Isabella he found the little woman around whom he could build his little nest.[2] Blinded by love and desire, he did not see her shortcomings nor the inadequacies of his own fantasy. Thackeray soon returned to London with Isabella, who was expecting their first child. They lived with the Carmichael-Smyths, Thackeray's mother and stepfather, until Thackeray established himself as a journalist able to support his growing family.

Anne Isabella Thackeray was born on 9 June 1837, shortly after Victoria came to the throne. She was named for both her grandmothers, and this heritage of English decorum and Irish volubility proved to be more than symbolic for her.

Early in 1838, the Thackerays moved to 13, Great Coram Street. For Thackeray it was a time of great domestic happiness as well as professional growth. He was fulfilling his young man's dream of marriage and parenthood; he embraced the challenge of Grub Street with enthusiasm and vigor.[3] In May of 1838 the first part of the "Yellowplush Correspondence" appeared in *Fraser's Magazine,* followed in July by the birth of a second daughter, Jane. Thackeray's and Isabella's letters are filled with the joys of marriage and the delight of watching a precocious first child develop. Most of Anny's memories of Isabella are those of a happy, loving mother who danced and sang and played the piano.

The first tragedy to mar Thackeray's fairy-tale existence occurred in March of 1839 when Jane died. Soon Isabella was once again expecting a child, and Thackeray began to notice but did not understand the insufficiencies of her character. However, it was not until after the birth of their third daughter, Harriet Marian, on 27 May 1840, that the greatest tragedy of their lives emerged and ended the happiness of their married life. A postpartum depression after Minny's birth (as Harriet Marian was called) drove Isabella to two attempts at suicide.[4]

Unable to work, with an infant, a small child, and an increasingly mad wife to care for, Thackeray moved his family to Paris, where his mother and stepfather provided a home for his children. Thackeray traveled from one country to another, trying to help the alternately raving mad or catatonic Isabella. This "year of pain and hope"[5] (1840–41) tempered Thackeray as he searched his guilty soul for the part he had played in Isabella's downfall. Her weakness of personality, her inability to cope with reality, her limited intellect, were all burdens she could not overcome. Added to these was the anxiety of being both wife and mother. When Thackeray accepted the doctor's diagnosis that Isabella could not live at home, he placed her with Dr. Puzin in Chaillot, where she lived until 1845. At that time he brought her back to England to live in a cottage in Camberwell with a companion. In this way Isabella lived out her life; she died in 1894 in Leigh, Essex.

In 1849 in one of "Mr. Brown's Letters to a Young Man about Town," Thackeray wrote: "I don't think they [women] have fair play. . . . I don't think they get their rights . . . enslaving them as we do by law and custom . . . it is for our use somehow that we have women brought up; to work for us or to shine for us, or to dance for us or what not . . . it was we who made the laws for women."[6] Thackeray understood Isabella's position but not until 1849, after the fact. He recognized her shortcomings as well as her goodness and he remained always a little in love with the woman she was not, as well as what she was. He wrote, "I like this milk-&-water in women — perhaps too much, undervaluing your ladyship's heads, and caring only for the heart part of the business."[7]

As for Anny, she was his child of love. Jane had died before she was a year old; Minny was a sickly, crying child. Although she was not the cause of Isabella's illness, her mother's madness manifested itself after she was born. It was unavoidable that Minny's birth was linked to Isabella's madness. Yet, they were both Thackeray's adored children. Anny was to remain his "fat lump of pure gold,"[8] and even though he insisted that he loved Anny and Minny equally, his partiality for Anny was obvious. She was so much like him: "a chip of the old block,"[9] intelligent, outspoken, and sensitive, and with a talent for writing. She was the reminder of happier times, when he had luxuriated in a wife and a home. For Thackeray divorce was impossible, and so he lived on to the end of his life, in a vacuum, a married bachelor determined to make a home for his children.

For six years, from October 1840 through late September 1846, Anny and Minny lived in Paris with the Carmichael-Smyths, except for holiday trips around Europe. Thackeray's mother was a strict Evangelical, a beautiful woman with a private court of worshiping friends and an adoring husband, Major Henry Carmichael-Smyth, a former soldier in the Indian Army. Living on a retired major's half-pay, he and his wife were a serious, dour couple who set about raising Thackeray's daughters with much love but little laughter.

Mrs. Carmichael-Smyth's letters reveal a remarkable woman. On her young granddaughters she bestowed the maternal love they needed, yet she imperiously ordered them about, laying down rules for them at long distance. Devoutly religious, she insisted they attend church every Sunday. Anny's hemming of endless tea towels is a further result of Mrs. Carmichael-Smyth's Evangelical predilection for work, even for nine year olds.

While Anny and Minny were living in Paris, Thackeray visited them, but the trauma of losing Isabella was intensified for Anny by Thackeray's frequent disappearances. He dashed in and out with laughter and excitement, wrenching visits that were difficult for father as well as children.

In 1845 FitzGerald described Thackeray as "writing hard for half a dozen Reviews and newspapers all the morning; dining, drinking, and talking of a night."[10] He visited Isabella regularly at Camberwell, but his life was essentially that of a bachelor. Whatever other arrangements he made, he was discreet. Accepting the fact that "the poor dear little soul will never be entirely restored to us,"[11] in 1846 he ended his rootless, lonely life. He wrote, "I am child-sick."[12] Over the objections of his mother, his daughters came back to London to live with him at 13, Young Street, Kensington.

The nightmare journey that had brought the two little girls to Paris was vividly described by Anny in the 1864 journal, and revised in the 1878 journal. For three-and-a-half-year-old Anny this coach trip was a haunting experience to which she referred often in adult life.[13] Uprooted a second time in their young lives, Anny and Minny entered the house on Young Street as dutiful children, returning to a father they loved but barely knew, leaving behind the grandmother who had reared them.

After Thackeray's mother brought the little girls to Kensington, she stayed on a while. She then returned to her husband in Paris without a farewell to her granddaughters. Thackeray was later to leave for America without saying good-bye to his children, feeling the experience too painful for him to do so. For Anny, such stealthy departures were bewildering and unsteadying, reminiscent of Isabella's disappearance. Still, though heartbroken at Mrs. Carmichael-Smyth's sudden departure, Anny's common sense as well as her sense of humor asserted themselves.

An emphasis on separation can be seen in Anny's discussion of her reading. Even as a child, Anny was steeped in the literature of the period. As a nine year old, Anny was reading *The Lay of the Last Minstrel,* and *Dombey and Son* (Letter 6). Her critique of *Dombey and Son,* chapter 18, carries an almost verbatim report of Florence's plea to her father (after Paul's death) and his reply to her. This critical and cruel relationship of father to daughter obviously had a special meaning to Anny. She is reassuring herself that this scene could never be reenacted between Thackeray and herself. As sensible as she was, and as loving as Thackeray was, she feared that she would lose her father as she had lost her mother. Later, in her diaries and biographical introductions, she recognized and acknowledged how honorably her father had managed his burden and how much he had loved his children.

Not wanting to part with his daughters, Thackeray spared them the limitations of a Miss Pinkerton's academy for girls. Whatever they had lost in Isabella, they were now under the aegis of a person of superior intellect and sensibility. In their motherless state, the little girls accompanied their father to many places otherwise out of their reach. Later on, Anny became Thackeray's hostess, enlarging her circle of friends to include the great.

Mrs. Butler (Mrs. Carmichael-Smyth's mother) came to live with her grandson and his children on Young Street in order to ward off possible gossips about a young governess living in a motherless home. Thackeray tried to hire unattractive-looking women in order to satisfy his mother's sense of decorum, but they often turned out to be unattractive in other ways as well. The problem of finding a good governess for his daughters was to plague Thackeray throughout their childhood.

As time passed, Anny missed her grandmother less and became more attached to Thackeray. In addition to educating his daughters, Thackeray made companions of them, treating them as young ladies instead of children. Of Anny, Thackeray wrote, "in 3 years she will be a charming companion to me: and fill up a part of a great vacuum wh exists inside me."[14] His daughters were the anchors, the domesticity, the substitute "little queens"[15] for everything he had lost when Isabella had left his home. To the end of his life, their welfare was his chief concern.

Thackeray's opinion of Anny during this period underwent a subtle change. From the beginning, he thought her bright. In a letter dated 23 July 1846, he described her: "she is going to be a man of genius." However, he criticized her character, "I would far sooner have had her an amiable & affectionate woman."[16] After his children came to live with him, only his evaluation of Anny's character altered.

In March 1847 he described her as having "a delicate soul. . . . What a noble creature she is," and again in May of that year he talked of "Anny's great noble heart & genius."[17] In January 1848 he wrote, "my dear old Nan goes on thinking for herself, and no small beer of herself — I am obliged to snub her continually, with delight at what she says all the time."[18] That spring, he wrote about Anny's "strong critical faculty" as well as her "generous and loving and just" nature.[19] Describing their journey on the Rhine in July 1851, Thackeray said, "Anny is famous . . . always magnanimous and gentle . . . a little affected & ostentatiously useful — her reasoning being 'I am very plain & clumsy, I must try & make myself useful & liked by helping people' & so she did with all her might."[20]

By 1849 Anny was "a great sensible clever girl, with a very homely face, and a very good heart and a very good head and an uncommonly good opinion of herself as such clever people will sometimes have." His single-sentence description of Minny was "Minny is very well for cleverness too as children go."[21] His preference for Anny, here as elsewhere, is obvious.

Inevitably, Thackeray became disappointed in women he loved, but not in Anny. He confessed that he liked "second-rate books, second-rate women, but first-rate wines."[22] His mother bedeviled him with her religion and her refusal to treat him as a mature man. His wife had not been able to cope with the love and life he offered her; Mrs. Brookfield's timidity did not allow her to repudiate her husband; Sally Baxter would prove too young. If his mother smothered him with her love, the others were too mediocre to rise to and accept his love. But with Anny, his love was returned and acceptable; she was clever, good, and adoring. Early on, in Young Street, Thackeray wanted a wife; later on, just before his death, Anny wanted a husband. But for the time being, they needed and complemented each other.

Anny's early maturity and maternal feelings are discernible in her attitude toward Minny. Later on Minny asserted her independence of Anny, but while they were children, Anny assumed the role of the mother and Minny that of the child, as in Letter 6.

Because so few letters by Minny are extant, Thackeray's evaluation of his youngest daughter must fill in the missing data. At first he thought her better natured than Anny, but by 1851 he changed his mind.

> Minny keeps all her claws for poor Nan. It's all smiles & good humour for me. The little hypocrite! . . . She has little Beckyfied ways and arts. It's almost disloyal the way in w^h I find myself observing her; . . . Minny's jealousy pains me — She is envious of Anny . . . snappish with her before strangers.[23]

A harsh estimate by a father of a daughter, but Thackeray as always was honest and he read her character without sentimentality. Just as his laudatory estimate of Anny was unclouded, so was his measure of Minny.

To Anny, the life she and Minny led with Thackeray in Young Street was filled with excitement and novelty. After the austerity of the Carmichael-Smyths' home, life at Number 13 with its rotating governesses, its outings, its garden, people coming and going, and Thackeray's awesome presence, presented a kaleidoscope of adventure to the nine-year-old Anny. An extrovert, she accepted all the friendship and love that was offered. For Thackeray, having his daughters with him was a joy, but undoubtedly a chore as well. Occasionally he indulged his habit of escaping to an inn to work in England and abroad.

In 1848 Thackeray and Mrs. Jane Octavia Elton Brookfield, wife of his Cambridge friend Reverend William Henry Brookfield, reached an understanding. Estranged from her husband, she needed a friend, while Thackeray without a wife became enamored of her. She was his "beau-ideal."[24] While Anny and Minny were on holiday in 1849 with his parents, Thackeray contracted cholera. JOB, as Mrs. Brookfield was called, nursed him back to health. However, the following year a daughter, Magdalene, was born to her and her now reconciled husband. Thackeray still visited and wrote to JOB constantly. This intimacy proved too much for Brookfield and he forbade Thackeray his house. Granted that there was not much a dependent Victorian wife could do under these circumstances, Mrs. Brookfield's conduct toward Thackeray was insensitive. There is no proof or likelihood that they had been lovers, but Thackeray suffered greatly when, under her husband's direction, she spurned him. Begun in August of 1851, *Henry Esmond* bears the marks of his thwarted love for Mrs. Brookfield. Gordon Ray's analysis of Lady Castlewood points out how Thackeray sublimated his feelings for Mrs. Brookfield and revenged himself on her by making her the older heroine who loves and is ignored by the younger hero until the very end of the novel.[25] However, for Anny and Minny she remained all her life the loving and beloved Mrs. Brookfield.

The texture of the Thackeray household comes through most significantly in the letters Anny wrote as a child to her grandmother in Paris. Anny outlined the trips to church, the state of nature in the Kensington house garden, Thackeray's comings and goings, including his progress on *Vanity Fair,* all of her feelings in her new life. These letters contain a great degree of sophistication, revealing her intuitive grasp of people's emotions and motives.

Anny's childhood experiences, her remembrance of her life with her father, were narrated in the 1864 journal, then in the 1878 journal, and finally in the Biographical Introductions to Thackeray's *Works.* Each time her views underwent a slight revaluation as she weighed and assessed the same scene from a different vantage point of increasing maturity. She further interpreted several biographical events when she shaped them artistically into scenes for her novels. However, here in her first known letters is an uncensored, uninhibited version of her life as she perceived it.

Anny's early letters reflect many of the qualities that her letters, her journals, and her novels would manifest throughout her life. Perhaps most apparent at first glance are the lack of dates or misdating, the frequent spelling errors (commented on in Letter 8), the lack of full stops, and the use of dashes. These idiosyncrasies of punctuation give the letters a feeling of breathlessness and of energy and joy in life. In Letter 1 her grandmother warns Anny "never to keep anyone waiting," but Anny always seems to have been late, and in her journals she reveals the pain that her father's criticism of this trait caused her. Conscious of her own feelings, she wrote about them, as she did in

Letter 4 to her grandmother, "when I saw your letter on the table I felt ashamed and thought that you ought to have seen the same but though I tryed ever so much I could not." Anny shows her awareness of her failures and indicates the high standard she set for herself. Her revisions show her attempting to describe as well as she can, an ability she would retain through her life.

The early letters also reveal Anny's psychological and observational acuity. Anny's gossip and her analysis of people's characters appear to be more than the work of a nine year old. Living in the society of her grandparents and their friends for six years, she had fallen into the habit of listening to and observing her elders. Her best writing would later reveal a special talent for observation, both visual and oral. Anny's daily intimacy with such things as their pets and untended garden, including the "yellow lillies in the garden . . . [that] shut at night" (Letter 9), and her telling descriptions of them, became a part of her professional style. Some of her opinions may have been Thackeray's or what she thought them to be. Her succinct dismissal of her governess with a curt "Bess canot bear to teach" (Letter 5) is an astute appraisal. Thackeray was soon aware of Anny's ability to judge character. In 1848 he wrote, "Anny has already taken Captain Alexanders [*sic*] measurement."[26] Her opinion conformed to his own.

That Anny lived in the home of a writer was evident in her explanation of Thackeray's latest chapter (35) in *Vanity Fair* (Letter 10). Anny was sensible enough to understand that her rendition of Thackeray's woodblock was merely "something like" her father's. Her narrative of chapter 35, "something like" as well, was remarkable on several counts. Anny proceeded with no hesitancy or awe to describe what her father had wrought; without embarrassment she acknowledged that her father's drawing was "much better drawn" than her own.

This habit, like Thackeray's, of including sketches in her letters, continued to the end of her life. Thackeray's insistence on drawing lessons for his daughters was justified in Anny's case. The sentence "she has (the French girl) got sabots on" displays Anny's understanding of sentence structure: she used parentheses to eliminate any ambiguity about who "she" was; Anny's use of the word "sabot" demonstrates her familiarity not only with the French language but with life in France. She draws sound conclusions about the narrative from the woodblock; her resolve to keep the chapter's contents secret in order to guarantee the sales of the numbers is amusing and wise.

Earlier she may have thought Thackeray was Jesus Christ when he made his whirlwind visits to the Carmichael-Smyths in Paris, or even have seen him as Jupiter[27] in his later dealings with Dickens and Yates, but at this time, Anny wrote of a father who happened to be a writer. There was nothing exalted in his calling or in his perception of himself, or in Anny's view of him. Writing was part of Thackeray's life as it soon became part of Anny's. Even in her juvenilia one can recognize a nascent writer. She enjoyed writing, and although she sometimes wandered in her narrative, her explanations of what things are and how they work, and her insight into human nature, were developing tools of the storyteller. Anny can be seen to be conscious of her inheritance from her father when she signs her poem written to Amy Crowe (Letter 11) "A I Titmarsh," using her own initials, but her father's nom de plume.

The early letters as a whole reveal a busy Thackeray, working and caring for his daughters. No mention is made by Anny of her mother, and as became more apparent in her teenage letters, her dependence on her father grew. The little household, sometimes chaotic, sometimes melancholy, cohered and became a family, because this was what Thackeray wanted—this was his duty as he saw it.

To the mature Anny, looking back on it, life in Kensington not only carried with it the charm of childhood memories but always represented another way of life, when bustling London had not yet encroached upon the farms of Kensington. In her novel *Old Kensington,* Anny fictionalized her activities at 13, Young Street. In the 1878 journal she told her niece, Laura, "all that part of our lives I have written about in Old Kensington." Although in the novel she presented a delightful evocation of Victorian childhood, a solemnity dominated the portrait. When writing about Young Street in her novel, Anny was an artist, distanced by art and maturity. However, life—reality—was often very exciting for young Anny and Minny, even though the missing Isabella cast the potent and unhappy aura over their lives that Anny the novelist understood and emphasized in *Old Kensington.*

LETTERS 1–11

From Mrs. Carmichael-Smyth to Anny and Minny

Letter 1
Ray/Morgan

17 Rue des Vignes
Mardi
[Postmark: 27 Nov. 1846]

My own precious Nanny & Minny & Everbody Here I am with dear G.P.[1] very snug & warm; for it is much warmer than at Kensington. We left Boulogne at 7, & were very nearly too late for the train, from being half an hour after our time: and I cant tell you how many evils would have happened, if they had not waited for us: in England they w^d not have done it, so mind Nanny never to keep anyone waiting, it is so easy to be ready — You may think how happy dearest G P is to have his old Wife back, & we have talked so much about you all. This is a pretty little apartment, for him & me, with such a lovely view, & we could see to read at ½ past 5, when I thought my pretty maids were jumping about by gas light. Tell G. Mamma,[2] G P has taken a very pretty apartment in Beaujeu, Avenue Chateaubriand & whenever she feels strong enough to get as far as Folkestone, she could wait for a sunny day there, cross to Boulogne & sleep, go to Abbeville in the 11 o'clock Dilly, sleep there & take a carriage to Amiens, all the diligences pass Abbeville in the night, either at 8 or 2 — she must sleep at Amiens & come without fatigue to Paris. Abbeville to Amiens is 4 hours — We can go to Beaujeu when we like, it is only the little difference of a few days here, so you must pack up her things & mind please dear Bess[3] to keep her from any packing — it is so much better in the train carriage than the dilly that I wish her by all means to go to Amiens in a carriage because she would have bustle in getting out at the Chemin de fer — My last day at Twickenham, put me off many little commissions, but what I most regret are some warm stockings for GP which I will thank G Mama to bring. They will not be dearer at Kensington I think than elsewhere, large woman's size of soft lambs wool, & a roll of shoe ribbon. if she puts 3p' in her box & 3 in

Flore's[4] there is no danger [shoe ribbon this breadth] I wish dear Annie you would write & tell Aunt B:[5] of my being safe at Paris — write clear & tell her all the news — & ask Papa to take you to call on Mrs Dance[6] to say how sorry I was not to have called on her, but that I was ill the day after I saw her & a great many things prevented It is raining & I dont know if I can get to the post — GP & I are so snug here, & we talk of you always, & I think it is such a comfort to talk with our pens. I long for the time when my Minneks will be able to write — till you have a governess. I hope you will every day do your sums & writing — & Sunday write me what the sermon is — that is, what you understand it to be — the 2 prayers I wrote for you are to make you think of what you ought to pray for; every thing I know is better said in different parts of our Church service, but we cant turn to that, & I want my children to feel that "in every thing by prayer & supplication to make their requests known unto GOD," it is their duty & comfort — I shall begin very soon to write a journal for you — tell dear Bess I am going now to see Maria[7] & take her things Give my love to Mrs Gloyn:[8] & thank her & every one who is kind to my precious ones — & tell Papa to kiss you 10000000 times for Grannie[9] & you can do so to him — & GOD bless you & bless you

       tell P love I send his
       letter today

GP will write next time his love & kisses

Dearest Bess Thinking over again upon the precious ones — a word of Mrs Hollingsworths[10] governess occurred to me w^h spoke so much — "it is not what children learn as lessons Ma'am, it is the charity, honesty teaching, by example more than precept" — how much good sense there is in this — As the old Man preaches it — God by with you in y^r excellent work.

       Yr Ever Aff–
       ACS

To Mrs. Carmichael-Smyth

Letter 2　　　　　　　　　　　　　　　　26th November
Ray/Morgan　　　　　　　　　　　　　　1846

Dear Grannie

I canot tell you what I thought on Monday. Bess came in and began with aint you happy Grannie is going to GP Fancy him siting by him self by the fire — She then told us about your going — what should I do without you — how happy GP would be — I was happy [*sic*] — so unhappy I could not cry but it is all gone now and I am not unhappy a bit: we took your note to the Scots to day — we are all well now Bess has been very unwell so she went to bed we went yesterday to Lilla's[1] — and amused ourselves very much —

Thanks for the pretty book I have not finished the lay of the last minnestrell[2] yet I am writing this with the pen you gave me I had the large one Minnie is so fond of her book she is reading it for hours at a time we all send our love to GP and Grannie Granmama made punch stop and we saw it she made a funny mistake at dinner John[3] asked about you and so she said you were quite safe and she said in answer to his question if you had a stormy passage, why the sea was so calm that they were bufetted about by the waves — , my how was that GM, why the sea was so calm that the wave where very high tell GP that I have been working pretty hard at his chain[4]

To Mr. and Mrs. Carmichael-Smyth

Letter 3　　　　　　　　　　　　　　　Saturday the 5th
Ray/Morgan　　　　　　　　　　　　　December 1846
　　　　　　　　　　　　　　　　　　　13 Young St Kensington

My dear M^r and Mrs Grannie GP —

I hope you are very well. I am and every body too GM is much better Bess was not very well yesterday but she is quite well today We went to Mrs Beyne's[1] to spend the day on Thursday and amused ourselves very much she is another cousin of papa's Mrs Prime[2] her Mother took us with Mrs Beynes little girl, she has got 2 children, a girl and a boy, to Madame Tusades Wax works[3] which are very prety one of the figures used to sigh but she was broken on Monday so the keper told us, there were two Princes [?] a Gent — and a lady who noded their heads — one of the groops was Prince Albert the queen and their children Prince Albert has got his arm round the princes Royal her sister I forget her name is standing on the sopha with her doll in her hand the Quee [*sic*] has one hand up and is reproving her daghter for making a noise to awake the baby on her lap — is not it a prety Groop I forgot the prince of wales that is standing beside her

you can easily imagin an emense hall or home [?] filled with all the historicall references you can think of. there are a number of babies We went to the Crowes[4] on Sunday they lend me the 1st 3^{d} 4th and 5th Vol^{s} of the robinson Suisse[5] but 2^{d} is missing it is a <u>very</u> pretty book they played and sang a goodeall Eugenie has got a very fine voice Minie has been washing her eye with Flore[6] and it is quite clean and not inflamed as usuall Bess told me to tell Maria that she began her note but could not finish it because her finger hurts her so — Minie's thing in her hair is a great deal better too, one minute after, instead of being better it is gone. I have began the dumpling net[7] it [*sic*] prety well advanced I wrote or began my journall but I canot manage it Mrs Gloyne gave Minnie a pair of sisors as big as that the london Newse came today —

Monday the 7th

I dated my letter wrong as it was the 5th I went out with Elisa[8] where I left of [*sic*] I got y^{r} letter this morning, last Sunday not the same we went to the Crowes but the text was put ye on the whole Armour of God[9]

Florie has just been in & I have been listing her all your messages here are hers Remerciez votre Grané pour moi et dites lui que Je'spére qu'elle sera bien contente pour moi et ma petite fille[10] — I wrote to Aunt B.[11] when you first left she is very well and has sent you a not [*sic*] by GM — I have got a little seall for Laure and a brooch for Flore — wich I have given her — I have not got any Christmas book we have got the wollen stockings for GP. Papa is not gone to Brighton [*line crossed out—illegible*] — We went to Mr Dances yesterday. Mr Dance is not very well We went to St Marks yesterday and all the servise was such a sleepy one if not chaunting that I cant not tell it to you Mrs Gloyne [*word illegible*] each a savings box saving bank written on it Flore has just siesed the Constitutionelle she has carried it away a great many loves to every body M^{r} GP I dreamed that you had the gout and came to see us thanks for y.ʳ letter Mʳ GP M.ʳ Haris¹² is y.ʳ glue pot now you have not written as you promised

---

Kiss to my Suse¹³ Goodby lara I shall answer y.ʳ letter soon

Annie

Dear Grannie I have mad [*sic*] a mess the part under the stroke is a letter to lara but now I am going to put it in an envelope thanks for haveing given Maria the work bag — what do you think I had best get for the remanig party of the Colmaches and for Miss Susse by remaning I mean whom I have not written to.

Mini sends her love¹⁴ GM told me to tell you that she gave her love and was losing all this fine weather [*four or five words illegible*]

My dear Laura I thank you for your note and basket

My dear laura I thank you for your kind note and basket Mʳˢ Colmache¹⁵ will bring you a seall it makes a very good impresion I hope you are very well. We [*word illegible*] love to monsieur Moris¹⁶ Mademoiselle Pauline

---

I have done half y.ʳ Chaine and almost Grannies net good by everybody — Annie

I have not got laura's basket but I do a If [*sic*] I had.

To Mrs. Carmichael-Smyth

Letter 4	Saturday 26th December
Ray/Morgan	18<u>4</u>6:

Dearest Grannie

A merry Christmas to you and GP and every bodie will not you write soon to us? WE send you kisses in plenty¹ And I am afraid the letter will be 2 weight with them. we have gone to such a number of invitations this week on Monday to Mʳˢ Fanshaws² on Christmas Eve to Mʳˢ Coal³ and yesterday at M.ʳˢ Crowes — What have you got for Christmas?

We have had a Bonbonniere⁴ Bess told me to tell you that she sent her love to you and a kiss to Maria Wednesday we went yesterday to M.ʳˢ Ervings⁵ and there was a party in the evening and we danced and amused our selves very much if you had but seen Minny in hight of a galop with little Master Loe⁶ all her hair flying about her and looking so pleased their was a magic lantern to and one at the New Years day before breakfast images and a pink sheet and it opened slowly opened it self and became a full flower.

This letter was began the day after Christmas day but since that We have got your letter I could not finish it yesterday for I went out with Bess to see M.ʳˢ Wadelle⁷ And we staid there I do not know why but when I saw your letter on the table I felt ashamed and thought that you ought to have seen the same but though I tryed ever so much I could not

My dear grannie & GP

love to every one and dear M.ʳˢ Auber⁸ to there is a little velvet for her did you get the locket with our hair as you do not wear lockets put it in your desk so that you may see or think you see us in it tell GP to take away that beautiful ribon from his eyeglass and put my square bobbin chain in its place I do not think he will lose his glass as it is pretty strong thank you for the presents you have given to the Medams Colmach we have got some nice little note paper Bess was so angry with the Weights [?]⁹ But they are gone now loves to old friends and kisses to you from

Annie

To Mr. and Mrs. Carmichael-Smyth

Letter 5
Ray/Morgan

13 Young Street
14ᵗʰ January 1846¹

My dearest Grannie And GP —

Many thanks for your letter which I have just received and I shall try to write this so as you can read it you will get the nets from Nina — and Maria is to make them up Give her a kiss and tell her that I will write to her but it is fair she having write to me I have got a new white frock and Minnie has mine made up for her only think it was not a bit to big for her except the bodice wich was to long but the wast was just the size Minie can read the printed letters very nicely and I think reads better by a goodeal though you must give her the merit of getting on by her self for Bess canot bear to teach and Grandmama makes her read to her the service or psalms wich are to difficult for her She has bought her a coppy wich would be more for me than for her and the lessons are printed in it

and instead of the first or 2^d class it is the 8th as for Flore one day i went our with Mrs Gloyne when I thought she was going the day after next, and bought her a scotch peble broach and gave it her as a parting present thinking that she was going so soon but Grandmamma did not go Minnie gave her a pin —

Did I tell you about the coungerer we saw on New Years day he was given a ring put in a wine glass then covered it with a pocket handkerchief and put the wine glass in a box after some time he took out the box opened it and took out another box opened that one took another anso on till at last he took out a very little one and out of that the ring was not that curious I have got all your letters in my desk I am reading the 2^d Chapter of St Luke when Jesus was found in the temple with the Doctors of Divinity.

love to Mrs Auber [*word illegible*] Miss Hammerton &^{ct} and every bodie I wish you would not look so cross every morning at the head of the table sometimes it seems to me[2] you smile when I do, very hard indeed but that is only my fancy there is a little lone letter for Maria we are going to a party this evening Grandmama has given me a white frock of Book muslin Maria will tell you all about it

                 Goodbye dear Grannie
                 Annie

Do you observe the kises on the newspaper in the shape of little seling wax dots
Mademoisales Thackeray presents ses complement a Madame Smithe et espere qu'elles aisant le plaisir de la vior a printemps prochain.[3]

                        Minnie and Annie MINNIE[4]

1840–1851

To Mrs. Carmichael-Smyth

Letter 6
Ray/Morgan

13 Young St.
Kensington
26th February Friday
1846[1]

Dearest Grannie
The murkiness just now has been so great that Bess at an arms length could not see Grandmama who was sitting very near her. I can tell you that though you <u>could</u> see the bookcase I could not say what sort of books were in it. we went to se M.[rs] Crowe on Monday week poor Minnie fell in to the fier and burned her arm She was a blind man[2] and before we could catch her she was in but it was not bad Bess put some wadding on it then some gold beter skin[3] afterwards. 2nd of March it is now much better though not quite well the dining room is being white washed the contents of Minnies letter are My dear Granny I send you my love And a kiss to GP there is an hippodrome here Minnie these letters wich are marked I made but the [word illegible] is a very nice one Poor Minnie was very much disappointed when GM said that you would think she was making a game of her while Minny spent her last half hour before going to bed on it when you write write her a little note because it will be as hers but put a seal or wafer that she may open it when doctor Quinn[4] sent her her medicen he adressed it to Miss M. Thackeray But she thought it was a letter from some bodie and almost cried when she found what it was but she did not I made the pen with which I am writing and have mad some very good we went to M.[rs] Scot[5] and [word illegible] a Capt. Haris[6] Miss Scot has got a little cousin with her for she had been some where to some shire but I forget the name is it true that you have got up a subscription for the poor I wish I could send you a shilling I would but I canot in a letter I am knitting a pincusion for papa the third number of Vanity fair is come out[7] poor little paul in Domby is dead but the Father is so unhappy and unkind to poor Florence They went to brighton and Paul is so fond of Florence he goes to Dotor Blimers school and Miss Corniela Blimers gives him to many lessons and becomes ill and dies when Florence goes in to his room she said Papa papa speak to me dear papa what is the matter Said he sternly. Why do you come here what has fritned [sic] you and then Water who saved her you know goes away[8]

I bought GM a spectacel case which cost 6 pence. I have now 4 shillings   Minnie has given me six pence.

I do not know why from the maner She writes   It seems to me as if Aunt Mary[9] disliked us so though I am fonder of her than ever I can not help being very fond of her   Mrs Parker[10] had as always been very unwell indeed thoug she is none the worse for it I hope you are very well and dear GP   the other day in the park sitting down with a saddle in checked trowsers and grey coat just like GP only when we came near the face was quite different   give my love to every bodie. Papa is just come home and is reading Punch   Minnie has got today some worsted to finish her kettle holder and Bess is going to teach her how to make your fring   I know bring the thread forward and knit 2   Miss Fanshaw is not coming I am sorry for it I wish when you had been here you could have come an see lord Holland castle[11]   it is very pretty   Many thanks for the violets   I did not open the newspaper   Grandmama said it was for me to write   the crocusses are comeing up   I will send you some when they are in flower and some evergreens have been put in the garden which looks very nice   We are all very well   give my love to Laura. Bess is gone out to dinner and it is 9 so good night Grannie

Annie

Bess has given me a wood pincusion[12]

Dearest Grannie   I had a long letter written before and I havenot sent [?] it for many reasons, I know it will give you pleasure to kiss your dear ones on both little hand [?] and as good as gold   my only fear is I shall become too fond of them, Mr Titmarsh[13] is as busy as he can be   And Grandmother is again quite well, I regret daily my incapability and repugnance to teaching, the former isn't to be cured, and the latter must be indured   I wish you [*word illegible*] send me one of the shaking [?] kettle [?] holders. My love to Mrs Auber she will know what I mean, dear GP kiss Grannie for me and I will pay you when we meet, adieu

Your afft Bess

Will you send the enclosed to Maria as soon as you can

To Mrs. Carmichael-Smyth

Letter 7 [April 1847]
Ray/Morgan

My dear Grannie Miss Drury¹ is come she is beautiful with large black eyes The second face is the most like She is very like you in manners We go and learn Dancing every Saturday at the Misses Henres [?]² we have I have not much to say we went to the ethiopians³ yesterday but I canot write now I mean when I am in a hurry GP's purse is not nearly finishe but I will get some [*word illegible*] paper and give you a long letter the ethiopians sang Lucy [*four words illegible*] and old tom tucker your too late to come to supper and many other thing

The crocusses are beatiful We are going to see you Annie I am writing a play about lady Inez Zollwig [?] but now I have no time to write it any more now I will send you our loves and hope you are very well We went other day out walking and of you we were talking We were talking of you and GP too

> Of you dear Grannie
> we're thinking
> Minnie and Annie

Give our love to Flore Marie
and my letter I send you the ethiopian serenader Bill⁴

To Mrs. Carmichael-Smyth

Letter 8 {April, 1847}
Ray/Morgan Thursday

My dear Grannie

We went today with papa to see the house of Lords[1] the new one I mean it was very handsome it is almost noth-  ing but gold the ceiling is done up in squares of oak I think and gold inside of the squares at one end there was some seats for the judgs and at the end for attorneys they wore such funny wigs made of horse hair there are ethiopian serenaderesses come out now so that the serenaders are all most forgotten in the placardes[2]

we attend to all your directions respecting G Mama [*sic*] give the cook and I now make it for her Will you give the enclosed to Flore kiss Mrs Gloyne for us Minnie is makeing great progress in her printing and reads very well she makes no mistakes about the words but is slow.

Mad. Sagnée, our danceing mistress says we are getting on very well the trees are buding and looking very bright and beautiful the  boots you got for me are not worn out yet — I have just had some new ones and some strawr bonnets too brimmers with white ribbon and pinck inside just in a simple cross we dig  every morning before our lessons for ¼ of an hour the roses are getting on very well G Mama had a letter from Che[3] this morning I canot think they talked about you Cherie did not even metion you perhaps Aunt Mary[4] did We do not get letters as often as we used but I do not write we have a goodeal to do now but I will write every week and then will expect a letter from you the Ribese⁵ a pinck flower is comeing up very nicely in the garden I do summes every day now not adition but muliption and division I forget if I have ever told you of our going to W____ I quite forget the name it was very pleasant and we had a nice walk and I came and went outside the carriage we saw a black swan today I donot think it as pretty as the white we went in to Westminster Abey but only saw a few tombs because service was going on I have not made a letter in Minnys note she invented and wrote it all herself

I have been writing to brodie⁶ it went of today an Aunt Becher's letter will be put in at the same time She is always asking after you — Uncle Arthur⁷ went away on the same day as M̲ʳˢ̲ Gloyne I will now tell you all we do in the day first we get up have prayers at nine but I will not have place here so good by dear Grannie

        Annie
        Give our love to every bodie

To Mrs. Carmichael-Smyth

Letter 9   [July 1847]
Ray/Morgan   Sunday

Dearest Grannie

I wrote to Mʳˢ Auber yesterday and asked her Mʳˢ Simpsons¹ address we went to church this afternoon the sermon was when Samuel asked Saul if the Lord liked burnt oferings better than being obeyed out of today's lesson he then said that some said that they where astonished that though Saul wanted so much to be forgiven that he was not and that his crime was not so great only to have pity but then he said that it was not pity as he distroyed those that where of no use to him and

only kept those that would be and he compared it to our own sowls that we pride ourselves in not doing things that we have no temptation to do and the little ones which we do.² The Parkers where here Saturday last and asked us to go there on Saturday of this week last time we had such fun and they have got some rabbits I do not like my sums not at all we have some yellow lillies in the garden and they shut at night We saw them shuting last night Miss Drury sayes that the convulvulesses³ will do the same Edward⁴ did not come on Friday to day is Monday I have not had my breakfast yet it is about ½ past 8 we are not at all early I sleep very long and do not get up though I can dress myself but I did this morning do you know we have another second cousin

Mrs Erving she had on the 1st of July a little boy I have not seen him yet it has just struck nine we have such [*ten words illegible*] GM is as usual and very week. Mr Dombey has married M^{iss} Granger — who is very fond of Florence When we come we will [*sic*] the numbers most likely to boulougne we have not had our dinner yet but I have donne my lessons I have donne Grannies bits of Noel and Chapsall⁵ and written some dictée and read in Grandfathers tales⁶ give our love to every bodie and to Chérie and Aunt Mary

In the garden this morning is a beautiful snake convolvulous come out and some verbena a red one not the smelling verbena but the flowering one it is scarlart Papa dines at home today for a wonder and nobodie to come and dine with him Mrs Parker has got such nice raspberrys She brought a basket of them to G Mamma who liked them very much and got more than usuall of them they were the first she had had

Annie

We have planted a dalia but Mrs Parker has promised us a good one Miss drury planted 2 slips of geraniums and the mignonette is growing up all very well one of the convollvulsous is out and a beautiful scarlart verbena we had a thunder and lightning storm last night with love to every bodie

Annie

Miss Avery[7] told me to tell you that she is horrified at the spelling and the writing I have practised on the piano to day. What a dear little [*line illegible*] Do not ask him to write to us tell him we will answer him and I will try and get some smart paper Ask him also to put a drawing at the bottom Give our loves to Mrs Gloyne do you see her often I did a sum to day it was quite right I miss GP & am going to make some book markers for you and GP.

To Mrs. Carmichael-Smyth

Letter 10 {July 1847}
Ray/Morgan

My dear Grannie we went to church this morning the sermon was about the wisdom of Solomon and the man without virtue there was no pleasure.[1] Sometime ago we went to see some pictures of which you will see an account in punch either this one the week before last's I am  not sure which perhaps the little Irvings will come tomorrow. we went to tea at Mrs Parker's yesterday we had some rasperrys of which  they had a great manny it is very hot today. Papa went in to the country on Wednesday and came back yesterday We went to gravesend. I think it will be in next V. Fair that George Osborne is killed and Amelia will have a little boy and Captn Dobbin will bring him a horse  while he is a baby I think it will be in Normandie.[2] I know all this from a picture on wood where Amelia is in widows weeds with a little boy and Captain Dobbin is coming in with a horse under his arms while a french little girl with cap on is trying to console her she has (the French girl) got sabots on Do not tell this to any bodie because it is a secret and if every bodie knew it they would not bye V. Fair. The picture underneath is something like it but the other is much better drawn. I wrote to Aunt Becher yesterday Mrs Auber has not answered my letter yet I must write again would not that black and white picture do very well for a gost the second gives a goodeal more trouble and not so good an efect

Monday I have just got your letter thank you for not believing G Mama that we write our letters on the slate before we send them to you for we do not. I have just finished the first chapter of Noel and Chapsal where

Tuesday[3]

They put a word wrong and they there are [?] some rules in the book and I am to correct it. The little Irvings[4] could not come yesterday. Mrs Scott has asked us to spend the day with Susy tomorow so we are going I have sent a news paper to Aunt Becher She has not been very well

it is so very hot today that we do not know what to do Miss drury has bought some blue muzlin to line our tippets[5] I have done a yard and a quater Give our love to every bodie and to dear Marie and Laure and Collmaches and every bodie tell GP that he must make haste and answer my letter but that it need not be in verse if he canot make one Good by Dearest Grannie

your
Anne

I miss GP Minnie will write to you I have knited a yard and a half of Mrs Aubers fringe.

To Amy Crowe[1]

Letter 11
Ray/Morgan

[c. 1850–51][2]

O! my Amy shallow hearted[3]
O! my Amy mine no more
Yestern we with Pappy parted
He for Gallia's barren shore
And to day I got a letter
Through a cloud a ray of light
It said "To Hampstead you can go dear
So fair Amy will you write
& tell us when it is convenient
We should to Hampstead take our flight
    A I Titmarsh[4]

2

1852–1858

INTRODUCTION

I should like a profession so much — not to spend my life crochetting mending my clothes & reading novels (Letter 17)

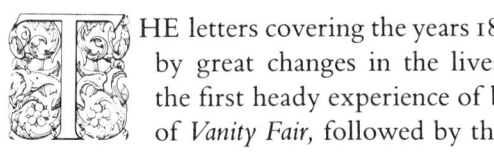HE letters covering the years 1852 through 1858 are marked by great changes in the lives of the Thackerays. After the first heady experience of being lionized as the author of *Vanity Fair,* followed by the solid success of *Pendennis,* Thackeray's position was assured. He now set his mind to earning enough money to replace his own lost fortune as a patrimony for his daughters. Although Thackeray was still in his forties, mortality began to weigh heavily on him. One of the reasons for this was his own ill health, exacerbated by a near-fatal bout with malaria in Rome in 1853. Another and possibly more powerful reason was his loneliness.[1] Despite his wholehearted acceptance of his role as paterfamilias, he suffered from the lack of a mutual love in a man-woman relationship.

It was not merely Thackeray's desire to make a fortune for his daughters that drove him to travel for his lectures. As Ray describes it, a deep restlessness and insecurity left Thackeray "permanently in need of reassurance [which he found] . . . in the companionship of a succession of women: his mother, his wife, Mrs. Brookfield, and, during his last years, his daughters."[2] During the period here under discussion, however, his daughters were as yet too young to be the companions he craved. Hence Thackeray traveled extensively, not merely for lectures or to further his work, but to satisfy his restlessness.

Because Thackeray felt the need to earn a large sum of money quickly, he plunged into lecturing. In the end he grew to hate it, but not before this highly remunerative occupation took him through England, Scotland, and twice to America. While Thackeray was thus traveling, Anny and Minny lived with the Carmichael-Smyths, as they had in earlier years when Isabella had been unable to care for them. When Thackeray returned from his lecture tours, his daughters accompanied him on holidays.

For Anny and Minny most of the results of traveling with Thackeray as a guide and companion were beneficial. Not only did they get to know their father intimately, but he was able to increase their knowledge of the world. The people they met became lifelong friends. In 1854 at Chateau Bréquerecque, Boulogne, they lived near the Dickens family. Kate Dickens became Anny's close friend. While in Rome Anny and Minny were taken in by the English colony living there and became regular guests of the Brownings, the soprano Mrs. Sartoris, her sister, the actress Mrs. Kemble, and the Storys.[3] Her stay at Chateau Bréquerecque so impressed Anny with its colorful peasant life that she used the location for *The Story of Elizabeth* and *Village on the Cliff,* and "Across the Peat Fields."

The first thing that becomes obvious upon reading the manuscripts of this period is that the letters are no longer a conversation among members of a tightly knit family. The majority of Anny's letters are written to friends who have displaced her grandmother as confidantes. Anny's correspondents are of two kinds. One group, consisting of Mrs. Fanshawe, Mrs. Stoddart, and Mr. Synge, are friends of Thackeray's. With the women (including Mrs. Synge) she is on an intimate mother–surrogate daughter relationship. The other group are young women of her own age, and interestingly enough, all are daughters of Thackeray's friends. This Victorian girl's choice of friends, as often in her age, was circumscribed by the people her parents knew.

Many Victorian practices surface in these letters. The morning after a dinner party, Anny brings leftover food, "mouldy scraps of things we could not get down our selves & treated three little boys in S.t Georges Hospital whose eyes lighted up at the squashy grapes and eager little hands stretched out" (Letter 25). The Victorian habits of bringing jellies to the sick and saying farewell to the dying, of wearing mourning and using black-bordered stationery, of clinically describing illnesses, are all part of the news (Letters 21–23, 25). With such preoccupation on the Victorian rituals of death, Anny was especially sensitive to Thackeray's growing ill health (Letters 17, 18).

Although Thackeray wanted to take care of his daughters financially, he treated them as adults and exposed them to the realities of life. They knew about his financial problems (Letters 17, 19, 20); they shared in the responsibilities of the family. Twice he promised to take them on lecture tours; twice Mrs. Carmichael-Smyth became ill and needed them to nurse her. Thackeray went alone while his daughters looked after their grandmother (Letters 21, 22).

Thackeray embarked on his first lecture tour in America on 29 October 1852. Before this, on 14 June, he took his daughters on a tour of Europe, but finding it "an endless leave taking" he suddenly "jumped off at Frankfurt and left them to their good old Granny: . . . It will be a year nearly before we shall be together again."[4] Trying to justify his absence to his daughters, he later wrote, "But we can't have all we want in life: its my clear duty to go fetch this money. . . . The months will pass over, and the duty will be done."[5] He outlined what their duty was: "you must speak French perfectly by the time I come back. . . . Learn dancing . . . and play me some good music when I see you again . . . . consider yourselves as at College; and work work with all your heart."[6]

When Anny realized the predicament she was in (alone with Minny and the Carmichael-Smyths), she rebelled. Thackeray would not be shaken from his resolve, and good-naturedly, Anny made the best of the circumstances. However, Mennecy, the village she lived in with her grandparents after Thackeray's departure, always had for her an association of gloom and misery. Yet, in her letter to her friend Laetitia Cole describing her travels, Anny dismissed the hateful town with "After our tour we went to Mennecy, & then came back to Paris" (Letter 12). When faced with the inevitable, Anny did the best she could to enjoy life. Her melancholy moods did not persist for long and once they were over she did not brood about them. This adolescent ebullience would later mature into an adult appreciation of life. After complaining to Thackeray about the separation from him, and Mrs. Carmichael-Smyth's high-handed ways, Anny settled in to enjoy Paris and she recorded, "the Champs Elysées w^h are as broad as three Oxford S^{t}s . . . beautiful carriages & horses trotting down the middle & such splendid gentlemen & ladies who look as if they had walked out of those fashion prints." Despite the fact that Anny outlined her busy day, the letter is not quite as open as it first appears. In addition to glossing over her stay at Mennecy, she does not complain about the confirmation *cours* she is forced to attend by Mrs. Carmichael-Smyth; these complaints are family matters and private—for her father's ears only. That this was her father's expectation is shown by Anny's report in her 1864 journal of her father's chiding her for talking outside the house. The phrase about ladies and gentlemen on the Champs Elysées is repeated. These fascinating people, supposedly closer to the company Thackeray kept in London, are the ones Anny would like to know, rather than her grandmother's old cronies.

The confirmation *cours* and religion in general became a great problem for Anny. An ardent Evangelical, Mrs. Carmichael-Smyth tried to impress her beliefs on her granddaughters. Younger and more pliable than Anny, Minny accepted what her grandmother preached. Anny, however, questioned every tenet, seeking clear and logical but less limiting answers. In dismay Mrs. Carmichael-Smyth complained to Thackeray, "poor Nanny's is a stiff heart of unbelief . . . I heard her declare that she 'did not care for the old Testament & considered the New only historical.'"[7] Applying to Thackeray, the oracle of last resort for relief from her grandmother's harangues, Anny received the following answer from him:

> I should read all the books that Granny wishes, if I were you: and you must come to your own deductions about them as every honest man and woman must and does. . . . And so God bless my darlings and teach us the Truth. Every one of us in every fact, book, circumstance of life sees a different meaning & moral and so it must be about religion.[8]

Thackeray outlined his beliefs and explained why he differed from his mother, but the choice, he insisted, was Anny's, and neither his nor his mother's to dictate. Anny answered:

> I am afraid Grannie is still miserable about me, but it bothers me when the clergymen say that everybody ought to think alike. . . . Monsieur Monod tells us things about the Garden of Eden, which he proves by St. Paul's epistles. I don't understand how God can repent and destroy His own work, . . . and it is things like these that they think one must go to hell for not respecting and believing. I am sure when Christ talks about 'My words' he means His own, not the Bible, as Grannie says.[9]

Mrs. Carmichael-Smyth's letters at this time portray a grandmother concerned for her granddaughters, a mother doting on her son, and a wife devoted to her husband. An intelligent woman, she wrote to Anny and Minny with intimacy and love, treating the young girls as adults, yet never able to admit their independence of her. Although she harassed her granddaughters over religious matters when they were living with her, there is no evidence of fanaticism in the letters. A strong woman, Mrs. Carmichael-Smyth did not relinquish her struggle for authority until shortly before her death. Letter 16 contains an indignant protest against the trial of Celestine Doudet, who was acquitted of murdering a young child in her care. Her forceful response, as well as her reticence, are indicative of her nature. No mention is made by Mrs. Carmichael-Smyth to her granddaughter that Doudet tortured this little girl and her sisters to prevent them from masturbating. The Victorian taboo against labeling masturbation anything but a heinous crime silenced Mrs. Carmichael-Smyth. But her outrage over the mistreatment of children and the widespread publicity of the case made it news she could not overlook.

In 1854 another great change occurred. The Thackerays moved out of Kensington to 36, Onslow Square, Brompton. Although they lived there until 1862, none of them was fond of the house, which lacked charm and grace. During their first year in Brompton, Thackeray added another member to his household. Amy Crowe,[10] daughter of his friend Eyre Evans Crowe, came to live with them. Six years older than Anny, Amy became at once the suitable and adored companion of Anny and Minny. Thackeray's search for the ideal governess had ended.

On his second tour of the United States (1855–56), he prescribed a course of subjects to keep his daughters busy, as well as a separate apartment for them. The flat was in the same building in which the Carmichael-Smyths lived, but this time Anny and Minny enjoyed a more empathetic chaperone in the person of Amy Crowe.

During these years many changes occurred in Anny's life and in her view of the world. In addition to the changes in Thackeray's literary position and the external changes of travel, foreign residences, and new abode and companion, Anny became twenty-one. She was now Thackeray's hostess and his primary amanuensis. These social and secretarial duties to her father were augmented by social work; yet the early rumblings of dissatisfaction with what she considered her useless life began to surface. Her cosmopolitan view of the world—her easy acceptance of all kinds of people and her awareness of the universe outside of her Victorian girlhood—dates from this period.[11]

Above all, Thackeray wanted his daughters to think for themselves. His teaching and her own questioning mind awakened within Anny great dissatisfaction with

> this ridiculous world with its absurd forms & twopenny tittle tattle. . . . O! if I was only a boy, I should make myself a clergyman in order to give a sermon wʰ would make their hair stand on end. . . . I am continually longing for something but I don't know what. . . . I should like a profession so much — not to spend my life crochetting mending my clothes & reading novels — wʰ seems the employment of English ladies unless they teach dirty little children to read wʰ is well enough in its way — but no work to the mind — & I don't want to write poetry & flummery . . . as my favourite Miss Martineau says it is far nobler to earn than to save. I think I should like to earn very much & become celebrated like the aforesaid Harriet. . . . (Letter 17)

When Anny fantasizes a position of power it takes the form of a clergyman. The fancy to be a clergyman goes along with a more possible ambition to be, like Harriet Martineau, a respected woman writer. Anny wrote this to Mrs. Fanshawe, a friend of Thackeray's and old enough to be Anny's mother. This last fact, however, did not inhibit Anny from giving the older woman advice. Throughout her life, Anny made friends regardless of age, sex, or position in life, treating everyone on the same basis.

In addition to giving advice, Anny asked advice of Mrs. Fanshawe, recognizing that she had "no one to talk to" about female considerations. Thackeray was, after all, a man; her grandmother was too old and opinionated; Minny was too young. What bothered Anny was growing pains—particularly those of an unemancipated Victorian young woman with an intelligent mind, who had been urged to think for herself. From today's vantage point, it seems inexplicable that Anny's writings have not been more thoroughly explored by feminist writers. She imbued her heroines with the same questioning of female inequalities that she had felt. In the end her heroines spend their lives in supposedly happy marriages, as did Dorothea Brooke and scores of Victorian heroines. The point is that Anny asked the questions and explored the options open for Victorian women, while she herself earned money writing until the day she died.

Anny's letters have a casual tone. The letters in which Anny is most confidential are those written to Amy Crowe. When writing to close friends, Anny's letters are full of enthusiasm and good nature. Not yet a writer, she exhibits humility about her craft when she tells another friend, Laetitia Cole, "I feel very much flattered at y.^{r} acting my play, & I think Mrs Smith a much better name than Castletoddie" (Letter 12). The play is lost in oblivion; perhaps rightly so. But in general Anny's writing was becoming more polished. A particular process of maturation was taking place. Anny was acting as Thackeray's secretary. She answered his mail (Letter 14); she took his dictation as he wrote his novels. Aware of words as she was, Thackeray's mode of composition, as well as the works themselves, must have made an impression on her. In Letter 12, in which she uses "very" four times, Anny noted, "What a quantity of verys." In describing a dinner at an inn in Le Havre, Anny wrote, "it was just like people in Pickwick," and her account of the scene is indeed Dickensian: "Mulligan poured out incoherently to the Hotel Captain who solemnly nodded his head every minute or two as if he were too wise to speak" (Letter 22). Her ability to encapsulate a scene in precise and telling detail became more striking as she got older. Writing Thackeray's words helped Anny see with his eyes and hear with his ears the real world around her. Telling a friend about one of her district pensioners, Anny used his vernacular: " 'Wouldn't it look orkard now for me & my old woman & pertickler, seein w^h we fears we must decline' " (Letter 25). In Letter 15, she described "a fine young Crimean . . . with one leg doubled up," and the horror of the Crimean War is brought home. She also sprinkled Yellowplush cockneyisms through her letters: Feyther for Father, Heving for Heaven, 'ope for hope (Letter 23), dele for little and prospex for prospect (Letter 26).

Life for his daughters centered on Thackeray and his work. When he finished a monthly number of his novel, they celebrated by going to the country for the day. Reminiscing later about Thackeray's dictation to her, Anny wrote:

> I remember writing the last chapters of The Newcomes to my father's dictation. I wrote on as he dictated more and more slowly, until he stopped altogether, in the account of Colonel Newcome's last illness when he said he must now take the pen into his own hand, and he sent me away.[12]

In Letter 24 Anny discusses the composition of *The Virginians*. The bustle and noise of Brighton, where the Thackerays were on holiday, "fairly drove Papa into Germany with his 'Virginians.' " The duties of being a father (and taking his daughters to Brighton) often conflicted with the demands of his profession. Telling a friend about the social requirements of Christmas, he wrote, "And how go away when the girls are invited to hospitalities? They are so happy and pleased that I must be so too; and ma foi *The Virginians* must wait for a day or two."[13]

In Letter 26 Anny discusses the Garrick Club affair with great candor. Anny and finally even Thackeray were both tired of the imbroglio. The Yates affair, better known as the Garrick Club affair, began on 12 June 1858 when Edmund Yates[14] published an offensive article about Thackeray in *Town Talk*. Because he did not know Yates outside the Garrick Club, Thackeray felt that his privacy as a member of a private club had been invaded and complained to the club after Yates had refused to apologize. The club demanded that he do so. Dickens (in a disturbed period of his life: he had just left his wife) took Yates's side. The club was adamant and Yates was expelled. When Yates realized that lawsuits against Thackeray and the Garrick Club were too expensive, he dropped the matter, but not until he had written a pamphlet again attacking Thackeray.[15] Because of Dickens's involvement in the affair, his friendship with Thackeray ceased. It was not until just before Thackeray died, and on his overture, that they spoke to each other. Because of the personalities involved, the affair was soon blown out of proportion, with people taking sides for or against Thackeray or Dickens, and not on the issue.[16]

Although their worldview was broadened through contact with their father's literary and social circumstances, the constant upheaval of moving out of their home, of leaving Thackeray, and of going to live with a more and more intransigent grandmother did not make for stability in the lives of Anny and Minny. Being older, and having had a family base of three and a half years of life with her mother, Anny was better able to cope with this problem. Still, in later years she wrote about Thackeray's first trip to America, "That whole summer of 1852 seemed darkened by the coming separation."[17] Thackeray felt that Anny's sturdy character would see her through adversity, but he was apprehensive about Minny. What manifestations of weakness Thackeray saw in Minny's behavior are not made clear, but it is apparent that besides being sickly as a child, she lived under the shadow of Isabella's madness.

Anny was changing from an adolescent into a young woman; only three years younger, Minny was still a little girl, the pet of the family, pert yet timid. Her letters to Thackeray while on his first trip to

America (Letter 13) are, as Thackeray described them, "funny little scraps."[18] Her love for Thackeray is underscored by her jealousy of his affection for any young girl other than herself. Minny harbored not-so-secret feelings of jealousy toward her sister. Minny's jealousy of Sally Baxter, the daughter of Thackeray's newly made New York friends, was pointed. "Miss Sally what an ugly name she has got fancy a Novel with Sally for the title" (Letter 13). Minny was maturing, but slowly, and if she thought deeply as Anny did, nothing of this surfaced in Minny's letters. Anny could admire Minny in a generous and openhearted way. In Letter 21 she wrote, "Dear old Minny's a trump isnt she." That Anny was also jealous of Minny can nonetheless be perceived clearly in her private journals of 1864 and 1878.

Thackeray continued to feel a special affection for Anny. His letters of the period are full of loving references to her. In 1856 he wrote, "What shall I do, if any scoundrel of a husband takes away Anny's kind cheerfulness from me?"[19] Later he would worry that no one had come to claim her. He always assessed her objectively: when she was fat, he called her "My dearest Fat";[20] when she turned out plain, he admitted that "Nobody is come after my homely girl who is the delight of her father."[21] He was proud of her growing writing abilities and the sketches she included with her letters;[22] he also admired her character. In 1858 he wrote, "As for Anny, she seems determined to be happy anywhere, and good tempered always."[23] Everything about her pleased him. He wrote, "there goes my Anny singing in her room, with a voice that is not so good as Adelaide Sartoris's but which touches me inexpressibly when I hear it."[24] Without a wife to act as buffer between him and his daughters, it was small wonder that Thackeray favored the more amiable Anny. "Annys happiness," he wrote, "makes almost me happy — unblases me when I am under the influence of it — ... I say to myself 'Good God what a good girl that is! Amen."[25] Ray states that "Thackeray's daughters gave his life its real focus after his return from the United States in 1856."[26] But Anny and Minny were growing up and would soon be aware that their lives now revolved around Thackeray; they wanted more than a devoted, loving, and famous father. Despite this, Thackeray continued to perceive his daughters as his "2 little wives," and for the time being Anny and Minny accepted the roles he chose for them.

With Thackeray lecturing and away from his daughters so much of the time, their correspondence to each other became significant. His letters to his daughters as well as two from Anny to him appear in Ray's third volume of *Letters*. This is not to say that Anny wrote only twice to her father during this time; rather the explanation lies in the fact that Thackeray was so delighted with her letters that he sent them on to friends to read. "My Nanny writes me the most delightful letters"; "I send you one of Anny's Isn't it a fine letter Miss Sara?"[27] To a friend he sends along "this enclosed letter of Anny's which I think you'll like to read. . . . Why, in 5 or 6 years, she will be able to do the writing business; and I can sit on the sofa as easy as the Professor of Deportment in Bleak House."[28] If Thackeray thought, hopefully or seriously, that one day Anny might become a writer, he did not push her into making a choice. In 1852 he even forbade her to write any more plays or novels.[29] Not until 1860 did she attempt any professional writing.

Anny's letters are honest, open, and thoughtful. To Thackeray in America she wrote, "I wonder what makes people cry when they are unhappy, and when they are happy too, and when they are neither one nor the other?"[30] In 1852 she described with exactitude and humor the parade for the emperor's coronation:

> There were soldiers all down the Champs Elysées and splendid aides-de-camps with feathers galloping about. Generals with their staffs trotting off to St. Cloud, regiments dashing by, all in the drizzling rain, and opposite a whole regiment of Dragoons, there was sitting one of Mr. Doyle's little dogs looking up at them, and nothing would induce him to move.

Ray explains that Richard Doyle "liked to introduce small dogs into his drawings."[31] Anny's letters reveal both the ability to express herself clearly and concisely and her facility at rambling on without periods or paragraphs to close one thought and open another. She was beginning to create art out of her life.

In Letter 17 Anny asks advice in seeking a profession. At the same time she refers to many novels and, as we have seen, expresses admiration for the woman of letters Harriet Martineau. By 1856 she admits an addiction to novel reading, English lady occupation or not. In Letter 22 she wrote, "I have taken to spending all the money I can lay hold of in novels." Even though she might be loath to admit it openly, it would seem that Anny had chosen her intended profession.

LETTERS 12–26

To Laetitia Cole

Letter 12
Ray/Morgan {2 Dec. 1852}[1]

Beloved Laetitia I am very sorry I did not write to you before, but I assure you I have a letter w.^h was never sent & that I was just going to write today when y.^{rs} arrived. I was very happy to hear of you & it was very kind of you to send a letter to me. We knew you had another sister because Miss Trulock[2] sent us a Times with Mrs Cole of a daughter in it & we were very glad & want to see Miss Rose[3] very much. What a quantity of verys. After our tour we went to Mennecy,[4] & then came to Paris on the 1.st of October. Now we work very hard & besides our walk I have only an hour in the evening to amuse myself. Grannie takes us to a Cour, that is a confimation cour, but as Minnie is so young she only listens as for me I have 5 or 6 pages to write twice a week a great deal to read besides. Also I practice a great deal & have just learnt a grand new piece w.^h goes up & down the Piano & shakes & runs & gallops & goes to sleep & bothers my fingers extremely. There is a piano under our room w.^h plays quite 4 hours a day & learns to sing besides, so you see we are becoming very musical. Minnie & I have got such a nice large room with such a gay lookout, we live very high up, up four pair of stairs but once you get here it is a very large & nice apartment. Yesterday :N:[5] was declared Emperor at the all Mayors, who are much grander personages here than in England. We saw him the other day in a beautiful coach & 4 horses & outriders & postillions, his hair has turned quite grey That is the only news I can give of him. Last week we had a g.^r happiness w.^h came by the post with the Miss Thackerays on the outside, all the way f.^m Hallifax Nova Scotia.[6] You may guess how glad we were. Papa had got there quite safely though with rather a bad passage & says he lived upon Champagne all the way out: & says every body on board was quite sick of the journey. I see I have made a pun but I didnot mean it. We have not been very gay. I have been to one party Grannie gives small ones very often when I beg very much to dance, & there are some little girls coming this evening. I feel very much flattered at y.^{r} acting my play, & I think Mrs Smith a much better name than Casteltoddie & Lieutenant Montagne a much more romantic one than Mrs Young's husband. I have just a quarter of an hour more before dinner, so I must make haste. You have been having floods & earthquakes & all sorts of things but there has been the most splendid weather here. Today we walked out in the Champs Elysée & I can't tell you how charming it was there with the very blue sky & the splendid ladies & gentlemen who look as if they had stepped out of fashion prints. I send you 3 little pictures for you Henny & Mary[7] & w.^{h} I bought to send by the Perrys[8] who have been here. Sunday. I wish you would come here & see us & Paris & my favourite Place de la Concorde. To get to it we walk down the Champs Elysées w.^{h} are as broad as three Oxford S.^{t}s, & trees & shops of toys & gingerbread & children & nurses & turnabouts,[9] beautiful carriages & horses trotting down the middle & such splendid gentlemen & ladies who look as if they had walked out of those fashion prints.[10]

From Minny to Thackeray

Letter 13
Ray/Morgan [Postmark: 12 Jan. 53]

My dearest Papa we were looking at a large box just now. and could not make out what was inside it & if you knew what a beautiful cake I suppose you have not seen it we are going to keep some of it for you and we are going to have a party for it. I dont think we shall ever be able to eat it it is so big and such beautiful gentlemen and grapes and above all a english cake & from an English papa.[1] We could not make out who it came from but at last we found a little piece of paper which A loves we are going to the Italian Opera to night we had an invitation to Mrs Lovets[2] but I think we like the Opera best Miss Shakespeare[3] is going too. it was Miss Dailey[4] who gave Grannie the ticket. Last Saturday we went to Besses & played at cards and we went to Mrs Corkrans[5] also. which we liked very much.

We are going to have a party & I am going to cut the cake I intend to make myself sick thats what the little Corkrans say & once they brought us a quantity of bonbons and made them selves so sick that in the morning we dident find one sugar plumb. Grannie & GP are dining out as Anny & I had lunched we left them. I hope your young ladies in the brocades are quite well, & particularly Miss Sally what an ugly name she has got fancy a Novel with Sally for the title[6] Grannie says I am to go to eat some pudding & I am very agreeable. thank you for writing to me I hope M.[r] Bellows[7] is bellowing good sermons we went to M.[rs] Corkrans to day she was ill & we met M[r] Corkran with all his children

Thats the Boulevards

 I don't know. how. he put his arm in that position. poor Aunt Ritchie[8] has been very ill she has had the jaundice she has had a picture taken of her which is very like her but they say it is too yellow she is much better now. They always send you their love but I have forgotten to give it to you before. I send you my love too so now Good bye I will tell you about the opera tomorrow.

HM Thackeray

To W. W. F. Synge[1]

Letter 14 [Postmark: June 1854]
Fales

My dear Synge
Can you use y.r interest to get a joint passeport for William Makepeace Thackeray Aged 42 as also for
Anne Isabella
Harriet Marian
Sarah Grey
Eliza Jordan
Charles Pearman[2]
(PS. We are going away on Saturday and are going to say goodbye to Bobby[3] & his parents one day this week. AIT)

And one also for the bearer M.r J A Sleap [?] my amanuensis.[4]

To Susan Scott

Letter 15 Feb. 18, 1855[1]
Berg

My dear Susie.
Im not going to make you any excuses for not writing before — I sh d have to say so much that it w d fill up the paper quite I have begun you ever so many letters w h have somehow never got finished, — I hardly know if this one will ever reach you. Miss Scott told us a great deal about you & Johnnie,[2] she says you are taller than I am, w h I don't quite like, & I am very glad to here what a poised [?] quiet studious young gentleman Master Johnnie has become, not caring for any thing but histories & grammars & such like useful entertaining things I think I have got a brother too just now, for Minnie looks absurdly like a boy with her short frisly curls.[3] I dont think Laure ever saw her like this or ever with her wig, w h I am happy to say is now lying in disgrace upstairs & only comes out for charades & dressing ups. Laure will tell you better than I can about Paris and Grannie & GP who dont change a bit & only grow kinder & dearer every year. Grannie writes us little leading articles about the war,[4] & she & GP hardly think of anything else. I hope you havenot

got any body out there. We met such a fine young Crimean at Paris one day, with one leg doubled up, I have not seen so many here, w^{h} I am not sorry for, it makes me perfectly unhappy when I see those poor crippled heros. We are very proud of our new house,[5] w^{h} is very nice & bright & clean. Minnie & I sit in state in the drawing room, & do our German Exercises, & we havent got a governess, but a very old friend,[6] to live with us, & as you may think we like it a great deal better. I think I must finish now as daylight & paper are lessenin [*sic*] every minute. Will you give Mrs Scott & Johnnie our love & believe me y^{rs} affectionately A I Thackeray

From Mrs. Carmichael-Smyth to Anny

Letter 16   [Postmark: 6 March 1855, Paris]
Ray/Morgan

Nanny dearest there wont be much in return for yr pleasant budget, my head is better but the old heart is very bad malgré all the joys I have in my darlings — but all resolves into "Lord be thou our pride" — GP has been out — 2^{m} since the fine weather & we have the sun so warm that we breakfast without a fire — the wretched Doudet[1] is acquitted, by 6 to 6 w^{h} is considered a verdict for the accused — there is a general indignation against her & the jury, & no scruples as to how the verdict was obtained — the death of Nicolas[2] has not caused half as great a sensation — Every body one met, Every shop keeper — had the same burst of indignation — What the 2^{d} trial may produce who shall say — a french Gent^{an} in the court said to Mr Chase, "I blush for my country" — & well he might — I spoke a good deal with Mr Rashdale[3] about Dr Marsden, he says a kinder "hearted, more affec^{tn} father does not live, sparing no expense, but weakly suffering himself to be alarmed by this horrid french woman upon a matter w^{h} he could not arrive at but through her — in all my experience of human nature I have never seen such an instance of malignity & practiced duplicity — I yielded half credence to her horrid reports of those dear children deceived by the power she seemed to have over them w^{h} made them speak as if she was kind to them" poor children[4] they will live down the calumny & so will their Father — Enough of horror — Yesterday coming out of Church who s^{hd} come up in his shovel hat but Arch: Allan,[5] whom I had^{nt} recognised at the sacrament & I wonder how he knew my old face so shrivelled up since 16 years — he & his wife are here on acc^t of their daughter at school very ill — "Why do English Clergy or gentry send their children to french schools? he said many kind things of you all — & looked as if he had sat for Dobbin — I think its very doubtful if Pauline will go to London after all — the musical world are delighted with her, at Hermanns Concert[6] she had a grand succés & again in a company all Artists who are charmed with the quality of her voice — They were at the grand affair of Prince Czartorisky's marriage to Miss Munoz,[7] who was in regal splendor with her horrid Mother — "It made one sick said Mad. C: to see people bending to that woman. I kept my fine form erect & my Eye stern & no Calmache de Vannessy[8] bent a knee — " how you'd have laughed at a scene with Miss Trotter[9] I was walking up the fbg[10] with Mrs Corkran who said "There's some one beckoning to you f^m a Carriage." it was the big Trotter, "Miss Doudets acquitted" — "is she I'm glad of it wretched woman for her punishment is her own conscience & may God forgive her" — "is that the way you judge?" "I can do no other, knowing all I do." Some circumstances proving her guilt & the terror in w^h she kept the poor children, from one of their own people who was not a witness — out jumps Miss Trotter "I wish I'd seen you before" "At any rate" said Mrs Corkran "There's a dilemma; if she's innocent the others are guilty." "Don't look at me in [*sic*] manner Ma'am as if I were culpable." Mrs Siddons[11] could not have given a more tragedy tone — deep, symbolical — poor Mrs Corkran hardly knew whether to laugh to cry; but she did smile, & Willie[12] looked as if he could have knocked her down; for my own part, I was so astounded I did not know what to say, but fortunately I thought of Miss Lask[13] & spoke of her, & we parted — "Isnt that a very wicked woman Mamma?" said Bubush[14] — This is all I can send you to day my dear darlings, only that I'm so thankful for Papa keeping well, & I think it was very witty of you giving him such a bedfellow w^h might have scratched his poor xxxxx

Now I'm going to see Mrs Allen & Mrs Gaskell[15] & GP will come out I hope for its sweet balmy air — GOD bless my dearest Maids if you see Mrs Robinson[16] give my love

We were not at home when her brother came — GP just awoke & sends you his love. I dont know what's become of Eyre[17] love to Amy Maria's Out & I'm y^r own old Granny

To Mrs. Fanshawe

Letter 17 [before 9 June 1855]¹
Ray/Morgan

Dearest A. F. I have a long letter for you in my desk but as you have so many bothers of y.ʳ own I won't treat you to ours. Sufficeth it to say that we have had a severe attack & three minor ones — I think we shall go to Paris very soon.² & Papa will be very happy for you to come into this mansion during our absence instead of letting it go to rack & ruin without any body in it — Write soon to me dearest creature we are so happy to hear f.ᵐ you & tell me who it is abusing you in Southton³ & what about I would bet six pence that its Miss Chamberlaynes⁴ or M.ʳ Fitzgerald⁵ — but pray stick up for yourself & don't bear it with Christian patience they will respect you a g.ᵗ deal more for it — also give them my compliments in a satirical manner — am I not talking fudge but you see its a comfort to fly away f.ᵐ this ridiculous world with its absurd forms & twopenny tittle tattle & say what comes first to our beloved aunts.⁶ O! if I was only a boy, I should make myself a clergyman in order to give a sermon wʰ would make their hair stand on end. When I heard to day some stuff about cherubs and cherubims & white clothes with crowns on for virtue; & frying pans for vice — I felt the greatest desire to start up & preach Nature & not what shall I call it — tracts Miss Holmes⁷ quietly says — you know we are infallible — & I quietly think I wish you may catch it. We are to be tremendously learned at Paris & follow Cours of literature⁸ &ct wʰ I like the idea of very much I cant make out what it is just now but I am continually longing for something but I don't know what, I hope it isn't f.ᵐ my favourite castle in Airing [?], pray tell me when thou writest. There is one thing wʰ seems delightful When we are old & go to parties with papa, & make breakfast & write for him — I should like a profession so much — not to spend my life crochetting mending my clothes & reading novels — wʰ seems the employment of English ladies unless they teach dirty little children to read wʰ is well enough in its way — but no work to the mind — & I don't want to write poetry & flummery⁹ — so I am in a fix what to do when I leave off lessons. Please write by my birthday & give good advice¹⁰ for I have no one much to talk to & I like my jaw very much indeed. Papa says in a few years we shall only have 200£ a year to live upon & as my favourite Miss Martineau says it is far nobler to earn than to save.¹¹ I think I should like to earn very much & become celebrated like the aforesaid Harriet who is one of the only sensible women living beside thee & me & 2 or 3 more I know. Give my very polite compliments to D.ʳ Wᵐ. Bullar[12] & thank him for forwarding or bringing this interesting epistle & give my love & this to Wose.[13]

y.ʳ Affect Niece
A Thackeray

To Mrs. Carmichael-Smyth

Letter 18   [Postmark: 16 August 1856][1]
Ray/Morgan

My dearest Granny. We are wondering very much where you are & what is becoming of you, & I am thinking that it can do no harm to send another line to Langen Schwalbach,[2] wʰ can but not reach you at the very worst. You didnt & I remembered afterwards that I didnt say anything about what we were going to do & go to. We were going to N. Germany & S. Devon when I wrote — to stay with L. Elgin[3] in Scotland to pay a visit to the Thackerays & the Pyrenees to stop at some quiet watering place in England or to Germany & learn artistic life or to Switzerland & write a number. So we set off to all these places last Friday — Amy to stay with Edward & then on to Eugenies (By the way do you know that secret, that he wants to marry Miss Wynne[4] only nobody knows anything about it except Papa who told us) and we began by the Thackerays at Bagshot[5] who were very kyind only it wasnt quite as good fun as the Coles. We took down grey gown & white barège & pink bows wʰ we gravely assumed for dinner & questo bothers me so that it is quite enuf to cast a shade over the pleasantest visit. That was sweet, pretty country tho where they are they have got a pony carriage, wʰ has one horse & 2 seats, & I drove round the corner & stopped & said wo, just as if one had been in the habits all ones life. I dessay riding about in the fly gave one some experience. Our friends the 2 Elder[6] girls were away so that we were rather disappointed the old genˡ told more stories than ever & Lady Eliz & her daughters [sic] just as kind as they always are. There was a man-servant of the name of Davis & another (from 6 to 7 or 8) called Tomkins, & when ever the genˡ said severely Tompkins — my lady speaks to you (T. was rather deaf) it always upset ones gravity somehow. Davis was a retired soldier with 3 clasps to his medal & quite a different party. Lady Eliz. said it was rather a bore to have such a hero in the house as all the maids were setting their caps at him, & he had proposed to two of them already. We only stayed there two days then we went to Winsor [sic] on Sunday — to S.t Georges Chapel where I felt dreadfully ashamed I got so muddled with an enormous prayer-book belonging to a K of the G.[7] & the chants & anthems that I could not find a single place, & a gentleman next me kept looking contemptuously over his folio to see if I hadnt got it yet. But o what a jolly place it is — Isnt it Granny — there were the old Winsor Knights in orders & old coats & the sun gleaming thro' the windows, & & you've been there & I neednt catalogue it, then in the afternoon we went & walked on the terrace & looked at the beautiful view (there I asked Minny why S.t Lukes was like Vevay & she said it was a wretched pun when I told her they were both pew-full).[8] & the sacred spot where Majesty descends. Majesty was somewhere else but the music played just the same. They told us that she'd locked up the P. of W.[9] for a couple of days in some room looking out on the terrace, & the second happened to be Sunday so when the people were all there walking about, our future Monarch came to the window & made the most hideous faces at his subjects & then put his thumb to his nose, while the unconscious Q. I suppose was calmly blessing them below. Papa has gone out in a cab with M.r Davison[10] — (for we are now in a very fine city, large & populous on the banks of a river We have a pleasant view of green trees from our windows w.h are all open to let in as much warmth as possible. We have just had a visit from Captain Mark[11] & Cheri. Cheri snubs us till we dont quite know what to do. I told him we were all alone w.d he come & walk in the Sq with us w.h he is to do if a visit he is going to pay is not at home. And there is a ring at the bell & I shouldnt wonder if it was him. I always make a point of calling him my dear w.h is a great shame isnt it. He gets on much better with Minny than with me I think. They have just gone off together in to the Sq. Min is about a head taller than him though he has got on a very tall hat. Minny has got one too and I am sure you w.d be reconciled to them could you but see how pretty my maid looks in hers Wednesday When Cheri came he didnt say do you like me to go with you but is my presence desirable — He brought us y.r address this mor w.h wed lost & U. C.[12] had luckily written down, they are all going off they dont know where under the care of M.r G. Wood[13] & as for us I think we like like this place so much, & have such comfortable lodgings & such pleasant parks to walk in that I shouldnt wonder if we didnt go any where farther. Papa is well again now but I daresay you guess he has had another sea-sick attack, it was only for one day one but as he did not feel well at Winsor he thought it w^d be better to come home,[14] & thats how it is we haven't been to all those jolly places. But we dont care as long as he only keeps cured & cheerful, & Mr Davison is going tomorrow to the Baron Osy, & what will you bet that we are not on board. No I dont think we will be there, so please write very soon to us at 36[15] & give us news of Major & Mrs Smyth if you should happen to meet with them. We made their acquaintance in Paris & found them very agreeable people. O you dear old Grandmother Goodbye & GOD bless you always. We have got some wedding cards from y^r favourite T. Fraser.[16] Shes married a Mr Urquart[17] in the harmy with some calabalistic [*sic*] letters after his name.

Little Edy Story came running up to kiss us in St Georges Chapel itself. Little Boy looks very pale & heavy & is expecting another brother immediately

One thing keeps us at home is that Pa aint got no money. Only £200 for the next 3 months isnt that little & my ball dress isnt paid for yet. New book is to be about J.J. Ridley — the rejected play worked in.[18]

To Amy Crowe

Letter 19
Ray/Morgan

SPA
Friday [22 August 1856][1]

Dear Amy,

Ecco un piccolo per dirte[2] that we're all right here at Spa, that we [*word illegible*] last Thursday three or four months ago that Calais was charming and all the little children made sarcastic remarks about our hats, while here we feel quite ashamed of them so brilliant & feathery & cocky & becoming are those of everybody else. Calais sent us to Ghent w^h is an uncommonly jolly old town with a moat & gables & convents & all the people wear crinoline. We went there with the Hawthor[3] of that conversational work Eyre lent you (w^h I read all Monday week I remember in the most desperate state of melancholy) Well he goes on just like Millemere & Dunnington[4] benevolently thrusting his opinion down your throat & wearing a very smart travelling costume as do his wife & Daughter. I remember he lay flat down on the sofa while we were at breakfast & informed me I never was tired & utterly worn out & then of course one felt quite young & ashamed of oneself. Then we went to Brussels & had a pretty stupid time looking out of window all day at a sentinel opposite & the pour-pour pouring rain. We had one damp mildewy deserted walk on the soppy paths of the dying park & werent at all sorry to pack up in a spendid new box the tray of the old one broke & the things to support it & the division, & the corners were bursting out & so we sold him for 8 franks & got a bran newer   Also Papa made us 3 presents 1 a soap-box 2 a soap box 3 22 volumes of Lamtine[5] rest[n:6] We begged him not but he would & so were in for it. The first sight w[h] greeted one here was a lot of crinoline, & 3 feet with heels out & Miss Piggo[7] & the proud girls walking back wards & for wards with the swells the 2[d] was M[r] Lytton[8] in a waistcoat all covered with red bees, & then M[r] & M[rs] Martin,[9] whom I think we will go & see today. Papa is very well & says this agrees capitally with him. M & me scrambled up some mountains yesterday & I think we shall be off again as soon as we poste questo.[10] were going to Dusseldorf f[m] here We have no news of Granny but we expect to meet them at every turn almost. I know you are having a capital time, so I wont write any more now & am always your affectionatest

AIT

There are jolly little children here   Are they as nice as Ginny & Amy, whom I dont send my love to because its a foolish practice but I dont like them the less for that.

To Amy Crowe

Letter 20   10th 7[br]/56[1]
Ray/Morgan   36 r. Godot

My dearest Amykin. I ain't got many things to write to thee, for this paper bothers me so that I can only think of it instead of all the clever things I would say upon foolscap & valuable information. This is only to tell you that our address is 36 r. Godot, & our health is most reassuring & our finances in a desperate state of confusion. Paris feels like a foreign city and travelling without our two dear old faces we had made so sure of, we never thought Marthas[2] so ugly before, as when it stepped out to greet us, as did Miss Osborne from the r d c[3] & the concierge in his blue velvet cap. Then we drove here very much out of temper & what was our surprise to find a brown young lady from India[4] who made us come away from our hotel Bristol & live with her here where we get up very late & go to bed very early, & are implored to eat cakes & meringues all day long by Felicie[5] who has a great many conversations with us & expressed the greatest contempt for Miss Burnett.[6] Miss Burnet is at Dieppe with her young charges I must tell you & Charlotte[7] & Budsworths[8] & Mrs Trimmer;[9] whose congestion is a much more serious affair than we imagined. As she now finds that she had been suffering from it for these last 20 years. Our Papa is still at Hotel Bristol we go & see him every day & have larks zusammen[10] We drove out in a little open carriage yesterday to the Bay, old Mr Browning[11] w^d be quite delighted with N I think if he c^d see all the new rivers & trees & pagodas & promenades w^h are springing up. Let me thee [sic], Minny wrote to you at Aix — isnt she a much faithfler friend than I am, & I suppose she told you that we dined every other day with the Rothschilds[12] there & went 2 to the play & to a concert & had very good fun till one bad day our poor papa got another & then & then we came away as fast as possible and as we wanted news of Granny & GP, & thought that they had not likely come back here to be with poor Major Robert[13] we came back here too & found them at Heidelberg. Poor Major Robert. I cant tell you how simply & unaffectedly his be [sic] his grief & goes about his dismal funeral business. Mr Fraser told us he had seen it in the paper at Aix & when we got here we found it was true & the poor kind little woman gone for ever. She died quite suddenly one morning. She had been out at the fire works on the 15 & getting up the next day fainted, & never spoke again, & died that evening. The little boy is at Lady Carmichaels & Frederica[14] at Grannys as I told you Frederica's a bore I think. So is Miss Mac[15] Swell Papa calls her who is coming to turn us out of our room poor girl Granny calls her, & so is the fact that we arnt to go nach Scotland mit unserin Vater.[16] I think we shall come here. That w^d be very jolly & then he'd fetch us & then I dont know what next. Granny & GP are having a very good time at Herr Werners Anlage, if you like to write to her & so are we with kind

Jane[17] & Felicie & do please write off this very minute & tell us thou art well & happy & ever our affectionate AMA Crowe. I dont think that a bit like & we kiss the little ones (we saw Amy in the Louvre yesterday) & Eugenie with all our heart.

From Anny & Minny to Amy Crowe

Letter 21   [Postmark: 26 October 1856]
Ray/Morgan

. . . theatres[1] & lecturing halls Endless copies & busts & skeletons beautiful garden to sketch in astronomy & geometry & everything possible going on inside. We went to the play last Saturday & woke Miss Douglas[2] who looked very handsome. It was the prettiest thing in the world Mids ^{mrs} Nights dream fairies & wood-scenery moonshine & sunrises. It was charming. I like Shakespeare very much indeed. But I dont like Mr Keene[3] in short sleeves & earrings. Dear old GP it makes ones heart ache to see him. The fever's worse & worse & she's down again lower than ever.[4] Its the pulsatelea[5] they say O Amykin I should like to swear a little at somebody. Minnys with her Its no use my going it only creaks, & when Mins tired she can come out & then Ill go. I dont know why people think fever so bad — [6]

My dearest Amy, Anny says Im to finish her letter & I think its time, but I happen to want to write to you myself so here goes 4.D. to days Sunday & Grannies better her pulse is only 100, 20bp[7] and sometimes not a hundred & now Ill tell whats made her better. She's wished for grapes two or three days but that beast Jah[8] said she might only have 3 & the other who is a fool said she mightened have any and last night she was very low and thought she was going to die, (but she always thinks so if she's at all worse so we dont much mind now, and poor soul she sent for Papa to say good bye, she would not see him for 3 days before that, and he cheered her up in no time and said that the 3 grapes was all fudge and he got her a great heap & she eat about a pound & thought them very nice & has been wonderfully well ever since wasnt that a good thing & now she's taken some magnesia. I wrote you another letter but I wont send it for this ones more cheerful as I was very frightened at first with poor Grannies dreadful screams and sometimes she is so low spirited and will tell us what we are to do when she is dead but now I know its all nothing but nervousness and I dont think there's the slightest danger. It is such a mercy that we came for poor GP. you may fancy what a way he is in, but Papa has cheered him so well, and he looks so happy now that she is better. Mrs Corkran was so kind and stayed here till we came. Please dear Amy write to us soon and often I assure it will be a great comfort to get a long cheery letter from all crossed.⁹ Im only afraid that poor Grannie may have a great many more palpitations, which perhaps are not very bad but they always make her so low, and then she screams out so, all out of nervousness for she has no pain what ever and then poor dear old GP is almost as bad as she is. You see Anny & I never nursed any one before and Im afraid we're very clumsy. So if you sugestions [*sic*], in that line to make say so in your next letter Eliza¹⁰ is as good as gold so is Martha but she snores Mrs Brice¹¹ came over with us, & at Boulogne caught a glimpse of Miss Markers¹² nose but that was enough for me so I cut

Papa is in with Grannie who goes on very well, my dear Amy its an awful long time since we saw you. Edward dined with us this day week in london I suppose he's at Moscow (I dont know how its spelt) now I should like to see you so much but as I cant please write to us. Im afraid Papa will have to go to Scotland very soon now. tell me some more about little nieces, we havent seen the Ritchie children yet but Charlotte or Jane¹³ come every day. Oh my dear Amy I shall be very glad to write and tell you that Grannie's well for GP's sake & for hers & for our, but I think it prudentest to expect a great many more relapses adieu mon cher chum

Je suis votre affectionate mais melancholy

PS. Grannys much better today, & O so hungry. Dear old Minny's a trump¹⁴ isnt she said A Amy do write soon

To Amy Crowe

Letter 22
Ray/Morgan

Hotel Wheeler
Havre
Friday
[after 21 Nov. 1856]¹

That is where your affectionate A & M are my dearest Amy, & where their Grandmamma is finding herself back again Thank God, & will leave her melancholies & unwellness we hope. She got better a great deal at Paris & then seemed to stop somehow and so we urged her off in the face of all the friends, & came away on Monday not without some secret trepidation on the part of those rash advisers who were bearing her off to certain death people told us. I wish to goodness they wouldnt give so much advice. She bore the journey famously slept it through & had a better night than she had had for 6 weeks she said & is really a great deal better. But you know after a nervous fever one need not be surprised at nervous attacks occasionally particularly when one has had them before the illness & that is what Granny will insist upon doing & theres no talking her out of it. She had a bad one last night the 1st for ten days, Eliza came & called me up, & there she was groaning & moaning & starting poor dear, & so wretched it became quite melancholico-comic at last. E is admirably good & sympathetic & patient, & respectful, & so Granny got calm about 4 and I daresay there wont be any more for another week or so. But except that, she is as well as you or I, & I dont think 4 or 5 hours melancholiness is such a dreadful thing do you? We want her to come to O. Sq.[2] again with GP & Im sure that w^d cheer her up. Its dreadful to think of going off and leaving them all by themselves those two dear old people & so we shall stay till Xmas at all events, & then our Father will be able to come over & then & then who knows. Only I should like to say howdy doo to my dear old Amy again Dont you think we have been quite long enough without seeing each other. Granny took her first walk today, its been such abominable galosh weather that she has been kept perforce to cabs and substitutes of that sort. But I assure you there is nothing equal to our old friends & I am certain she will eat a good dinner & be all the better. We have had two famous letters from our Father hes making 500£ he says and many more compliments than that fall to him & hospitalities. Middleton[3] seems to be a very jolly place & he says Fanny[4] was regretting us 3 very kindly indeed to him & sends you her love. But he's having a capital time out there & received a note of thanks from grateful Edinburgh for his admirable lectures. He sent us a little notice of G IV[5] w^h is very funny & good. Mr Corkran brought us the kindest notice of him in an Ed. paper w^h I never read the like of in all my life. Well then it is settled that he is to come back at Xmas to us, & to lecture as hard as he can meanwhile. Isnt it an odious business. We have been reading a disgusting book of Albert Smiths called Mr Ledbury[6] (I have taken to spending all the money I can lay hold of in novels) and theres a good deal of his show in it. One felt personally defrauded somehow when one came upon it. We are so idle here that we have not even time to read novels. Its very good fun as I think I have told you before, & this Inn is exactly like one of Mr Dickens's early novels. Nothing but the queerest snobs come here — Though its very snug & comfortable with a rosy chambermaid called Lucy, & passages w^h look into a covered court where the maids & the boots[7] are frisking about all day long G P and I dined at the table d'hote one day in company with 5 sea faring Captains (for the most part h-less)[8] & a sort of mad Mulligan[9] joined to the most graceful manners & the master of the Hotel a retired Captain carving at the head. The Captains were all joking one of em who was going to be married. And one wretched snob took some pie — & said Sweets to the sweet, while Mulligan poured out incoherently to the Hotel Captain who solemnly nodded his head every minute or two[10] as if he were too wise to speak. I havent room to tell you all the queer things they said, but it was just like people in Pickwick. Its so amusing in bed of a morning through the door, I heard a ruff voice asking his morning to be shown into to a gentleman called Gollegan, small fond of talking with a feminine voice, What a stupid letter I never has anything to say with a steel pen Granny is asleep on the sofa. I am afraid she looks a good deal older dear old soul It was quite odd just now she looked so like Grandmama come to life again. Minny has been drawing a set of the funniest pictures theres one [*sic*] the children swinging the cook w^h is capital & when the rope breaks & poor cookey comes to grief.

I really cannot stand the ink any longer its so comic that you cannot help bursting out a laughing. This is tomorrow. Granny had a capital night and theres a sweet soft grey veil out of window putting one in mind of dear old England. I'm sure it is not a foolish fancy, I feel it penetrating the pores of my heart. I am afraid my poor Mulligan has come to grief he tumbled down the hold of the Southton Packet last night & was brought back here & rubbed all over with mustard: Theres a good old couple staying in another room waiting for a steamer w^h has been out 80 days with their daughter on board, w^h they had been afraid was lost at first & theres an old lady in a braided wig — blk satin gown & yellow barege shawl w^h has a very sweet effect when it turns out upon the porte. Marias last note to me was dated one October at night & full of dark allusions, & disagreeable I thought. She said being without a maid she had really had no time to write to you. As I know what a lot you have to do dear Miss Amy I shall look out for a letter next w^k to y^r affectionatest Anne.

Letters 53

<u>dont write to us here</u>
We have faithful letters f^m our Tishy who is here a^b w^k at the D^rg Schools[11] & Uncle Chas seems to have some idea of coming over as A. Mary[12] is sick again. We have been seeing E. Thackeray at Paris who is really very nice & now that there is no more room I seem to remember how little I have told you. Bess & Maria [*word illegible*] are very busy with a lodger & no servant. We have had a little sort of tiff w^h is made up again. I didnt answer a letter of Besses, & so I pounced upon the opening I saw in M not answering you & we made it up[13]

How de do dear old Amy
Ive no paper nor time to say more than your affectionate[14]

To Amy Crowe

Letter 23　　　　　　　　　Paris. 28. 9.[1]
Ray/Morgan　　　　　　　[Postmark: Paris, 30 Nov. 1856]

My dearest A.M.A. I send you a dismal Havre letter and here I hope is a cheerful Paris one. We were so glad to see one f^m thee when we came back last night after our ten days with quite another Grandmother to the one who went away. Your note lay on the top of Mr Synges flowery handwriting & an invitation — if not engaged for tonight from Mrs Giles.[2] Mr Synge begged us to accept the blessing of an old man & says they've all had the influenza. Our dear old Feyther sends lots of letters & newspapers He's having a very good time still & all the places are bien [?] besides ever many more. Heving only knows when hes coming home again but Xmas I think & ope. Isnt it delightful about Mr Davison? Sir Henry Davison doesnt that sound harmonious, & 5000£ a year with a 1000 retiring pension[3] — My dearest Amy when Granny made certain arrangements why did we all burst out laughing at her. W. Ritchie the croesus was dreadfully afraid of having this offered to him, because he wouldnt have been able to refuse, & advocatgeneralism is a much better business still.[4] Then poor Monroe is dead.[5] I'm so sorry. I went to see her the last day I was here, one evening & Miss White[6] begged me to go in, & she was so changed & softened, & kind, poor soul, she took my hand & held it & seemed quite touched. Mr Chave[7] buried her the other day, & the 2 poor daughters are going away & I really am so sorry, arnt you rather? We have been grumbling at the rain w^h kept falling at Havre but it seems theyve been having snow here — Yesterday was charming & as usual the journey was capital for G. who was getting back into her painful nervous state of hers, so that we thought it best to move off again. She has put on her blk jacket with the worn elbows today & looks quite smart — I am speculating as to this evening. Dont you think the high white barège will be the thing? The Miss Burnetts have got black & red velvet bonnets & tight jackets & look sweller & scornfuller than ever. Mr Dunbar[8] is dying & it was the ugly one who was to have married him only he bullied her so, thats why she was so thin. Hennie[9] informs her faithful Minny that she had seen Mr Crowe at the D.C. & that this is her last letter as she has only 3^d of her allowance left, but she has begun to leave off butter so as to earn a little more. Laure has been playing in public for a 100 f^s. Papa doesnt tell much of his G.[10] that one doesnt read in Mr Cunninghame.[11] I dreamt of the Dickens's party you tell of last night. & we said yes you were quite right & that everything was settled between Kate & M^r W Collins.[12]

When you next write say if you are very jolly or if you begin to think youd like to come back. Granny has some notion of that sort in her head.[14]

To Mrs. Stoddart[1]

Letter 24
Ray/Morgan

36 Onslow Sq.
Sunday
[late August/early September 1857][2]

Dear Mrs Stoddart

It is very nearly bed time & I have only a sheet or two of very queer note paper at hand, but I hope you wont mind if I write to say howdy do to you upon it & to hope that you have been having as pleasant fresh breezes this summer as we have. We all went down to a place w^h I know its very snobbish to like, & took a very nice lodging at 126 Marine P.^{d} Brighton with no end of waves out of every window, & carriages & horses & Punch & Judys, & organ boys f^m morning to night. They fairly drove Papa into Germany with his "Virginians" who are bursting out next month in their yellow covers,[3] & I hope it will be all right now but I cant tell you the state of misanthropy & disgust into w^h they had plunged him It must be a great bore to be forced to write novels when one is so sick of them that one (Papa I mean) cant even read one without going to sleep over it. He is away just now, & we are orphans with a grandmother only, to keep house for, but we are looking out for him every day, & now that his book is coming out we know that he is obliged to return to his family whether he will or not. His Oxford bills have been just coming in, over w.^h I assure you he has been pulling very long faces.[4] I cant tell you how disappointed we were when he didnt get in. We minded it a great deal more than he did, but I think the bills affect him a great deal more than they do us. I thought at the time that I w.^d tell you what you might perhaps care to hear. When he came back after his canvassing he told us how scarcely any of the College servants voted for him except those of St John's But these all came forward, & when they did so it was not from any personal interest in him but for old times he said.

And now dear Mrs Stoddart I think I will say good night to you. Minny sends you her love by the name of Harriet, as she wishes to [*sic*] called now that she is grown up. Please write us another letter some day when it doesnt bore you & at all events believe me

      Affectionately yours
      AI Thackeray

To?

Letter 25   [before 10 April 1858][1]
Ray/Morgan

ill[2] till the Baker came and administered Salt — but tho' its much better Granny & GP have been telling me we ought to make away with it as its mouth might be poisonous & hurt the Mother & little browny — Papa is dining at Mr Delane of the times[3] he's done his months wk.[4] & seems now again a little bit better — Talking of dinners we had such a horror of a dinner last week. 18 people each more genteel than the other & Gray got bewildered and Charles went mad & Sims[5] floundered about among the dishes and the waiters danced wildly round emptying everything down the peoples backs such a harum scarum spill em tear em I never beheld in mortal life. But enough of this painful subject Next day we <u>charitably</u> went off with little mouldy scraps of things we could not get down our selves & treated three little boys in St Georges Hospital whose eyes lighted up at the squashy grapes and eager little hands stretched out — it made one quite melancholy feeling — poor children to see their fever stricken faces and their wan little fingers — two of them have been in bed three months the other is going to have his eye taken out & put in again & they say he will see better than ever. He is one of my district people.⁶ M.ʳ Molyneux's⁷ low church ladies are at work in it with little tracts.

You will sympathise with their horror when one old fellow made a mistake & gave them back one of <u>my</u> fellow visitors pamphlets with Episcopal seals and mystic signs & symbols & frantic high Church Doctrines instead of their own little converted niggers. This same old soldier of 80 has been at Waterloo & my colleague is most anxious that he & his old wife the char-woman shᵈ come & be confirmed next week & promises to hear him his catechism for the occasion. I went alone the other day & he rather timidly appealed to me — "Wouldn't it look orkard now for me & my old woman & pertickler, seein wʰ we fears we must decline" — He seemed very much surprised and immensely relieved when I said it was no affair of mine he must talk to Miss Hancock⁸ as she did the Religious part and I had only come about the soupe.⁹

To Amy Crowe

Letter 26   [Paris]
Ray/Morgan   [late Dec. 1858]

You dear old girl to write such a nice Christmas letter to us. Mine was written a week ago & I lost him as usual & so Mins went without. Even now I think I shall stop this for a day or two to let it tell you the end of everything. Fancy the first thing when we awoke yesterday morning, in comes Caroline¹ with a dele strip of paper. The pleasure of y.ʳ company is requested at 9.30. by a young fellow at the hotel Bristol.² First guess who it was & see if you are as clever as we were: My dear young fellow looked famous but he went away last night saying, I think I am going to be ill — Dont come up in the morning. But the breakfast was so jolly one could afford to cry at night, and as he didnt mention the afternoon I think we will go out & see presently on our way to Ch. Granny cut the p.³ pudding Sure enough — Poussiac & Frantz⁴ dined & our dear old Daddy who we hadnt heard about for so long that we began to think he was enamoured of being a batchelor that we should'nt hear any more of him. What he says (for hes come to fetch us back) is that he wants if possible to fight against y.^r coming to Granny as hes more soletary than ever & more away from home & that once you come she will never make a move for any body else & for me & Minny to leve without you aint a cheerful prospex — however I dont think or talk about it & leave the elders to fight it out between em. Granny comes out every day about 12 & goes to bed at 10½ like anybody else — of course she hasnt put a foot to the ground yet — but sits up & has been almost quite herself save for feverishnessesses. She wants to get up & carry her bed dreadfully poor dear. On the whole I fancy shes been lucky — her knee stiffness gives her more trouble than her hip now but all the Doctors say that always follows & will go away by degrees. I havent asked Pap yet how long he could stay it rather stuck in my throat yesterday & we aint seen him today — Just fancy what news he brings. Gray's going & Emmas gone[5] — Emma went he wrote because G & she quarrelled like cats & dogs & all of a sudden up comes Gray & says she is going too — that her sister has come to town & they mean to live together — She had not a notion of it the day before & he thinks that it was some strong expressions he used when he found no soap & dirty towels in his room. Or perhaps that she read a letter I wrote in w.^h I said I was in a great rage at Emma's going that she was in fact higher in the social scale than Gray & D. However it seems Emma went out larking & stopped away all night & said she was at her sisters w.^h she wasnt. Im beginning to hanker a little after poor Eliza again — Papa says he saw her at Mr Dillons[6] where she only gives ½ satisfaction about the cooking & looked so old, so miserable so dirty crying & wretched that it made him quite sick & he gave her a sovereign. Gray told him she was always thinking and talking about us. It seems to me very heartless & unkind of Gray to go & so heres an end to sinking down into our graves surrounded by attached and whiteheaded servitors. Its rather comic to have come to 3 men & no maids at all now. Mrs Russell[7] has lost her baby poor thing & been dangerously ill herself with erysipolas. Mme Marochetti[8] has got her 2 sons at home & looks very happy — Alice[9] is better but has been awfully ill. Such a wretched letter as I got from Louisa[10] — who says she behaved like a tigress all through but its a nice letter too — 8 pages of horrible metaphors & misery & description of illness (thats not what I mean by nice —) I was thinking of her re-enthusiasm for Papa who had sent wine generous wine w^h she poured like life down the lips of her darling hour after hour through the dark midnight watches — Jellys transcendant Jellies fit for Juno — w^h had sustained her own numbed heart & brain. She says poor Alice was burning with molten fire within while clay cold damps &ct. But its been typhus & a sort of diptheria & a dreadful abscess on her neck w^h burst inwardly & I cant go on with the dreadful list. Once she says she fell back fainting & Mrs Corkran thought it was all over. But however the swelling broke outwardly too & since then shes been better. What made it so bad was that she had inflammation of the bowels & together w^h wanted 2 opposite physics so they gave them both. Dont you think neither w^d have done as well. About the Garrick: its only ½ as exciting as it used to be.[11] Papas getting disgusted. Everybody's been bullying him about his susceptibility. Mr Dickens finding he w^d have to be put up in the witness box wrote off to Papa to say that could not the lamentable affair be arranged — That Mr Yates having rendered him a Manly Service in a Matter of w^h he had Cognizance he had &ct. Cant you fancy him & his gusto over Manly Service.[12] (It was going off from the smoking room at the G to tell all the stories Papa was telling of Mr Dickens.) I am getting confused & indignant Papa says the story is that Charley met his Father & Miss Whatsname Whatever the actress[13] out walking on Hampstead Heath. But I dont believe a word of the scandal — After all the stories told of us[14] we can afford to disbelieve it of other people. Mr Fladgate[15] always carries all the printed papers about in his pocket so as to have em constantly handy. He is quite affected abt it — I am 60 years of age — I shall see it thro' this crises he says & then retire from the Comittee {*sic*}. We went to pay Papa our visit yesterday and found him with a little leach. As soon as Granny is up we will go off again Everything is still uncertain. But we shall be going in a day or two & now can't bear to think of Granny left all alone — She said something delightful today about coming to Brighton for the Summer when the apartment is up in April. Wouldnt that be the very thing? It's charming to hear abt all the nephews and nieces & the red habit Shirt & the Christmas tree — We manufactured one for the Ritchies w^h we carried off in a cab Such a business it was, all the little nuts & bobbins rattling & tumbling about, & the candles & bonbons & rubbish — As I was staggring upstairs with l'enfant — the cab man called it — the door opened & out rushed the children whom we had imagined safe in bed. We had wanted it for Xmas day, but Charlotte wants to keep it till we dine & that wont be for some months I fancy.[16]

3

1859–1863

INTRODUCTION

I think for my part that we were all very old in those days & that it is now that we are very young. (Letter 36)

ROM 1859 through 1863 Thackeray's star was setting; Anny's, smaller and less brilliant, was rising. Thackeray was plagued with worries about his finances, his literary ability, and his health. He wanted to leave his daughters a fortune and to enjoy the remainder of his life. This necessitated that he earn more money, but his failing health and ensuing sense of desperation made the creation of a highly successful novel less likely. Within these four years Thackeray's health deteriorated rapidly, leading to his death on Christmas Eve of 1863. Besides accumulating a fortune for his daughters he was determined to leave Anny the legacy of a career. Anny had her first article published in the *Cornhill* in May 1860. He was proud to see his predictions about her talent come true. She, in turn, was modest about her success.[1] Once Thackeray was confident in his daughters' future, he appeared content to die.[2]

Thackeray's traveling was no longer frenetic. His failing health may account in part for this, but he appeared to have achieved an inner peace that resulted from his greater maturity. He built a new home, which he ironically named "Vanity Fair," and despite the great expense, he loved it. In Letter 34 Anny complains about the cost. She admits that even the beloved Palace Green "has its drawbacks," as the cost of the house escalated. "Papa has been really out of sorts J & G send in more & more bills 800 just come in for nothings — " They all

loved the house on Palace Green. Red brick, and built in the Queen
Anne manner, the house facing Kensington Gardens was (and still is)
beautiful.[3] Their happiness in it added to their delight. Describing her
feeling after a performance of *The Wolves and the Lamb* which was given
to commemorate the completion of "Vanity Fair," Anny wrote in her
diary, "I remember such an odd feeling came over me I suppose this is
the summit I shall never feel so jubilant so grand so wildly important
& happy again — "[4] And indeed Anny's jubilation was short-lived.
The Thackerays moved into Palace Green on 31 March 1862; Thackeray
died less than two years later.

His last four years were filled with close association with his mother
and his daughters. On 9 September 1861 Major Carmichael-Smyth
died. After the death of her husband, Mrs. Carmichael-Smyth moved
into Thackeray's home. With Thackeray as arbitrator she caused fewer
problems for Anny and Minny than when they had lived with her
years before. Even with a broken hip which had left her lame, Mrs.
Carmichael-Smyth was a vigorous, opinionated, regal old lady. In
1859 Anny was twenty-two and Minny was three years younger; they
could now be his adult companions. Because he was ill so much of the
time, Anny and Minny rarely left him alone; they visited away from
home one at a time.

Weekends were spent with such friends as the Trollopes, Rothschilds, and Knightons (Letters 32, 35).[5] Other trips were taken not
merely to accommodate Thackeray but also for Anny's and Minny's
enjoyment, for example, attendance at the Mount Felix Ball (Letter
28). Longer journeys were taken to Folkestone (Letter 29), and to
Europe (Letter 30).

For the first time, Anny and Minny wrote to each other because
they were traveling without each other. They each went to recuperate
from an illness; yet their primary concern in the letters was always
their father's health. Anny and Minny's relationship seems to have
been a good one, but Minny was still dependent on her sister (Letter
33). Anny treated Minny as the baby sister even in 1859, when Minny
was nineteen. In the 1878 journal Anny admitted: "I used to treat Minnie as if she was a very little girl always but one day she looked at me &
said You dont suppose Ainy that I dont know all the things you think
tho you dont say them." Minny exploited her little sister status when
it suited her, but was quite capable of being an adult at other times.

The letters written by Minny at this time show a young woman trying to be independent, yet often regressing into her former position of baby of the family. Anny's description of her, even by Victorian standards, is of a much younger girl. In an 1861 letter Anny characterized her as "nearly 21 and absurdly young for her age for she still likes playing with children and kittens & hates reading & is very shy tho' she does not show it & very clever tho' she does not do any thing in particular."[6]

Away for a month in Scotland for the frequently prescribed change of air, Minny's letters disclose, by 1863, an intelligent, witty, and sharp-tongued young woman. Her letters are lively and full of acerbic observations. For example, to Anny:

> I may as well write to you pour passer le temps as the french say. . . . Have something nice to eat prepared for me against my return Mind this & remember that I am now accustomed like Brownie to a great deal of notice . . . Theres a sweet oyster woman if you had a voice like a oyster what a comfort it w^d be to Papa — (Letter 40)

Minny also alludes to feelings of rivalry between herself and her sister that Anny only mentions in her journals.

Minny's visit to Scotland was a success. Thackeray wrote to his friend John Brown:

> I am very glad you like my little Min. With her and her Sister I have led such a happy life, that I am afraid almost as I think of it, lest any accident should disturb it. . . . I think she ought to come back to her Papa and sister. We three get on so comfortably together, that the house is not the house, when one is away.[7]

In *The Virginians,* begun in 1857 and finished in 1859, Thackeray portrayed his exemplary family the Lamberts. The Colonel and his wife live in harmony, understanding, and love. They have sons who are away at school; thus the two daughters, Theo and Hetty, complete the family picture. In a letter Thackeray wrote, "I am afraid the 2 Lambert girls in the Virginians are very like them [my young women], but of course deny it if anybody accuses me."[8] Although Anny is lovingly portrayed as Theo, the elder Lambert daughter, she is really a synthesis of eighteenth-century virtues, Thackeray's milksop maiden,[9] and Anny's real character "(with her usual propensity to consider herself a miserable sinner) always reproach[ing] herself" (chapter 92). In the 1864 journal Anny wrote, "Papa once said — not long ago — Anny always manages to reproach herself whatever happens." Theo's physical appearance matches that of Thackeray's dear fat old Anny. His description of the two Lamberts, "saucy Hetty or generous Theodosia" (chapter 23), is also reminiscent of the two Thackeray girls. In the Colonel's introduction of his daughters, he dismisses Hetty with a curt "Here is Miss Hester," but he affectionately lists Miss Theo with all her virtues, comic or otherwise. Thackeray repeatedly calls Hetty "saucy" and "Madam Pert," attributes jealousy to her (chapter 23), and indicates the Lambert girls' different reactions to a situation by recounting Hetty's anger and Theo's pity (chapter 62).

In *The Virginians* Thackeray is writing nostalgically, sentimentally, remembering what he experienced for only a short time—a happy family life which contained "among the blessings which Heaven hath bestowed . . . the love of a faithful woman" (chapter 21). Theo and Hetty are faithful to their father, but in a curious way which departs from reality. Theo marries, has a large family and lives in Victorian happiness ever after. In love with the obtuse Harry, Hetty remains an old maid devoted to her father. The course of Anny's and Minny's lives did not follow fiction, nor did Thackeray live long enough to see how his determination of the situation was altered by reality. While he depicted what he knew about his daughters, the young Lambert girls remain charming, natural, and honest. When they grow older and Thackeray turns them into stock Victorian heroines, they become dull. However, he always writes of them with affection and tenderness.

Amy Crowe had also become an integral part of the Thackeray household. Thackeray himself dubbed her "dear good little Dorrit!"[10] who was "so good and gentle that actually nobody in my family is jealous of her."[11] What Thackeray said of Amy was augmented by Anny's description of her: "one of the best and gentlest & kindest of women."[12] Anny's letters to Amy afford an honest assessment of the Thackerays because they describe a home with which Amy was familiar, while at the same time she was unhampered by family ties. Amy was and simultaneously was not Anny's sister. A greater freedom of exchange of ideas existed between the two than between Anny and Minny, because Thackeray the father never came between the friends. Amy's father may not have been very kind to her, but he existed; Thackeray was only a substitute and, given Amy's "little Dorrit" quality, no real threat.

In Letter 36, written to Amy in India where she has gone to live with her husband, Anny described the Thackeray household with the assurance that Amy will "know exactly what it is all like," comparing it with her life as a child: "I think for my part that we were all very old in those days & that it is now that we are very young." Still, there are problems: "it is not at all so couleur de rose." She explores her own feeling with a pen: "Isnt [it] a delightful comfort that we are all so happy together. I should be quite happy if it wasn't for those mysterious griefs of mine. There is rather a tragedy going on in the house." Abruptly she defuses the topic of her own griefs by speaking, not of *her* tragedy, but of one in which the housemaid has been caught pilfering. What her "griefs" are, she does not specify, if she knew them at all.[13]

Although Anny was launched on a career, she was not certain of its promise or even of its assured existence. Her beloved Amy was gone; her friends (many younger than Anny) were getting married; her letters are full of references to engagements and marriages (Letters 29, 30, 34).

In Letter 35 she described Amy's departure for India, "Yah what hateful things partings are." Anny had developed the ability to generalize from a specific situation. Perhaps Amy's departure caused her to remember the buried trauma of Isabella's removal. Anny's dark moods became more pronounced as she got older. However, she was aware of them and learned to deal with them. In Letter 28 she wrote: "This is an unfavourable day for my correspondents. I mean Im very grumpy & in the blues, so please dont fancy from the desponding tone of my letter that things arn't going very well with us, & that we arnt very grateful to Providence." After outlining all the externals that had gone wrong and how the problems had been solved, she added that "Now we are very jolly, that is as jolly as people are generally, when they have everything they can wish for, except M.ʳ Yates friendship." Her own state of being depended to a large degree on those around her; her answer to despondency was humor. She took a serious situation and laughed at it—often at herself. As in the letter to Amy in India when Anny denigrated her mysterious griefs by following the reference to them with the housemaid's tragedy, here she diminished her own problems with the reference to the Yates affair.

Anny's joke about the Garrick Club affair in her letter to Synge is a good indication that Thackeray, often thin-skinned where his honor and dignity were concerned, had finally decided to back away from his grievances. In an earlier letter to Amy Crowe in December of 1858

(Letter 26) Anny related with gusto the state of the affair, relishing all the gossip and hearsay; however, after a year of wrangling, public attacks, and private feuds, Anny and Thackeray as well were satiated with it.

Anny's letters to the Synges are chatty and full of reports about Thackeray. Although replete with details, the letters do not contain the confidences found in Anny's letters to Amy. In Letter 28 Anny described Thackeray's health: "Its all lemonade & giving up other more intoxicating liquors." About the Garrick club affair she wrote: "We are begging our Jupiter to keep in his thunder & not even read it [the Yates pamphlet] & as he has taken to paying great attention to what we say lately perhaps he wont." Yet no matter how indulgent a father Thackeray was, no matter how much Anny thought he was listening to her and Minny, she admitted to the Synges that they "let Papa do as he likes" (Letter 29).

Thackeray's closeness to his daughters is revealed by the fact that he discussed his financial and literary concerns with them. Anny knew about the arrangements Thackeray had concluded for his editorship of the *Cornhill:* "1000 a year for editing . . . & then he's paid for his articles beside" (Letter 31). In addition, she recounted his anguish at the lack of success of *The Adventures of Philip.* "Well then Philip is a regular failure if you know what it is to have a pianoforte played upon y.r nerves that is what Papa is going thro. Though he dont say much about it" (Letter 34). Because of the expense of the house and the failure of his new novel to make money, Thackeray was forced to "write like mad . . . wh isnt very favorable to composition." However, the real problem was, as always now, Thackeray's health. "These are all very trifling troubles if he could get 3 days of wellness I shouldnt care hes not worse than usual only more bothered." Once caught up in the fever of building his house, Thackeray spared nothing. He was resolute about leaving a fortune for his daughters. Tired and ill as he was, he drove himself, knowing that what he produced was not up to his usual standard.[14]

In a later reminiscence Anny disclosed that her father lived in "good company."[15] As a child she had been witness to his way of life; now as an adult she became part of Thackeray's world of "eminent Victorians." Still functioning as Thackeray's daughter, she also partook of the London season as well as of its cultural activities. Her description in Letter 36 of the paintings in the exhibition of the Royal Academy which opened on 2 May 1863 is sensitive and knowledgeable.

Another important factor in Anny's letters is her growing literary ability. Descriptions of both people and places became sharper and more focused. She dispensed gossip in narrative scenes, complete with conversation. Though her subject matter flowed in an unconscious stream from one topic to another without paragraphs, she was extremely conscious of her style. For example, in Letter 27 she wrote, "We thought of you on Sunday with very red noses & numb fingers & bad colds — that is us you know — not you." When the meaning was muddied, she clarified it.

Her ear for the vernacular in conversation (even in French) is sharp, as shown in the exchange between the Thackerays and the waiter and other travelers who share their journey. Particularly amusing is the Frenchman "with a fat old wife sucking liquorice big rings mittens dyed hair" (Letter 30). These descriptions—briefly highlighting striking characteristics, authentic sounding conversation, and suitable tone—are all reminiscent of Thackeray. Her thoughts, her judgments, are of course her own, as is her love of nature. For example in Letter 36: "Outside the moon was shining the stars blazing a beautiful soft little breezy wind came through the lilac trees. . . . It was a sort of poetry tonight in the middle of prosy everyday." Some of her sentences are still rough and unpolished (she was writing letters which were not for publication), but there is ample evidence that she was seeing and hearing with a professional's sensibility.

Anny's letters reveal a startling candor mixed with a pull toward exaggeration. Thus she writes in Letter 27, "I wrote you a letter last night full of such astounding news that Minny would not let me send it — So tonight I must send you a little word much more common-place & rather more truthful." And later in the same letter Anny insists that her story about Dr. Anslie was a "pure invention" of her own. Anny needed to find a format for her inquiring mind and her judgments of character that would not slander any of her acquaintances.

Many years later she explained to George Smith, publisher of the *Cornhill,* how her first article, "Little Scholars," came into being.

> I had written several novels and a tragedy by the age of fifteen, but then my father forbade me to waste my time any more scribbling, and desired me to read other people's books.
>
> I never wrote any more except one short fairy tale, until one day my father said he had got a very nice subject for me, and that he thought I might now begin to write again. That was Little Scholars which he

christened for me and of which he corrected the stops and the spelling, and which you published to my still pride and rapture.[16]

In his own *Reminiscences* Smith continued the story:

> Thackeray sent it to me and a letter containing the following passage: "And in the meantime comes a contribution called *Little Scholars,* which I send you, and which moistened my paternal spectacles. It is the article I talked of sending to *Blackwood;* but why should *Cornhill* lose such a sweet paper because it was my dear girl who wrote it? Papas, however, are bad judges — you decide whether we shall have it or not!"[17]

Describing three charity schools in London, the essay is simple, conversational, and without pretense. Although there is no Dickensian horror or shrill indignation at the poverty of the children, neither does Anny whitewash or falsify reality. She admires the efforts of those who try to alleviate the distress of the children and teach them useful trades, all the while being captivated by the children themselves. She informs her readers about how many children may be fed a hot lunch for one shilling. Without comment she tells the harrowing tale of a little girl and her drunken father; while of another group she writes: "Mr. Millais might make a pretty picture of the little scene."[18]

Of special interest is the third school Anny visited, one for Jewish children in the slums of Spitalfields. Whether Thackeray chose it for her is not known, but her treatment of this school is refreshing and strangely clear-sighted for a Victorian: "Little Jew babies are uncommonly like little Christians; just as funny, as hungry, as helpless, and happy now that the bowls of food come steaming in" (120). Anny speaks to the reader with a charming grace. It is indeed a "sweet paper." Thackeray recommended the article to a friend, "Read the Cornhill Magazine for May; the article Little Scholars is by my dear old fat Anny."[19] Having guided Anny's career, Thackeray was happy with her debut.

Several other publications followed in the *Cornhill;* Anny's first novel, *The Story of Elizabeth,* ran in the magazine from September 1862 through January 1863. "Little Scholars" with its honesty, clarity, and simplicity set the pattern for Anny's nonfiction; *Elizabeth* became the prototype for her fiction.

Anny's plots comply with many conventions of the Victorian novel. Her plots begin with a change in the life of the heroine, and then, like her father's masterwork, *Vanity Fair,* trace the vicissitudes of the lives of two women, one of whom is frequently more moral and seemingly more deserving of happiness than the other. Yet this heroine has some kind of moral lapse. Eventually, however, she rejects one suitor and is consequently married to the "right" suitor.[20]

With the exception of *Mrs. Dymond,* which is a full bildungsroman in that the heroine grows and matures into a woman, the heroines in Anny's novels reach only a partial awakening. They are passive Victorian ladies whose psyches Anny explores so that the reader understands them better than they do themselves. Anny's novels are notable for their sense of reality, for their evocation of the past, for their appreciation of nature, for their honesty, humor, and understanding of the predicament of many women in her age, and for their easy and graceful style.

It is striking that the heroine in Anny's novels is frequently an orphan. Although this is a common theme in Victorian novels (though in Thackeray it is Becky not Amelia who is an orphan), given her own parental circumstance it is understandable that Anny's literary mothers are usually absent, ineffectual, or cruel, so that the heroine sometimes must mature within a single-parent home and often will have difficulties owing to this limitation. There is perhaps in Anny's history also a personal reason for the repeated usage of dead fathers in her novels: such a close daughter-father relationship as she and Thackeray had can bring with it a need to keep the father absent or, symbolically, no longer existent in order to avoid any threat of unconscious incest.

Interestingly, *The Story of Elizabeth* was attacked in *The Athenaeum* because the reviewer found that it "turns upon a subject which is, or ought to be, quite inadmissible for a novel: the antagonism of a mother and daughter, both rivals for the love of the same man. . . . it trenches on the sin of incest." The reviewer does not seem to understand fully the dynamics of the relationship, but shows proper Victorian outrage at the tone that Anny adopts toward a man who entices three women to love him. Reviewers of Thackeray's first novel, *Vanity Fair,* also objected to the mocking tone of the author. Looking toward Anny's future, *The Athenaeum*'s reviewer admits that "there is enough in the author to make us wish to see it come to perfection."[21]

Despite *The Athenaeum* attack, *The Story of Elizabeth* was generally well received. The plot hangs precipitously on chance—yet there are passages of great authority. Her descriptions of the household of Pasteur Tourneur, the man Elizabeth's mother marries, and of his preaching are striking. Modeled on Monsieur Monod, the minister whose *cours* Anny was forced to attend by her grandmother in Paris, Tourneur possesses the right proportions of cruelty and pride underneath his charismatic religiosity. The meanness of the strict home bears the touch of authenticity. Anny's probing of Elizabeth's psyche uncovers pertinent questions. Elizabeth "could not have told you herself—what she wanted, what perfection of happiness, what wonderful thing."[22] Unsure of herself and outmaneuvered by her mother, Elizabeth allows the older woman to sever her relationship with her lover, Dampier. After an almost fatal brain fever, Elizabeth and her lover are reunited. On this simple domestic tale Anny has superimposed her knowledge of the Calvinist Parisian society, and an exploration of the two women's inner lives. Although Elizabeth is the heroine, the mother's mature discontents override the daughter's adolescent problems.

Strangely, the novel ends on a melancholy note, despite the fact that Elizabeth and her husband are walking in a moonlit garden. The last paragraphs describe Elizabeth's mother as "haggard and weary," her husband as "old and worn" (194). Told by a narrator, the last sentences of the novel read:

> I looked back for the last time at the courtyard with the hens pecketting round about the kitchen door; at the garden with the weeds and flowers tangling together in the sun; at the shadows falling across the stones of the yard. I could fancy Elizabeth a prisoner within those walls, beating like a bird against the bars of the cage, and revolting and struggling to be free.
>
> The old house is done away with and exists no longer. It was pulled down by order of the Government, and a grand new boulevard runs right across the place where it stood. (194–95)

The narrator looks at the present and sees within it the past which Elizabeth escaped and the future which will destroy all outward signs of the present. Elizabeth the prisoner escaped into the arms of Dampier; Anny had no such hero. As Lady Dampier, Elizabeth forgets her earlier questioning; life with Dampier fulfilled her tentative quest for a "perfection of happiness." For Anny, her quest was just beginning. Her heroine was typically Victorian; Anny was not.

Both George Lewes and George Eliot have left interesting comments on *The Story of Elizabeth*. Lewes was editor of the *Cornhill* at the time it was publishing Anny's novel. He wrote: "But I am savage with Miss Thackeray—she has gone abroad without sending the finale to her story and without letting me know how much it will make. Chip of the old block!"²³ Eliot, however, was more appreciative of Anny. She wrote:

> We send to-day 'Orley Farm,' 'The Small House at Allington,' and 'The Story of Elizabeth.' 'The Small House' is rather lighter than 'Orley Farm.' 'The Story of Elizabeth' is by Miss Thackeray. It is not so cheerful as Trollope, but is charmingly written. You can taste it and reject it if it is too melancholy.²⁴

Eliot's admiration of Anny's writing increased with the years, until in 1875 she wrote: "I am obliged to fast from fiction, and fasting is known sometimes to weaken the stomach. I ought to except Miss Thackeray's stories, which I cannot resist when they come near me—and bits of Mr. Trollope, for affection's sake."²⁵ This is indeed praise from the most intellectual of Victorian novelists.

An earlier short story published first in the *Cornhill* in 1863 titled "Out of the World" uses a variation of the two-women plot. Roberta keeps house for her brother Dr. Rich, who marries a spoiled patient, Horatia. What she needs is an occupation, he tells her, "Don't most women? . . . Don't I find you all like prisoners locked up between four walls, with all sorts of wretched make-shift employments, to pass away time? Why, this room is a very pretty prison."²⁶ Alluded to at the end of *Elizabeth,* the theme of woman as prisoner is here openly stated both by the doctor and Horatia. Cut off from fashionable society, she leads a "Petit Trianon existence" (139), and Rich realizes his mistake. "The two pictures [each had of marriage] were not in the least like one another, or like the reality even" (138). Disaster follows and Rich dies. Although at first overcome by grief and guilt, Horatia returns to her old life. Anny concludes with a conventional happy ending of marriage for Roberta, but her handling of Horatia is unconventional. Given a chance for a fuller, richer life, Horatia cannot live "out of the world." Anny explains her title: There are "people of the world" (that is of society) and "people out of the world, . . . Horatia was a small person of the world" (109). In the end she consciously returns to her useless, frenetic existence. The absence of resolution of Horatia's problem echoes an immaturity similar to Anny's at the time she wrote the novel. The story is slight, but Anny's questioning of a woman's role in society is valid. Out of her own strivings, Anny fashioned a narrative with a prickly ending and a heroine conscious of an unresolved problem.

For the last six months of his life Thackeray was busy writing *Denis Duval*. He worked on this historical novel with renewed artistic vigor; the opening chapters prove that his imagination once again matched his skill. In the eulogy Dickens wrote for the *Cornhill*, he spoke of Thackeray's daughters: "In those twenty years of companionship with him, they had learned much from him; and one of them has a literary course before her worthy of her famous name."[27] The future would prove Dickens right.

LETTERS 27–40

To. Mr. and Mrs. Cole

Letter 27
Ray/Morgan

36. Onslow Square. S.W.
[before 6 March 1859][1]

My dear Mr. and Mrs Cole. I wrote you a letter last night full of such astounding news that Minnie would not let me send it — So tonight I must send you a little word much more common-place & rather more truthful — Everybody sends you their love & is charmed to hear you are getting well & journeying pleasantly. We thought of you on Sunday with very red noses & numb fingers & bad colds — that is us you know — not you — & we pictured Mrs Cole in a light muslinette & Mr. Cole in his shirt sleeves sitting in an Italian temple on a marble bench eating ices. Tishy[2] came to lunch with us off roast Beef and Papa paid her so many compliments about her blue ribbons &ct that I began to tell her she had best go home & see how her brothers & sisters were getting on. And then we went for a walk in the H.G.[3] Crowds of fashionables — three young men from Harveys — an old lady in a fur jacket — an old gentleman who stood stock still for ten minutes looking at us thro' his eyeglasses until little Manson Craigie[4] cried out [sic] I say old feller dont stare!" upon w^h he meekly put them up and went away — and then a couple—such a sweet couple — this is for Mrs Cole because a stern masculine intellect would despise the feeble gossip — The big Hairy Hat young man with the pipe & little Miss I think who called him "Tom." Tishy said. — then there was Capt Fawke.[5] O O cry the little Craigies is that the man who invented the umbrella! . . . and a hundred other people besides. Grannie has just come home from Southampton where she went to see Edmund[6] off — poor Mrs Craigie breaking her heart abt him   Mrs James Wilson[7] was on board with a daughter & going to Malta & I think that sounds rather pleasant. Today Mary[8] came to see us looking very bright & nice & we had a walk to Harveys where we spent some of our 2 Papa's money & Tishy we were told was going to stop at home all day and make Gingerbread nuts for tomorrow. That sounds like the Queen of Hearts doesnt it? I told you in my letter yesterday that D.ʳ Anslie⁹ had been taken up by the police after partaking too freely of the champagne at Mr. Theggelas [?] [*word illegible*] breakfast but that was a pure invention of my own and a shameful thing it is to spread such unfounded reports. His Aunt came to see us the other day the dearest nicest bigottedist little Catholic. She is going to take us as a great treat to the convent of the poor clares¹⁰ who never lie down & pat about on stones all the winter. I wish by the by I could manage to tell you how cold it has been and as for my showerbath Burrrrroooooooooooo. Papa has been pretty well all this time & comes down to lunch saying quite cheerfully "there's a deuce of a row going on upstairs between Emily MacWhirter and Eliza Baynes"¹¹ and then he goes off on his own devices & we see him no more. I went to call at M.ʳˢ Brookfields¹² on Saturday and found her with a beautiful sort of violet Toga she had made

& designed herself entirely. Its a gown but there are no seams & long graceful folds & I assure you the effect is perfect. I think a livery of this sort for the young ladies at the Museum would be most desirable but of course if the plan should be adopted I shall expect something for my idea. M.ʳ Brookfield is going to stop at Lady Dorothy Nevilles¹³ with whom they have struck up & Magdelene¹⁴ is busy decorating her room all over with painted paper butterflies with the wings turned up to look natural. That puts me in mind of a letter f.ᵐ Mr. Cayley¹⁵ wʰ I didn't but Amy providentially read in wʰ he says he is very much obliged to M.ʳ Cole & tells us confidentially that he is persuaded there is a market for his wares & that he shall get ten pound for the Honeycomb pattern. M.ʳ Bell¹⁶ says nothing & so I am beginning to quack. Grannie is having a little dispute with us about Molyneux clock wʰ we say is a quarter of an hour slow She says all the other clocks are fast but all the clocks I am afraid say it is time to go to bed & leave off talking to you. I have been writing ever so long and I have not said half as much as I could do if I could be with you for 5 minutes at Florence. But we do hope you are enjoying yourselves & were you not delighted about your eldest little he-pig at Woolwich¹⁷ and all the others looking very well & fat & ready for killing — or killing other people rather & we send our love and I am always yʳ affectionate

Anny TH.ʸ

P.S. Monday morning 8.30 a messanger arrives f^m the Secretary of the Guy Fawkes Committee to request me instantly to pay up my subscription

To W. W. F. Synge

Letter 28
Fales   Sunday. March 6. 36. [1859]

My dear Mr Synge.

   I have been looking about all over the house for thick paper to write to you upon & give my news such as it is. This is an unfavourable day for my correspondents. I mean Im very grumpy & in the blues, so please dont fancy from the desponding tone of my letter that things arn't going very well with us, & that we arnt very grateful to Providence. First of all that Papa is really a little better. Its all lemonade & giving up other more intoxicating liquors, next that we are home again, for I think I havent written to you since Granny broke her hip & Min & I went to Paris to nurse her & Amy to Wales & Papa ill here and everybody wretched. Now we are very jolly, that is as jolly as people are generally, when they have everything they can wish for, except Mr Yates friendship. The lawgoing has been given over. It w^d have had to go into Chancery w^h is expensive & so a abusive pamphlet is coming out.[1] We are begging our Jupiter to keep in his thunder & not even read it & as he has taken to paying great attention to what we say lately perhaps he wont. I needn't tell you how glad we are to have news of you (even thro the N. York Paper) & how we are beginning to want you back again. One goes on very well for a little time when one is away oneself & quite miserable, but now that we have time to look about us we are thinking that we want you all back very much & that you have ben junketting about with plenipotentiaries quite long enough.[2] I want to see my God son[3] too & question him in his catechism. Only I dont think his mother w^d stand it. The Mount Felix ball this year went off famous. Papa behaved nobly. took us down dined at Oatlands P^k Hotel. Went with us stopped till 4½ slept at OPH.[4] Came back to town next day. As for Partners we had 22 each, & really liked it as much as last time. I dont know if other people did though & Mrs Sturgis[5] as I was going away said. Ah. We wanted Mr Synge to set it going. I have been wishing for him constantly this evening Its not been the same without him. and then she said it over again to somebody else. The Russels⁶ were in the house. Katey looking <u>really</u> extraordinarily good looking. I was quite surprised & wondered whether it was her. a high wreath. bright colour & white dress & flirting rather with Mʳ Crawfurd.⁷ I shᵈ have like to pull his nose (only please this is confidential) there was some mystery or other. Everything has been on & off again between him & Lily⁸ & the poor child looked so awfully wretched & miserable that it almost twisted ones heart to see her & there he was gallivanting about & spiting her. Its a shame, because <u>his</u> side broke it off, & I am sure he's bad natured. John was frisking about & flirting also a good deal with Lou⁹ while Mʳˢ John looked on benignly thro an eyeglass She was beautifully dressed, exceedingly bumptious and I really think one of least prepossessing women I have ever come across. Mʳ Felix has on his brass buttons. He had a white waistcoat & a black neckcloth — Harry had a white neck ribbon & a black waistcoat. May had no end of partners Miss Gordon¹⁰ was there not so handsome as last year Miss Holland Lady Holland in flimsy [?] satinet. Col. Hamley of course & a little old comic Mʳ Alexander who is perfectly frantic about Mʳˢ Julia¹¹ & has seen the Colonel very near indeed. This little O.C.¹² danced the highland fling (so did I with Arthur Prinsep¹³ <u>danced</u> everybody down) We met Mʳ Alex. a day or two ago. Ah! said Minny there is nobody so handsome here as a certain lady we know Mʳ Alex. I dont know who you mean said he, but if it is the most beautiful of natures works & the most charming & amiable of her sex with whom there never was anyone to compare — Mʳˢ Russell Sturgis in short; I quite agree with you. He wears pumps with large bows Mʳ A does &

a wig with a curl on each side of his head. The fashion is really very comic, & we cant help laffing at him for it. Our Coles came back from Rome, by the same post wʰ brought your two last letters. They went for their Fathers health wʰ was quite broken with hard work & so he & Tishy & Mary packed up 3 little carpet bags & set off on their travels. I am trying to remember how many of your friends we have seen but weve been extremely quiet & hardly met anybody. Mʳ Abbott I saw one day at Mʳˢ Elliots¹⁴ & had a little talk with, his uncle dined with us, a charming old gentleman we both fell in love with. Florence Proby¹⁵ came to tea with us (I just rather think we missed you then — it didn't go off half as well; though we had a grander tree & a Magic Lantern in Papa's room)

Letters 75

looking very very smart in little white silk boots. Uncle Arthur[16] has been very nearly put into prison by M.ʳ Isaacs over the way (this is also confidential) Fardel[17] goes on being ridiculous the winter has vanished & everybody is coming out in large white linen umbrellas lined with green Please bring it home with you — there came a ring at the bell & M.ʳ M.ʳˢ [*word illegible*] walked in, very glad to get news of you; it was six o'clock & I felt very guilty at only having tea to offer him as Papa & I were going out to dinner. He's been ill with a cough he told me & sent his very best messages to you. Minny is upstairs studying astronomy, Papa is not up & is reading the Times, Amy is improving her mind at the window and I am everybody's mouthpiece when I tell you that we wish you health & happiness & good luck & lots of money & are yʳˢ affectionately. 36. Onslow Sq.

To W. W. F. Synge

Letter 29   Pavilion. Folkestone
Fales   Aug. 27. 1.5 p.m. [1859]

Abominable brass band shreeking discordant polkas, vessels swinging in the port. Old gentleman with yellow waistcoat & umbrella under his arm walking across the prospect [?] Papa wild in next room Virginians (No.24) brought to a sudden stand still Sunshine hills ladies in Spanish hats, gentlemen, [*two words illegible*] masts lamp-posts, young lady in No 8 writing to gentleman at the other side of the world. Who she wishes back again with all her heart, & so do her

relations who are also stopping at Folkestone & taking their pleasures. When we opened yʳ letter & found that instead of saying I shall be home on the 14 with my wife and children & y.ʳ Godson, it was only I have been ill & am seedy still I neednt say how sorry & provoked we were but I hope my dear M.ʳ Synge you will be all right again long before this sheet of paper has travelled out to that mysterious country you write from and that the next time we see y.ʳ writing it wont be shaky & wont give us bad news about you any more. I gave y.ʳ message with the figures to Papa who says he <u>has</u>

written. Hes in very good spirits & jolly today at last thank God. His No. is finished, he's recovered f:^m his last attack of Spasms I think he's really better of those & though constantly ill one way or another we aint ½ as anxious as we used to was. As foir the V.^{gns 1} Its a great comfort theyre over — Satdy R.[2] will be in to them as sure as eggs is eggs, Sat: is very welcome for though I own theyre stupid & uninteresting theyre gentlemanly & dignified & a man can't be lively for ever. (We went out fishing at 8 o'clock this morning & brought home two small fishes & I still feel so sick I hardly know what I am writing about & so if I am not lively w.^h I ought to be, its only a temporary stoppage) I suppose you will laff to hear of Mr Crawfurd's marriage. I did as I perfectly well remember abusing him to Miss Ford w.^h ought to be a lesson to one never to speak ones mind ab.^t anybody to anybody else particularly if theyre privately engaged to be married. Mr Abbott is also spliced to his cousin Miss Smyth[3] & Mrs John Sturgis has got a baby. I forget which sort. We have hardly seen anything of them this y.^r She asked us once to dinner & we cdn't go & she couldn't come to us when we asked her, but we saw em out once or twice in white & green & diamonds & dear old Stister Murgis in a clue boat with bass bruttons. John looks 20 years older & Lou Perry has been going to be married, but there was some hitch about money & I dont know how its ended. Y.^r uncle came & dined with us one very hot day when the ice didnt come till dinner was over & ladies & gentlemen & dinner were all melting away. he was as kind & pleasant as ever but a talkative Baronet shut him up so he only looked pleasant through his little eyes. We have been coming out very strong in Baronets all middle aged bachelors, there's one of them very nice here who we see all day long; not middle aged of course or it w.^{dn't} be the thing but 60 or so we breakfast & walk & dine with him & let Papa do as he likes, & go over to Hythe where they practise musquetry & drink tea with Granny & GP every day who are living there for the present.[4]

To Amy Crowe

Letter 30
Ray/Morgan   [16 September 1859][1]

My dearest May Anne. This is Sep.^{br} 16 Thursday I think more or less. I'm writing under a nice cool arcade of columns with lilac trees

growing I have got 2 dz. great mosquito bites round my poor little eyes. We have been O jolly to Blgne[2] as you know thence dash across Paris (only dining there also an amazing little cafe by the J des Pltes[3] to Tours; w{h} we reached at 3 o'clock the morning after, & where we had peaches for breakfast & saw a nice smiling old city with gardens full of flowers & turrets & not very many people, and from Tours another long day to Bordeaux w{h} we reached one night with all the stars shining & the South seemed to begin, black eyed folks a great Bustling station & then splendid, long quais & bridges & rows of lamps handsomer almost than Paris: We drove off in state to a filthy hotel decorated with dahlias & Laurels & dirt & slop & pails in every corner & were shown into some swell apartments reeking with dinner, & no wonder. I thought I'd fling open the window & enjoy the lovely evening & it only looked into the passage with half dozen people coming & going & all staring in & so though we dont like making a fuss we weren't sorry when Papa asked for another room upstairs for us, a little step, but a great blue sky with stars & tall houses opposite where we saw them all at work in the morning. Young lady with black hair & yellow handkerchief cames looks out spits into the street. Old lady in a peignoir brushing her combs ditto, femme de menage dusting & brushing, femme de chambre coming & going with caps &ct. The old Lady came out very smart when her toilet was completed & sat the whole day long at her bed room window. On Sunday we got into the old Bordeaux w{h} is very curious & striking brown red light & shade Amazing old women in great white caps little Murillo boys & a funeral 30 young ladies in black & bottines[4] tripping along after it with their hair parted on one side, parties playing at dominoes in the by streets a couple of ancient churces & a tower: We descend? Qu'est qu'il y'a Des Cadavres M. parfaitement conservés.[5] But we didn't w{h} I wasn't sorry of. We'd been to some wine vaults in the morning quite awful enough goodness knows with rampant fungii & creeping & slimy & oozy horrors till just as you come out its a perfick vertigo of em layer over layer. As for the bottles, you have seen bottles & can imagine them. And indeed as we each walked along with a candle in a little procession we thought we had seen enough long before the entertainment was over. We stayed at Bx 2 days in wh time the dahlias & Laurels wh were only stuck up for the Kg. of Belgium, not the mere luxuriance of the South as I fancied at first, had time to fade & look more and more untidy & we were very very glad to get away from all the grub to Toulouse for wh Papa had a fancy. I never saw a charminger road no — not anywhere — Vines and ancient villages all along the way & miles & grapes

& aboundings, in fact very much what I have so graphically represented in the accompanying sketch from memory. Flocks of turkeys pigs and queer interiors. But all this jolly business stops at Toulouse where theres a very nice inn with Algerian curtains & a very nice dinner (by the way we had none for 3 days or only such a scamper that it scarcely counted) & more peaches. Theyre a sort of mixture of grapes & apricots very tough.⁶ Toulouse is like Neuilly like Courbevoie only uglier but they are very kind folks whereas at Bordeaux they actually glared at us in the streets. The quai at Bdx is a wonderful sight there are queer gay painted flat bottomed barques with country folks on board wh look like scenes at the play. One awful old woman dressed in yellow was crouching all by herself at the prow of one of these, & it was piled & piled with great onions behind, you can fancy with the blue for a back ground what a bit of colour it made. Papa called her The Lady of Shalott.⁷ The next days journey was a very queer one the lovely South of France is perfectly hideous & horrible (here came a long drive by the sea limpid blue with lilacest hills & mermaids dashing against the rocks & now only half an hour to tell a thousand things.) To go on with the Sth of France its covered like snow with miles & miles of chalky dust so thick on the ground the men & women the trees that you see no colour except this dismal whitey brown paper colour in wh everything seems to be

carefully wrapped up. We passed Carcassonne standing like this in a vast plain black ruins with the sky beyond & night (as you observe coming on — that was awful enough but when we got to Narbonne where we had meant to stop the great mouldering dust the silence the awful black lonely towers black & Moorish & ghastly beyond description, when we saw all this we dashed down some dinner with a lot of Spaniards (N. is close upon Spain we were very near going) & getting into the train again went on to Séte where we thought we sh^d like some tea. Little old teapot standing all by itself in the middle of the table. Here waiter, du lait du sucre du pain et du beurre s'ilvouspl: "Nous n'avons pas de lait Mademoiselle. (Min declares I mildly replied in English French O n'importe) bread & butter then. Nous n'avons pas de buerre Mademoiselle. il n'est pas bon dans ce pays ci.⁸ & so we sopped our bread in the nastiest tea very pale rather sweet & with an indefinable dusty mouldy taste. Very nice family travelling the same way, old lady in red feathers uncommonly confidential How dirty one gets travelling to be sure (if you c^d have seen her you wouldn't have said no) And how expensive the washing is. I never have any done. No. I calculate and bring all I think I shall want with me from home. You see I wear a black petticoat, whipping up her dress and if I get to any place I slip a white one over it. But she was very good natured & not a bit X when a lady travelling with an invalid husband in a night cap upset a bottle of wine over it. Another queer little man got in with a fat old wife sucking liquorice big rings mittens dyed hair. M. said he La Ferrance démande la guerre perché l'Angleterre sostine a garder et proteger les coquins qu' ont voulu agragoener [?] notre empreuer Monsieur La Ferance J'indigne. M. la Fernace vous fera payer votre ostination avec les dernieres gouttes de votre sang⁹ & he clenched his hands & jumped on his legs & we burst out laughing. Voila la quatriéme¹⁰

stationg says his wife quite placid — Then he told us that he had been up in a baloon & down at the bottom of the sea in a diving dress he had himself invented & that there are lovely grottoes covered with coral & grapes & raspberries w^h go squash if you bring them up & that he supplied the Navy & was going to build a Hotel at the B. de Blgne. Veux tu du Regliss Fillo!¹¹ to the fat wife who w^d just point her wishes & then he'd execute them. J'parie ché c'est le cousin J'parie ché c'est son chapeau dant c'te caléche says she. and then he very grand, Ce sont nos parents qui viennent nous chercher dans leur voiture a eux.¹² Bonjour Monsieur Bonj^r Mesdames. After Séte it grows very pretty again you skirt the sea now — then you pass Nimes Arles & Montpellier all dusty & wrapped up in in brown paper. You know how Nathalie[13] goes on I'm sure she never was there But if it wasnt for the dust Nimes & Arles too w!! be charming places & lots of flowers grow I fancy. Tarascon is perfectly charming. You come to a river & to a little quai again, & on each side of the river is a hill & on each hill an ancient town with convents & a castle on the brow & spires & old brick walls & by the way Tishy & Mary[14] have seen Tarascon but I don't fancy they can have taken the drive at Marseilles that we did this morning. I think it beats Naples blue & green & lilac & heavenly tints all over. Tomorrow we are going post to Nice. 4 horses 3 outside one (Sims) in. We are at the Hotel d'Orient. We went out this evening to go to the play but lost our way & came home again. We dined at the table d'hote today. There was a tall gentleman in spectacles & 2 yng. ladies all over mosquito bites besides ourselves. With a little bottle of ammonia wh they keep dabbing on. And we were rung in to dinner by a tremendous bell & you may fancy how foolish we looked at the 3 plates. I who had thought of putting on a silk dress! I sh!! think theyre only full when the boat comes in & out. We met that woman with the fish this morning & then a donkey. I can't draw donkies very well & then an old woman sitting in a basket with great melons to sell & then a monk & then two bare legged Arabs & the queerest spelling. ici on donne a

boire et a manget, & a boire et a mangé[15] I've seen. And now as we must be up very early in the morning good night dear Amy — I hope you got all safe & dont know where to tell you to write we are going to Turin I think perhaps Poste Restante, Geneva at once addressed with a T not 𝒯 w!! be the safest so goodnight & goodbye. Pls Enclose this to Tishy with this scrap as I havent time to write two & with love to E. and all the little letters I'm always y.r afftest

A.I.T.[16]

To Mrs. Synge

Letter 31
Fales

36. Onslow Square S.W.
Feb. 5 Sunday [1860]

My dear Mrs Synge.

 Two days ago Mrs Proby came to see us & brought us some very good news of you all. — Says she "I'm glad to be the first to tell you that our friends are coming back" & I needn't add how we were the people to be glad to hear it. I want to see my little Gilbert[1] very much again & his parients [*sic*] & brothers & sister & so this is a little congratulating letter to the family from the other one in Onslow Sq & not a mere gossipping one, & as I expect it to be answered in person I dont write to Mr Synge but to you — who I find by the way do write to <u>other people)</u> <u>Miss Russell</u>[2] told me & we meant to concoct a joint letter & <u>screw</u> one of you when we heard you were on y^{r} way home. Miss Russell & Minny & I sat up till 2 o'clock one night in the haunted room at Mt Felix[3] telling gohst stories & talking about things in gen^{l}. We paid such a jolly little 3 days visit — no Whites no Perrys nothing to put one out it was all just exactly perfect & I dont know when we have had such a pleasant time. Mrs Sturgis looked so kind & handsome, Miss Russell & her brother were so friendly (& we always thought her a little trump you know) & all together it was just what we all wanted to set us up again. We have had a g^{t} deal of illness in the house since I wrote me & Amy was the victims. first I took ill abroad[4] & was awfully bad so that I almost thought I should never get home again, that was a mistake however Im glad to say but I didn't get well till Amy fell ill w^{h} the doctor first said was small-pox w^{h} gave me a turn & cured me. This was a false alarm, & another mistake but mild typhus, or typhoid fever is bad enough & now after 2mth ½ she's not herself again. That same kind Mount Felix has had her down for the last ten days & I xpect her back with her hair grown long & all right again.[5] Katey Russell is still there — you know all abt. Harriets wedding of course — thats the only one I have to tell you of I think. — poor Mrs White has had a paralytic stroke, Hervey is as fat & friendly as ever, Hoddy Toddy has turned into the very sweetest little boy, May's[6] hair is quite long, old nurse gong on just the same — & really their kindness about Amy has quite touched me. Col. Russell[7] is good looking, rather slow, sensible, quite a contrast

to the other Col. who by the way I heard Miss Warren⁸ speaking most
unkindly of & indifferently at wʰ I winked my i. I'm sure you will like
to hear abt. the 90,000 & 100.000 copies of the Cornhill. Only I dont
think it pays much the expenses are so great that after 50,000 I fancy
it doesnt pay at all. Advertisements dont pay after 50,000, & then are
given gratis. Of course Papa gets his 1000 a year for editing & it doesn't
affect him directly & then he's paid for his articles beside. Its famous
occupation for him suits & amuses & interests but isn't so profitable as
old business⁹ used to was. However on the strength of our reduced fortunes we have set up another hoss, & the open with the 2 little cantering
mares makes a very neat & creditable appearance & yʳ sons Godmother
means to call & fetch him in style one fine spring morning when you are
all safe back in Cumberland Street. I dont think except once to call on
Mʳˢ Proby we have been in that way since you left — stop once — to
yʳ house Miss Vincent¹⁰ having told Grannys husband's nephew's wife's
mother that you were back in the old place again. Granny has got a snug
little house in Brompton Crescent where we go & see her everyday. Eyre
Crowe has some sort of place with Mʳ Cole. We saw Lᵈ Kilmarloch in
Regᵗ Street 2 days ago who made a beautiful bow There's a row in the
Cabinet.¹¹ Tories are coming in they say. I like a shindy & am yʳ most
affectionate

         AIthackeray

From Minny to Mrs. Carmichael-Smyth

Letter 32   Saturday. 36 OS [1861]¹
Harvard

My Dearest Grannie We found your note yesterday when we came back
from Waltham² where we had 2 such pleasant days, it is such a jolly
place, a nice old fashioned red brick house with a pretty garden. All
Mʳ Trollopes servants are tremendously Irish & the greatest fun in the
world, especially old Barney the groom who has only one eye & joins
in all the conversation & one only regrets that one cannot understand
a word he says. We had 2 delicious drives in an Irish jaunting car; it is
the County of John Gilpins³ ride & I think we must have looked very
like that famous family, all packed in the Car, with Mʳ Synge trotting

in front on a mare his coat tails flying in the wind. It is quite pretty to see the children riding down to little Gilbert, they all seem to take to it quite naturally. Old Barney was anxious to make the baby ride & saw that his 2 young masters both rode before they were a year old & as this Baby is 14 months old I suppose he s^d have taken him out with the hounds. I went to Mrs Craigies last night expecting to find Addie (?) & the girls but they had not arrived. I am glad that you don't think of staying with Mrs Green[4] at Boulogne for it would surely be very dismal & you had much better come back here — Anny doesn't like her shower bath at all. She also takes some medicine with a villainous smell — but I think she has been much better since the last 2 or 3 days. Papa is not very brilliant. London is beginning to fill. It is superb weather we had not had 2 such days as those at Waltham all the Summer With best love to the children & AM & UC.[5] I am always my dearest Grannies

HMT

From Minny to Anny

Letter 33   Saturday
Ray/Morgan   1862

My dear Anny

many thanks for your fond letter I am glad that my bag and you arrived safe — pray take care of these both — & write and tell me all about Mr Tennyson[1] & what his wife is like & his little boys, & his house — Now dont make y^rself in the least unhappy if I tell you that Papa is not well I have just been to see him & he says it is a <u>very</u> little attack, & he has got the papers & I think he will be well tomorrow but I shall not be able to write to you because there is no country post — but on Monday I will write & I shall be very angry if you are at all unhappy & dont enjoy y^rself, for really he is very little ill. Isabella Irvine has been here so happy with a bit of news Mary Irvine is going to marry her brother Octavius,[2] & Mrs. Kemble[3] has been here and she frightened me because she said I kept contradicting myself — So I did; and I have found a school that I think will do for little Quin [?][4] at 15 a year, w^h is 6^s & 6^d a week, at least I think so — and if old Miss Cripps[5] doesnt send a better one I think he had better go there — Give my best love to

Mrs Cameron⁶ & I assure you Papa is not at all sad, he said so himself Mrs Kemble said that Freshwater was not in the least like Holland — Oh she confused me so — but I have no time to send you any more — Ella⁷ is coming to see me tomorrow directly after Church She writes that she is desperately fond of this new one — I shall be so glad to have her again — We dont miss you at all — Browny⁸ & pussy are quite well, & Piggy <u>will</u> suck my fingers, I wish she wouldn't. Bobby sits on the fender rail & Billy & Coo are much as usual.

Good bye

To Amy Crowe

Letter 34
Ray/Morgan [Postmark: London, 15 Sept. 62]

Dearest Amy — Come any day you like for I dont think we shall go away again — I'm sorry youre so melancholy dear — Why a year ago you could not have written a sadder letter. I think Autumn makes people dismal I suppose theres a dark side to everything — Even Palace Green has its drawbacks as you will see on the other side of this paper[1] My dearest Papa has been really out of sorts J & G[2] send in more & more bills 800 just come in for nothings — curtain, making up old carpets & that crooked looking glass. Well then Philip is a regular failure if you know what it is to have a pianoforte played upon y.^r nerves that is what Papa is going thro. Though he dont say much about it. Dear Papa Well then he has had to take half the American money & he wants to write like mad & put it back w^h isnt very favorable to composition. These are all very trifling troubles and if he could get 3 days of wellness I shouldnt care hes not worse than usual only more bothered. Granny isn't very well but so kind & coming soon — We told Edward when we saw him at Folkestone that Eugenie[3] could be more charming than anybody in the world & also more aggravating — We were rather frightened at the collision & Minny kept saying there never were two sisters more unlike. I was rather surprised to hear of things going on smoothely — but dont let her make fun of him to you. He isnt a bit clever but we should be dull enough if we had to build a fortification or put out a gunpowder magazine. And I think it was very clever of him to fall in love with you.

I wonder will you be really more happy? I think so when the first dismalness of going away is over — We too shall be very dismal & at sea without you There's a lot of places I want to go to (out pops <u>my</u> particular little selfishness) & Minny quite declines. She very amiably came to the dispensary yesterday for M.ʳˢ Homers [?][4] and we made friends with the charmingest handsomest young Doctor with manners exactly like M.ʳ Travers[5] — only rather better who gave us everything we wanted, I wonder what sort of day we shall have tomorrow at Lydy's — Herman is supposed to be in love with Miss Kate Terry[6] they correspond & he has bought her two pears at 8′-each. M.ʳ Prescotts[7] want flowers I had no time to send it yesterday. I'm ashamed to tell you what we did — dont look at the seals — Im thinking about Eugenie I quite understand her impatience — theres so much in being of the same clan after all that of course does not influence her. Give her my love I dont mind her knowing what I think, because I'm honestly fond of her — But I dont think she makes enough allowances for other people — & forgets that they have batteries of nerves, as well as she herself. On second thought please say nothing at all as that is much the safest course in life.

Y.ʳ Affe A.T.

To Mrs. Synge

Letter 35　　　　　　　　　　　　　　　　　Thursday, Jan. 22ᵈ
Fales　　　　　　　　　　　　　　　　　　　[1863]

My dearest M.ʳˢ Synge.

M.ʳ Synges letter & the beautiful bit of coral & Guy's letter[1] have all come — and this morning we are very melancholy for we got up very early and went to say Goodbye to Amy Heaven speed her dear little soul. It <u>is</u> dismal to think that we are parted for ever,[2] but Im very very thankful to know that she is happy. She looks it. So bright and pretty & smart And Edward follows her about with admiring eyes. We went to the play last night. It seemed somehow as if she was you — Yah what hateful things partings are. We saw Fechter[3] in <u>the duke's motto</u>[4] — I cant try to tell you the story, he disguised himself as a humpback, in the most extraordinary manner he talked about a shile! a baebe! a lapsdog — he fought lots of duels & married the Bebe in the end —

& then we had — who do you think? — Lord Dundreary to dinner last Sunday.⁵ He is perfectly charming. Fair, with a curly moustache, well made & well dressed, quick & decided, & what is so funny he takes Lord Dundreary off. He says he is going to write a new play, with a tragedy of Sam's⁶ in it w:h is to be acted on a little stage on the stage. And he says if ever we have any more theatricals he will come & act for us. It would be quite a treat he said to do something that <u>wasnt</u> L:d Dundreary but we only mean to have some more acting by <u>way of</u> a finale when we go away into a little house — How provoking about your ship — Dear me! I hope it has come to hand by this time and what a pleasant little glimpse of the children Guy's letter gives us, walking up the hill & saying they can see Gardner & England. How does M:r Synge like being Godfather? Did he give H.M. a mug & will he hear her her catechism? I assure though I make jokes people are very much impressed when I tell them. So many folks ask after you & they all say it sounds delightful only that is quite different from having to live with the Savages. Amy is going to Folkestone & Paris, & then on Monday they go to Marseilles & on Thursday embark on board the Vechi

And we are going down M:rs Trollopes tomorrow w:h is great fun, to & dances & shall come home on Saturday & then on Monday go to the Rothschilds again, at Mentmore.⁷ M:rs Caulfield⁸ is to be there. I have got a new pink gauze and a lilac, & a violet silk for every day & I think it will be rather fun. We have been getting some presents lately — a delightful set of photographs from M:r Fred:k Chapman⁹ & I cant quite remember anything else. Except 2 most lovely tinkling chandeliers from M:r G Smith.¹⁰ They are up in the drawingroom. We have come back to the side of the house lately the weather is cold & we have all got a sort of general family influenza. Rap taptaaptap — there comes dear old Brodie. Do you remember our old nurse & there she is & Brownie staring just as if she knew I was writing to you & Minny doing her Latin She works very hard at it — I meanly gave in. Grannie is still here & we all jog together quite snugly. Ah! dear! Amy's gone right away. I'd forgotten all about it for the last five minutes (Brownie has turned right round with her legs <u>towards</u> you & has gone to sleep again. Papa instead of writing his great thundering book is thinking of a shorter one¹¹ first¹² I'm not sure that I am glad theres no end of sensation novels coming out. A certain Miss Braddon¹³ seems to have it all her own way. We have been making immense friends with the Charles Collins' Wilkie's brother & Kate dickens as was. & I must tell you, one  day M.ʳ Julian Fane[14] came to see us we all felt our hearts break on the spot. Young Jim Carmichael[15] called a day ago & Minny met M.ʳ Jervis[16] at a party. He was very nice she said & talked to her. And we have had a grand reconciliation with the Erskine Perrys. Do you know that the Sturgis & M.ʳ Guthrie[17] & Miss Kate Perry[18] are all going to Rome (not roam?) Dont I sound pleasant

 Ella Merrivale[19] comes home today f.ʳᵐ her young mans father's house This is Kate Collins not in the least like who is sitting in Brodie's vacated chair And Papa is walking up & down in his dressing gown & talking about a childs book of nursery rhymes. Tell M.ʳ Synge this is all the literary news I can send him. Give the dear little people my love & Good bye dearest Mam & write soon to y.ʳˢ

Affectionately always
Anne T.

To Amy Crowe Thackeray

Letter 36   [6 May 1863][1]
Ray

My dearest Amy I have begun as usual ever so many bits wʰ I never can find when I want to go on. What jolly 2 delightful letters, & do go on writing them they are so werry velcome. I can imagine you quite; in full dress in the morning with all the young officers with their swords sitting round & making conversation — Isnt it different from all our humdrum years & years together? Minny & I get immensely excited, as all your visitors come pouring in I dont take the same deep interest in F.^t W.^m [2] w.^h Grannie & Mrs Craigie do but I think I can see it when I shut my eyes. What are you doing at this very instant I wonder? My dear old girl I wish I could see. Now when I tell you that I am in my room at my Davenport that Minny is upstairs cutting sticking plaster because she has cut her little fingers, that Papa is in his study smoking and thinking, you know exactly what it is all like. Could you draw us a sort of plan of where you live or wouldn't Edwd like to do it for us — that w.^d be very kind now — and tell me what you wear of an afternoon & all that & then I shall know. How funny about Dr Charles.[3] Ask him if he remembers telling us how to make noses when we were all very young. I think for my part that we were all very old in those days & that it is now that we are very young. We dined at the Wilsons[4] on Mayday. Mrs Sartoris[5] was there it seemed like a little slice out of the past; tonight we dine at our ArchBishops & last night we all three dined at Julias[6] & met a Major Noran[7] very fat f^m India, Mr Rogers[8] the good liberal costermonger clergyman. What a shame it is he is only a curate after 20 hard years of work. But his reward is coming & he shall be invited to palace Green. My Elia as Minny calls Miss Steuart[9] came to dine on Monday & we all went off to the SKM.[10] to see the jewels & the company & to hear the band perform at intervals of 5 minutes The company was so very small posing that we thought it a great privelege to be let into a little gallery with the band. But O. Clang Bang Bong our heads went round & round — We rushed to the farthest corner, all the people down below looked up & [*two words illegible*] because they thought we were the R!deref[11] family. Bong Bang Clang & the doors we locked & we couldnt get away You never heard anything so horrible. And as for the jewels they were all gone except one very small & extremely ugly brooch. It was worth no end of money that was some consolation. Outside the moon was shining the stars blazing a beautiful soft little breezy wind came through the lilac trees — Mr Cole walked home with us with Hennie & Alan & Bartly & Isabella & Mrs. Corbiere.[12] It was a sort of poetry tonight in the middle of prosy everyday. Somebody — O it was Miss Steuart — was saying that Sir John Simeon[13] had told her how sorry he was you were gone. He said he was not quite sure of the name but he

Letters 89

meant the Watteau-Lady in the writing cap that was so becoming. Of course in India people wear bows behind. & nets & curls all round like M.^rs M'Callum.^14 But Im quite sure they dont wear caps any more. Julia Sterling^15 has set one up & Im still looking in the shop windows for mine. On Sunday (Im going backwards) we drove down to Richmond.^16 Mr Morgan John^17 on the box looking as spruce as possible, Mr Collins & Papa & me &M^18 inside. We dropped them at the Star & Garter & went on to Mrs Prescotts to dine & to sit out in the verandah looking across the garden. That was another garden day — all this sounds so delightful that it must make you long to be back in England, instead of w^h though it looks charming on Paper I think I have (nearly) cried three times this week. Once with vexation for someone offered us a £1000 a year almost for the house unfurnished & went away & came back never no more & then once — I cant write such nonsense all the way to India — & I am ashamed of the third time too So you see it is not at all so couleur de rose as the paper & a person who has such misfortunes as these to contend with is indeed to be . . .

I went upstairs there & put on all my clothes to go out. But reflecting that Mrs Gurney^19 is coming to lunch I took them all off again. Last week I worked so very hard finishing a stupid long story squeezed up into a short one, w^h is stupider if possible, that I am taking my eees this week & enjoy it immensely It — the story is called the arbour at the end of the garden — thats all & you will see it in the Cor if they putt [sic] it in.^20 I must tell you about the pictures We went the opening Day^21 Hennie & Minny & I, walked & got there at 12 & were not too much crushed up — There was so great a crowd around Eyres picture that I could not get to see it quite. I don't think I like it quite so much as de Foe. I have not seen what the times says.^22 Everybody is amused at Vals picture w^h the times says is ugly w^h considering the model was unjustifiable. Mrs Prinsep was the model. They meant to call it Guinivere & Lancelot at first but this was thought inadvisable as it was Mrs Prinsep, & then when the picture was quite finished they changed the subject and called it something else. That seems queer art doesn't it?^23 Mr Millais little girl is the prettiest dearest little picture that ever was painted. She is sitting in a pew with a pair of Mrs Millais beautiful

 yellow kid gloves beside her & listening with all her eyes. Then he's got the Lions den I dont care for so very much Little boys & girls creeping from under the piano & then he has got a lady with a mermaids gown in the moonlight — I couldnt see that enough either to tell you how I like it. It is very weird & odd & silvery.[24] M.[r] Hunt has a little funny King of Hearts not bigger than this sheet of paper; a little henry the 8 on a green field playing at some game, and a very uninteresting (they all call it 'very fine') portrait of D.[r] Lushington.[25] M.[r] Walker has chosen a charming subject a Lady frozen up in the snow with her dying infant[26] & imagine! M.[r] Cole has sent two funny little etchings. The 'to let' is up in their house & they move in a month; our successors have got rose coloured blinds in the drawing room & seem to be making themselves quite at home. I feel as if they had no business there — M.[rs] Freake[27] has been given a tremendous music. A Duke to play the drum Honorables fiddling lords trumpetting Everyone says there never was such beautiful music Isnt this like a paris correspondent letter? Now I must go on to the <u>on dits</u> You know about <u>Lou Perry & this handsome rich aimiable clever M.[r] Ricardo</u>,[28] & do you know the Sartoris' are enormously rich now, with a fine place in Hampshire and has Minny told you about Mr Ross & Miss Rosey Smith.[29] Its only a rumour. Lolla Sterling[30] comes to see us very often and we always talk about you, & I give the Coles some of your letters to read because they like it. Heres my poor Tishys note. Isnt it sad? Dont you think Mr Corbière must have some intention if he always meets them every where & walks & so on. I am afraid he is a rather[31] vulgar person & so I hope almost that there is nothing in it. Mrs Trollope is in town — Minny says I like her to agravate my sister & Papa has been asked to meet them at about four places & says theres a good deal of sameness, & he doesnt want to meet them very much oftener. Granny writes such dear kind little letters Isnt [*sic*] a delightful comfort that we are all so happy together. I should be <u>quite</u> happy if it wasn't for those mysterious griefs of mine. There is rather a tragedy going on in the house. Ellen has taken gardeners money out of her drawer & tells fibs like a little Sophia[32] about it I dont know what to do. It is horrible to send her away isn't it — but if she wont confess? Grey as usual has been describing all she has felt on the occasion — I got a dear little letter from Mary Irvine who seems very very happy, &

L.! John[33] came to lunch one day and has given us a very charming old picture of my Fathers Father. Its over the door in the back drawing-room. In the corner by the chimney where you always sat I have stuck a little frame of the Virgin (one of those photographs) & M.!ˢ Cayleys little carved bracket. It looks very furnishing, the chief Baron has come home & lives in Papa's study, & the pretty little glass out of our O S[34] bedroom is over the drawingroom book case & looks ever so much nicer than that round one   There are 2 disgusting columns put up in the dining room I am sorry to say, on each side of the marble table   it makes it look like a cemetary we want papa to have our names engraved & I think that's all.

Mind you go on telling us about the people & then we shall get to know them. Cap.! Twyford[35] is our last — Edward knows him, he is very funny & at home calls the servants by their names and spends the morning. He has not yet confided all about his heiress but he is very near it & I shall be delighted to listen. I felt as if I was you the other morning with young officers dropping in to lunch. Col. Hamley[36] came one day looking quite young & handsome. How very odd it is that men seem to get younger as they grow older   Why even My Min is beginning to look old & that does make me sad. She has certainly got fatter & stronger & has cream for breakfast & so I hope & will continue. We been reading <u>at odds</u>, & Carlyle[37] who I suddenly find I can understand, & yesterday we went with Lady Low & Selina & sat in H.P[38] and saw the people go by. Sir James Colvile Sir Arthur Buller[39] &ct. Isabella is married Ella writes so happily. Her great friends are Merolla's[40] do you remember M.ᵐᵉ Merolla at Paris. Its her son, & we are going to have one last dinner party & then pull in. The Milnes. Col Greathed. the Lows the Troubridges — Sir Ar.B. & I think thats all.[41] Edith Procter[42] is coming to spend the day tomorrow   today that great bothering Catholic bazaar is going on & we must I suppose go there. M.ᵐᵉ Marochetti wroted & begged us & it is a bore. Poor little Manson[43] has been desperately ill but he is all right again. Miss Fagan[44] is staying there — My love to Edmund if you see him, I hope you will see some of our cousins & write & tell me all about them. You know your letters are 10.000x more amusing to us, than ours can be to you because you know all about us & our friends & we dont yet know about y.!ˢ.

Your fetch[45] isn't going to India   I had never thought of that, what fun it will be to give letters of introduction to you when our friends go out. Little Charlotte still wears her velvet frock & goes to tea at the

Coles where a young gentleman she says plays to her upon a sort of flute. This is Alan[46] on the Jews harp. She also says I have a dear Papa wots gone into the city — she stopped in the Park one day & said this to two very grand swells. Julia saw she did not quite like it. Poor Mr Pollen has been dreadfully ill, he was a Julias last night so was Mr Doyle so were their adored M.^{r} & Mrs Martin Smith[47]

The dinner party guests are the Leechs[48] who really have one every other day — little Booge talked about Edward at Folkestone, & Mr Herbert Wilson asked about you & Mrs Wilson talked about Mr. Creyke[49] & said he had always a photograph of himself in his pocket. Did Minny tell you Lady Palmerston[50] asked us again at last & we couldn't go! Papa was at the Acad. dinner P of W[51] broke down in his speech but went on again very cheerfully & speaks with a slight German accent.

Now it is lunch & I must finish goodbye my dearest woman. My love to Ed. Papa wonderfully well but doesnt do much work. Y.^{r} dear AIT

To W. W. F. Synge

Letter 37 [19 July 1863]
Fales

Dear Mr Synge. We got your kind letter two or three days ago with the Kings card of acceptation [*sic*] in it & it made me feel very guilty for not having written before. How thankful I am you're all all right.

We are going on just as usual, pretty well, & rather happy. Papa is hard at work upon Denis Duval w.^{h} is the name of his new book. Not a long one & historical & very interesting I'm glad to say. But I'm sorry to say he has written himself into two bad fits of illness over it so that I owe it a grudge already. This is Sunday 19 of July. We put off going away it is so pleasant here, we sit out in the gardens & enjoy the lovely weather [*inkblot with the words "Brownie jumped up"*] & of a Sunday I see about ten Saturday reviews sitting under the trees alongside of ours Grannie comes & goes, she goes, tomorrow to Paris for ten days. We find it very dismal when she is away & no Amy & all alone of an evening if the other happens to be out. The Collins' are our greatest allies — They dined with us last Sunday with Mr Morganjohn[1] who said he had at last written to you, & let us into the secret of the Fair Haired young lady we used to be so curious about. Minny is quite well again, but she has been out of sorts all summer & we have been quite quiet for sometime past. Poor Tishy Cole had a fearful illness brain fever & was as bad as bad c^d be, but she too is all right although still away getting strong & recovering from the affects. We are going down to [*word illegible*] spend the day with her on Tuesday. The Merivales[2] have broken up house & gone for 2 years alas. There seems rather a dispersion of old friends Of Amy we have the best news they are going up country to Debroghur[3] but Colvin[4] & Co will always reach them Calcutta — She wrote & told us how excited she was to find Major Synge[5] in the Forty when she & Edward set up there — We went & called upon the mess [?] at her request because she wanted to see him, but as nobody returned the visit he got disgusted [?] & wouldnt go any more. Hearing however that Major Synge was going away she sat down & wrote him a note saying she was a very old friend of yours & wanted to see him very much & would he come & call upon her. She says she got a very kind little note but he had to leave that night or something & so I believe they did not meet after all but I'm not sure. She seems very happy & is very well & says the people are rather astonished at her very English ways walking & not going to sleep &ct. Calcutta is not like London as far as society goes she says. One day she saw poor M^r. Reddie[6] Mrs Sturgis' flame do you remember. But he was walking with Lady Trevelyan[7] & she didnt like to stop him. Mrs Sturgis asked us to go down to Walton last week but we couldnt manage if Minny was ill & Papa got an attack There was a Regalia & crowds of people Miss Perry told me about it. She is very enthusiastic about Lou's[8] intended Mr Ricardo. She says he gets more & more charming. Miss Crawfurd it seems to me is hardly used by fortune but she looks very jolly notwithstanding & is constant to Dr Manning.[9] We dined at Richmond yesterday with a M^r or Captain Darkwood[10] who has just come in to a fortune & very good naturedly spends it on his friends & treats them to peaches & allsorts of good things. He is a big dark man & yet so curiously like you, that Minny & I were both quite struck by it. I saw your Jugles [?][11] the other night looking <u>extremely handsome</u> her hair has gone up & she told me Bobbie was on his way home w^h I cant imagine to be the case. She is stout & looks ten years younger Can Major Synge be coming home? —

I am very sorry for the poor Bishop We have been making friends with the Archbishop of York. & so have the Trollopes who dined there last week. M.[r] Trollope dashed up in a hansom looking very jolly & is going abroad somewhere higher that the something to get out of the way of his fellow creatures — He is the kindest & friendliest soul — I havent seen her for a long time. I like his books very much indeed. There is one of Henry Kingsleys called Austin Elliot[12] w[h] Ive been reading w[h] is rather jolly & everyone has got the Bossu the original of the Dukes Motto[13] We want to go to Tom Taylors ticket of leave man very much.[14] on Friday we are going to Faust the opera,[15] w[h] has had a great success. Madame Rulor,[16] Id have given my eyes to see, but I have kept my eyes, & not seen her We did get to hear Jenny Lind.[17] We had a melancholy little conversation afterwards with M.[r] Collins about the people whose day is past Kingslake[18] du Chaillu[19] Raphael nothing lasts more than ten days. We are all unhappy at the terrible American War[20] — Is there never any end to it — Backwards & Forwards its like the ebb & flow of the sea

Goodbye and my love to M[rs] Synge (Who <u>could</u> help appreciating her) and my love to the dear little chickens

M.[r] Lucas[21] is going to marry a very nice young lady [*two words illegible*]

From Minny to Thackeray

Letter 38
Ray/Morgan

Clatto[1]
Cupar, Fife
[Sept. 1863]

My Dearest Papa

I do think it was very kind of you to send me a letter — I hope you liked my pictures? Wasnt it nice of M.[r] & M.[rs] Mener[2] to take such pains with them all for the sake of pleasing you — Every body has been so kind to me, & I have got so fond of them all — except when they sing hymns, which I cannot quite join in. I am very sorry that I cannot get home till Monday instead of Friday, but it is better I think, that I should go with the Lows, as I dont know of any one else going — the Gen' has promised me that he has quite settled to go on Monday and they are so very kind to me[3] — I wish Papa that you would tell Anny not to want me till Monday for it makes me uncomfortable that she should & it wont be very much longer — & I shall never never never stir from home again — Oh Papa what nasty things they have for breakfast do you [*sic*] those things like pale eels stuffed with garlic I am afraid that you w^d rather like them — What a funny old lady Mrs Ferrier is.⁴ I wonder if you are fond of her? — The Blackwoods⁵ brought me to her at the ball & she said that you were notorious & charming — Miss Janie⁶ wasn't there for she is still in weeds but Mrs Blackwood says that she has quite got over it — Isnt it nice — It wasn't Col Hamley or anyone who knows us, who wrote the review of Eliz^b in Blackwood but Mrs Oliphant⁷ — Mr Blackwood told me that he heard her praising it one day & instantly told her to write a review of it w^h was kind of him so I am glad to go there — They live 2 or 3 miles off — and I shall go there from Monday till Wed^y and then come back here and if I can stay with the Lows till we go to London — I do not much want to go to Dr John Browns⁸ but if he seems to wish it much I will — for I would not offend him for the world — Goodbye

My dearest Papa

I am very sorry to send you such an untidy letter but I have got someone to post this in the country & am in a g^t hurry.

From Minny to Anny

Letter 39   [Sept. 1863]
Ray/Morgan

M^r & Mrs Miller & the dear crabbed old Sheriff went off this morg — the bride in a huff because Augusta & I praised the Miss Moncrieffs who evidently were sorts of rivals of hers in Edinburgh — and she made such unkind remarks about them — that I told her that they were girls who w^d be thought a great deal of <u>even</u> in London, w^h they would — Oh dear; says she, they are by no means thought much of, in Edinbro — <u>we</u> consider ourselves in a far superior social position, do we not Mrs Patten¹ — yees yees my dear Mrs Miller, says M^rs P who always agrees with every one — in fact I did not get on very well with Mrs Miller, for she gave herself airs & I could not help showing her that I did not think her at all a swell last night I must say, that she was rather nice & she owned that tho it was delightful being at the Top of every thing in Edinbro, when she came to London, she found what a narrow stupid little groove she had been moving in — & she wished for a little expansion & universality. Really these Scotch people are great muffs — I asked Mrs Patten if she knew Mrs Millais, Oh dear No says she, Mrs Millais is not visited in the County at all — So I supposed that it was on account of Mr Ruskin[2] — but Mrs Patten said that it was nothing to do with Mr Ruskin — but her relations were not people that the County families could associate with in fact her father was a writer[3] What that is I do not know, but they assured me that it was not at all what my father was — Can you fancy these stupid County people, not making much of a genius like Mr Millais who passes many months in the midst of them — of course I dont wish to say any thing against my very kind host & hostess — Mr Patten I am sure you w^d like, he gets quite ill with laughing & Mrs Patten is a character & amuses me immensely — Mr Moir[4] told me before he left, that if any thing should happen to prevent D^r J Brown from ciceroning about on my Edinburgh day — I was to be sure & send for him — he is very shy tho he is a Sheriff & I was rather surprised — I have got to go & be photographed again Mrs Mercer[5] has sent to me to come because my other has gone wrong I hope it will hold up for me to walk today — the hills have their lovely bloom on them again this morng — Why will you go racketting about in that way — The Workhouse, Mrs Senior[6] & Julia, all in one day — of course you have headaches — Look here tell me if you w^d like me to come home without going to the blackwoods — at the beginning of the week — I send my [*sic*] to Papa.

I am y^r dear
Minnie

I shall write separate to Grannie you neednt shew this

From Minny to Anny

Letter 40   [Edinburgh]
Ray/Morgan   [Sept. 1863]

My Dear Gal —

   I am sorry that you did not hear from me yesterday but in honour of our departure from Clatto I don't think the post went. I really felt quite melancholy at leaving it, as if it were my own Country Seat. It looked so dismal at the end with all the basons & jugs packed up. It finishes up all of a sudden everything shuts up & all the servants drive off in a bus to the station & we in the Carriage. It was very rough in the carriage by the way & Augusta & I were quite poorly Paul wears a most disreputable travelling costume in Mad de C's style he looks like a gambler in it his master & mistress are distressed at his appearance but too nervous to mention it — The poor little page was sadly sick during the horrid passage & we were all uncomfortable D.r John Brown & Nelly met me at the station — Nelly is a dear little thing — I must tell you that I wrote to Eugenie[1] & told her to settle when I was to go to her & when I was to come here I shall end by stopping here altogether & I am sure that I am very glad if it gives them the slightest pleasure — I can see that this is a very very melancholy house — especially I should think for poor Nelly — I was afraid before I came of seeing poor M.rs Brown, but she can neither move nor speak and is quite helpless in her room — I don't know whether you will get this letter much before me — but I may as well write to you pour passer le temps as the french say — I am going presently to see Eugenie & the Lows & Minnie Senior & the dear old Sherrif. The Low girls are very much bored at the Edinburgh Hotel I am very fond of the Lows — I shall not be sorry to see Brownie & pussy the day after tomorrow. I dont think I have any more to tell you except my love to Papa D.r John Brown sends you his bitterest hostility[2] — Have something nice to eat prepared for me against my return <u>Mind this</u> & remember that I am now accustomed like Brownie to a great deal of notice — I have been invited to 3 parties to night one with the Lows one with the Browns & one with Eugenie to dear dear M.rs Kinglakes sister[3] — Theres a sweet oyster woman If <u>you</u> had a voice like a oyster what a comfort it w.d be to Papa — he will be pleased to hear that I shall join him in Scotch[4]

4

1864–1865

INTRODUCTION

> *And so out of all the dear life long talk one remembers two or three disjointed words here & there a look & tone — But I think there is something greater still — a sort of certainty of Love far far beyond our deserts — perhaps it may be ours even now — God knows I at least cannot be more unworthy of it than I was then (1864–65 Journal)*

ANNY began keeping a journal about a month after Thackeray's death.[1] The journal contains reminiscences of Anny's life from the time she was three years old. Described are not only events but feelings, as Anny remembers them and tries to analyze them. The recollected happiness of joyful occasions is often aborted by her present feelings of loss and sorrow. The above entry from the 1864 journal is characteristic of its content and tone—showing her pain, her love, and her feelings of guilt.

At the time of Thackeray's death Anny was twenty-six, unmarried, intellectually unchanneled, rebellious against the rules that bound a Victorian woman. Thackeray had been the center of her life. It is not strange then, that with Thackeray's increasing illness, Anny would panic, her jealousy intensify and focus on anyone or anything that threatened to take him from her. It is also understandable that his illness and death would bring on a sense of guilt over the moments of distance from her father caused by her generally unrealized desire for independence or her minor failures—for instance, her repeated lateness. At the same time she was so close to her father that she naturally worked out some of her complex feelings toward him after his death by, in effect, trying to replace him, a more successful act that combined fidelity *and* independence. She assumed his role in the family, looking after Isabella, protecting Minny, dealing with Mrs. Carmichael-Smyth. In addition, she confirmed this new position by becoming the family breadwinner.

Before her father's death Anny was, while clearly an intelligent young woman, a dilettante writer and volunteer social worker who bemoaned her fate much like Horatia in "Out of the World."[2] After his death, she assumed responsibility for her family and for herself, and she began to write in earnest. In the 1864 journal she searches not only for her dead father but for her living self.

Anny used the journal as a means of exploring her inner self and facing her personal devils. While she was pouring out her anguish in the journal, she had assumed Thackeray's position as head of the household. The weaker Minny remained a child under Anny's protection; Isabella, unmindful of the family tragedy, lived on, needing care and supervision. The sorrowing Mrs. Carmichael-Smyth grew more menacing in her religious mania. Thackeray was aware of the clash of wills between his mother and his daughters, particularly with Anny. In the 1864 journal Anny revealed Thackeray's doubts about his mother and daughters living together once again. He had said to Anny: "it will be a very dismal life for you when I am gone. I have a great mind to put it into my will that you are not to live with Grannie." His forebodings about the difficulties of the three women living together was borne out after he died. This was the real world Anny faced and dealt with, while in secret she examined her past, reconstructing her shattered life in the only way she knew: through the pages of her journal.

The 1864–65 journal is not one based on daily entries; the writing spans more than the year and a half. Anny not only covers her own life from her birth to the time she writes her last sentence, but she moves back into Thackeray's youth. Time is elastic; wherever her thoughts take her, she is present. She tells stories within stories. She remembers a specific occasion when Thackeray told her an anecdote about his past. In this way, the journal concentrates on feelings, wherever and whenever they occur. The alternation between time periods is further complicated by Anny's abrupt swing into the present tense when describing events in the past.

At times she appears desperate to put into words every picture, every word, every mood she can remember about her father, often insisting that he is still alive. "Papa has beautiful white hands with pink knuckles & long nails — . . . His eyes are so soft & large . . . his voice is low & gentle . . . he holds down his cheek to kiss & he presses our foreheads." For a grieving Anny, this is the way Thackeray *is*—and always will be. Only renewed realization of loss brings her back to reality.

In addition to its value as a record of Anne Thackeray's lament for her dead father, and as a more generalized work in terms of the basic father-daughter relationship, the journal serves as a source book of intimate details concerning Thackeray himself. Conscious of his failing health, Thackeray appeared to be taking stock of his younger days. The glimpses he gave Anny of his youth prove extremely revealing. " 'I am sure I must have been a most affected boy' . . . Papa said he never would ask anybody's name." He inspected his past actions impartially. "I have never done anything wrong in my life. Only once when I was a boy I did not pay back some money as quickly as I might have done. I kept the ten pounds for three months after I might have paid it." He recounts events from his youth: how he had as a boy set by "a secret store of brown sugar" in a book; how he dreamed that the devil had gotten his nose and how he hid under the sheets; how they had made the coach ride to Paris when Isabella had gone mad. "He said Bhuu — What a terrible night that was —" Anny recounts that ". . . Papa has told us how one day he was at his desk writing when Brodie came & asked him for some money & he changed the last five pounds he had to give it her, and we children were in one room crying and Mamma was raving in the other."

Anny's descriptions of her father are equally valuable. He "liked going to the play"; he did not like "cutting his nails"; when she expressed a desire for a shawl, he went to Marshall & Snelgrove that very day and bought her one; he was guilty at times of personal stinginess as well as of confessing that he swore at his clubs (a fact he was not ashamed of).

Anny's descriptions of his physical appearance are rich with detail.

> I can see him passing his hand through his hair laughing at the children pouring out his tea. . . . Then he liked pacing across the room & counting his steps from one place & another . . . his smile is extraordinarily sweet his voice is low & gentle.
>
> I can see him swinging his arms as he walks   I can see him looking out over the ship sides & placing his spectacles that are always slipping.

These are memories of a daughter who was in close contact with her father; these are also a novelist's telling particulars about the living Thackeray. He was no myth to her, no immortal; he was gentle to the cat; he came downstairs in his long dressing gown; "Brilliant conversation bored Papa he liked easy going talk"; he called her his "blessing"; he pronounced a sham benediction on her; he liked old curiosity shops and silversmiths; he always made jokes; when she bored him he would caution her "vous Radotez ma chère — & laugh so kindly"; he fell asleep and snored at the Athenaeum and at St. Paul's. "When we used to come & stand near his chair he had a way of putting up his hand to us backwards. Dear hand that was never closed never withheld. I am aching to touch it to speak to him once more." Anny moves from a physical description to symbolic meaning, to a personal revelation. Despite her grief, she was developing as a writer.

Although Anny reveals many of Thackeray's work habits and literary opinions, she focuses mainly on Thackeray the father and her relationship with him. To jog her memory about details of their life she refers to his diaries as well as her own.[3] These entries keep alive for her the past so that it does not disappear as Thackeray did. At the start she despairs of capturing his essence. "It does not sound the same when it is written down," she laments. The outmoded theory of Thackeray the cynic is denounced; Thackeray the clubman and bon vivant did not exist for Anny. What emerges is Thackeray the loving but fallible father, generous friend, and dedicated artist. She does not inter the bad with his bones, does not hide his faults and flaws as she knew them; for her his good far outweighs them. He gave her the "certainty of love," and with that gone, her inner life collapsed. Although she was able, outwardly, to function as the head of the family, she became deeply troubled.

The natural reaction to the death of a father was further exacerbated in Anny's case by her feelings of guilt. Several reasons for this suggest themselves. In many ways Anny was still immature, and her childlike regrets for having been "wicked" stem from this immaturity. She also suffered from strong feelings of disloyalty to her father which can be ascribed to her wish to become independent while at the same time she found herself unable to act. Her writing at this time suggests another cause of her feelings of guilt. Despite the fact that Thackeray wanted her to have a career and suggested the topic for her first published article, she believed that, in some way, she risked usurping his calling. Her deepest feeling of guilt was provoked by Thackeray's death itself:

she was alive and he was dead. In addition, she was troubled by the feelings of jealousy she had experienced over her father.

The depth of her self-blame was nearly overwhelming. She bewailed her unworthiness, castigated herself for her jealousy:

> Here once for all I will write down in case in after life I should ever ever forget or forgive myself.
>
> That in these last days I think I must have been almost out of my mind at times. I can remember thoughts so impatient so unloyal so irritable & wicked. An absurd jealousy & suspicion had seized hold of me. The Last day my Father lived I went to church & prayed so fervently for myself to be delivered from it, that I did not think to pray for him.

Despite the fact that she recognized after his death how upset she had been at the time of Thackeray's last illness, she judged her own actions harshly and without forgiveness. Thackeray had recognized this tendency in her toward self-flagellation. "Papa once said — not long ago — Anny always manages to reproach herself whatever happens. . . . I remember he said on my last birthday You are reproaching yourself about every thing today —" Although Thackeray had detected Minny's jealousy, toward Anny's either he was blind or he chose not to see it, or perhaps she was able to hide it. It would take many years for her to forgive herself and accept these emotions as natural. Only in her last novel, *Mrs. Dymond,* does a heroine of Anny's learn generally to accept her own frailties and to relinquish the attempt to be a model of perfection.

Anny's jealousy appears to be free-floating in that it had no specific focus. It was entangled with guilt, and other feelings of unworthiness and "wickedness." Up until the last year of her father's life she had been able to keep all these destructive responses under control. However, when he became threateningly ill more and more often, her fear of losing him made control impossible. In the journal she realizes that "he was never well all this year." Some references seem clear and others have the authentic vagueness of someone struggling to understand past behavior. After Thackeray's last carriage ride, Mrs. Carmichael-Smyth, sibyl-like, had prophesied:

> 'I could not bear to see the carriage drive up with Charles & Sims in their great black wagon
>
> I said 'What harm could that do us' or something of the sort but I did feel a chill & at night when I went to the Coles with Katie I was so very wretched & I did try not to be jealous

> And then next morning Fanny said M.ʳ Thackeray is not well Miss, & I went into his room in a sort-of rage of sorryness.

Frightened at the unsubtle allusion to a funeral coach, Anny tries to dispel this image but cannot. At the Coles' the sight of a family consisting of father, mother, and children underscored the frailty of her own family structure. She became envious of what she did not have as well as wretched over what she was afraid to lose. The "rage of sorryness" that tortured her when she found out the next morning that Thackeray was ill was caused by the guilt she felt in this implicit criticism of her father.

The Yates affair had elicited an earlier wave of jealousy and guilt: "As we were coming home in the dark at Knightsbridge we met the Collins who said he had been to see them, to show them something wʰ M.ʳ Yates had written. I pray God to be forgiven for my wicked anger and absurd jealousy." Anny was angry at, and jealous of, a situation that became the focus of Thackeray's attention and that caused him discomfort and pain.

Thackeray's work was often a source of difficulty for Anny: "Papa once said to me, not pleased, — I find you have been complaining out of the house to two different people & expressing your desire that I should leave it — I said Yes, I had always said so to him that I could not bear to see him work when he was ill." Understandable as Anny's concern for Thackeray's welfare may be, complaints to people outside her family were inappropriate. From Thackeray's point of view, Anny was interfering in his life. Her undue distress at his working when he was ill once again suggests guilt feelings. And to add to her burden, he was working to accumulate a fortune to leave to her and Minny. Therefore, believed Anny, she and her sister were responsible for hastening his death.

At the start of the journal there is a paragraph that has no reference to anything before or after it and that suggests Anny's jealousy of her sister. Further isolation from the paragraph which follows it (by a space in the folio) contributes to the evidence that Anny stopped writing at this point. It is one of the rare instances in which Anny presents an anecdote out of the past without any commentary in the present: "Grannie said one day that Minny had a pretty voice & I said <u>has</u> Minny got a nice voice & Papa said Min has a very sweet little pipe of her own." Anny exhibits tremendous willpower. She reveals the episode but she does not articulate her jealousy. Her halt in the narrative at this point is a compelling indication that her thoughts proved to be too difficult for her to handle. Minny's jealousy of Anny showed itself in overt actions; Anny, however, was ashamed of this same feeling toward her sister and tried to repress it.

One of Anny's earliest memories included Minny in a negative manner. At times of stress, old patterns of behavior reassert themselves—the child in us gains sovereignty over the adult. Ray notes that Anny

> Throughout this period . . . was haunted by a vivid memory of early childhood, Thackeray's putting out the light in the stage-coach to punish her for being naughty during their journey to Paris in 1840 after her mother's madness had declared itself.[4]

At the time she was a child Thackeray had put out the light in the coach as punishment for her making the baby cry. Minny was therefore the cause for the light going out in the coach, or so the child Anny thought.

In her journal Anny, childlike, fears "Has the light gone out now for us, because we were not quiet & good?" Minny's weakness and her grandmother's intractability made it imperative for Anny to have the adult in her assert supremacy over the child. It was necessary for someone to take charge of the Thackeray affairs, and Anny was the only one capable of it.

In a letter dated 1 May 1864, Anny wrote: "My little Minny is asleep now too sad to keep awake tonight — But she is much better thank God & the aching leaves off for a while now & then — Only she looks thin and so wan at times that I can't bear it, but thank God she is much better."[5] Despite her old jealousy of her sister, Anny loved Minny. What had been an older sister's protectiveness before Thackeray's death turned into maternal feeling as Anny looked on Minny no longer as a sister but as a daughter. Anny's own distraction was apparent in the repetition of "she is much better thank God." Outwardly Anny worried about her more fragile and delicately balanced sister; inwardly she agonized over her past sin of jealousy. Anny loved Minny, but as a rival for Thackeray's affection she fought unconsciously for supremacy over her younger sister, recording naively Minny's "failings." In real life Anny was caring for Minny, Isabella, and her grandmother; in her journal, she pushed them aside. When they impinged upon her thoughts, she was impatient for them to leave—to make room for Thackeray and Anny.

Anny begins her journal with a memory from her childhood. "Papa called Minny Min & me Nan very often." In addition to re-creating her father, she is trying to establish a separate identity for herself. However, she still clings to Thackeray's definition of "Nan"—and this despite his desire to abdicate his role as arbiter. "When I asked him a question he said I leave it to y^r own excellent understanding   It was a sort of little joke because I wanted him to settle always   One day he laughed & said I defy you to get anything out of me." Thackeray had learned from his mother how difficult it was to withstand a possessive parental relationship; he wanted his daughter to become independent and make decisions for herself. Anny was reluctant to take the step out of fear of replacing him, or perhaps she wanted to but felt it was disloyal.

Anny was no beauty; Minny's appearance was about average. They were both intelligent and moved in good circles, daughters of a famous father. Yet neither of them had received serious offers of marriage. Did Thackeray's dependence on them, real or imagined, keep them aloof from eligible young men? Did Anny's assumed position in the family triangle keep her unapproachable? And possibly the fact that Isabella had gone mad such a short time after her marriage acted as a further deterrent to marriage for her daughters. In the journal Anny records two comments made by Thackeray on his daughter's marital status, "Once Papa said to us — I think you girls ought to marry so that I should have some grand-children. I once said Papa you dont want us to marry do you & he said quite hastily but looking around, Certainly not." Thackeray answered Anny's question with haste and embarrassment because he did not want to appear to be blaming her for the lack of marriage offers.

For Anny, the memory of Thackeray and his views on children attaches to those about her marrying, and then once more to his love for her and her feelings of unworthiness. "God knows I at least cannot be more unworthy of [his love] than I was then." Following a blank space is a paragraph beginning, "Papa is always so easily pleased." The importance of Thackeray's pleasure, meaning his approval, is excessive. "Papa always liked everything we did, & we never liked anything much until we knew he approved."

It is perhaps now impossible to recover, if it ever could have been clearly known, the reasons for this somewhat extreme dependence on the father, even for activating her own experience. Perhaps in some complicated way her possession of her father's attention—the mother being removed from the scene—left her also too dependent on him even as it allowed her to be very close to him.[6]

Anny used the journal to examine her relationship with Thackeray. However, it was inevitable that references should be made to Minny, Isabella, and Mrs. Carmichael-Smyth. Those to Mrs. Carmichael-Smyth are negligible; those to Isabella and Minny seem neutral but under examination prove to be negative. For example, Anny wrote: "Mama went out of her mind," "Mama was raving," and Thackeray "talked about Mamma." Anny offers these statements as simple matters of fact; she never reveals what she thought or felt. In contrast she discussed with interest Isabella "looking a little shocked" over Thackeray's reaction to the Bible story of Abraham. Thackeray talked to her about her birth and how Isabella almost died because of the malpractice of a homeopathic doctor. Surely this would cause complex responses in any child, but again Anny made no comment.

Another telling anecdote Thackeray later used in *Denis Duval:*

> He said he thought of a little story I had told him of walking on the sea shore with Mamma & she held me by the hand & once pulled me in a little way, & then her love struggled with her madness & so we came back safe. . . . I remember someone said Papa was coming down to us — but this was 24 years ago.

Thackeray recalled the story told him by Anny, but whose interpretation was it that Isabella's love for Anny overcame her madness? Anny was barely three years old when the incident occurred; it seems more likely that Thackeray made the judgment. Anny inferred that Thackeray was coming to rescue her. She dismissed the whole incident with "— but this was 24 years ago —" Again there is no comment from Anny in the present.

Anny's relationship with her mother is hard to assess. From Thackeray's and Isabella's letters to Mrs. Carmichael-Smyth, Isabella emerges as a gay, indulgent mother who sang and played with the baby Anny. Their relationship was of such short duration, though important, that Isabella's absence takes on more significance than her presence. Not until after Isabella's death is Anny able to express sympathy and sorrow over Isabella's plight. Here in the journal, Anny's silence denotes great turmoil about her feelings for her mother. As the goodness of Anny's early memories about her mother faded, what remained was the void left by her absence, and the guilt and hostility attendant on it. Added to this was her guilt at having had the father to herself and having let him die.

Anny's sense of having been "wicked" and needing forgiveness permeates the journal. "Dear Papa where you are can you hear, can you see us — If with my whole life I could tell you once more that I love you & know that you forgive me." After these sentences there is a pause in the manuscript. This indicates a reinforcing of Anny's guilt at not having loved him enough. If she had, if she had told him so, then, like a talisman, it would have warded off his death. Not having done so, she repeatedly asks his forgiveness. Throughout the journal she lists her transgressions. She "forgot Papa's bag"; she "always kept him waiting"; she "bothered him about his cheques & retrenching & moving." Relentlessly, she calls herself to account for her evils.

> If I remember how often I misjudged how impatient how cruel my thoughts were it seems as if there could be no peace or forgiveness ever again. . . . Only one lives on & one does not guess at the great pit into w^h one is falling down lower & lower & suddenly your life seems to stop all the great clouds roll away & you find yourself in a hell of your own making.

She has lost her chance to change her ways.

> still I pray that I remember the wrong . . . the love was so part of us both that we did not think of it — or I at least until it was gone — . . .
> I wish that I could live my life over again — only just a little wiser a little more faithful & tender.

She excoriates herself for her past commissions and omissions. But she is also bewildered by the present: "my dear Papa O my dear O what shall I write — O what shall I feel If I am happy I am forgetting you — If I am aching for you I grow sick with grief." And yet for all her breast-beating, Anny was aware that Thackeray knew how much she (and Minny) cared for him: "We would have blacked your boots you said to some one & indeed indeed we would."

The journal has a remarkable structure. Unplanned as it was, it nevertheless contains the resonance of a sonata form. Divided into two parts or movements, the coda was written a year later, after the death of Mrs. Carmichael-Smyth. The first movement rises to the crescendo of Thackeray's death; the second descends to Anny's aftermath of grief; the coda balances the pattern with resolution and acceptance.

In the first twenty folios Anny weaves back and forth between the past and the present. Finally she recounts the sequence of Thackeray's last days, culminating in his funeral. With extraordinary force the current narrative begins to dominate the past memories, until finally, in the last nine folios, only the present remains. The tempo quickens, the details become more precise, the writing more taut and economical.

Anny's memories glide between her past as a little girl and the present. Chronological time does not exist as she recalls episodes which follow her personal inner logic. Fuguelike, the episode is repeated, with variations. On the first folio she moves from the time she was "little" to "lately" to "not so long ago." In most cases she begins with a scene out of the past that modulates into the present and ends, inevitably, with her father's illness and death. An example of this is found in the following episode, which starts with Anny as a little girl; the incident is repeated "until now almost," when she "cannot bear to think that quite of late it has not been quite the same."

> When we were little girls Papa used to talk to us a great deal and tell us about the Bible and Religion. . . . He used to talk to us of a morning after breakfast in his study & of an evening after dinner smoking his cigar & we generally sat on the floor & listened to him. That has gone on until now almost. And then we would give him a chair for his legs and a little table for his candles & he would presently nod to us and go to sleep. I cannot bear to think that quite of late it has not been quite the same.

This is followed by a discussion of Thackeray's religious beliefs. Then dipping back into the past, remembering Thackeray's reaction to the story of Abraham and Isaac, Anny writes, "The last time we went to church together was that day at the Temple." A lyrical description of the church service, the tea attended afterward, ends:

> And Papa laughed because we were so pleased and happy and looked at the pictures on the walls. Is it ungrateful to be so sick with grief — Perhaps even when we come out of this Temple we shall find him gone on a little way before us and waiting to lead us out into the open air.

At this point Anny leaves a double space in the folio as if actual time had elapsed in her writing. The next paragraph treats of an entirely different topic. These spaces in the manuscript, often as much as half a page, and in two instances a page and a half, occur when she is overcome with emotion. Such abrupt halts punctuate the manuscript with escaped feelings she is trying to master. The two long hiatuses appear after each of the two parts. There is no way of knowing the period of time during which she ceased to write, but that she was overcome with emotion at each point is evident.

Although the two parts of the journal are similar in construction, there are many differences in content due to Anny's changing state of mind. Begun a month after Thackeray's death, the first part is written in the earliest stages of shock and mourning, while the second part, dated 15 April, is dominated by Anny's introspection and anguish. Suffering from even stronger feelings of loss, she is more able to articulate her emotions than before.

Another notable difference lies in Anny's modes of recollection. In referring to an old diary, she writes:

> In one place I see — 'forgot Papa's bag — ' It was the day Amy went to India I went & knocked at his door in a fright next morning & when he did not answer I thought it was that he would not let me in — I remember how ashamed I was when I saw him, for ever thinking he w$\underline{d}$ be angry; he wasnt a bit.

The notation in Anny's 1862 diary jarred her memory about the incident.[7] She examined it, recalled her mistaken fright about Thackeray's reaction as well as her needless shame, but she was no longer worrying the subject. Many of the remembrances now end in more reasonable and distanced analyses. However, she continued in some measure to find fault with her past actions and to wish that she could "live my life over again — only just a little wiser a little more faithful & tender." She grappled with everyday life, but the hysteria within her was not placated, nor did the self-flagellation abate. The second part of the journal is a conflicting combination of more thoughtful analyses and more anguished loss.

Thackeray's real-life predilection for "water and milksop" maidens led him from Isabella to Jane Octavia Brookfield, known as JOB; and later to Sally Baxter, a different type. But they all disappointed him. Isabella went mad; JOB preferred her husband to Thackeray; Sally married a Southern gentleman. Only in his fiction could Thackeray manipulate his paragon. By the end of *Vanity Fair* Amelia Sedley becomes a "tender little parasite."[8] Lady Castlewood, the older woman, pines with unrequited love for the young Esmond. In the 1864 journal Anny admits that Thackeray "liked JOB best of all women," "that after all there was no one like her. So tender so womanly except perhaps you girls." Of all the women Thackeray had loved—his mother, Isabella, JOB, and Sally—none had remained true to him. In the journal,

Anny writes that she should have been "a little more faithful" to her father; actually she remained faithful to him until she was forty, when she married.

In *The Virginians* Thackeray writes that Rachel Esmond "would have jumped overboard if her papa had ordered."[9] Anny's reference to Thackeray's belief that his daughters "would have blacked his boots" is an ominous variation of the statement about Rachel Esmond. As a five year old, Thackeray had been parted from his mother in India and sent to England. Perhaps this desertion by his mother made Thackeray sufficiently distrustful of women as to view jumping overboard or polishing boots as positive acts of fidelity.

In the second part of the journal, Anny's inward journeys appear to be less painful than before. Although she continued to write of Thackeray using the present tense, she seemed to be searching for happier memories. On her last birthday Thackeray had accused her of reproaching herself too often. Despite this reproof Anny wrote, "But O what a happy day it was all the same." Philosophically she added, "It seems no use to reproach myself about Papa. It does not make me love him more."

In the first part of the journal Anny made no mention of Thackeray's work. She did refer to his decision not to write for the *Realm,* and to his discussion of the Bible as literature. In the second part of the journal she recalled his comments about *Esmond, Pendennis, Philip,* and *Denis Duval.* She revealed how he had "a superstition to write a little every day"; how he "made little sketches in the air" with his finger. In the beginning of her journal she envisioned Thackeray the father to the exclusion of all else; only in the second part was she able to recognize Thackeray the writer.

As time passed Anny referred more and more to her diary and to Thackeray's. "Papa has written in his book Dined with girls at Star & Garter." This short sentence was Thackeray's only comment on Anny's birthday. For Anny remembering, it became a day of great importance. She fleshed out Thackeray's brief entry with a detailed description of the people they met, the dinner they ate, the carriage ride home "past the river through the clouds & clouds of mists . . . in the calm summer eve[g]." Anny's reference to Thackeray's entry in his diary was confirmation of her memory. Assuring herself of the past, Anny tried to rescue herself from the present.

Often, having consulted his diary first, she then described the event Thackeray merely noted. "On the 15 June Lady Trowbridge & Sir

R. Murchinson are written down." She recalled that she had accompanied Thackeray and that he took sick, necessitating their return home. Retreating to the halcyon days before her father's death, she relives them less than she did in the first part of the journal and instead recounts them.

Occasionally, however, Anny still resorted to living in the past. In May she wrote in a letter, "To me the dead are dearer than the living and more alive at times." [10]

The journal memories referred to here are followed by a blank space; a new paragraph begins, "We have been so disturbed & unhappy that I have left off writing for this last fortnight, but I will try & never do so again for the words fade out of ones memory with time, sometimes they seem far far away sometimes I almost seem to hear him speak." Anny does not divulge why she was so disturbed and unhappy. What follows in her journal are several of Thackeray's reminiscences of himself as a boy. This allows Anny once more to escape her present as well as her past.

The first two entries in her notebook dated 1864–77 read:

> 1864. This sad year began at Freshwater. It was bitter weather Minnie & I were in Mrs. Camerons cottage. She was goodness in person Alfred Tennyson used to come & see us in his cloak Harding Cameron used to come & try to interest Minnie in particular. I remember the cold & the nights. I seemed to see funerals passing along the downs — the rocks & the waves wailing against it were always consoling.
>
> 15 Jan
> We came back to London to Katie Collins house. Everything seemed empty [11]

From January through September when Anny and Minny moved into their own home at 16, Onslow Gardens, they traveled from the home of one friend or relation to another. From Mrs. Cameron's at Freshwater, to the Collinses in London, they went to the Ritchies at Henbury, then back to Freshwater, to Putney Heath, then to Mrs. Sartoris at Warnford. In August they joined Mrs. Carmichael-Smyth at Arromanches in Brittany, and this proved to be the most difficult time of all.[12] As Thackeray had feared, each day brought "terrible religious discussions," wearing down the already burdened Anny and the delicate Minny. "Grannie looks very ill. Minny says she herself is half mad . . . We want to do our duty, [but] seeing no one makes it so much worse . . . [I feel] torn & crazed between the two dear ones, . . . so miserable & so fearing for the future."[13] A few days later Anny wrote: "I am crying Minnie is crying Granny is crying & thinking of GP. How very miserable we are. What can we do?"[14]

The present life which Anny found so difficult was not only one without Thackeray but also a rootless, bleak wandering about. Affairs had to be settled: the house on Palace Green and its contents sold; the estate settled (Thackeray had died intestate); his copyrights sold. These were practical matters, distasteful to a grieving daughter. However, Anny was in control of her life now. Decisions were forced upon her; she became self-directed. In a letter to Mrs. Baxter, she wrote on 24 October: "we must look about I suppose & find something to do & to be interested in — It is very difficult — I try to write a little but I have nothing to say —"[15] Thackeray, the huge father-mother-teacher figure was gone; Anny turned to the only thing she knew how to do—writing.

In the Baxter letter Anny says she has nothing to say, but she *is* writing. She was also writing in her journal and had been since the end of January. The journal became for her a book of sorrow, a receptacle of her self-incrimination, self-examination, and self-revelation. From this she advanced to letter writing, and then to writing for publication. In letters like the one quoted above, Anny spoke openly and without reserve. Perhaps it was easier to do so with Mrs. Baxter, whom she had never met and from whom she was separated by an ocean. Nevertheless, and for whatever reason, Anny did reveal her innermost thoughts to Mrs. Baxter, her father's old friend.

> I know Papa was tired & that he did not want to live except for us & yet my heart sickens & aches & I feel that he might have been with us now — . . . I woke up with a start saying to myself It has only been a dream & it is not true. It makes one so humble & so ashamed to hear of his tender goodness & to remember his unceasing love & partiality — & it is like a sort of torture now to remember how little we understood it[16]

The fact that she wrote about herself in letters (and not in her secret journal) made her thoughts at once more acceptable. By verbalizing her transgressions to another person, she began to forgive herself and to accept her past actions. At the end of October, her period of intense mourning was nearing its end.

It is illuminating to examine the endings of both movements or parts. One can readily observe at what point Anny regained a balance and perspective in her life. The first movement ends in a dream of great anxiety and sexual content, followed by the discovery of Thackeray's death, another short dream, and finally his burial.

> That morning I dreamt I was with Papa climbing a very high hill. We went higher & higher so that I had never seen anything like it before. And Papa was pointing out something to me w^h I could not see & presently left me & I seemed to come down alone. He said write to Mr Longman. I said I have written.

What Thackeray was pointing to, which Anny could not see, was the new land—death—which he entered and she did not. Her coming down the hill alone confirms this. The dreamlike quality was made to seem real by Thackeray's referring to a real person, Mr. Longman, and her father's request that Anny write to him to break an engagement. Dutifully she had anticipated his wish. Although the sexual content of this dream cannot be ignored, it is not relevant at this point.[17] The importance of the dream, for Anny's purpose in the journal, is based on her anxiety and apprehension that her father had died during the night, and that what she had experienced was an intuitive foreshadowing of his death.

A space in the journal is followed by a short paragraph in which "Charles the servant met me He is dead Miss he said He is dead / Then Grannie came from her room." This is the climax of the journal, perhaps of Anny's very life, yet she takes the time to identify Charles as the servant, to record "he said" in its proper place, and to describe the direction of Mrs. Carmichael-Smyth's entrance. These details indicate how hard Anny was striving for objectivity, for the distancing necessary for survival.

The next paragraph describes the dream she had two days later in which Thackeray asked her, "Are you sick my child." Even in death Thackeray remained for Anny the loving and caring father. At the cemetery she "felt as if my head was on his breast. And it seemed as if he was with us the whole time at Kensal Green." Although dead, and the cause of her grief, he was the only one who could understand it.

The entire recital of these last days is told in a straightforward, unembellished style. She held on to the actual facts of those terrible moments when she learned that her father was dead. For example, she "went out of [her] room to the landing & Charles the servant met [her]." Even when time had passed and she knew the truth, she clung to details in order to make it real: exact place (the landing), exact person (the servant). During these later months of loss she lived in a push-pull exchange between present and past. The journal illustrates this exhausting pattern: no sooner did she go forward than she was pulled back, by some reference or some memory. "Sometimes he gives us a sham benediction & stands in an attitude. Only the shamness is realness & the Blessing is there." At this later date she was, at least, able to accept his blessing. Yet she comments in the present tense on what has happened in the past. Symbolically, she takes him from death and places him, once more alive, in the living center of her life.

As time continued to widen the distance between her and her loss, she was better able to remove the blocks against reality which she herself had constructed to save herself from pain. She could, step by small step, see the past as the past and, in effect, leave Thackeray behind.

Earlier, she made no comment at all on his death; how she had felt, what had happened when she knew he was dead, and, most likely, even saw him dead. The two days before the funeral were relegated to a locked cell of silence within her. Deliberately, she chose the burial of reality over the more painful burial of her father. As the journal nears its end, Anny is sufficiently distanced to reveal an incident at Onslow Square in which she referred to Thackeray's severe illness in 1849. Like her father, she uses this illness as evidence of a step along the way toward his eventual death, so that the death, approached slowly, will be less of a sudden shock—an event met in stages, therefore less overwhelming. With his help in the past, she was able now to recall the time when, alive, he had blessed her and spoken his thoughts about dying. "Papa said next morning That as he was in bed the night before & as he was looking about & thinking how comfortable it looked, he could not help wondering. what the end of it all would be, & whether this was the room in which he would die one day." In this entry Anny uses the past tense: "Papa said." She can bear, now, to separate life from death; she can recall a time when her father *was* alive and relinquish her wish to place him in the present. It is also significant that Thackeray is the giving father, sensitive to Anny's attachment to him, preparing her for a reality which he believes she will find difficult to accept.

On 29 September Anny and Minny moved into their new home at 8, Onslow Gardens. Mrs. Carmichael-Smyth joined them two weeks later. Now frail and sickly, she had exhausted herself in grief over the deaths of her husband and son. Chastened by sorrow, she became easier to live with. Anny wrote in her diary on 26 November: "I went for a little walk with Grannie. She said she had changed her mind about many things, especially about religious things, and that she could now sympathize far more than she had once done, with what my father used to think and say."[18] Less than a month later Mrs. Carmichael-Smyth was dead. She died quietly and without any warning. With the exception of the cloistered Isabella, Anny and Minny were now bereft of family.

Scarcely four pages long, the last part, or coda, of the journal is dated "5th June 1865," less than six months after the death of Mrs. Carmichael-Smyth, and almost a year and a half after Thackeray's death. It is no wonder that Anny lamented, "We sometimes wonder if one of us will die next Christmas." Yet for all her cataloging of Thackeray's friends who had died within the last year, and her comment that "Today I have felt like Job," this last part of the journal is not as grim as it is sad. Anny and Minny have learned to accept the trials of life. "Yesterday Minny said to me Anny how can you dare to complain? — our small troubles we can forget & our greatest sorrows are our greatest blessings — Her words have been ringing in my ears ever since." After the deaths of their father and grandmother and the loss of Palace Green, little troubles were meaningless. Once Anny and Minny had been Thackeray's blessings, now he was theirs. Anny wanted to be relieved of sorrowing. If Minny could not completely rescue her sister, Anny was ready to submit to religion: "the future came not as we had expected it but as I had prayed for I think somehow our prayers are answered . . . I used to think it would be a sign that our failings towards our Father were forgiven if my dearest Grannie were to go at peace with us at hand." And Mrs. Carmichael-Smyth went in just such a way. She had loved her granddaughters; she had also caused them great anguish; but at her death, Anny recalled only her kindness.

This section ends with a reminiscence of a recent trip to Cambridge where Anny and Minny visited Thackeray's old rooms.

> It was like feeling nearer to Papa to go & see his youth with our own eyes — It was like living then & when we came back here it seemed as if we had travelled from one century into another almost. . . . A kind sick clergyman . . . remembered him in M.r EFG's rooms quite well, & again drawing pictures at a water party.

Thackeray and his youth are beginning to recede in time from Anny's conscious memory, "from one century into another almost." He will always remain a part of her life, but she is opening to the reality of separation. The journal entry ends with a young Thackeray visiting

FitzGerald and drawing sketches at a water party. For Anny this picture of a youthful, carefree Thackeray is especially attractive. Perhaps her guilt at having "replaced" her mother leads her to think of her father before he was married. The relationship of father and daughter, fraught as it always is with danger, was in Thackeray's and Anny's case particularly difficult.

Faced with this burden, Anny turned for refuge to her personal religion. She searched for and found a Bible text: "Have mercy . . . blot out our transgressions — but many are in my — And I pray that for once my gratitude & love for the Father of my Father & of us all may be true & from a loyal heart." Thackeray is still uppermost in her mind—she prayed to the Father of *her* Father, as if God could have validity only when linked to Thackeray. She had not overcome her self-doubt; she believed herself guilty of transgressions, hoping that her love "may be true."

However, the tone of these last pages differs greatly from the two main parts of the manuscript. A year and a half had passed since Thackeray's death. If nothing else, time had helped to assuage her grief. Her inner strength, common sense, and essential optimism made her recovery an eventuality. When she began to write about her grandmother's death, Anny had already withdrawn from the journal and was looking at its contents with objectivity. "I cannot help writing a word in the book where my poor sick heart tried to write its pain. I am not once going to read what I wrote I am only going to say that even after such sorrow & darkness as ours has been a light comes." Anny recognized how the journal had served her, but she no longer needed it. She shed her mourning clothes and sought resolution to her time of pain; she felt able once more to partake of life. The period in which she had written in her journal "seem[ed] like twilight when I think of it."

Anny called the 1864–65 journal her "clasp book" because of its brass clasp. It was a secret diary, as holy as a confessional, as private and complex as an analyst's couch. As long as she had need of it, she clasped it to her, pouring into it her innermost feelings. After she had written the final words, her "loyal heart" turned outward to the world. While Thackeray would remain the most decisive force in her life, she would, henceforth, seek a self who would grow beyond the past toward a future of its own. In times of great distress, she would return to the solid presence of her father and be again comforted as his "shadow."

Important as the intimate record of a great artist, the journal also stands as the lament of a grieving daughter for a loving and beloved father. Not only by the words, but by what is omitted, by the unvoiced recriminations, the silent and often unrecognized anger, by the childlike need for more and always more love, Anny's 1864–65 journal becomes the pivotal effusion of her psyche. Undisciplined, her sorrow had brought forth words and thoughts she no longer wanted to read or deal with. In the future, these feelings would find their way, transmuted, into her novels. The party celebrating Thackeray's move to Palace Green had been the happiest moment of her life; the 1864–65 journal represents the intellectual climax of her life, and is the forerunner of her career.

What she had begun tentatively while Thackeray was alive, she performed resolutely after his death: she became a writer. Often working on more than one project at a time, she wrote continuously. On backs of envelopes, scraps of paper, odd sheets of stationery, and in notebooks, she sketched ideas, scenes, first drafts. Then too there were her letters. Even given the fact that the Victorians were a people who communicated by letters, Anny's output was prodigious. Once she was able to deal with the immediate shock of Thackeray's death, the event released her in a vast resource of creative energy.

Although Thackeray protested that he wanted her to think for herself, he nevertheless wielded the power of a strong father. He told her when to stop writing and when and on which topic to start again. Doubtless it was good literary advice; nevertheless, he was making decisions for her. She needed to please him—never understanding that his love would not have stopped at her independence. Doing what she thought he wanted her to do, not what *she* wanted to do, promoted her feelings of hidden anger, which in turn produced dissatisfaction with herself. She was caught in a vicious circle of unhappiness feeding on unhappiness. When Thackeray died she was truly grief-stricken. Yet his death released her to a significant degree from the unhealthy syndrome in which she was trapped.

No longer able to turn to Thackeray for advice, she had to decide where she and Minny were to live, how to deal with her mother and grandmother. Letters 42–44 to Mrs. Henry Cole illustrate how Anny emerged from her grief to become stronger and more able to take charge of her world. Always irrepressible, she met the challenge. The restraining influence that Thackeray, in all his love, held over her, was gone.

The letters Anny wrote soon after Thackeray's death differ from the 1864 journal. They illustrate, clearly, her belief in the "necessity for self control" (Letter 43). This struggle is evident in her letters, whereas in the journal she wrote from an unguarded position. Nevertheless, disjointed phrases and fragmented thoughts find their way into the letters. As time elapsed, Anny gained more composure, and the tone of her letters changed.

When berated by Mrs. Cole for her neglect of Mrs. Carmichael-Smyth, Anny held fast to her resolution that her "<u>first</u> duty in life is to try & make my sister as happy as it will ever be possible to be, & my <u>second</u> to comfort & take care of my poor dear old Grannie. . . . but from her letters I cannot understand what she w^d like" (Letter 43). Distracted by her exaggerated sense of duty to her sister and her grandmother, Anny never considered her responsibility to herself. The jealousy and wickedness for which she castigated herself in the journal only made her sense of duty to her sister more imperative. The letters show that although she made an intense effort to gain control over her sorrow, her life was deeply affected by it and by all the concurrent emotions.

Anny's desire to hold on to something material—a book, a teapot, a sugar bowl—that had once belonged to Thackeray is poignant. Still bedeviled by remorse Anny nevertheless functioned in the world and showed more signs of overcoming her grief than in the journal.

By 1865 Anny was once again out in society but not yet fully recovered. "Minny goes out into the <u>big</u> world much more than I do It depresses me so that I always shirk it when I can" (Letter 49). The letter is, however, cheerful and full of orderly plans for social activities. Her period of mourning almost over, Anny was on the threshold of resuming her life. Written in 1865, Anny's prayer (50) shows the struggle toward accepting her limitations and her life. In the last line she combines the past with the present and asks for blessings of the dead as well as the living. The note added in 1875 emphasizes the earthly happiness she eventually would count as hers.

JOURNAL

Ray/Morgan
MA 4500[1]

> 'Good Will' he was to all men here
> O keep our Saviour dear [?]
> O weep my Muse on Thackerays bier
> All suddenly his reign had ceased
> Yet not untimed Deaths call was given
> For bidden to an Angel-Feast
> He kept his Christmas day in Heaven

January 28. 1864.
Anne Isabella Thackeray[2]

Papa called Minny Min & me Nan very often. When we were little he used to call Minny Finniken & me Buff and sometimes Frederica & Louisa. He called Pussy Louisa & gave her his fish at breakfast & took her up very gently & put her outside the door when [*sic*] would not leave him alone. Papa has had a little tea pot to himself & the times & some fish & and his big chair at the top of the table & he has come down in his dressing gown & slippers & stooped for us to kiss him. Once or twice lately he has had some cocoa, but he made a face & said this wont do I must have some tea. After breakfast he has gone up to his room & stayed there or come down again into his study until Luncheon. One morning not long ago (after he scolded me that time for being always late) I was down a little early & I went out into the garden to say my prayers & after a minute I looked up & saw Papa looking at me through the dining room window & then I went in quickly & clasped him round the waist as we have always done. Minny could not reach round. The time Papa scolded me — it was six months ago I think — or less — he said I have asked you in vain for years & years to come down at nine o'clock — It has chipped off a little piece of my affection for you. When I am gone you will remember this & do it — but then it will be too late. That was dreadful & though I answered quite cheerfully I thought about it until I could not help going up to him in his room & crying a great deal & saying Do forgive me Papa He smiled & left off writing & held out his hand & of course he forgave me & I think that is what he did.

One day he talked to me a good deal & then he smiled & said "& I am sure if anybody where to ask me which of you two I love the most I could not tell them" He has so often said he was so glad we suited him. What should he have done with a stupid son for instance.

Papa has said God bless you to us all our lives Pray God he says so still.

Sometimes he used to say Godblesh³ an' he will. That was what Biddy the Irish apple woman used to say to him because Papa gave her sixpences & shillings now & then. (She said God help you when we passed her stall the other day). And then when he went to bed he used to say Bong Swaw, or stoop for us to kiss him if he came in with us. And sometimes he said Goodnight my Shildren and Goodnight my blessings. & Ta ta And he always walked up his wooden stairs & shut his door with a push.

It does not sound the same when it is written down

One day not very long ago I came into the diningroom & Papa was sitting looking at the fire — I do not think I had ever seen him like that before. And he said I have been thinking that in fact it will be a very dismal life for you when I am gone. I have a great mind to put it into my will that you are not to live with Grannie. Papa said very often at my death or when I drop & at my vale . . & once he said Why should not we sell off the house & everything in it & go away Somewhere. And then he used to tell us about his will. He said he had not signed it yet because he wanted something altered he said. I have left Amy £500 and now she will not want it now,⁴ & when I asked why he should make a will at all he said "because of your Mother — I cannot afford to give her a third.⁵ Grannie ought to have something, unless she gets her pension, and then she wᵈ be better off than you two

One day I took a walk with Papa & we presently met the little Normans⁶ in a procession, nurses & babies travelling along one of the new Roads by the Exhibition.⁷ And then Papa said 'Who's this? — I wonder who this is. Charlotte 'You are Annieminnies Papa' & then Annieminnies Papa took out his purse & looked untill he had found three little silver threepences. One for Charlotte one for Archie & one for Georgie & he said, Charlotte look here, when you go home you must say to your mamma

> A gentleman met me
> And gave me a kiss
> And afterwards made me
> A present of this,

and then you must hold up the threepenny piece   So Charlotte said Yes and Archie & Georgie each held their sils[8] very tight & Papa & I walked on. Charlotte ran after us to ask are you going to my home? — w$^\text{h}$ amused Papa. Only Papa was always amused by little children.

I told Papa that one day I should come home & show him some money & say a gentleman met me & gave me a kiss & afterwards made me a present. Papa said "I should like to see you — ." Grannie said one day that Minny had a pretty voice & I said <u>has</u> Minny got a nice voice & Papa said Min has a very sweet little pipe of her own.

When we were little girls Papa used to talk to us a great deal and tell us about the Bible and Religion. He was always more reverent than anybody I have ever known about things w$^\text{h}$ ought to be sacred. He used to talk to us of a morning after breakfast in his study & of an evening after dinner smoking his cigar & we generally sat on the floor & listened to him. That has gone on until now almost. And then we would give him a chair for his legs and a little table for his candles & he would presently nod to us and go to sleep. I cannot bear to think that quite of late it has not been quite the same. He has dined at home very little & I was hoping only the other day that we should soon be going back to our old ways.

Papa said that he could not picture to himself any scheme of a future existence that was in the least satisfactory. But he said I am quite content to wait & see. And he bowed his head.

He said that Molyncaux and his set seem to treat the Bible as if it was God Almighty. It is perfectly preposterous the way they go on about a collection of Oriental fables & histories. Papa said I think that S$^\text{r}$ John was a gentleman that he liked the Epistle of S$^\text{r}$ James the best. That it would almost seem as if the simplicity & stupidity of the disciples had been purposely exaggerated in order by this simple artifice to heighten the superiority of the Personnage whom they surrounded.

They could not understand the plainest things. They were always asking stupid questions. — That was a long time ago. He said the other day that he should call himself an Arian,⁹ only the fact is he said I go a good deal farther. He often said that he ought to have been a clergyman but unfortunately he c^d not take in the 39 articles. He said that one or two whom he had known, owned when they were hard pressed that they could not understand certain passages. Papa could not bear the story of Abraham. He used to say that one day when I was a little girl he came in & found Mamma [*sic*] about poor Isaac in her sweet voice & that I burst into tears & stamped & flew into a passion. I can remember it quite well too. In a window in the drawing room in Coram Street and Papa taking me up on his knee & Mamma looking a little shocked. Papa said that never was anything more outrageous & unjust.

Once he said hesitating that he thought he c^d recognize the Sacred character of the Divine Personnage. Latterly he let us talk & only said I am quite content to wait & see. The last time we went to church together was that day at the Temple¹⁰ the

Lady Colvile came with us. I don't think Papa minded at all, but at first he said it was quite a different thing from going alone with me & Minny It was all bright & Autumn brown. We were a little late and we drove through the Park to the Athenaeum to pick him up. I saw him through the window and then he came and said only twenty minutes late but he did not mind, and it was O so pleasant. We stopped at the Temple Gate & sent away the carriage and Young Herman¹¹ came with a big stick to meet us.

But it was so late that we could not get in at his side and so we went over to Papas side & he let us in. They sang Rejoice and again I say unto you Rejoice then they sang the evening hymn and when it was over we waited a little while and then when all the people had drifted out we followed. We could not sit next Papa and I tried to see him once or twice during the service but I could not. Only when we came out of the church there he was waiting for us as I knew I should find him. Standing quite still with his back turned to us until we should come up to him. And as we came out into the open air he began to chaunt Rejoice and again I say unto you Rejoice and then he said — How beautiful that evening hymn is . So simple and unaffected & so entirely to the purpose. It says just what is needful and no more. The sun was setting over the garden & the river and everybody went away through the courts and archways but we went and walked along the terrace and down some steps into the garden. It was all golden & shining, when we came out of the lamp-lit church & the organ was booming & the people we [*sic*] passing out and the sky was very bright & warm & red, but in the garden by degrees the twilight came and the lights faded out of the sky and the river.

We went up some twisting stairs into Young Herman's room where tea was ready spread for us. And Papa laughed because we were so pleased and happy and looked at the pictures on the walls. It is ungrateful to be so sick with grief — Perhaps when we come out of this Temple we shall find him gone on a little way before us and waiting to lead us out into the open air.

Tonight I suddenly remembered how Papa said the other day he was standing by the chimney in the dining room. 'I am sure I must have been a most affected boy.' I am sure I was. I remember going to see an old lady once and behaving in the most absurd manner. He used to tell us what agony of shame he went through on one occasion when he called upon somebody and was found reading the names written on the trunks in the antechamber. Papa said he never would ask anybody's name There are people whom he speaks to & whom he has known for years but whose names he does not know. Once or twice he said he did not know if he was going mad but constantly people took off their hats in the street whom he did not know in the least.

And another day — Again two fellows took off their hats to me — one was on Waterloo bridge and another in Oxford Street. I am certainly going mad. Papa liked the old curiosity shops so much and the silversmiths We have been with him very often. I wish so that I could remember some of the funny things he used to say. Papa always made jokes. I used to want him to be pompous but he never never was anything but himself.

The other night we had a talk after dinner about our summer trips & the happy week at Paris and then Knightons & Frystone.[12] Papa took up my diary for 64 and said next year begins with a Friday. And I said little thinking — Papa I assure you Friday is our lucky day Indeed it will be a happy year. The new cook had sent up a nice little dinner on Friday w.h pleased him & put us in mind of the Cafe's at Paris & I think that is how we came to talk about them. There had been some talk of our going to the Coles but we were vexed with ourselves for having been out all afternoon & said we w̲ᵈ not go. Papa got up and went into his study. I am so glad we stayed. Before he went to bed he came in for five minutes & I thought then that he saw how sorry we were to have left him. On Sunday morning I went to breakfast with the Seniors after early church I do think it was a little that I wanted to be more cheerful & to talk to him. He was standing at his end of the table when I came in to lunch and carving for himself. After lunch we sat by the fire, we three & talked to one another. We talked about Mamma and about Mʳˢ Brookfield & Papa said that after all there was no one like her. So tender so womanly except perhaps you girls said Papa. And then we talked about Mamma & Papa said, how when I was born he knew nothing about it & the homeopathic doctor nearly killed her,[13] & he sent out & brought in another who only was in time to save her life. About four o'clock I went into the drawingroom and found Minny crying She said she could never bear to hear us talk about these things. And then the Collins came & Wᵐ Craigie & we went out a little way together & called at the Kurzons[14] & came home Papa came into the drawingroom again the door and to open [*sic*] & My daddy wᵈ stride in in his long dressinggown, all that week. And Mʳ Cayley came & asked him about the Realm & wᵈ he write.[15] Papa said he could not undertake to do anything for a newspaper, his own work was as much as he cᵈ accomplish. Then he looked at the device and talked about an orb & got up to fetch a book in his study about it,[16] with some old fashioned drawings. Mʳ Cayley was to come back to dinner. I said I was going to the Leslies[17] & Papa said to me 'You are not going are you?' And I said — I suppose I must as they sent for me. I thought you meant me to go. Papa said 'no I had nothing to do with it' — I was so sad, so silly, so foolish, that I felt as if I could not bear to be at home.

When I came home they were all waiting for the carriage to take Katie back.[18] I was very happy & began to tell them all about it, & so thankful to be happy again, & as I was telling them I caught sight of Papa's face in the glass. Dear face turning away because he was smiling so tenderly, as he often had a way of doing. And I thought to myself now that is all I want & I went to bed so happy. Papa & Mʳ Cayley went into the study. I cannot remember if I said a regular goodnight.

That afternoon Papa said to Mʳ Collins come up into my room and I will show you something — Mʳ Collins has since told us that he noticed that Papa was quite tired & out of breath when he got up stairs.

On Monday morning I went into Papa's room early and I remember that he was so gentle that I could not help a sort of pang. There were only some horrible kidneys for his breakfast. But he said it doesnt matter. He lunched with us & we talked about the dinner-party the day before. Papa said about the Realm I cannot see any demand for it — & then he said how nice M.ʳ Merivale had been the night before. I said you must have a drive all by yourself in the carriage. He liked going alone or with us only sometimes, but he did not like to go if Grannie didn't And as we were going out Papa came walking out of the study saying, I came to see if the carriage was there   Minny & I crossed the road & Papa looked after us & stopped behind. It was the only time almost this ever happened & I thought so then to myself.

As we were coming home in the dark at Knightsbridge we met the Collins who said he had been to see them, to show them something wʰ M.ʳ Yates had written. I pray God to be forgiven for my wicked anger and absurd jealousy.

When I saw him next morning he told me of a nice article in the Star. I told him I had seen it — he said "There should be some sort of answer I suppose" — I said something about the Yates affair, & he told me then he was going to leave it alone — He had partly written an answer but he would not send it. Then he told me to find a Milton. I brought him one odd volume after a long search & he balanced it in his hand and said this is just what I dont want. I want Miltons Epitaph on Shakespeare.[19] Thinking it hopeless I went to breakfast leaving Fanny[20] looking. She found it & gave it to Grannie who took it in.

I heard his step overhead as I was sitting writing in my little room. I waited for the first time in my life I think to finish before going to him. When I did at last he was gone out in the carriage they told me. We went out about 3 — Miss Davison[21] detained us, had she but stayed a few minutes longer — Papa came home just after we had left very gently & sad & cold & asking for something warm. There was only some brandy & water wʰ Fanny prepared. Grannie said, 'I could not bear to see the carriage drive up with Charles[22] & Sims in their great black wagon

I said 'What harm could that do us' or something of the sort but I did feel a chill & at night when I went to the Coles with Katie I was so very wretched & I did try not to be jealous

And then next morning Fanny said M.ʳ Thackeray is not well Miss, & I went into his room in a sort-of rage of sorryness

And Papa who lay very still with large-large eyes took my hand in his & said — It can't be helped darling. Then he added I did not take enough medicine last night. I have taken some more I shall be better presently. Thank God all my wickedness went away & I stood by his bed forgetting to go & only thinking of him. Then he put up the paper to his mouth & signed to me to leave him.

About three o'clock I heard him coughing.

The doctor said he w^d be all right in 24 hours. I went out in the afternoon for a while & coming in the man told me he was much better. And then I thought all was well.

That morning I dreamt that I was with Papa climbing a very high hill. We went higher & higher so that I had never seen anything like it before. And Papa was pointing out something to me w^h I could not see & presently left me & I seemed to come down alone. He said write to Mr Longman.[23] I said I have written.

I was just dressed when there was a strange crying sound in the house & I went out of my room to the landing & Charles the servant met me   He is dead Miss he said He is dead

Then Grannie came from her room

And two days after, as I was lying asleep O so heart weary I thought he stood by my bedside & said Are you sick my child.

His coffin was so long it was like him & I felt as if my head was on his breast. And it seemed as if he was with us the whole time at Kensal Green[24]

I like to think of one evening a little time ago when he was undergoing his treatment & Minny & I sat up in his room while he was at dinner. We cut up his chicken for him into little bits & his saussage & then he said I must have some more & some more and we said O no Papa but we cut it up & gave it to him all the same. And then Papa used to say You may now leave me my blessings.

Papa once said — not long ago — Anny always manages to reproach herself whatever happens. It seems no use to reproach myself about Papa. It does not make me love him more. I will try please God to do as he likes & to love him always I pray God to make us always love him so that at the end we may meet once more & be his children still

I remember he said on my last birthday You are reproaching yourself about every thing today — First about Anslie now about Miss Davison. But O what a happy day it was all the same.²⁵ We went by the Kensington train to Richmond & we walked along the terrace to the Park. There was an old flowery gentleman sitting on a bench. Papa said he had once been very rich & in the heigth [*sic*] of fashion and that there was still a sort of faded splendour about him. He & his brother were the illegitimate sons of two great people but the world had gone wrong with them.

We walked in the park and met Mr Anslie who was going to India very melancholily Papa said he felt very guilty at not asking him to dinner, only it is not the same as ²⁶ dining together & it w^d spoil it quite said Papa. Then we dined together in the coffee room of the Star & Garter There were two old ladies drinking cups & cups & cups of tea. There were some Scotchmen toasting one another — a clergyman & his party who presently simpered away It was such a bad dinner Papa said, but we liked it so much all three of us. Then Papa called a little open carriage & we drove home past the river through clouds & clouds of mists, & coming through Birnes & over the bridge. And all the people were out in the street at Kensington & we got home in the calm summer eve^g. Papa said he could have walked almost as quickly as going by the slow stopping little Kensington train. Papa has written in his book

Dined with girls at Star & Garter. Next comes Clifford Trafalgar ²⁷

On the 15 June Lady Trowbridge & Sir R. Murchison are written down.²⁸ I went with Papa in the carriage & he said he felt so unwell & sick that he really thought he must go home, w^h we did. But we enjoyed our drive all the same & he said as soon as he turned back, he felt quite well again. On the 17th we dined at Mr Grant Duffs ²⁹ Papa says it isn't M^r he cares for so much as M^{rs} ³⁰ On Friday the 19 we dined at Mrs Walters & went to the Donnes.³¹ Papa liked the dinner at the Walters, & said it was nice to see all the Times people rally round their chief. I think he said Mr Walters was quite stupid & good humoured & quite good company enough.

Then the next day we drove out with Papa to Bedford Row. We waited for him in the sunshine outside, and he came down after some long while with ever so much money — Mr. Trollope following — & I think Papa said part of this represents our trip — I remember making room for him as he got in All the people with their papers passing up the street — the clerks nibbing their pens — the cabs waiting here &

there I think we must have driven in the Regents Park after that but I cannot quite remember

We have been so disturbed & unhappy that I have left off writing for this last fortnight, but I will try & never do so again for the words fade out of ones memory with time, sometimes they seem far far away sometimes I almost seem to hear him speak
Papa said
I have never done anyone a wrong in my life. Only once when I was a boy I did not pay back some money as quickly as I might have done. I kept the ten pounds for three months after I might have paid it. Speaking of some family affairs he said that very time I had my illegitimate sister Mrs Bletchenden's money in the bank & though I was in the greatest straits at the time I never thought of touching one penny of it.[32]

Then Papa used to tell us how he lived at Paris for a whole month upon five pounds & bought a waistcoat out of it —

On Saturday before he Died Papa told us that old familiar story at dinner. Here once for all I write down in case in after life I should ever ever forget or forgive myself

That in these last days I think I must have been almost out of my mind at times. I can remember thoughts so impatient so unloyal so irritable & wicked. An absurd jealousy & suspicion had seized hold of me. The Last day my Father lived I went to church & prayed so fervently for myself to be delivered from it, that I did not think to pray for him. I was over-anxious & over worried by little things Papa once said to me, not pleased, — I find you have been complaining out of the house to two different people & expressing your desire that I should leave it — I said Yes, I had always said so to him that I could not bear to see him work when he was ill.

Papa said, It is absurd to expect a man to give up work at fifty. If I live I hope I have ten years more work in me. But he forgave me then as he always did.

Papa said he had a superstition w^h was to write a little every day — were it only a line. — I can see him pointing now with his finger to the two or three little words some times he would shew us a few lines & say, There, that has been my days work I have sat before it till I nearly cried & nothing would come. One day lately he did a famous Long piece four or five pages

I think I like best to think of him shaving. When we were such little girls we used to go in & watch him. He could shave most beautifully & quickly — he mixed the soap with his little old silver brush & wiped it on his shirt sleeve off the razor. When the old soap glass was broken one day, Papa used the silver top for the lather. He used to laugh at the silver tops on our table, & he used to say the girls have taken an old dressing case of mine & set it out in state. Papa always liked everything we did, & we never liked anything much until we knew he approved. Now all the people he liked seem (now, as then so much more near us than our own friends. Papa liked M.ʳ Leech as much as anybody & M.ʳ Collins & M.ʳ Neate[33] & M.ʳ Merivale Old Spottinose he used to call him. Brilliant conversation bored Papa he liked easy going talk He liked Professor Owen & the old Dean of S.ᵗ Pauls & M.ʳ Bell.[34] We used to have discussions over M.ʳ Bell — Papa used to call him a handsome young fellow with turn down shirt collars. & he used to ask Katie why she hated him so. Then Papa liked JOB best of all women, but he was fond of others of Marianne Irvine, of Emmy, of Katie of Tishy Cole. Of M.ʳˢ Whitmore of M.ʳˢ Jackson.[35] He had a charming way of saying — How dydo my dear I am very glad to see you again — He was fond of Adelaide Procter, and Kate Perry & then there were many whom he liked — M.ʳˢ Mansfield M.ʳˢ Stephenson M.ʳˢ Vivian M.ʳˢ Denman[36] & a good many of whom he was fond without exactly liking — They bored him so often —

When I bored him he used to say — vous Radotez ma chère[37] — & laugh so kindly. Papa used to laugh out at things which children said to him. When he offered little Granville Cole a sixpence, the child said very gravely Spose you was to give me a sillen? — Papa often said that.

Last year when we went down to Blendworth[38] there was a pretty dirty little girl in the carriage we tried to amuse her & shewed her pictures, & presently Papa said Shall I show you a lovely green bird with a beautiful yellow nose & he took her up in his arms & held her to the window to see a parrot who was travelling up to town & looking out of window. Then the little girl made a grab at Papa's spectacles. He said children always try to pull off my spectacles & then he told her about the monkey at the Zoological Gardens.

When Papa was a tall young man with black hair & an eyeglass I can remember how we used to hold his forefinger when we walked out with him. He always talked to us very gravely as if we were grown up women then, lately I think he spoke to us as if we were children & he used to say come along my little dears.

The first time I remember Papa is standing at his knee & asking him to tell me the name of my doll and Papa said this is Miss Polly Perkins I think.

Then I remember him in the stage coach after Mamma went out of her mind. He was very grave & when I kicked & talked he told me I must be still or I should wake baby, & when I still went on he said he must put out the light if I was not quiet, & then still I was not quiet & the light suddenly went out. Has the light gone out now for us?[39] because we were not quiet & good — I pray that the sun may rise & a day of peace & forgiving & love for weary aching hearts once more.

When I talked to Papa about that journey he said Bhuu — What a terrible night that was — there was a french man in the corner chattering with his teeth & saying J'ai la fievre mon dieu J'ai la fievre but he was kind afterwards & held Minny while Brodie was attending to you.[40] Papa has told us how one day he was at his desk writing when Brodie came & asked him for some money & he changed the last five pounds he had to give it her, and we children were in one room crying and Mamma was raving in the other. My poorest dearest — Was it more terrible than it is now for us — I think so for at least this is peace sometimes. Terrible & awefull though it be. Last year on Christmas day we took a walk with Papa in a bright sunshiny morg and we went to Little Holland house & saw dear old M.ʳ Prinsep in a sunshiny studio being painted by M.ʳ Watts[41] As he just now came to see us it seemed as if Papa must be with us still. It is so strange to see one person after another but not Papa.

Papa said when I drop there is to be no life written of me, <u>mind</u> this & consider it as my last testament & desire. Today I do not remember many things he has said. I can see him passing his hand through his hair laughing at the children pouring out his tea from his little silver tea pot — I can see him looking at his dear face in the glass & saying I am sure I look well enough dont I. Then he liked pacing across the room & counting his steps from one place & another, he couldnot go on writing as I am doing now, his spectacles were moist if I asked him abt little Janey[42] — Papa has beautiful white hands with pink knuckles & long nails — he says he cannot bear to cut them, he kept saying that he would get no new clothes this year but that next year he wd have some done up. His eyes are so soft & large with falling lids his smile is extraordinarily sweet his voice is low & gentle with a manly tone in it but when he is not well, it seems to lose the <u>ring</u> he holds down his cheeks to kiss & he presses our foreheads.

I can see him swinging his arms as he walks I can see him looking out over the ship sides & placing his spectacles that are always slipping I can see him waiting for us at a little table with the dinner spread, with his legs crossed & reading the paper & then he turns it to the other side. He orders what we like and a pint of claret for himself he says take away the cheese how I see it all — he looks in the paper for a play for us to go to — this year he said to us when I asked him if we should go abroad or not

It is very foolish of me but I cannot bear to part from you. Yes pack up your things & come along. Dear Papa where you are can you hear, can you see us —

If with my whole life I could tell you once more that I love you & know that you forgive me

When I came back f.^m Brighton not long ago Papa came out in his dressing gown & opened the door for me & I placed the lilis I had bought for him in his arms He was amused at all the things I had to tell him — a certain <u>part</u> of me is shut up for ever. Nobody else can I talk to as I talked to him. Then I shewed him the prayerbook I had bought for Minny. I began to draw black lines along the red letters & Minny scolded me. Papa said you have rather improved it but that is quite enough.

We sat in the morning room and the sun shone & I talked & talked

The other day I had been reading Esmond[43] & I said to Papa that I thought he was very like Esmond and Papa said He thought he was perhaps only Esmond was a little bilious fellow. Papa used to say that Esmond was never a favourite with the public. Papa was quite fond of his characters they seemed alive to him & he used to wonder whether he should meet them ever One day he says at the cider cellar there was an old man with his hat cocked & a little cape — the very image of Costigan.[44] Papa said it seemed to him wonderful at the time but presently the Captain turned around & offerred to treat him to a glass of anything & Papa said it was like a miracle It was the voice & the brogue of Cos.

He drew Pendennis from Mr Hannay[45] — the face I mean. I remember coming in to study at Kensington — in Young Street — & finding Papa drawing him in the window Papa liked the Little Sister but he used to say that Philip was a failure — he was sad about it and he said he was determined that Denis Duval should be a Great Success. He talked [sic] us about it a good deal Agnes the heroine[46] had one or two names, but Papa said she sh^d be Agnes after all — it was an ugly name but there were 2 St. Agnes's & it was convenient for the working of the story And he I think said he should take a voyage on board a man of war to learn all the nautical phrases Papa was so sorry for the poor crazy lady in Denis Duval.[47] Think He said he had thought of a little story I had told him of walking on the sea shore with Mamma & she held me by the hand & once pulled[48] me in a little way, & then her love struggled with her madness & so we came back safe to the little white house in w^h we lived.[49] I remember someone said Papa was coming down to us — but this was 24 years ago —

Papa often spoke to me about my handwriting & asked why it was necessary that I should write in such enormous characters — he called Minnys a funny little fist & screwed up his fingers & pretended to write as she did & laughed. Papa used to beat upon his thigh sometimes & say it was quite numb — That always made me uncomfortable — he said lately it had become worse.

He used to paint his pretty pictures and say "I had much better have left it alone I have only spoilt it. There is one we have w^h I shewed him & said I should get framed. Papa said Ah that is clean because I did it twice over

Mrs Brookfield was telling us today how one day she & Magdalene met Papa in Pall Mall & walked along with him a little way And she says they met M^r & Mrs Garden[50] on their road, & that the one interest Mrs Garden has for her is that she has shaken hands with Papa. When we used to come & stand near his chair he had a way of putting up his hand to us backwards. Dear hand that was never closed never withheld. I am aching to touch it to speak to him once more. In his books there is written at the end House. And as he wrote it he said — that is about the last cheque I ought to draw this month — and I was so glad when he said it for I had bothered him about his cheques & retrenching & moving until he had almost ceased for a time to speak to me of money matters.

A little way back is Marshal & Snelgrove. I had asked him for a lace shawl & he went with Minny & walked there all the way and bought the pretty white lace & brought it back

One night — it was like a funny dream. We had been out to tea Minny & I, & Mrs Dalrymple[51] brought us back in a cab to the gate — It was after 12 & we c^d not get in & the cab drove off & two soldiers came up talking very loud and just at the moment when I was going to get frightened up came another cab, out of w.^h stepped a tall gentleman with a g.^t bundle of asparagus in his arms all in the moonlight — And then all in a minute the tall gentleman was Papa & we <u>were</u> so glad, & the gate was opened & we all passed in together — Once I walked home from the Collins with him & that was very very nice — & my last walk God help us & give us strength to walk alone now for a little I seem to remember every step as we went along by that path w.^h runs with the Remington Rd to Hyde Park Corner where Papa called a cab — He said I shall have to go on with you all the way to Poland Street — I said I should be quite safe alone And so at the corner of Regent S.^t he left me & paid the cabman to be civil to me & to take me to my workhouse.[52]

Mrs Brookfield asked me yesterday if I remembered dining at the Whites years & years ago — Papa and the grnup folks dined downstairs & we children were up in a nursery — Mrs Brookfield says that all the time Papa fidgetted & waited & would not eat any dinner until they had sent some up to us & he said at last to Mrs White first the poor little people upstairs When are they to have their share — And then when the people said O yes by the way what shall we send some roast beef Papa said — <u>I</u> should say veal pie —

That was when we lived in Young Street. We came when I was 9 & Minny 6 Papa was not at home when we arrived but early next morning when we were half dressed & the maid was tying out strings he tapped at the door and came in & took us in his arms. Everything seemed so strangely delightful — the volumes of Punch on the drawingroom table the delightful Keepsake books in their red covers with the lovely ladies the old schoolroom with the book case & the cupboards — and Papas room with the vine round about the window & the sun pouring in.

April 15. Putney Heath.

I have been looking at one or two old notebooks out of my davenport Instead of writing about Papa it is only about myself but — I see heren there delightful drive to Hampstead with him & walk in the Park — Papa dined at home. I remember the drive to Hampstead — we were trying to find out Mrs Procter, & when we asked our way to Oakhill everybody said, What name was it — Papa said that was the way they knew nothing about the way & so invariably asked the name out of mere curiosity and when they went on bothering he said Jones — So Sims went driving about saying very loud Can you inform me where a party of the name of Jones is living. When we got to Mrs Procters at last they were in a terrible fluster — Mr Forster[53] has sent to say that he was coming & so we drove off quite quick only laughing rather at their predicament   In one place I see — "forgot Papas bag —" It was the day Amy went to India[54] I went & knocked at his door in a fright next morning & when he did not answer I thought it was that he would not let me in — I remember how ashamed I was when I saw him, for ever thinking he w^d be angry; he wasnt a bit, only said I had better write to Mr Phinn [?][55] & tell him how it was.

When Papa came in and found us working strips,[56] he said most useful or sometimes Thankyou — And when he held up his old carpet slippers and said are not these pretty slippers, he used to add my daughters worked me a pair but these answer my purpose quite well   When I asked him a question he said I leave it to y^r own excellent understanding   It was a sort of little joke because I wanted him to settle always   One day he laughed & said I defy you to get anything out of me   Papa always liked going to the play. We used to dine rather early, and the cab used to come & Papa used to say have you got the glasses or we used to Pick him up at the G[57] or the Atheneum. I can always see Papa going up the G steps and walking away, or at the Atheneum he was oftenest waiting for us. I wish so I had not always kept him waiting — it spoilt many a pleasant drive we might have had — The last time we went to the play together we did so like it we first went to see something of Byrons,[58] but they w^d not give us good places & then we went on the Strand to Miriams crime.[59] And it was so nice and Papa so well & in such good spirits. I remember now — only I cant think of it — that he was <u>never</u> well all this year, he said Life at this purchase is not worth having — If it was not for you children I should be quite ready to go.

At the play that night he lent me his spectacles to look through & fell in love with a most hideous creature & I said O! there is such a love. In the second little piece I do not know how it was going — Papa said he thought it w^d be as well not to stay & see & the actress gave such a bewitching ogle that Papa jumped up in a fright and we all filed out. Afterwards he said — I hear that after piece at the Strand was quite moral & proper & that we might have stopped to see it quite well —

The other day opening one of his old School books he found a secret store of brown sugar w^h he had hidden away — It was the thing to do in those days, he said You put by y.ʳ store and then you had the gratification of coming upon it unexpectedly — Papa said it was scarcely sweet at all.

One night Papa told us he was lying in the dark with one hand outside the bed, pointing up in the air. And suddenly he thought to himself, now what w.ᵈ happen I wonder if the Devil were to come with a pair of nippers & take hold of my finger." So then he put it under the bedclothes again. But then he suddenly remembered that he was not safe even then for the Devil might still come with a pair of nippers & take hold of his nose. So we asked Papa if he put his nose under the bedclothes. But he laughed & said No not his nose. One day when I was a little girl I was dreadfully frightened by a story he told me of a man whose nose had been broken for years & years, & one day when he was blowing it, it came off in his hand, & Papa waved his hand. I felt a little Thrill of horror & thought Papas was coming off. Papa couldnt bear cutting his nails — He had a favourite barber who used to cut his hair, & where he went for a very long time, & always took a cake in his pocket for the mans little children — One day he found that this wretched creature, always charged him twopence more than anybody else who went to the shop. Papa said it was not the twopence but it was the ingratitude which shocked him so. He never went there anymore though he was very sorry for the poor little children. I know he once sent us to Greenwich in the carriage to take a big cake to a funny little boy who when he asked him his name, said Master Snooks & stood like the clown he had seen at the circus the day before. Once Papa said to us — I think you girls ought to marry so that I should have some grand-children. I once said Papa you dont want us to marry do you & he said quite hastily but looking around, Certainly not.

And so out of all the dear life long talk one remembers two or three disjointed words here & there a look & tone — But I think there is something greater still — a sort of certainty of Love far far beyond our deserts — perhaps it may be ours even now — God knows I at least cannot be more unworthy of it than I was then

Papa is always so easily pleased. He likes everything that people do for him Gardner[60] washed two little dirty gold tables we had & made them shine Papa was quite charmed & said once or twice Have you seen how smart the gold tables look — Go up and see. Then his new paper pleased him and the red carpet on the stairs & he said Stephenson had only charged £19 for the whole job — he did not think it dear. He would pull the ragged threads off his coat & turn out his elbow and say is not this a handsome coat? — One day he came down with his shirt sleeves carefully turned back. It was a stinginess he said, he was going out to dinner & he did not want to put on a clean shirt — he used to laugh at his swearing & say that in after days we were to say that we were sorry to say our dear Papa used sad language at times. The young fellows he said never swore — It is only us old ones who damn and swear — to hear some of them at the Club is perfectly awful Papa said all the waiters at the G were always eager to serve him tho' he only gave them five shillings now & then — At the Athenaeum he always went to sleep in the library — one day he said he was horribly ashamed he woke with a loud snort — Everybody must have heard him. He said one day when we picked him up that the old dean had always something ready & appropriate — He met him & told him how he had fallen asleep at S.t Pauls and then the Dean said a little verse about the curates eyes, you never saw.

We went to S.t Pauls Emmy Papa & I by the underground railway Papa bribed a beadle who put us into the Deans box all carved oak soft cushions dust and darkness. Then the choir chanted the Psalms the people knelt & bowed their heads. Once in the Psalms Papa pointed to And he shall run to & fro & howl like a dog,[61] & said Beautiful Beautiful shaking his head. I cant help laughing, but when he went to sleep in the soft cushions & gave a little snore, I was obliged to touch him & wake him up. We said our prayers laughing but with all our hearts — Numbers of people with much greater pretensions to piety were asleep all around about Young Mr. Milman[62] droned on & on, it was like reclining on luxurious sofas, — through the arched aisles the light fell shadowing — And my dear Papa O my dear O what shall I write — O what shall I feel If I am happy I am forgetting you — if I am aching for you I grow sick with grief

If I remember how often I misjudged how impatient how cruel my thoughts were it seems as if there could be no peace or forgiveness ever again. And yet I do think I loved you — We would have blacked your boots you said to some one & indeed indeed we would — Only one lives on & one does not guess at the great pit into w.h one is falling down lower & lower & suddenly your life seems to stop all the great clouds roll away & you find yourself in a hell of your own making. Still I pray that I remember the wrong because it was new & strange & that the love was so part of us both that we did not think of it — or I at least until it was gone — a little way only a little way.

I wish I could live my life over again — only just a little wiser a little more faithful & tender.

One Sunday we drove down into these parts, we called at the Owens who asked us to dine and we walked with them in their garden. Two little boys were rushing about with switches & cut the Professor over & over again. He only smiled very goodnaturedly & moved a little uneasy. Then they tried Papa I knew they w:d not do that a second time — He never w:d allow a liberty, — & he turned around & said 'No that is rude you must not do it, & took the switches away out of their hands. Then M:r Phinn asked us to dinner, & then we drove on through a lovely landscape Papa liked it so & made little sketches in the air with his finger & at last we came to Heaths [63] to whom we were engaged to dine. Poor old M:rs Hampstead [64] (Papa called her) we all missed her jolly old welcome, but it was nice too & we sat on the terrace Minny & I & Fanny Rose Owen. The gentlemen talked over their wine.

Papa used to like to tell us how one day he took M:r Heath aside, & said I have an important question to ask you, Tell me where do you get your teeth! — And old M:r Heath immensely flattered, burst out laughing and said My dear Sir look here, & they were every one his own.

Papa used to carry his sham vel [65] about in his waistcoat pocket. There was one so shabby, and so ugly I always said, that I gave it away a little time ago. Papa only laughed when I took it, & said it was a very handsome waistcoat & he wondered we did not think it pretty

Tonight looking at the animals I seemed to hear him saying Brownie has again mistaken the nature of my apartment. I can hear him say little everyday things which seemed so familiar they must needs go on for ever. To imagine their ceasing never occurred to me. Bring my bag to the club. Drive to the Athenaeum Sims. Has anybody got a needle & thread, & then I'm sick — I'm sure I don't look very ill — I was at a concert last night when he had been to Evan [66] — Papa says to me so often. I want to know what has become of all my penholders, O no of course nobody takes them —

Sometimes when we go into his room of a morning he puts out his [67]

hand & feels for his spectacles & then he says now I can see my daters. Sometimes he gives us a sham benediction & stands in an attitude. Only the shamness is realness & the Blessing is there.

The first night we slept in out new house in Onslow Sq. I said to Papa who was sitting in the corner in his little study — I am so glad you did not die when you were so ill[68] We should never have known you then or learnt to care for you & Papa said — a little hurt & yet touched too — I have thought so myself but I do not think it right ever to talk sentimentally about ones feelings. Papa said next morning That as he was in bed the night before & as he was looking about & thinking how comfortable it looked, he could not help wondering. what the end of it all would be, & whether this was the room in which he would die one day.[69]

Monday 5th June 1865.

I have been sitting in the corner of the room where Grannie died[70] & such a peace & rest has come over me after the long disquiet that I cannot help writing a word in the book where my poor sick heart tried to write its pain. I am not once going to read what I wrote I am only going to say that even after such sorrow & darkness as ours has been a light comes. Yesterday Minny said to me Anny how can you dare to complain? — our small troubles we can forget & our greatest sorrows are our greatest blessings — Her words have been ringing in my ears ever since

After a long year that seems like twilight when I think of it, we came in October to this little new house of ours. It was all bright & alight with flowers We thought we should have found it dark & dreary but we almost cried for joy instead of sorrow to be at home & with Papa again

All the terrible time of Arromanches was over. I think we were mad almost I was torn & crazed between the two dear ones & was foolish & hasty but O so miserable & so fearing for the future — and the future came not as we had expected it but as I had prayed for I think somehow our prayers are answered. I believe though it frightens me to believe — in the constant will & Almighty Patience with our short comings.

I used to think it would be a sign that our failings towards our Father were forgiven if my dearest Grannie were to go at peace with us at hand

And she went in one night like the awful night at Kensington.[71] We spent a long happy Sunday evening together She said she was not very well but she was so sweet so tender that it seemed like old days. She told us all the dear old stories once more — Her youth her happy time at Bath India & the Grandfathers [72] — I will write it down one day perhaps but today I only want to tell of her last love & last words

About 9 o'clock we had a little supper. It was like the last meal Kate Perry used to tell us of when she spoke of her sisters death. Grannie God bless her broke bread & gave it to us, she only took a little broth herself but for us she was looking for the nicest little bits & I remember thinking how she looked at Minnie with tender eyes of love. At 10 o'clock — we had ceased talking & I had read from the Christian Year for the day [73] & she had been reading the Psalms to herself for the last time. She got up & looked at the clock & said it was time for bed. Then she gave me a great long tender kiss & then another & went away and as she went I thank God that I remember saying thank God in my heart.

And then as we were sitting by our fire we heard a little noise & a minute after Fanny called us — And all was over.

The night Papa went, was a very terrible one when it came round again — The men were busy in the house & we sat upstairs in our bedroom with Jane Ritchie who had come to us dear woman, in our wretchedness.

Just about the time, Minny had fallen asleep — suddenly my anguish went away The room seemed to grow light a strange brightness & perfect peace & happiness came over me — Minny began to smile in her sleep. I think the brightness of their love must have fallen upon us

We sometimes wonder if one of us will die next Christmas So many old friends have gone their way this year. Poor Sims to whom we said goodbye Mr Prescott & Admiral FitzRoy [74] both by their own hand. Dear Mr Prescott that was a real sorrow Mr SpringRice [75] is the last friend we have lost.

He died at sea quite peacefully with his daughters & his wife about him

I have just taken down Grannie's bible & seen a few words that Job spoke in his utter desolation — Today I have felt like Job, so much is gone & yet all is dearer & nearer only that is gone. It seems to me at last as if more happiness & more peaceful times were in store Amen if it is so, if not pray God to make us know him as we should know him love him as we should love him, & wait in peace & trust until the end. What it is, this great end is very awful to realize, sometimes I feel as if it was our home, & then again as if it was only a strange country — But this is the strange country please God.

When we were at Cambridge the other day, we found out Daddy's name written in the old college books, many more of the old familiar names that are now dying out — dear M.ʳ SpringRices — it was like feeling nearer to Papa to go & see his youth with our own eyes — It was like living then & when we came back here it seemed as if we had travelled from one century into another almost.

Papa left Cambridge about 31. His name is first put down in 28 — Whewell was his master,[76] & we passed his rooms without knowing it! — A kind sick clergyman who was there remembered him in M.ʳ EFG's[77] rooms quite well, & again drawing pictures at a water party

My heart is very full & I have been looking for a text. I have only found Have mercy upon O lord according to greatness of thy loving kindness blot out our transgressions[78] — but many are in my — And I pray that for once my gratitude & love for the Father of my Father & of us all may be true & from a loyal heart

LETTERS 41–50

To Lady Stanley[1]

Letter 41 {1864}
Huntington Library
HM 6965

My dear Lady Stanley Your letter seemed to comfort us & warm us for a little as the goodness of the people Papa cared for can do sometimes

He used to say to us that you were always a good friend to him & kind & faithful. It is impossible to write only I wanted to say this to you. Minny & I send you our love for that kindest letter. Your sincere

Anne Thackeray

Please give our love to Miss Stanley & say thankyou for us.

To Mrs. Cole

Letter 42 {1864}
Ray/Morgan

My dearest Mrs Cole

I have just remembered a little old thick green book in Papas bedroom with Private written by him upon the back It was as well as I can remember in the book case near the window & rather high up — but I am not very certain. Would you dear Mrs Cole put it safe away & lock it up — I am so afraid of valuers or servants &ct looking into it — Is it very silly. I am sure you will not mind my troubling you.

Dear Tishy sent me so long and a nice a letter about the wedding, & do not you think it was kind & charming of Mary to write us a little word from Folkestone?

Minny & I have been writing to Grannie about taking a little furnished house for a month instead of our all stopping about here &

there — We are good for nobody just now & it seems a pity to waste kindness & hospitality w.h we should like so much some day. We think lodgings w.d be such a confusion & with maids &ct the other w.d be as cheap I think for us 5 people.¹

Dear Mary how very very happy & good & tender they both seem. God bless you all prays

y.r affectionate
Anne Thackeray

To Mrs. Cole

Letter 43 [1864]
Ray/Morgan

My dearest Mother Cole

<u>Of course</u> we mean to try & do our duty by Grannie.

I had already written twice to ask if we could be taken in at her lodging but I could get no answer.

We felt very guilty when we came here, but we were so nervous from constant society & necessity for self control that I am very glad we did come, & now we are quite ready for anything. You know we went to Henbury¹ entirely to be with her & I c.d not help her coming away, but she always had such a dislike to the idea of <u>our being alone</u> that we did not like to insist upon it till now. You know that I am not dishonest or apt to say things of myself that are not true, & now that Papa is gone I feel very strongly that my <u>first</u> duty in life is to try & make my sister as happy as it will ever be possible to be, & my <u>second</u> to comfort & take care of my poor dear old Grannie. I cannot help the first being the pleasantest — it was pleasantest always to be with Papa & yet it was the most right. It makes me very unhappy to thing you & M.rs Brookfield & Grannie evidently think me wrong — we are only too glad to live with Grannie if she will like it, but from her letters I cannot understand what she w.d like except going to live abroad. But I daresay it will be all right when we come tomorrow —

Goodbye my dearest kind friend — I keep forgetting that I shall see you quite soon. Your affectionate

Anne Thackeray

To Mrs. Cole

Letter 44 Botley Station
Ray/Morgan [1864]

My dearest Mother Cole. I wonder what we should do without you? — There is another box at Lubbocks[1] with <u>my things</u> & a tea-pot I should like to sell as we shan't want three

I suppose the dear kettle had better go — but couldn't we put a reserve — say 40 or £50 upon it. I think Papa gave £40 for it.

Perhaps the little sugar bowl gilt inside may be in the box Papa always used it & so we want to keep it We only want to keep 2 little fillagree small baskets[2] We dont care for the big cake basket. We packed up & came off in a fluster this morning & I find if I dont write here at the Station without the list that you will not get it.

Perhaps if we sell my teapot we c^d keep the cup, but I dont care very much for it & Mrs Cole shall decide only we want a little Relic or so — To look as if we had seen better days.

Im afraid poor dear Granny is very hurt & disappointed that we have put off coming & indeed I am too not to come to her, but Minny got so <u>pale</u> & <u>limp</u> at the notion of coming back just yet that I had not the courage to force her. I dont think Granny knows how miserable it is for us: Father, home all vanished in one moment, — or she would not think it heartless to shrink so from coming back before all this last horrid thing is over.

Mrs Brookfield says she met Mr Cole who she thinks is <u>quite an angel</u> he is so kind to us & it seems to us that there are indeed one or two angels walking about & comforting & helping — Here is the list — There is a little barrel beer-pot mug I should like to send Edward — &

Goodbye dearest Mrs Cole we shall come to town on Thursday week — as our lodgings will fit in to then

I send my best love & to Harry arent you proud to have a son major? Im
always your affectionate

AIT

Mr. Sturgis has sent us a offer f^m America. £100 & perhaps farther profits if we will give our sanction to a collected edition of Papas books

1864–1865

To Jane Shawe[1]

Letter 45 [Putney]
Ray/Morgan [19 May 1864]

Dearest Aunt Jane. I read your kind letter in the railway yesterday. I went to Mrs Coles on some business & found it there. We are at <u>Putney</u> in a little cottage called Heath Cottage, w^h has done us a great deal of good & been like a good friend to us. Grannie is at Paris & we are thinking of going over to her as soon as we have got things straight but everything has to be waited & waited for.

We have got a house to live in close to Onslow Sq called Onslow Gardens — It is very fresh and open & though there are a good many rooms they are not large ones. Theres a balcony & a bath and a little study for me to write in someday — at all events to write my letters & improve my mind.

We are both quite well though Minny is very very thin — I hope you & M.[2] like this fine weather as we do it seems to comfort and soothe & bind up ones aching wounds somehow.

I have been reading in the Times how at the great literary dinner yesterday[3] the Prince of Wales spoke so very very nicely about Papa and after him Ld Stanhope[4] & Mr Trollope and Ld Russell[5] whom he knew. Did you ever know your Father — You do know alas what a weary life it is for lonely women to lead[6] — I mean to be very busy & think of other peoples aches as much as I can. Granny has a great scheme of a cheap-food kitchen in Chelsea like the Glasgow one. Did you ever read Robertsons sermons[7] there is a little passage in one of them w^h seemed to comfort me one day when I wanted it very much — It is on a favourite text of yours I remember

Beloved if God so loved us[8] It is the one, almost only struggle of Religious life to believe this — In spite of all the seeming cruelties of this life in spite of the clouded mystery in which GOD has shrouded Himself in spite of pain, & the stern aspect of human life & the gathering of thicker darkness & more solemn silence round the soul as life goes on, simply to believe that GOD is Love & to hold fast to that as a man holds on to a rock with a desperate grip when the salt surf & the driving waves sweep over him — I say that is the one fight of Christian Life compared to w^h all else is easy. When we believe that human affections are easy — It is easy to be generous, & tolerant when we are sure of the

Heart of God. Minny said abt this (as she always call [*sic*] me) Ainy — I like much better to see the little animals all so wonderfully cared for and the little birds & the chickens than to read vague things about rocks

Our little chickens have come to such a sad end The hen sat & sat & sat for days & the rain came & then the fine weather & at last one morning there was a little yellow bright eyed creature & then another o so pretty — That brute Brownie — opened the door of the coop took out our pretty little things & ran off with — the hen flew after her, pecked screamed got the chicken back again but it died just after; well then we didnt know & left the chicks & the eggs together under the hen, & she not being able to manage so much at once trod on the two others & they died in Minnies hand. Poor little Hen was miserable would go on sitting on one old addled egg wouldnt eat wouldnt come away, until at last we bought some little chickens three weeks old, slyly took away the egg & popped them in.

Old Hen went about as proud as possible scratched nice little holes in the earth for them to bathe in, broke up the food for them to eat clucked & tucked them under her wings because you see she thought they were so very young & tender they must be kept quiet — she didnt understand they had already seen life & were 3 weeks old, but they were all so happy — We went to London yesterday on some worrying business & only came home quite tired out & disheartened about seven o'c — What do you think — The poor Hen was dead, someone had opened the coup w^h I had shut when I set off Brownie had bided her time rushed at her — & there were the miserable little chicks squeaking & quaking

Brownie slinks about all in a sort of lump When we look at her she turns her head away she sits on the stairs not daring to come in to the room & we cannot forgive her yet & speak as if nothing had happened

+ Do you know if Uncle Arthur has got anything??[9] I saw him once he was very kind & jolly

Goodbye dearest Aunt Jane
We send you our love

I'm y^r affectionatest
AIT.

PS. Minny sends you her love.

+ Yes! He has got a very good wife,
One of the greatest blessings in life,

Of brains he has an excellent store,
And — a great deal else — I say no more!

To Mr. and Mrs. Synge

Letter 46   Putney
Fales   May 20th [1864]

Dear Friends Your kind letters touched us & comforted us but indeed we knew that they were coming & that you were thinking of us in our bitter pain — Of Papa always & always — The worst is over now please God & five months have passed away of such pain that we try not to think of them but if we had died of grief it would not have been enough for the dearest & tenderest of Fathers. As for dying that would have seemed easy enough & it was living wh seemed so terrible at first. But it is mercifully allowed that one does not realize ones loss & we even now forget often & often, & indeed we cannot feel that he is not with us at times — nor do we try not to think so — Please God we shall hear his voice see his dear brown eyes & feel his Fatherly blessing in our hearts until our lifes end — He always hoped to go as he has gone Thank God it was all peace & silence, he had not moved that is the one comfort in a terrible darkness — We thought it was only a little attack — perhaps we too may die all alone[1] — I had always so hoped to die with Papas hand to hold — It makes me sick now to think how blind we were — we would have it he was better — & indeed he had had no attacks this autumn but he was constantly ill in one way & another & yet so brave & bright at times & so very tender but it has been a sad & anxious time & though we would have it he was better we were thoroughly wretched & did not dare to look forward. Minny was out of sorts & I made her go away it seems hard to think of now but with all the bitter bitter sickness there is the unspeakable peace and comfort of having had his love for our very own of looking forward to the happy day when we may meet again without fears & forebodings to make the brightness so dim.

    Everybody has been very kind to us — we have been here at Putney for the last month or more & Grannie has been at Paris — Now as soon as we have put a few things into a house we have bought close by Onslow Sq — we think of going to her & going to the Pyrenees for wh she has a great fancy — And indeed we rather dread settling down, though we longed to have a home of some sort to come back to.

We are both quite well & so is Grannie — Minny made me very anxious for a time she got into a dull sort of way but I think please God there is nothing amiss[2] She is only delicate & very thin & easily tired —

The last time papa spoke of you all he said what a nice letter — WWF had written to him —

It was a comfort to get Amys letter & yours for a long while after as if all was well with us. They are still at Dibrugarh I am sorry to say & tho' he has leave to exchange he can find no one to take the place. However Amy has her little girl to comfort her — Edward says he did so hope to show her to Papa — If we do go away we shall not come back to England until the beginning of October — Some friends of Grannies will be going with us & we hope that the Collins' may come How good they have been to us — and the Coles & Mrs Brookfield and everyone Mrs Trollope came to see us the other day — they are both as kind as friends can be. But there is very little to be done for us except this wonderful & <u>warming</u> kindness w^h has helped us through so much. Mr Smith too has been so very very good to us Once some of Papas letters were sold in a drawer & Minny & I were rushing about nearly crazy to buy them back — We found that he had been beforehand & done it all for us without a word[3]

Now I think it is a pity that so very much was sold but at the time we did not care I used to go & try to chose [*sic*] & I only got into a sort of stupified state. There is enough left I think for a house — Papa always liked to talk about his sale so that we could not bear that it should look <u>shabby</u>. The drawingroom w^h you never saw furnished looked so very pretty — Papa used to walk up & down in his slippers & dressinggown & say What a pretty room it is to be sure — I am sure every body must allow <u>that</u> —

Charles has got a good place at the Museum & Sims is with an old lady Gray had left us just a little while before Gardener has been so very good I shall never forget how she rushed off through a storm when we were waiting at some little railway station on our way to the Isle of Wight & came back with brandy & all sorts of things to warm us quite wet through herself. She & Fanny are both going to stay & we shall have a cook & Grannie is to keep house besides at least that is the scheme we have made.

No 8 Onslow Gardens it is called & please write there It is a new Sq behind the church — a continuation of Onslow Sq. Good night and God bless you & keep you & we send you our love & we miss the dear children and I am your   affectionate

AIthackeray

When is Bobbie[4] coming back? — We shall always have a room for him.

To Miss Boyle[1]

Letter 47	8 Onslow Gardens
Huntington Library	November 2^d [1864]
HM 15293	

My dear Miss Boyle

Thankyou for your letter — It was very good of you to think what this would be to us. It is a great great loss & grief — Papas friends are like a little bit of himself somehow

What it is to those, who have lost the tender & noble protector & husband & father, makes ones heart sicken to think of. At times the poor wife[2] is delirious with anguish but Last night I went to her & she was much more composed & quiet than when I first saw her God help & comfort her. I am going to see if she will see me today & I will tell her all you say Time seems so very very long when every moment is a pain that I think she feels already as if it had all happened long long ago instead of only yesterday.

He was up & in the dining room on Saturday — about 5 o'c he went up into his shed for a little & then said that he was not well & instead of coming down he should go to bed. A little later his favourite sister came into the room & Mrs Leech was there & suddenly He is fainting — the si[3] put out her arms & he I am going — & smiled — God bless him & died

Ones heart is very full It would be a comfort if one could do anything for her We shall all love his children for their Fathers sake, & we ourselves for our Fathers sake who loved him so much

Mr Leech said once or twice that he should never rally from that shock He was very ill & low & nervous — Papa was thinking about him & talking to us, not a year ago & telling us how serious he thought it was

I am fidgetting & longing to have news of Mr. Collins I am afraid this will be a great blow to him

Goodbye and thank you all [?] again

We felt somehow, so sure that everyone cared about Papa that those who spoke — or those who felt it, but did not speak of it to us seemed to us to be acting only in kindness — We want him so much now to go & comfort Mrs Leech. He could be so tender & so cheerful too

I think I told you once how he showed us your little nephews letter — half touched half laughing as it was his way.

Yours sincerely
AIThackeray

To Mrs. Synge

Letter 48
Fales

Brighton Dec^b 28. 1864

My dearest Mrs Synge

We have had another sorrow & my dearest Grannie is gone. She died quite suddenly on the Sunday before Xmas She had said good night quite well & in good spirits — while she was undressing Fanny left the room for a minute or two & coming back almost immediately found that all was over. We had been dreading Christmas for weeks past, but we did not think what a second Christmas it was to be. And yet strangely to ourselves even — though the last semblance of home & protecting love is gone — this new sorrow seems to have eased the weary pain w^h has ached & ached all this endless year. I think now, even if one of us 2 were to die the other would almost feel as if she had only gone home For home does seem there more than here at times Grannie was buried on Christmas Eve — but all our strength & courage failed us & we could not go again, it was this day year that we left our Father there. We came here a few days ago with my cousin Jane Ritchie — I think for the present we shall live on in Onslow Gardens — the future must settle itself — I have no heart to make plans or schemes.

Dear little Bobbie[1] was so bright — I thought as I put my arms round him & kissed him how you must envy me — It was a real comfort &

pleasure to see the dear little face again quite unchanged only a little bit more mother countryised. We were to have arranged before this for some little expedtions together but all our plans were changed Now Minny thank God is looking & feeling quite strong again & I still hope he will come & stay with us before he goes to Charterhouse.

I want Mr Synge to do me a kindness w^h I am sure he will if he can — Would he let us know whether he thinks there is any chance in the Sandwich Islands[2] for my Uncle Arthur Shawe It seems impossible for him to get even a bare subsistance here He is about fourty, well mannered & trustable — he had to leave the army in consequence of a jollification three years ago, but he has never transgressed since then — he writes a fair hand though he is not very eloquent with his pen, he understands his own trade perfectly, & if there was any chance ever so small in the Honolulu Police or Army it would be quite worth his while to go out — Mr George Smith advised me to ask Mr Synge — if he can help me I needn't say how grateful we should be. I wonder if we shall see him in the Spring I have just been reading in the Cornhill Magazine that the Queen[3] is really coming over.

I am so thankful to hear that Gilbert[4] is well again — I wish you were coming too Of all the household that you left, there are only us two & Fanny left. Gardiner gave me warning a little time ago. I was very much hurt and disappointed for I had thought she really cared for us: but I believe she had long wished to go into the country.

We sometimes feel almost inclined to go away & hide ourselves somewhere, but people are very kind & we should break all the old threads & so we had best struggle on until use and peace come to make our lives less sad. Miss Perry was telling us about Walton the other day. Katie Russell was there she said — it brought up old days very keenly as she said it — Amy[5] writes so happy that it is a comfort to think of her, her baby is very pretty & a funny mixture of the Father & Mother. Allahabad — India or care of Mess^{ers} Colvin & Co Calcutta is their address, the latter is the safest perhaps. I do not wonder that you cannot read her writing, we are only beginning now to make it out. And now Good bye in [*word illegible*] & Godbless you all in the New Year — Your affectionate

Annethackeray

Please if you can don't forget Uncle Arthur

To Mrs. George Baxter[1]

Letter 49
Columbia

[c. 1865][2]
16, Onslow Gardens
S.W.

My dear Mrs Baxter

    I have been away & my answer has been delayed a few days & I do hope that it will not miss the mail. I cannot tell you what a real <u>delight</u> & pleasure it gives us to think there is a chance of welcoming dear Miss Lucy[3] in our little blue room — I am so <u>very very</u> very[4] glad to think that she has almost made up her mind to come or rather that <u>you</u> have for her & Minnie says "Anny ain't you glad — & wont it be delightful to see her. I know we shall be very fond of one another —" and that is something enormous from Minny who never <u>says</u> much only thinks   Dear Mrs Baxter I know it will be good for her & we wont let her get tired or overdone — We are going away for a month somewhere in the suburbs f^m the 20th of May to the 20th of June, but we mean to come up & see pictures &ct — then we shall have a fortnight before we go to Switzerland here at home & Im sure Lucy will like Bromley where we think of going it is only a few minutes by Rail & O dear me how I wish it. About gowns, I think you will know better than I shall for Americans dress so much better than Englishwomen — I suppose for Switzerland 2 walking dresses & a silk one & a cut square or sort of demi toilette & a stout one for rainy days is about what one wants — in London an eveg dress is always useful, though in June we dont go out much   All our dinners &ct come before Easter — after Easter a very fast set of country people come up to town, & the residents who are not quite grand & in the world go to see pictures & sit out in Kensington Gardens & are much more quiet in the heigth of the season as it is called than before it has actually begun. Minny goes out into the <u>big</u> world much more than I do   It depresses me so that I always shirk it when I can, but I <u>promise</u> that Lucy shall see everybody interesting & Tennyson too — if we have to make a pilgrimage on purpose

    I only came back yesterday — little Margie[5] met me with little arms open — said Aunt Annee — do 'ou lub me <u>vedy</u> muss — I hear her chattering away upstairs now & I send you a very bad photograph of her & Minny — We are such shocking bad housekeepers & never make brandy peaches, but I do hope Lucy wont miss them very much — I do hope she wont mind Bromley   I have looked out at bricks for the last few months until I dont feel as if I could bear it any longer & am longing for trees & commons   Goodbye dear Mrs Baxter it is so good of you to trust us enough to think of trusting us with Lucy   I promise you to take as much care of her as I do of Min & Im

Yours affectionately
AIT

Were here already   How fortunate that I happened to write about how charming that y^r cousins should be coming   Dear Lucy please give her my best love & tell her how happy she has made us — I wont write to her now but I will by the next mail.

{A prayer written by Anny}

Letter 50   9 June 1865. AET. aet.[1] 28
Ray/Morgan

Pray God be our helper & keeper now that we are alone in the world & that troubles & bewilderment & remorses have come round about us   Pray God make us humble & true & thankful for all the love all the mercy which has been shewn to us

Pray God teach us to feel thy presence comforting us & surrounding us — Teach us not to fear the great chill Death & uncertainty which awaits us all — Make it into a home when we have reached it at last

Pray God if it be thy will give us someone here to love & to go to, if not teach us to be content & not to desire as a right the inestimable graciousness & manifestations of the love w^h come in different ways to each one of us

Teach us to love make our hearts burn with truth   help us to work & to live from a higher point of view than we have done hitherto

Help to help others a little — to remember our own shortcomings to try for truth in all things to be pitiful & gentle

Our Father thou hast allowed us to come to thee. I think I feel in my heart that it is no presumtive [*sic*] fancy but that the spirits fashioned by Thy hand may look to their creator as their Home.

Pray God bless Papa & Mama Grannie & GP & us two & little Jane 1875.[2] Since then what dear ones have come to bless us Leslie[3] & our little Meme[4] & Anny & Margie[5] & My Richmond & Pinkie[6] too & the love of friends

5

1866–1877

INTRODUCTION

*now that I k̲n̲o̲w̲ all my life contained, it seems to go back &
back into the p̲a̲s̲t̲ & bind it all & heal its bitter ache (Letter 65)*

DURING the years 1866–77 Anny's personal life was turbulent, yet her literary career was highly productive. In addition to numerous articles, she published eight books. Busy writing and sought after by editors, she traveled for pleasure, for her health, and to write. Like Thackeray before her, she took off with the chapters of her novels due for serial publication and, like her father, she always managed to get them in on time. While enjoying a busy life of travel and creativity, Anny wrestled with her misfortunes. She wrote: "We dreaded this Christmas but the children helped us through—last year Grannie died . . . Then dear Amy died in India & then a cousin."[1] Despite these deaths, which exacerbated her grief for Thackeray, she began to write brighter, more optimistic letters to a wide circle of people, including Tennyson and Browning.

Since Thackeray's death, Tennyson had become Anny's mentor, and more and more often, she returned to Freshwater and its soothing natural aspects and to Tennyson's salutary warmth. Something of the nature of their relationship appears in Anny's *Records of Tennyson, Ruskin, and Robert and Elizabeth Browning,* published in 1892. Anny's first recollection of Tennyson was "when she was propped up in a tall chair between her parents" (39). On her first visit to Freshwater, she described walking with Tennyson "along High Down, treading the turf, listening to his talk, while the gulls came sideways, flashing their white breasts against the edge of the cliffs, and the poet's cloak flapped time to the gusts of the west wind" (43).²

Another time, the poet, nearsighted, asked her "to look and tell him if the fieldlark did not come down sideways upon its wing" (51). On still another occasion, Anny joined the Tennyson family in attending a performance of *Hamlet*. At the play's end the actors, still in costume, joined the poet in his box. Anny described the scene:

> The whole play seemed to flow from off the stage into the box . . . I could scarcely tell at last where reality began and Shakespeare ended . . . here were the players, and our own prince poet, in that familiar simple voice . . . explaining the art, going straight to the point in his own downright fashion . . . carrying all before him. (59)

Anny's essay about Tennyson (like those on Ruskin and Browning) is not chronological, not critical, but wholly anecdotal. To her, Tennyson was a lifelong friend, a man she had loved and admired.

After the deaths of Thackeray and Mrs. Carmichael-Smyth, Anny had established a shaky refuge. Although she remained close to her sister, Minny's engagement and subsequent marriage to Leslie Stephen caused a rift in the relationship between the sisters. In her journal for 1866, Anny wrote: "Two days after Minny's engagement, Tennyson came and I asked him to help me with the last paragraph of my book *The Village on the Cliff*. I was overwrought."³ It was more than Anny's last paragraph that needed help. She was "overwrought" at the prospect of losing Minny. A portion of the final paragraph of *The Village* reads,

> And Nature, working by some great law unknown, and only vaguely apprehended by us insects . . . brings about the noblest harmonies out of chaos. And so, too, out of the dire dismays and confusions of the secret world come results both mighty and gentle. (318)

With Tennyson's help, she sublimated her feelings, losing herself in her book.

Whatever advice Tennyson provided, it is not unlikely that Anny's unconscious dictated the end of her novel *The Village*. Although Anny and Minny did not resemble the heroines of *The Village*, the circumstances in which the heroines find themselves at the end of the novel were similar to those of Anny and Minny. The sad ending in Anny's novel reveals the bereft heroine facing a life of loneliness. Anny herself may have given up hope of ever marrying, especially since her younger sister had married before her; and now, after the death of her father, her life's focus on her sister was becoming blurred.

At the time of her engagement, Minny wrote, "I hope never to be separated from Anny, except perhaps during my wedding tour. I am sure she will have no reason to regret this change in our lives."[4] Though loving, Minny's statement is more wish than practicality. With the addition of Leslie Stephen to the household, the sisters' rapport lessened. The household no longer revolved around Anny and her career. Stephen was a demanding, donnish, penny-pinching husband, and though he admired Anny, their temperaments clashed. Anny wrote, "[I] am generaly flourishing except in one way it begins with an L & finishes with a e" (Letter 51). Surrounded by Minny's happiness, Anny's loneliness and her need for someone to love who would love her became crushing, especially when seen in the light of Stephen's revelation in his *Mausoleum Book* that "Minny had begun to think that it might be as well for Anny to take a house of her own" (23). Stephen continued disarmingly by admitting his faults: "I had a perhaps rather pedantic mania for correcting [Anny's] flights of imagination and checking her exuberant impulses. A.[nny] and M.[inny] used to call me the cold bath from my habit of drenching Anny's little schemes and fancies with chilling criticism" (23).

It is well to consider the fact that Leslie was too fond of Anny for Minny's liking, and not the reverse. In a letter to Anny, Leslie admitted:

> You know that I cant speak to you when you are here. I cant even write very easily; but I must say one thing. Of all the good you & Minny have done for me . . . you two have been a new influence in our family & thawed us all with kindness. When I laugh at your sentiment, dont fancy for a moment that I ever do or can forget, what I owe to it in making my relations to my mother easier & better. I wont say any more; perhaps I shall never say as much again. (Letter 59)

As scrupulously impartial as Thackeray had tried to be, he favored Anny. Now Minny had a husband of her own, and as much as she loved Anny, she wanted Leslie exclusively for herself. Again, in the *Mausoleum Book,* Leslie confessed: "Anny's aggressions were not very irritating, and that she was like a person forced to live in a den with a fretful beast and persisting in stroking it the wrong way" (24).

The problem was that Minny did not want Anny stroking Leslie in *any* way.

What really rankled with Stephen was that "Anny was always the aggressor and could not keep silence" (24). He wanted to be the master of their home; Minny wanted to be its mistress; yet Anny was ruling them both. Despite the fact that they all loved each other, they had created a ménage à trois that was bound to fail. While Thackeray lived, Anny had been the adored daughter and sister; upon his death she assumed command of their home, and made all their monetary decisions. But in 1867, after Minny's marriage to Stephen, he took over control of Minny's exchequer. A receipt showing a repaid debt to Thackeray is signed by Anne Thackeray and Leslie Stephen for H. M. Stephen (Letter 52). As a good Victorian wife, Minny had relinquished her economic rights to her husband, leaving Anny with yet another loss of purpose.

Shortly after their marriage, the Stephens planned a trip to America. Anny refused to accompany them. Minny wrote to Mrs. Baxter in New York, giving three different reasons why Anny could not accompany her and her husband. Anny offers no excuse for staying behind except: "I think I am right" (Letter 53). That a problem existed is obvious; for Anny, separation from the newlyweds was necessary. In the same letter Anny continued, "Leslie too is a dear good old fellow & he adores Minny in his silent dobbin like way," but she could not help being disturbed by his masculine presence. "Leslie on the other side is smoking his pipe." In 1870 she again noted: "dear old Leslie works away & smokes & writes & smokes till I can scarcely tell w^h is him & which is his pipe" (Letter 54). Although Thackeray had smoked cigars, Anny never complained about them. Stephen's pipe became for Anny a bothersome habit. More likely, she resented his pipe as the symbol of his assumption of the role of master of the house.

Anny separated herself from her sister in her writing and in her relationships with other people. "Miss Thackeray" became part of the London literary scene and artistic salons. In 1870 George Lewes wrote: "At the dinner was Annie Thackeray, Mrs. Procter, an American lady, Butler Johnstone, Kinglake, Lecky, Rosetti [sic] Arthur Russell and a crowd in the evening."[5] Not only Anny's inclusion in such a distinguished company of Victorians, but the fact that Lewes lists her name first, testifies to her importance within the group.

As with Tennyson, Anny enjoyed a long and warm relationship

with Browning, assuming the roles of a bright daughter and a charming companion. Never a sycophantic follower, she endeared herself to these older men with her cleverness, wit, and perception. Asking favors of Browning, she perceived exactly how far she could go in her requests.

She had known and admired Elizabeth Barrett Browning when the Thackerays had lived in Paris and later in Rome. In her essay on the Brownings, Anny quoted "a girlish note in [her own] old diary: 'I think Mrs. Browning is the greatest woman I ever saw in all my life.'"[6] Always in search of maternal tenderness, Anny was impressed by Mrs. Browning, the mother whose son Pen was constantly by her side. Anny's mature judgment in the essay assesses her schoolgirl partiality for the poet: "I don't think any girl who had once experienced [Mrs. Browning's friendship] could fail to respond to Mrs. Browning's motherly advance" (130–31).

In 1872 Browning and Anny rented houses near each other in Calvados, Normandy (he in St. Aubin and she in Lion-sur-Mer). It was there that Browning conceived the idea for his narrative poem *Red Cotton Night-Cap Country,* which Anny titled for him and which he dedicated to her. In a letter written in 1872 from Lion-sur-Mer, Anny described the village:

> It is close to the place we came to ten years ago nearly with Grannie & where I wrote The Village on the Cliff here nothing seems changed. There are the cotton nightcaps & the melons & the bathers; its a sort of Pompei with little feasts all the way down the street & great shining fish coming up out of the sea & tumblers & a gladiator or two & the most astounding chatter & barter. (Letter 57)

The cotton nightcaps are also noted in *The Village*. However, because of the gory nature of Browning's poem, about a sensational contemporary suicide, he amended the title to *Red Cotton Night-Cap Country*. The poem is not one of the better received of Browning's works. Attacked by the critics for her part in its composition, Anny was indignant for Browning rather than for herself. He, in turn, was indignant for her: "Indeed the only sort of pain that any sort of criticism could give me would be the reflection of any particle of pain it managed to give *you*." Used to criticism as he was, he continued: "Remember that everybody this thirty years has given me his kick and gone his way . . . but any poke at me which should touch *you* would vex me indeed—" (*Records,* 181).

INTRODUCTION

As Thackeray's daughter there was bred in her an independence of spirit and a nonchalance in dealing with Victorian men of letters which enabled her to be good friends not only with Tennyson and Browning but also with Carlyle, Ruskin, Darwin, Arnold, Swinburne, and later James. At the beginning of her essay on the Brownings, Anny wrote:

> The sons and daughters of men and women eminent in their generation are from circumstances fortunate in their opportunities. From childhood they know their parents' friends and contemporaries, the remarkable men and women who are the makers of the age, quite naturally and without excitement. . . . the friends existed first; then, long afterwards, they became to me the notabilities, the interesting people as well, and these two impressions were oddly combined in my mind. (129)

This "oddly combined" attitude augmented by her own abilities made her a suitable companion for these men.

Between 1866 and 1878 Anny published eight books. The three novels are of particular interest because heretofore her fictional efforts had been short, episodic forays into the lives of her characters. In these novels Anny tried not merely to lengthen the tales but to impose more form, continuity, and plot sequence on them.

First published serially in the *Cornhill*, *The Village on the Cliff* (1867), *Old Kensington* (1873), and *Miss Angel* (1875) are domestic novels. But as always in Anny's writing, there is a great deal going on beneath the everyday surface. Although the chief occupation of Anny's orphan-heroines is to find a husband, they all work, as governess, painter, farmer, volunteer. The usual machinery of the domestic novel abounds: the love triangle; the lost inheritance regained; the pretty, noble heroine; the romantic hero; the conscious class system; the neatly packaged happy ending. Anny brings to this formula a style and psychological approach that are peculiarly her own. When she was a young girl traveling through Europe, she depicted scenes in her letters almost as if she were painting them. Quick impressionistic strokes caught pictures seen from a train or a coach window. In the same way, she captures a place, a feeling, or a mood in her novels. In *The Village* the hero Richard Butler wanders about Caen

> in this pleasant confusion of sight, and sound, and bright colour. . . . [he walked] round and about, stopping at every corner, looking into every church, noting the bright pictures, framed as it were in the arches, staring up at the gables, at the quaint wares in the shops; making mental notes of one kind and another, which might be useful some day. (27)

Butler is a Pre-Raphaelite painter, storing details which he will use one day. This is what Anny, herself, did. Of Petitport, a small seaside resort in Normandy, she wrote: "The horizon is solemn dark blue, but a great streak of light crosses the sea; three white sails gleam, so do the white caps of the peasant-women, and the wings of the seagulls as they go swimming through the air" (7). In the sharp visualization of the three white sails, the white caps, and the wings of the seagulls, Anny paints a picture realistically, yet she is also impressionistic when she describes the birds as "swimming" through the air, not flying. With deft touches she etches in sky and sea, linking them together with the waves, women, and birds. All the universe—inanimate nature, animal life, and humanity—are part of God's plan for a peaceful Sunday afternoon. This is not a static view, but rather more like one frame of a moving picture, captured with painterly words.

Anny unreels other pictures in a slow, leisurely expansion of detail and idea until she reaches the perfect metaphor for Caen: "a goblin city" (26). Her use of the present tense in description creates a sense of immediacy, echoing the 1864 journal, in which the present tense served to evoke for Anny a Thackeray still alive. The narrative happened in the past, but the nature passages present an ongoing phenomena.

The Village is recounted in the first person by a narrator, Miss Williamson. Anny uses this same spinster in *Miss Williamson's Divagations, The Story of Elizabeth,* and *Fulham Lawn.* One may speculate that Anny consciously or unconsciously chose the name William-son, thus reaching back to William Thackeray and the son he never had. Miss Williamson (or Anny) was indeed following in her father's literary footsteps.

In *Old Kensington* the descriptive passages follow the form of those in *The Village:* the short, impressionistic sketch and the longer mood-building scene of nature combined with place. However, there is a special ambience which Anny conveys in this novel. Set in the Kensington in which she had grown up twenty-five years earlier, the novel is a long reminiscence through every street and house and by-lane that she remembered. It is nostalgic, filled with an innocence, a serenity that was no more and perhaps never really was.

Although the setting is the Kensington Anny knew as a child, the circumstances of the heroine's life are similar to those of Anny's when she lived in Paris with her grandmother. Both heroine (Dolly) and author suffer from the effects of an absent mother. They are relocated, at the same age, to live with elderly, childless relatives. Dolly's father dies, while Anny's father saw his children only sporadically. For Dolly, as well as Anny, life was austere, adult, and gloomy. In addition to the remembered sadness, Anny was depressed by her life at the time she was writing the novel. Living in the home of a younger married sister with a newborn child must have been trying. Despite the happy ending, the novel, like most of Anny's writing at this time, bears an imprint of bittersweet melancholy.

Even more interesting is the parallel structure of *Old Kensington* to *Vanity Fair*.[7] In reliving her life in Kensington, Anny also seemed to be reliving *Vanity Fair*. She follows the lives of two heroines, Dolly and Rhoda, one good, one bad, as their fortunes rise and fall. Instead of being killed in the Napoleonic wars, Anny's George dies in the Crimean War. Just as Dobbin waits for Amelia, so Raban waits for Dolly. Rhoda is no Becky Sharp: there is little joy in her, but she is drawn with psychological acumen. Unlike Becky, she ends her days living on the charity of Dolly, the friend she has wronged. Dolly is a milk-sop maiden, but with a difference: she undergoes introspection leading to growth and some change.

Probably she did not consciously set out to copy the structure of *Vanity Fair*. Yet it was part of her consciousness when she began to write about her experiences in Young Street. Fact and fiction—Young Street and *Vanity Fair*—were inextricably fused together. Her father's novel was part of her life, not only in the reading of it, but through its actual creation. When she remembered posing for Thackeray's drawing as one of the two little girls packing up his puppets, was she Anny of Young Street or a character in *Vanity Fair*?

Both books are domestic tales with strong traces of the historical novel. Both novels include characters with ties to India. Both contain memorable minor comic characters; both are without true heroes. The triangle-scene climax in *Old Kensington* is not as dramatic as that of Rawdon's discovery of Becky's liaison with Lord Steyne; Anny is quieter and more overtly psychological in her handling of Dolly's discovery that her fiancé loves another. She walks out of a concert hall, leaving him in the insinuating hands of Rhoda. Yet there is nothing of the corruption and evil of Lord Steyne about these two; they are weak people, who, having put all their faith in the power of money, are unable to stand up to adversity. Although Rhoda gets her just deserts, it is Thackeray who moralizes; it is Anny who analyzes. Thackeray gives us a sparkling cross-section of hearty Regency England; Anny's view of Kensington is charming but somber, and it is not knowledgeable about all classes of society. Instead, she examines the motivations of several women of the same class.

At the time *Vanity Fair* was published, Thackeray was thirty-seven years old; he had lost his wife to insanity, he was the father of two children, and determined to make a home for them. At the time *Old Kensington* was written, Anny was thirty-six years old and well on her way to becoming a spinster. Thackeray was a man of the world who picked up the pieces of his life and tried to make the best of what was left to him; Anny had suffered grievous losses, but she had not yet lived. The world of *Vanity Fair* is complete—containing as it does both good and evil; the full world of *Old Kensington* is yet to come. Thackeray had lived his life; Anny's is yet to come.

The last chapter of *Old Kensington* is entitled "The Play Is Played, the Curtain Drops," and is based on the final words of *Vanity Fair*, "our play is played out." These in turn are similar to the opening line of Thackeray's ballad "The End of the Play," "The play is done; the curtain drops," printed at the end of Thackeray's Christmas book (1848–49), *Dr. Birch and His Young Friends*. I do not presume to compare *Old Kensington* with *Vanity Fair;* the first is a moving novel about an appealing young woman, the second is a masterpiece. Yet, despite its inadequacies, *Old Kensington* is worthy of its place in the direct line of descent from *Vanity Fair*. Like it, *Old Kensington* is a panoramic view of a time that is no more, about characters who are always with us.

Anny's peculiar novelistic talent lies in her depiction of the psyches of female characters.[8] Soon after her engagement to the worthless Robert Henley, Dolly lies awake thinking.

> She had found out, by her new experience, that Robert loved her, but in future that he would rule her too. In her life, so free hitherto, there would be this secret rule to be obeyed, this secret sign. Dolly did not know whether she resented it. . . . Dolly, conscious of some hidden weakness in her own nature, deified obstinacy, as many a woman has done before her, and made excuses out of her own loving heart for Henley's selfish one. (252–53)

Here Anny is not leaving "the mysteries of womanhood to be described by some interloping male," as Richard Whately described authoresses, but doing it herself. Toward the end of the novel, when Dolly admits that she loves Raban, he refers to her as the prize. Dolly thinks that "perhaps the prize isn't worth having, . . . she was only thinking as she stood there of all her friend's long fidelity and steady friendship" (526). Like Amelia, Dolly sees, at last, the worth of her patient lover, but unlike Thackeray's heroine, Dolly proves to be a real prize. Amelia is "the prize [Dobbin] has been trying for all his life." Thackeray, and Dobbin, know that she is a "tender little parasite," and Dobbin declares that "the prize I had set my life on was not worth the winning."[9] Early in Anny's novel, Raban calls Dolly "a beautiful sour apple" who will "want time and sunshine to ripen and become sweet" (110). This touch of the sour apple is exactly what is missing in Amelia. Anny understood that some women could and did grow and ripen.

Miss Angel is Anny's one attempt at historical romance. Set in the eighteenth century, the novel interestingly depicts the life of a female artist, Angelica Kauffmann. She becomes the overnight sensation of English society and is nominated a founding member of the Royal Academy. The novel is steeped in eighteenth-century lore: coach tours through Italy with outriders and quaint hostelries, great balls, powdering rooms, visits with Samuel Johnson and Queen Charlotte. Anny refers to and quotes from the Rossi biography of Angelica Kauffmann, but with several changes from real life (as far as Rossi describes it) in her fiction.

In real life, through the intervention of friends in high places, Angelica received an annulment of her disastrous first marriage. Because female artists were a rarity in the eighteenth century, "[t]raducement of [Kauffmann's] character was an occupational hazard.... The myth was that she was a flibbertigibbet who spent most of her time flirting."[10] In Anny's novel Angelica waits for the fortuitous death of her first husband and then enters into a happy union with another artist. In *Miss Angel,* not only does Sir Joshua Reynolds paint Angelica's portrait—as he did in real life—but he is made her unsuccessful suitor as well. Anny comes closer to portraying the real Angelica Kauffmann than did the petty gossips of the eighteenth century. Anny's heroine is a hard-working serious artist, an intelligent woman capable of holding conversations with Goethe. Hurt by the posturing and obeisance intrinsic in the role she assumed in order to become a painter, she turned to her art. Understanding the value of creativity, Anny wrote:

> The sympathies and consolations of light, of harmony, of work, are as effectual as many a form of words. They are *substitutions* of one particular manner of feeling and expression for another. To hungry, naked, and imprisoned souls, art ministers with a bountiful hand, shows them a way of escape (even though they carry their chains with them).... Angelica was

never more grateful to her pursuit than now when time was difficult on her hands. (135)

For Angelica, as well as for Anny herself, work was the only anodyne for troubled times.

In his chapter on contemporary novelists in his autobiography, Trollope adds "two ladies" to his list "in order that I may declare how much I have admired their work. They are Annie Thackeray and Rhoda Broughton." He continues:

> Miss Thackeray's characters are sweet, charming, and quite true to human nature. In her writings she is always endeavouring to prove that good produces good, and evil evil. There is not a line of which she need be ashamed,—not a sentiment of which she should not be proud. But she writes like a lazy writer who dislikes her work, and who allows her own want of energy to show itself in her pages.[11]

Trollope, whose own psychological acumen was profound, nevertheless shows himself not fully sensitive to the psychological depths of Anny's female characters. Underneath the sweetest and most charming of her heroines was a repressed turmoil. Her heroines do not explode; they come to quiet realizations; and continue to measure out their lives with teaspoons. Her female characters do not include a Lizzie Eustace, a Mrs. Proudie, or a Lady Mason. These are all extraordinary women. Anny's heroines are good women, ordinary women trying to understand themselves and their worlds. Anny brings them to life, "quite true to human nature," and shows that even the simplest of them is important in her hidden complexities. Anny reaches down into herself as she constructs a heroine. If she did not create dramatic women as Trollope did, she created, with an honesty that a woman could easily perceive, the reality of a young, vulnerable, inexperienced woman.

Trollope equates Anny's casual, colloquial prose with laziness and absence of style, but her distinctive manner serves her purpose. Her wanderings and leisurely asides, her ample descriptions of nature, her slow unraveling of motives, are as pertinent to her stories as the narrative and enhance her analysis of character. Never the omniscient writer, she is rather a friend sharing a psychologically acute tale, talking directly to the reader in the manner of an oral storyteller.

Anne Thackeray—as a writer and as a spinster living in her sister's house—found a kindred soul in Jane Austen.[12] In notes for her essay on Austen, Anny quotes Richard Whately:

> Authoresses can scarcely ever forget they are authors. They seem to feel a sympathetic shudder at exposing naked a female mind. They leave the mysteries of womanhood to be described by some interloping male, like Richardson or Marivaux who is turned out before he has seen half the rites & is forced to spin fr. his own conjectures the rest. (Letter 55)

At this time Anny, unmarried, knew little about men, nor did she have the ability to understand them in the way that Trollope understood women. However, the empathy that Trollope brought to his female characters was not an intimate knowledge of the female psyche, but rather a more general understanding of the human condition. Anny was deficient in her portrayals of men (until she wrote *Mrs. Dymond*); her heroes are one-dimensional. But in her female characters she exposes "naked the female mind." They question their given positions in life and search for new roles as Anny herself had done.

> There are two great classes of women—those who minister and those who are taken care of by others; and the born care-takers and workers are apt to chafe in early life, . . . Something is wrong, . . . hearts beat passionately, boil over, ache for nothing at all; they want to comfort people, to live, to love, to come and go, to feel they are at work. (109–10)

Anny was a caretaker, and so were her heroines, who wanted to live and to love.

Many of Anny's heroes at this time wander aimlessly and passively; in a sense antiheroes, they are the centers of actions done for them, the inheritors of fortunes, the recipients of good, rather than the initiators of action and of life. Catherine (the second heroine of *The Village*) sends Butler back to Reine, the woman he loves. Catherine serves the same purpose of getting the two lovers together as Mrs. Hilberry (modeled on Anny herself) does later in Virginia Woolf's *Night and Day*. Without Becky's wit and good humor, Reine is the same kind of strong, self-sufficient, and steely young woman—a loner out of her class, fighting to survive. Like Becky she says, "I am no angel," but then she adds, "We in our class are not like you others. . . . I cannot dissemble" (200). Here Becky and Reine part ways.

Anny's females have fragile egos; they are victims and as such often cannot free themselves. When they do, they turn to a more loving and honest suitor, but they never become whole in their own right or fully emancipated. They still define themselves as their men see them. Anny called her women to account for cowardice and foolishness, but rarely did she attack a man for his defects. What she dealt with was a woman's faulty response to a man. In *The Village,* Anny states, "Women usually respect a man when he is angry even when he is in the wrong" (106). For Anny, a woman's cowardice was far more damaging to her than a man's wrongdoing against her.

It is intriguing to consider why George Eliot found Anny's novels to her liking. She wrote: "I am obliged to fast from fiction, and fasting is known sometimes to weaken the stomach. I ought to except Miss Thackeray's stories, which I cannot resist when they come near me—and bits of Mr. Trollope" (Haight, VI, 123). And again two years later Eliot wrote: "I know nothing of contemporary English novelists with the exception of Miss Thackeray's and (a few of) Anthony Trollope's works" (VI, 418). Indeed, Eliot sent *The Story of Elizabeth* to a friend along with copies of *Orley Farm* and *The Small House at Allington* (IV, 209). Of Anny's novel, Eliot wrote, "It is not so cheerful as Trollope, but it is charmingly written" (IV, 209). In a diary entry for 19 April 1878, Eliot recorded having read "Annie Thackeray 'The Village on the Cliff'" (VII, 22).

From George Eliot's references to Anny's novels, there appears to have been something more appealing in them for her than being "charmingly written." I propose that Eliot recognized a woman's insight into a female character—that one step more into a female psyche than a male writer could take in order to expose "naked a female mind"—which Trollope, also presumably chosen by Eliot for his psychological insight, did not sufficiently recognize. In her essay "Silly Novels by Lady Novelists," Eliot insists that "women can produce novels not only fine, but among the very finest;—novels, too, that have a precious speciality, lying quite apart from masculine aptitudes and experience."[13] Anny's "precious speciality," her psychological insights into her female characters, combined with her ability to express them, rendered her different from the usual Lady Novelists, and therefore readable to Eliot.

Anny wrote many fairy tales that are reworkings of old tales set in Victorian times. The giants and monsters are industrialists, fanatics, grasping misers, and the unloving. The disasters they create are personal as well as public. Not fairy tales for children, they are cautionary lessons for adults. As moral as Thackeray, Anny lacked his light touch and irony to make her message palatable. The fairy tales are, however, extremely imaginative in applying myths to the morass of Victorian society.

One essay of all those written in this period must be considered. Anny rewrote "Toilers and Spinsters," first published in the *Cornhill* in 1861,[14] for inclusion in her 1873 collection of the same title. Some grammatical changes are incidental. Additions occur in the explanation of advances that had taken place in the realm of women's work opportunities and facilities, for example, the establishment in 1873 of the Berners Street Club for women (9).

At the end of the 1873 rewrite, Anny acknowledges that Thackeray "wrote a title to the rambling little paper" of 1861 (23). Though the two versions are similar, there are some interesting additions. In the earlier paper Anny asks for more and better jobs for all women who want to work. She asserts that a spinster can enjoy the world as well as a married woman—and even as well as a man!

> What possible reason can there be to prevent unmarried, any more than married, people from being happy (or unhappy), according to their circumstances—Are unmarried people shut out from all theatres, concerts, picture-galleries, parks, and gardens? . . . Does Mudie refuse their subscriptions? . . . May not spinsters, as well as bachelors, give their opinions on every subject, no matter how ignorant they may be. . . . I know of no especial ordinance of nature to prevent men, or women either, from being ridiculous at times. (23)

The great problem for single women (as for married ones) is "want of adequate means." "[S]urely it is the want of money, and not of husbands," Anny continued, which brings with it great unhappiness. Women must be trained in order to enter the work force, and "every woman in raising herself may carry along a score of others with her" (8). Anny also suggests a club where working women may go for a decent meal, a glass of port, and a quiet reading room. From today's vantage point, her requests seem modest indeed, but in 1861 they would have appeared radical had they been written by anyone but Miss Thackeray. She was asking for many more job opportunities for women, for greater social equality between the sexes, and for recognition of a woman's human rights. It was of supreme importance for her that a woman be allowed to earn her own living.

The changes made in 1873 are significant because Anny herself realized that she was writing from a "double point of view and from the two ends of fifteen years" (24). After acknowledging the changes which had enabled more women to earn their own livelihoods, she continues:

> What Arnold did for schoolboys and schoolmasters, inventing freedom for them and a rescue from the tyranny of common-place and opposition, . . . some people have been trying to do for home-girls, schoolgirls, and their teachers, for whom surely some such revolution has long been needed. (29)

She asks:

> What is it, then, that we would wish for. . . . Eyes to see, ears to hear, sincerity and the power of being taught and of receiving truth; . . . by being taken out of ourselves, . . . do we most learn to be ourselves and to fulfil the intention of our being. (30–31)

Anny's original premise in 1861 was simply to open the way for better job opportunities for women and to establish eating clubs for women. In 1873, she asks not only for more and better education for women but for the right of women to declare themselves as women —to come into their own and be themselves. Her scorn at the failure to expand the suffrage to women is clear, though the subject is relegated to a footnote added in 1873. Noting that the "apathy of 'half the women of England' who do not care for votes, and whose supineness in the Attorney-General's eyes is a good reason for not giving the Franchise to those persons who *do* happen to care for it," she protests. If the Victorian woman

> is able to rule her household, to bring up her sons and daughters in love and in truth, and to advise her husband with sense and composure, she may perhaps be trusted in time with the very doubtful privilege of a 5,000th voice in the election of a member for the borough. (11–12, n. 1)[15]

Whatever the limitations of her manifesto, it must be remembered that Anny was writing before there was much feminist discussion. In 1861 she had begun a little paper about spinsters; in 1873 she brought the essay up to date. That women should be able to work and be better educated was their right, not because they were women, but because they were human beings. This is one of the significant beginnings of today's feminism. Virginia Woolf's *A Room of One's Own* is a natural descendant of her Aunt Anny's "Toilers and Spinsters," albeit with a difference in focus.[16] After Leslie Stephen had been a widower for three years, he married Julia Duckworth. Virginia Stephen (Woolf) was their daughter. Anne Thackeray was a friend of both Julia and Leslie Stephen, and visited them often in their home at Hyde Park Gate. Because she was Aunt Anny to Laura Stephen (Minny's daughter), she became Aunt Anny to all the Duckworth and Stephen children. For the young Virginia Stephen, Anne Thackeray was a powerful model of a female writer.

In "Toilers and Spinsters" Anne Thackeray spoke for the common, untalented spinster; in *A Room of One's Own* Virginia Woolf spoke for the elite and talented artist. Anne Thackeray hoped that a woman would be given the opportunity to earn her own living; Virginia Woolf asked for five hundred pounds a year to be given as a legacy to enable her artist to work. Anne Thackeray was a Victorian Lady who frequented the best drawing rooms in London; Virginia Woolf was a rebel from Bloomsbury who had been denied admittance to the Oxbridge Library. Anne Thackeray, later Lady Ritchie, spoke for the poor; Virginia Woolf the radical spoke for the elite. What must be remembered is that Anne Thackeray and Virginia Woolf were part of the same family, the same Victorian class. Anne Thackeray worked within its parameters; Virginia Woolf turned her back on Hyde Park Gate and all it symbolized for her. Yet, paradoxically, it was only the intellectual elite, but still an elite, she cared about. Anne Thackeray's essay broke ground; Virginia Woolf's became part of the feminist vernacular.

Anne Thackeray's "little paper" bears looking into; it shows the fifteen-year evolution of a working writer, unhampered by societal strictures. By being herself and examining the world from her unique perspective, Anny had developed a devoted following of friends and of readers. Yet in the midst of her literary triumph came personal tragedy.

Before the birth of her second child, Minny died. Anny was now indeed alone. At times of crisis we often revert to behavior of a previous critical time. When Minny died, Anny's guilt, not only at being alive but at the jealousy she could not suppress at Minny's good fortune, added to the burden of true sorrow she felt about the loss of her sister. She reverted to her suppressed feelings of sisterly jealousy over Thackeray and back even further to her primal jealousy against her mother over her father. "I think I am writing to tell you that Papa is dead. It always seems to be that come back, not anything new," Anny wrote in Letter 62. Bereft now of Minny, Anny mourned once more for Thackeray.

Among Thackeray's papers, Anny had found "Adieu," a poem by Carlyle, copied out by Mrs. Brookfield (JOB). On the envelope Anny had written:

> Written out by JOB
> Kept by my Father

> When Minnie died
> I used to read it & read it.¹⁷

Anny had to learn the bitter lesson of saying "Adieu forever now" to all those she had loved.

In another letter written in October of 1876 to George Eliot, Anny is still grieving. In discussing Eliot's newly published *Daniel Deronda*, she wrote: "I hope you are pretty well & rested from y.^{r} work — I have felt it come Very home to me — it is the first book I have ever read without Minnie & does not seem to me quite a book so much as something w^h has been" (Letter 63). Eliot wrote to John Blackwood, "What a blow for Miss Thackeray—the death of that sister to whom she was so closely bound in affection" (Haight, VI, 200).

Minny's death was indeed a blow to Anny but in another way it served to hasten her liberation from several Victorian mores. She was forty years old; her mother was insane; her father, grandmother, and sister were dead; her nearest relatives were the dour Leslie and her mentally deficient five-year-old niece, Laura. Taking into consideration her warm nature and her need for love, the time was ripe for her to find a husband. Instead, she was found by Richmond Thackeray Willoughby Ritchie, the son of Thackeray's favorite cousin, William Ritchie. Educated at Eton, Richmond was a King's scholar and a Newcastle medalist; later he entered Trinity College, Cambridge, on a scholarship. He was brilliant, serious, handsome, and completely enamored of his famous, worldly, and elder cousin. Richmond's adolescent worship turned to love. Encouraged by Anny's need of his adulation, he was determined to marry her. How could a sensitive young man find her anything but captivating when she wrote him such letters as this one from Interlaken:

> How I wish one could send all that one sees to you and to all other poor hard-working people who really want it! I should like to send you a pine tree, a bunch of wild strawberries, and a valley of sloping, nodding flowers with thousands of glittering spiders' webs, the high up snows and far below lakes and yesterday's yellow evening, dying rather sadly behind the pine ridge and the misty Stockhorn.¹⁸

She called him her "dear Tonic," and her "blessing," a nickname used heretofore only among Thackeray and his daughters.

After the devastation of Minny's death, Anny and Leslie learned to live together. When Richmond Ritchie's visits to the house became insistent, Leslie protested. He found them together in the parlor kissing, and like an irate father or spurned lover, he demanded that a decision be made. After all (even years later) Leslie wrote, "It was clear that a long engagement would be very undesirable. She could not afford to waste time."[19] Anny was forty, Richmond twenty-three, and still at Cambridge.

To the consternation of Richmond's many friends, who were foreseeing a brilliant academic career for him, he forged ahead with his intentions. Leaving Cambridge, he entered the India Office as a junior clerk. On these expectations, coupled with Anny's earnings from her writing, they were married. On 2 August 1877 George Eliot wrote to a friend:

> And Miss Thackeray's married today to young Ritchie. I saw him at Cambridge and felt that the nearly 20 years' difference between them was bridged hopefully by his solidarity [sic] and gravity. This is one of several instances that I know of lately, showing that young men with even brilliant advantages will often choose as their life's companion a woman whose attractions are wholly of the spiritual order. (Haight, VI, 398)

Eliot was not aware of how prophetically she spoke, for Anny's marriage was to anticipate her own two years later, in 1880, to John W. Cross, twenty years her junior.[20]

Richmond was tall, good-looking, and a Thackeray. He was old for his age; she was young for hers. He assuaged her reawakened grief for the loss of her father. When questioned by a friend about her feelings for Richmond, Anny wrote that she loved him "but not well enough to refuse him."[21] To her old friend Hennee Synge, Anny wrote:

> I knew yr kind heart would understand & sympathise with the strange happiness which has come so unperceivedly into my life. Richmond has been away ever since it was settled so that at times I almost imagine it is all a strange dream. But it is no dream & no vague story — all is true all his goodness & faithful affection & now that I know all my life contained, it seems to go back & back into the past & bind it all & heal its bitter ache. (Letter 65)

Literally she went "back and back," doubly safe in the love of a male Thackeray, who would help her to lay to rest, for now, her longing for her father.

Winifred Gérin believes that *From an Island,* written at the hectic time directly before and after Anny's engagement, is "as near to being a little masterpiece as anything she had yet produced."[22] Gérin praises Anny's analysis of character and her sense of place. The novella also has great biographical interest because of the time in which it was written. Struggling with the problem of the suitability of her approaching marriage, Anny had to deal with criticism about the seventeen-year age difference between her and Richmond. In the novella, the heroine almost loses her husband, but he returns to her strong and loving. In reality Anny feared that she might lose her new-found love. While in this dilemma, Richmond sent her a telegram explaining that he had reconciled his mother to their engagement. Seemingly joyful, Anny accepted Richmond and his love for her. Her true feelings of fear and possible loss were relieved in the happy ending of her novella—in effect, her wish, her hope, rather than her certainty.

The setting of the story is Freshwater, to which Anny escaped from her trials in London, while the great house of the painter in the novella is that of the Tennysons (Farringford), in which she places the entire cast of Tennyson's family and friends. Eleven years after Tennyson had helped her with the ending of *The Village on the Cliff,* and again with Tennyson's guidance, Anny transposed her life into the fiction of *From an Island* and accepted her great good fortune. She wrote to a friend:

> If it were not Richmond, I should be afraid to take such a life's gift, but he knows his own mind so clearly, that this blessing of affection seemed to have lightened the darkness in which I have been living, and now at least I feel as if it were ungrateful indeed if we did not take the happiness which has come like a sort of miracle.[23]

Once again, there was a blessing in her life; nature had worked its miracle.

Anny's inheritance from her father was vast, and she had enriched her share in her own unique manner. She had inherited his friends, like Browning and Tennyson, and then gone on to forge her own relationships with them. She had inherited some of his ability to create unique and compelling novels, essays, and letters. Out of her own life she had created art. Thackeray's works and Thackeray himself were a part of Anny's life. When writing to announce her engagement (Letter 64) she compares her situation to that of two of her father's literary characters and then had wondered how he himself would have responded to the news. Anny had also inherited her father's love for domesticity and for children, and she fulfilled her desire for a family in an unusual manner. Anne Thackeray's letters of 1866–77, as well as her professional writing, show an author who has learned her craft and a woman who has come into her own.

LETTERS 51–65

To W. W. F. Synge

Letter 51   [1867]
Fales

What a delightful amusing letter you wrote me my dear WF.[1] & how glad I was to get it I hate writing so & have had so much to do lately that pen & ink always make me sick & that is why I have not answered before. I had a most delightful trip & am generaly flourishing except in one way it begins with an L & ends with a e — I send you all my best love & should like to see you again very much. I am going for a little bit with Minny to some baths w^h she has been sent to, for she has been ill & is still far from strong & cant walk a quarter of a mile. It is rather tiresome to pack up again so soon — Cant you Come & lunch one day — we dine out Im afraid almost everynight — say Chuseday or Wensday <u>if</u> you are in town

> yrs ever with love
> to dearest Hennee[2]
> <u>AIT</u>

To W. W. F. Synge

Letter 52   8br[1] 23 1867
Fales   The Eyrie,
                                                     Henley-on-Thames

Received from WWF Synge Esq. seventy five pounds being payment in full of all owing by him to my Father.

> Anne I Thackeray
> Leslie Stephen (for
> H.M. Stephen)

To Mrs. George Baxter

Letter 53
Columbia

[July 1868]¹
Oatlands Park Hotel
Walton on Thames

My dear Mrs Baxter

Your letter came yesterday when Minny was in London buying her little provisions for America, & I could not help opening it & beginning to cry over your dear kind familiar handwriting — It was a happy little cry making me feel that my dear was indeed going, but going to find one place at least where she would be at home & at peace with friends of our dearest Fathers choosing I know you will be so good to her, & indeed I do believe that seeing you is one of the very most [*sic*] things w^h take her to America. I feel as if a little bit of my life & ease of heart was going & yet I think I am right to stay behind — She is so true & clear & she looks with such simple bright eyes that I dont even feel as if I could keep my conscience straight without her for very long — Leslie too is a dear good old fellow & he adores Minny in his silent <u>dobbin</u> like way — This little note of mine will be brought out to you by a young friend of ours, of whom my Father was very fond, & he longs to make your acquaintance & I think I may introduce him to you. His name is Herman Merivale, his sisters are both in America & his father has just come back. Mr Merivale the father is Under Sec^{ty} for India — As I write there is a grand talk going on across my paper. Mr Appleton² is making out their route for them & leaning across the table, Leslie on the other side is smoking his pipe & asking questions Minny in her blue cap ribbons is opposite to me & writing it all down Outside theres the garden & the birds all singing in the sunshine. It seems like a little bit of USA here, the Storys are delightfully companionable, Mr Appleton as kind as kind can be, & there is a nice Mr Dexter³ who can talk to us about all of you & that is always a bond. How I wish your Lucy would take courage & come. She & I would go to Rome together & make all sorts of nice little expeditions & then I would come back to America & give her up safe into your hands. Dear Mrs Baxter it makes me so happy to think of Min quiet & safe with you & coming back to your home from various expeditions to tell you all about her impressions & to ask your advice & help in her various schemes & difficulties Theres nothing she thinks so pleasant as home & quiet & she hopes everybody <u>except</u> you will ask her to meet people & that you will never have anything but a home welcome for her

I am going off to Switzerland with my cousins for a fortnights trip the very day they start. I hope I shall meet Mr Longfellow[4] there & his daughters We shall be a large party & I mean to try & be as happy as I can & then to come back here & write my book until I see them again. My children are growing up into dear little companions now & Margy puts her arms round my neck & says Poor dear Aunt Anny I will 'em your handkerchiffs & make your tea when I am big. I send my love to Lucy & I am Dear Mrs Baxter

Affectionate
Anne Thackeray

To Lucy Baxter

Letter 54   [1870]
Columbia   Elm House. Wandsworth
       <u>Sunday</u>,

Here is a quiet Sunday morning dear Lucy for me to write & tell you how I thanked you for your last kind welcome letter I wish I was a better correspondent. I <u>think</u> my letters & then naturally they dont go. But now that I have come away into a more tranquil life I shall have time to write <u>once</u> at least to each of my friends. London is my home & always will be, but its almost too big a home for a person who isnt very decided or rich or strong & who has no good excuse for saying so. I have had to set up <u>health</u> but that <u>is</u> rather nonsense for I am quite well & only get knocked <u>up</u> if I do too much. However having set up health & a little convenient neuralgia — I have come off here for a fortnight to write all the morning & to my friends on Sunday.

I wonder if this is like an American house-hold. There are M.^{r} & Mrs Senior. She sings like a bird & has beautiful golden hair & has one big son at Oxford. Then there is old Mrs Senior very old & very ill with little funny rows of white curls — Then there is Mrs Hughes ye Mrs Seniors mother in whose room I am established — She is a brave old lady the mother of Tom Hughes the M.P.[1] you may have heard of — All round the room hang the pictures of a whole past away generation, & of her own sons — three of them are dead — They were g^t friends of

Leslies — his pupils at Cambridge. Then there is Hastings Hughes[2] a widower with 4 little children & a governess who also lives in this funny old Elm House & there is a long garden and beyond it a great wide plain crossed by railways that puff & scream & throb like the waves of the Sea. All the morning I write (only I am sorry to say nothing but <u>mice</u> come out [*sic*] these mountains of mss) & in the afternoon I think I generally go to London & see Minny for it is only a little way, & these whizzing trains are always ready to carry one off. (As I dip my pen into my inkstand I think that Papa's pen used to go into it once when he used to write to you) — I had a long talk about you the other day with Mr Bingham Mildmay[3] who took me in to dinner at Mrs Sartoris — I dont think I like him <u>very</u> much, tho' when he talked of you — all that bit of him was very very nice. Only he is so completely <u>alive</u> — & when I talk to people like that I feel as if I was little more <u>dead</u> than them & as if in that sense I had got on ahead of time. but it <u>may</u> be only fancy and[4] I suppose the meaning of life is to <u>live</u> & to <u>do</u> & that is better than feeling. He said I was to send <u>the</u> very <u>kindest</u> message I liked to your mother & you. I said I should <u>say</u> he remembered you. Mrs Mildmay is rather thin long faced & <u>aristocratic</u> looking — I wondered if she knew all about you all but I did not ask her. It was at Mrs Sartoris, there were diamond ladies & satin ladies — I had my best gown on & was deeply interested by the arrival of Lady Herbert of Lea[5] in a sort of beautiful sateen [?] like dress & wreaths of simple false plaits — what a shame of me — I cant scratch it out, as I ought to for she was <u>very</u> kind & said would I become a Catholic? & that she had reviewed all my stories in the Tablet.

<u>long time after. Easter Eve.</u>

I thought my beginning of a letter had gone to India dear Lucy & I looked for it in vain to send it off I am home again for a few days on my way to the Isle of Wight where all my cousins are, & my friends Mrs Cameron & our Alfred. He is not like Papa & yet he is in some ways, in a sort of simplicity w^h I think belongs to all really great men & I find myself turning again & again to Freshwater. Two days ago I went to see the dearest little American Lady for whom all our hearts have ached — Mrs Kühn[6] whose husband was killed at Rome out hunting. She & he were both great friends of mine at Rome. I daresay you will know of her, Minny fell in love with her twin sister in America. I wish you could see her going out smiling in blue satin. She looks bright & pink & happy thank God & dear old Leslie works away & smokes & writes & smokes till I can scarcely tell w^h is him & which is his pipe. They send all love & true greetings to you as I do. Did you ever get my book.⁷ It was sent addressed to you to the care of Messrs Putnam New York — a long time ago. This is just such a spring day as I remember it was when I wrote to you begging you to come to us that eventful summer when we went to Switzerland & met Minnys fate. Everything & nothing has happened since then — I only wish there was ever ever a chance of your coming to us even as much as there was then the Butlers⁸ are coming over Mrs Kemble writes — I have a presentiment that some day we shall know each other — and I neednt tell you that such as it is, our shabby little sunshiny home is yours dear Lucy always & at any time I went on Monday last to see the children — Little Anny wanted to come back with me very much — I feel rather frantic at times (but only for a minute or two) when I think of the slippery hold I have of everything I love⁹

it is a mistake — if it were only for this life it wouldnt matter but this is only an abstract speculation & means no more that it expresses And now I must finish dear Lucy & once more good bye. And with my love to your mother Believe me always

Y^rs affectionately
AIT

PS. I was ashamed of my abstract speculation & tore it off. So please forgive in [*word illegible*]

Memorandum

Letter 55 [Memorandum] Frognal,/Torquay¹
British Library {c. Spring or summer 1871}²
Add. Ms. 45741; 230–33

As I must leave off being young, I find many douceurs in [*sic*] — for I can drink as much wine as I like³ You will kindly make allowance for any indistinctness of writing by attributing it to this venial error.

    She⁴ never grizzled over her state, nor allowed her conscious superiority or intellig [*sic*] to claim distinction in her home. Tho an artist, she had no artistic temperament

An oblique reproach upon me.

Brought up in a kind of atmosphere wherein convention in the things that matter was omnipotent No "isms", & dogmatism is as hard to discover as scepticism.

Esther of Splendeurs[5] — Miseres de Courtisanes loves Lucien with a far more chaste affection than many a correct heroine. Mistresses of famous men not sensual M$^{\underline{me}}$ du Châtelet's relations with Voltaire based on affinity of lit. taste & critical appreciation more than phys. attraction.[6] Aspasia intellectual not sensual[7]

Whately remarks[8]
Authoresses can scarcely ever forget they are authors. They seem to feel a sympathetic shudder at exposing naked a female mind. They leave the mysteries of womanhood to be described by some interloping male, like Richardson or Marivaux who is turned out before he has seen half the rites & is forced to spin fr. his own conjectures the rest.[9] Woman rarely possesses the power of laughing at her own misfortunes. Humour the principal ingredient of the philosophic temperament Who is more humourless than the notoriously funny man? A large bulky figure (says Miss Austen) has as good a right to be in deep affliction as the most graceful set of limbs in the world.[10] She stayed in Hans Place.

To George Leslie

Letter 56
Princeton
AM20792

16, Onslow Gardens
S.W.
[1872][1]

Dear Mr Leslie[2]

I have been wondering what picture you are going to be kind enough to do for me for the second part — if by chance you were to do the little bit where Dolly throws a snow ball at Henley,[3] this is to say please that he is rather tall & inclined to be stout. I have always imagined him with fair hair & a composed expression & clean shaven with small barrister-like whiskers —

Please remember me to Mrs Leslie & believe me

Yours sincerely
AIThackeray

To Mrs. George Baxter

Letter 57
Columbia

Lion-sur-Mer[1]
August 17. [1872]

My dear Friend. A sort of fatality has prevented me from writing to you for a long long time & even now I am almost afraid that this one of my many letters may never reach you — But I have seen Mr Strong[2] & heard of you f.^m him & I must try to write once more though I am ashamed to say that after he left I searched through the house in vain for the little card he had given me with y^r address. Minnie says perhaps by sending this to y^r niece it may reach you, & so my letter shall go to Minnie in Cornwall first before it starts on its journey to America.

Dearest Mrs Baxter how can I write to you of this terrible & unexpected sorrow[3] Your life seems to me one long sorrow & one long love. How Papa would have felt your loss. I remember so well how he came back describing you all, & telling us that perhaps your son was coming to stay with us for a long time & we have the picture still in the old book at home & I can hear him telling me y^r childrens names & ages, how he loved you all. My heart aches as I think of you & I send you, dear unknown familiar friend my love & truest sympathy.[4] Words dont come very easily but they mean that our hearts are with you & dear Lucy & the past which is so much my life & my present, that it comes before me far more vividly than do these little Norman Gables & corners & the voices in the moonlit court.

Minnie is in Cornwall in a little green gably house, & I have come here with the children for an unlucky whooping cough made it risky for us to be in the same house with little delicate Laura — (here I must tell you that indeed I wrote to tell you of her dear little existence but something as usual must have happened to the letter)

It was such a pleasure to me before we left London to see y^r brother & to hear of you, & to try & trace some likeness to the face I have always imagined to be yours. I was less fortunate in missing your niece to whom I wrote to the address she gave, but my letter of course came back through the dead letter office.

This is another green over grown place with a garden & an old Marquise in a camisole & the little Norman church chiming in the sunshine & moonlight & the dear little girls scampering about very happy as I need scarcely say. I have also a bright young couple of cousins here with some more sweet little God children of mine & the old Marchioness & I contemplate our respective families from the two ends of the garden. It is close to the place we came to ten years ago nearly with Grannie & where I wrote The Village on the Cliff here nothing seems changed. There are the cotton nightcaps & the melons & the bathers; its a sort of Pompei with little feasts all the way down the street & great shining fish coming up out of the sea & tumblers & a gladiator or two & the most astounding chatter & barter This morning I quite frightened a poor old thing with pots of butter by saying do ask the real price I am so very busy, & have no time to beat you down. I found I had quite hurt her feelings. I must finish this tonight & take it into Caen tomorrow where they will know the way to America — Here the good old woman who keeps the stamp shop can only send to England & Paris & Switzerland at the farthest — Today I sent a little scrap for Leslie who is at Zermatt now & who wanted a holiday for he was so thin & so over-worked when I came away that I was quite unhappy about him.

Minnie is looking very well & thank God the little one is growing & getting stronger She can almost walk & almost talk & she is the most tender little heart. She has a little look of my dearest Father sometimes [5] but she is even more like Leslie She is so fond of music & sings with happiness when the sun shines or when her Mother takes her — My last letter was full of poor Minnies troubles with a little donkey whose Mama gives Laura milk for breakfast It was rather affecting & that is why I will put the little letter in if I can find it.

I should <u>dearly</u> like a letter from you or Lucy now & then though I know that with you as with me writing makes but little difference, but still I do long to hear from your own self how you are & all of you — and goodnight dear Mrs Baxter & God bless you & yourn. & help you & keep you prays

Your affectionate
Anne Thackeray

Please write to 16 Onslow Gardens

To Robert Browning

Letter 58　　　　　　　　　　　6. Stanhope Gardens
Yale　　　　　　　　　　　　　 Wednesday
　　　　　　　　　　　　　　　 12.3.1873¹

My dear M.ʳ Browning

This is too provokingly absurd & disappointing & tiresome & not to be thought of. I <u>am</u> so sorry for you. I cant imagine anything more maddening. What should I do if after all our work & trouble anything so impossible were to come & stop one, but I do hope the counsels will find out that it is all nonsense² — Who ever heard of any Frenchman except M.ʳ Milsand³ who ever read an English book, & besides — after having it all in the papers — It sounds too absurd altogether. Meanwhile I want to see the book more & more & do please dear M.ʳ Browning relent & send me the proofs & most most sympathetically

　　　　　　　　　　　　　　　　　　　　　Yours sincerely
　　　　　　　　　　　　　　　　　　　　　<u>Anne Thackeray</u>

From Leslie Stephen to AIT

Letter 59　　　　　　　　　　　8 Southwell Gardens
Ray/Morgan　　　　　　　　　　South Kensington
　　　　　　　　　　　　　　　 1.1.74

Dearest Anny,

This is my first letter this year & I send it to you with all appropriate good wishes. I only wish that it could be more cheerful; but that is out of the question just now.

Poor little Laura is still coughing & it is a severe trial for Minny. I dont believe that it is really anything to trouble ourselves about much. The doctor has been here this morning & promises that she shall be better tonight; he says that it is merely a cold & with no bad symptoms; & moreover she is quite cheerful & always playing with her toys. It is all the more pathetic to look at her dear little face & see it always cheerful though she is tormented by this hideous cough. And Minny is made so nervous by it that I have great trouble in calming her at all. I hope she will be better by the time you return; but I tell you of new trouble — wh. I have not diminished because I think you would prefer it.

The sheer melancholy weighs upon us at times. I fear — I cant quite say how much I fear or precisely what: but I fear at least that we shall all have to look back upon this time as a very solemn one. No words can say how beautiful my mother seems to me now; or how kind & good she is. But I seem every day to have less hopes for any length of time. I have lately observed more distinctly an uncertainty of mind, wh. is so gentle that it is hardly painful except as a symptom; but I cannot but think of the time when she will no longer be present to make us better whenever we see her.[1]

You know that I cant speak to you when you are here. I cant even write very easily; but I must say one thing. Of all the good you & Minny have done for me, there is one thing for wh. I shall love you as long as I have any love left in me. It is that somehow you have not only comforted my mother during her last years, but you have brought me nearer to her. I am sometimes saddened when I think of her fondness for me & think how little I used to deserve it. Latterly I hope I have been better to her, &, if I have, it is chiefly because you two have been a new influence in our family & thawed us all with kindness. When I laugh at your sentiment, dont fancy for a moment that I ever do or can forget, what I owe to it in making my relations to my mother easier & better. I wont say any more; perhaps I shall never say as much again.

Goodbye dearest Anny & the happiest of all possible years to you

Your affte
LS

I think I have rather exaggerated darling Memee's[2] ailment It is rather very vexatious than serious.

From Robert Browning to AIT

Letter 60
Baylor

19. Warwick Crescent, W
Jan. 29. '74

Dear Miss Thackeray,

I feel properly humiliated. On referring to the Poem, I find the line to be simply

"Far from the shore, far from the trembling throng"[1] — & so forth. How the other reading got into my head, I can't guess. Do forgive my blundering memory!

Ever truly yours
Robert Browning

From Robert Browning to AIT

Letter 61
Baylor

19. Warwick Crescent, W
Dec. 4. '74

Dear Miss Thackeray

We never got any note, or you should have been properly thanked, depend on it: Sarianna[1] will call with this & tell you so. I ought not to go out, I believe, but how can I deny myself so great a delight as to do as I am bidden so kindly?

Ever yours most truly,
Robert Browning

To Mrs. George Baxter

Letter 62
Columbia

[Dec. 1875]

My dear Mrs Baxter

I knew you would write to me when I looked at my half written letter to you. I think I am writing to tell you that Papa is dead. It always seems to be that come back, not anything new.

About my darling I have no words & I am still so unaccustomed to it that I dont feel I think very much — only that I have the tenderest faithfullest most unspeakably loving sister that all one ever ever had She was expecting her confinement & well comparatively speaking & she talked quite cheerfully w.h she had never done before of her dear little baby, & one day I went away for a night —

You see it is my Fate — & she was dead when I came back next day, with tender closed eyes and a face so radiant. It was Papas illness killed her not her little baby, w.h never was born, some convulsion. — We had no parting only she had been so very tender — like a mother

Poor Leslie has been so good but so wrung & strained & theres plenty to do for a time till our turns come. The card said your Lucy had oh! such lovely eyes: and you two have gone through this & other sorrows all your lives — But if death is only our dearest it seems to lose all its terrors. Of course Leslie & I are going on together with Meme & I shall have the children & everything I ever wanted, except the light & warmth & tender blessing of our home w.h came f.m her.

Y.r affectionate
old old friend

To George Eliot

Letter 63
Berg

11 Hyde Park Gate South
October 17. [1876]¹

My dearest M.rs Lewes. I have had a letter from an American gentleman who has been to see us once or twice — & please would you be so very good as to read it — & if you wouldnt mind — let him come one Sunday to see you. I sh.d be so obliged — He knew Leslie & my Minnie in America

I hope you are pretty well & rested from y.r work² — I have felt it come Very home to me — it is the first book I have ever read without Minnie & does not seem to me quite a book so much as something w.h has been.

I hope to come & see you in a few weeks — but for the present, I am thankful for a bad cold w.h gives me a real reason for keeping quiet Little Meme has been very well all the summer, but she is not quite right just now. Nor indeed is her Father — but he is coming to see you & I am sure you will do him good & M.ʳ Lewes³ too.

Believe me

Yours very sincerely
Anne Thackeray.

I have a great happiness in Margie and Annie who have come for two years.

To W. W. F. Synge

Letter 64
Fales   [1877]

My dear WWF

I had hoped so much to have seen you this time but I am going away again today & I only came out [?] for one night — for Leslie sent for me to settle [?] something —
Dear WF. I am going to marry Richmond Ritchie¹ who is years & years younger than I am but who has cared [sic] me so long & with such wonderful fidelity & unchangeableness that I have no courage to say no to the happiness it will be to us both to belong to each other It is much nearer to Lady Maria than to Lady Esmond² only then his feeling has been like Esmond, without any Beatrix or change for nearly seven years I have wondered & wondered what My Father would have said — I think perhaps — if he had known all — he might have agreed³ Leslie has been so, so, kind & M.ʳˢ Ritchie has agreed most anxiously & affectionately & will you tell Hennie with my love f.ᵐ

Y.ʳ affect old Friend
AIT

To Henrietta Synge

Letter 65
Fales

11 H.P.G.S.
[May 1877]

Dearest Hennee

Thankyou. I knew y.^{r} kind heart would understand & sympathise with the strange happiness which has come so unperceivedly into my life. Richmond has been away ever since it was settled so that at times I almost imagine it is all a strange dream. But it is no dream & no vague story — all is true all his goodness & faithful affection & now that I <u>know</u> all my life contained, it seems to go back & back into the past & bind it all & heal its bitter ache — Margie & Annie are so good about it They are to stay on with kind Leslie & my sweet little Meme will have her 'chicks' as she calls them to keep her company — I have been looking at little houses all round about Young Street is now so grand that they ask 500 for 2 years lease I am very busy arranging all sorts of things but when I can & when Richmond can spare the time (for he is just coming up) I or we will come gladly & spend a day with you — Mama is now at Wimbledon & I go to her when I can, she has got the most charming little house there, & we are to be married in July,[1] & R^d will begin his India Office quite directly — he is coming up on Friday & do tell WF[2] with my best love that I shall be at home all the mor^g & dearest Hennee I give you a loving enfold & am y.^{r} affectionatest

AIT

6

1878

INTRODUCTION

> when My darling [Minny] died I heard his [Thackeray's] voice saying poor Nan but now I think we shall all be together again some day, & if it is not God's will, at least it has once been his will to make us all, & when I think of them & of Richmond & of you my dearest children I don't know how to thank God
> (1878 Journal)

ALTHOUGH it covers much the same period as the 1864 journal, the 1878 journal is strikingly different. In 1864 Anny had just begun to write seriously. She was a distraught daughter mourning for Thackeray. By 1878 Anne Thackeray Ritchie was a writer of some note. As the wife of Richmond, she was expecting her first child. Time had alleviated her grief for her father and even for Minny. However, Thackeray, and to a lesser degree Minny, were still important to Anny. Indeed, this journal, ostensibly written for Minny's daughter, Laura, is really an epistle to Thackeray and Minny. Anny writes an *apologia pro vita sua* in two senses: this is the story of her life; it is also an apology to her father and her sister for the happy life she is leading. They are both dead and she, Anny, is alive and has had the good fortune to become a writer, a wife, and a mother-to-be.

One significant difference between the two journals is that the 1864 journal was written for no one to read—not even Anny herself—while the 1878 journal is addressed to Laura. The earlier journal is an effusion of emotion; the later one is a conscious piece of writing. For a parent or a close relative to write a family history was a common Victorian practice. What is strange is that Anny writes as if Laura were a normal child who is going to lead a normal life. Until Minny's death, Laura appeared to be normal; at least there is no intimation in any letters or journals that she is not.

However, after Minny's death there was a marked difference in Laura. Whether this was due to the loss of her mother or whether it was the onset of mental problems is all conjectural. Overly sensitive to the fact that his mother-in-law, Isabella, was insane, Leslie Stephen harbored "the vague dread . . . . [of] hereditary taint."[1] Like Stephen, Winifred Gérin believed that "[t]he terrible heritage feared by Thackeray for Minny . . . had mercifully passed over one generation, to blight the next."[2] However, Laura was declared mentally deficient, while Isabella had drifted into schizophrenia only after suffering postpartum depression.[3] As she grew older, it became obvious that Laura, for whatever reason, was not normal. In Stephen's description of Laura in the *Mausoleum Book,* she was first a "backward child," then "mentally deficient" (44). By 1878, when Anny wrote this journal, she must have been aware of this. Yet, Anny ignores her niece's abnormalities. In describing how she came to write *The Story of Elizabeth,* Anny tells Laura that "perhaps [it] will amuse you to read [it] some day."

Anny persists in writing the journal as if Laura will lead a normal life. "If my Meme lives to be a woman & to marry, it must be somebody good who speaks the truth & who tries to help others." In this journal Anny recasts the truth in order to be of help and comfort to Laura. For example, Anny emphasizes her own childhood misbehavior in order to reassure Laura that her misbehavior is not unusual. Anny wanted to let Laura know that life was worth living however difficult it may seem at the moment.

At this particular time, when Anny was expecting a child who would be Laura's cousin, the prospect of hereditary mental disorder (as it was considered in those days) was too dreadful for Anny to contemplate. And so Anny, usually so honest, would not recognize that Laura was mentally deficient or, even worse, tainted with Isabella's madness. In this journal Anny refers openly, but in vague terms, to Isabella's illness. After Minny was born, Anny writes, Thackeray was "in great trouble" because of a "deep sorrow." Later, Anny explains that "[o]ur Mama was ill" and the doctor said "it was better we should not go & see her"; still later she confirms that "[m]y Mama was ill & away." Even if Laura had been a normal child, Anny would have found it difficult to explain Isabella's schizophrenia to an eight year old. The journal, however, was written to be read not only by Laura the child but by Laura the woman, as many revelations of an adult nature show. Anny's ability to discuss Isabella could be due to the fact that Anny was expecting a child, and sympathy and love for her mother were reawakened.

On the surface, the mood of the journal is charming and delightful. In order to make one incident more pleasant, Anny alters facts. In her description of their nightmare journey to Paris after Isabella went insane, Anny writes: "The next thing I can remember is being in the dark in a diligence & the baby was crying & I began to cry & my Father struck a light to cheer me up. There was a sick man in the corner moaning & then the dawn came." In the 1864 journal Anny explains how Thackeray blew out the light because she would not stop crying and then she mourns: "Has the light gone out now for us? because we were not quiet & good — I pray that the sun may rise & a day of peace & forgiving & love for weary aching hearts once more." In the 1864 journal Anny prays that "the sun may rise," but in the later journal she states that "then the dawn came." With adult wisdom, and happy in her new life, Anny provides a happy ending to a painful episode in her life.

In the earlier journal Anny is still enmeshed in overwhelming guilt and acute sadness at the recent death of her father. In the later journal time has lessened her guilt. In general, most of the incidents Anny recalls in the later journal are of a pleasant or happy nature. Even those that are not take on an acceptance colored by time. Anny, the mature woman of forty-one, writes that M. Monod "was a good man & did his duty & when he preached to us, it was not what he said but his whole heart & life that seemed to reach us." This is a facet of Monod that Anny can only concede twenty-five years after the fact. Her grandmother's Evangelicalism, reinforced by the French preacher's sermons, had been the scourge of Anny's young life. In the 1878 journal she acknowledges that Monod's theories were at odds with those of Thackeray and of Anny herself. Her earlier passionate denial of Monod's religion has dissipated. Instead, she carefully examines the man's motives and his intentions. Her need to assert herself, to strike out for independence, is gone. What emerges is a more levelheaded and dispassionate appraisal of her earlier life, an appraisal composed by a professional writer.

All of Anny's memories are not happy ones. Nevertheless, in the retelling, they lose the horror of childhood miseries. She relates quite matter-of-factly how naughty she was as a child and what punishments were meted out to her; she does not dwell on the injustice or the unhappiness. For example, "Grandmama [Thackeray's grandmother] was very unkind & always scolded me . . . I was very naughty . . . I ran away three times . . . I must have been a very discontented child . . . I was always in disgrace." Aside from running away, she never mentions the crimes which resulted in the following punishments: "I was shut up in a cupboard . . . I was shut up in my room . . . I was whipped." None of these punishments, it must be noted, was administered by Thackeray. Most of her infractions stemmed from unhappiness. She ruminates that she was "out of temper & jealous & suspicious"; repeatedly she remarks how unhappy she was. Much of her anxiety was due to Thackeray's absence or illness, but a great deal of her unhappiness was part of growing up, made more difficult by Isabella's absence.

Despite the fact that Thackeray's daughters came back to London to live once more with him, they could not shed their feelings of insecurity. "[W]e could not bear the manservant whose name was Samuel James. He was very clever & very fond of Papa & he was always thinking what he could do for him, & Mommee & I were afraid that Papa would like him better than us." As an adult, Anny adds, "Were not we silly little girls?"; but as children Minny and Anny no doubt suffered. Here again, Anny alleviates the pain of the past with an adult amelioration.

Just as Anny was jealous about Thackeray's manservant, she was even more jealous of Minny. Anny recounts an early dream about Minny when she was still a baby. "One night I dreamt somebody had cut the babys two little feet off & I scrambled out of bed & went to look at her & O I was so glad to see her warm & sound asleep. I had never loved her till then but then I loved her." Aside from the violence in the dream, what is most striking is that after the dream Anny loved Minny. Was it the relief she felt because Minny was uninjured and that she, Anny, had not harmed her? Jealous as she must have been over a new baby, she could for the first time love her. Or perhaps Anny *had* to love Minny in order to keep herself from committing a crime against her. In any case, it is apparent that the incident was one Anny did not forget. She does not mention this dream in the 1864 journal, most likely because it was too painful for her to deal with. However, in 1878 the dream has metamorphosed into a memory with a happy ending—Minny was unhurt and Anny loved her.

More noticeable in this journal than in the 1864 journal is the constant upheaval that Anny and Minny endured. Aside from Isabella leaving their home, they were yanked back and forth between Thackeray's home and the Carmichael-Smyths.' Not only were their guardians switched, but their place of residence changed. The continual parade of inadequate governesses added to the predicament of the shaky household. Anny dwells on their life as children; she reveals two little girls, on the one hand oppressed in the home of the Carmichael-Smyths, on the other hand spoiled and petted by Thackeray and afraid to believe in the permanence of life with their father. Even after they were teenagers their life of vagabondage continued.

But in remembering her life for Laura, Anny reshapes it to make a happy story by relating (in addition to unhappy events) how they used to go to "childrens parties in white muslin frocks, to Mr. Dickens & Mr. Macreadys"; how they read "piles & piles of the most beautiful delightful wonderful fairy tale books"; how Thackeray bought them "2 wax dolls" and gave them "bigger helps of jam" and took them to see the Diorama and the Colosseum. Even this recitation of the delights of childhood is shadowed by the fear that Thackeray will spend too much money on them, and yet they are memories of a loving father doing what he could for his daughters. Anny admits that she thought, when she was very young, that he was Jesus Christ. Anny the woman understands that when Isabella left their home "Papa was very lonely at times for we were only little girls." Her own life until she married Richmond was much like Thackeray's—she had her work, Amy's children to care for, but no one to love. Now married to Richmond, she could fully appreciate the void that had been in her life, and which existed in Thackeray's once Isabella was gone. This unclouded view of her early life lends a maturity to the vision which is absent in the 1864 journal.

However, in other appraisals of her life, she is still trapped in her early sense of guilt and wickedness. Her repeated self-accusations of being naughty are vague and unsubstantiated (except for her running away), merely declarations of bad conduct. Was she in reality so naughty or does she only think so? Does she think it is wicked to enjoy the good life when Thackeray and Minny are dead? Particularly in the case of Minny, where Anny is still not able to deal completely with her jealousy, there appears to be a problem. The sisters loved each other: "we had lived just the same life together like the married .... we were not much parted." But Minny married and before she died was on the verge, according to Leslie Stephen, of asking Anny to set up a home of her own. Anny's jealousy was not a new feeling—it is apparent in the 1864 journal in unguarded bursts. "What a pretty little girl your sister is" someone tells her, but there is no reply or comment from the adult Anny. Of the young woman Minny, Anny writes, "All of a sudden yr Mama had become quite grown up & so pretty & beautiful that people hardly recognized her." This is praise of a rather dubious nature. Although Anny recounts disagreements they had with other children, she does not remember any differences with Minny. Anny remembers Minny crying, throwing a shoe at the housemaid, hiding from Thackeray, but never doing anything wrong to her personally. Anny's memory is here exceptionally selective and this in itself may be cause for further guilt. Anny's guilt may have stemmed from the perception that despite the fact that Anny was naughty and Minny good, Minny died and Anny is alive. In writing this journal, Anny tries to come to terms with her guilt. By accepting her jealousy, she can dissolve her guilt, and really love Minny. In understanding herself and her motives, she is able to recognize that none of these feelings are absolutes and that none of them can be completely eradicated, only deactivated. In discussing Richmond, she writes: "I think that is religion, to be true & good & that is why I love your poppee because he is sincere & so thank God is my Richmond who married me when I was so ill & old & unhappy & who has not loved me a bit the less for that." Anny finds it necessary to explain why she married Richmond. She apologizes for cutting short her grief and for finding happiness. After Minny died, Anny heard Thackeray's voice "saying poor Nan but now I think we shall all be together again some day, & if it is not God's will, at least it has once been his will to make us all, & when I think of them & of Richmond & of you my dearest children I don't know how to thank God." Anny was now ready to lay away her guilt and accept the realities of her present good life. As for God, she could only hope that He, along with Thackeray and Minny, would approve.

In the 1864 journal Anny reviews her life with Thackeray. There is no chronological sequence to it; her feelings and thoughts lead her into examination of past events without any regard to when they happened. In the 1878 journal Anny makes a strong attempt to impart a narrative sequence to occurrences. She is telling a story using chronological ordering. For example, on the first and second pages she wrote, "The first time I saw y.ʳ Mommee . . . Then I can remember her as a little baby . . . and The next thing I can remember." She also tries to anchor events in time. She explained that in "1848 there was a revolution in France & people were afraid that in England too all sorts of terrible things wᵈ happen" and "The Crimea was the autumn after our winter in Rome. . . . It must have been the following summer that the still more wretched news of the Indian Mutiny came to us in beautiful sunshiny weather." She took note of these great historical events as they affected her life; they were signposts for personal occasions.

Although she changed facts of the incident in the coach to Paris, she usually did try to be scrupulously honest. However, she did not wholly trust her memory. In 1869, she wrote from Rome, "Yesterday was like one of the days one remembers, but the thing is one doesn't remember it!"[4] Aware as she is of this, she tries in the 1878 journal to verify facts. "I must get my dates into order for I find I cannot quite remember when everything happened." And at a later time someone, probably Anny herself, inserted dates and clarifications in the journal.

How important getting things right was to her in the 1878 journal is evidenced by the changes made in the manuscript. In the 1864 journal three deletions occur: two are grammatical and only one is a suppression of fact, probably made at a much later date: "The little Ritchies were with us." In the later journal there is a conscious groping after the factual truth, while in the earlier journal Anny searched through her feelings for verities. In the 1878 journal "our governess was now called Miss Trulock" is crossed out and in its place is "We had a governess called Miss Alexander." This change and others like it are not important in themselves, but they show how consciously and honestly Anny was trying to re-create her life with Minny; she was also the artist writing a unified and logical piece of work. All of her work from this time forth is that of a writer of integrity, conscious of her craft.

Because this journal was written by a writer, not by an unhappy daughter as the earlier journal was, Anny included lyrical descriptions of occurrences, places, and people. Of her first tour of the Continent with Thackeray, Anny wrote:

> We went to Vienna & to Venice & to Milan & we lost our shoes & our shifts & our collars & I think we came home with very little besides a chessboard in our trunk. But it was all so lovely & so wonderful the things we didnt lose were the pictures & the places I can see them now after all these long years & years when I look for them.

Another domestic account deals with her first sight of Rome where the Thackerays spent the winter of 1853.

> It seemed all golden like the great picture at Venice when we landed at Civita Vecchia. . . . I daresay it all looks just the same blue sky & beggars in the sun & shadows & lovely old sloping ruins & arched palaces. As we got to Rome it was evening & papa said Look out there is St Peters. & we looked out & a great dark <u>living</u> sort of dome seemed to hunch up its shoulders as we drove under the stars

When Anny revisited Rome in 1869 she wrote that Rome is "a great deal bigger, grander, <u>Romer</u> than we remember it even. . . . I find one of the odd effects of Rome is to set one longing, I don't know for what exactly."[5] The vistas of Rome, both physical and psychological, were more accessible to the adult than to the young girl. The Eternal City also weighed heavily on a spinster with no one to follow her in the historical continuum, which was so palpable in Rome. But in the 1878 journal, none of this complicated adult feeling surfaces in Anny's remembrance of Rome, where all has become light and beauty.

In addition to providing descriptions of events and places, Anny displays her skill in presenting portrayals of people. One of the many governesses who cared for her and Minny was "a funny little short long nosed punch like woman." A fascinating example of how Anny reworked idiosyncrasies of real people she knew into characters for her fiction starts with some thumbnail descriptions of friends in Mennecy when she lived there with the Carmichael-Smyths. Of an actual acquaintance Anny wrote, "There was M. le Maire who used to come in & squint & sing till one couldnt help laughing." This profile prefigures the character of the mayor, Fontaine, in *The Village on the Cliff*, but instead of singing badly, Anny's hero plays the cornet badly. In her novel, Anny takes this mere suggestion of a character and builds him into a sympathetic, vulnerable human being. In "Across the Peat-Fields," a short story published in 1881, Anny uses the same basic Frenchman, also called Fontaine, but here he becomes a fussier, more comic secondary character who plays the fiddle, also badly.

Her stay in Mennecy furnished her with the embryos of other characters: Major Carmichael-Smyth evolved into the narrator's granduncle in "Across the Peat-Fields"; and a neighboring playmate became her heroine Pauline. In the 1878 journal the passages referring to these people she knew read like sketches for her fictional portraits. In the opening paragraph of "Across the Peat-Fields," Anny writes that it is

> a story in which some true things were told with others that were not true, all blended together in that same curious way in which, when we are asleep, we dream out allegories, and remembrances, and indications that we scarcely recognize when we are awake. Story-telling is, in truth, a sort of dreaming, from which the writer only quite awakes when the last proof is corrected. (145)

This is the technique that Anny uses to record the story of her life in her journal of 1878.

At the end of the journal, Anny describes her life with Minny until the famous housewarming of Palace Green in 1862. This event, with its glowing fires, opulent food, and distinguished guests, went on for two days. It was the high point of Anny's life and centered on the production on both nights of Thackeray's play *The Wolves and the Lamb*. "I suppose this is the summit. I shall never feel so jubilant so grand so wildly important & happy again."[6] Surrounded by the beauties of the new house Thackeray had built, Anny was virtually its mistress: "it seemed too delightful to think that we were really & truly going to live in this beautiful place & be young ladies & have fun & society & see life." Her memories of the housewarming and her part in it are so happy that she is able to praise Minny and her performance in the play with only slight jealousy.

Anny "ordered the supper" and received the company, which meant that she greeted the guests, most likely standing by Thackeray's side. For Anny at that time, this was the "summit." This tableau then, is the ending Anny chose for her life with Thackeray—a happy ending rather than one culminating in death, as in reality it did. Anny describes their life at Palace Green for another page and then abruptly ends with an unfinished sentence, "Cousin Emmy came to stay with me while [Minny] was away. & y.ʳ . . ." The journal proper ends here with an unfinished sentence but with a completed idea. The journal is a unified whole, beginning in 1840 and ending in 1862, which was exactly the time span Anny chose for her narrative.

Descriptions of two additional scenes written on the same loose paper, but perhaps written by Anny at a later date, are folded with the pages of Anny's journals. The first relates to a memory from when Anny was a very young girl, a story of sorrow becoming relief. One autumn, Anny, Minny, and Amy Crowe were enjoying a holiday in Wales; Thackeray was on the Continent; the Carmichael-Smyths were in Scotland.

> When one day about 3 o'c . . . I saw a little telegraph boy coming along the path . . . I thought it was bad news of my Papa & I hardly could open the paper But the telegram was from Grannie in Scotland dear kind old GP had died quite suddenly. & so we packed up & set off that evening. It was a long long tiring journey & we were very sad & still very frightened about our Father . . . then we went to the inn still very frightened . . . & we said our name was Thackeray . . . the waiter said There is a gentleman of that name in bed upstairs. . . . then we rushed into Papas room & there he was quite well & sound asleep.

A journey such as this—to attend a funeral—for two Victorian women, alone, aged twenty-one and eighteen, was a frightening experience. Of the major's death Anny writes that "[t]he first break that came in our home was when our kind old Grandpapa died." Anny insists that "the first break" to the Thackeray family was her grandfather's death and not Isabella's illness, which necessitated the dismantling of their home in London and Anny's virtual loss of her mother. Even in retrospect, so many years later, Anny cannot recognize Isabella's insanity for the tragedy it was. And despite the sadness of losing their much loved GP, the trip ended happily because Thackeray, well and sound asleep, was waiting for them.

A final, fragmentary page of writing, in Anny's hand, depicts a beautiful scene of Anny looking out a window and watching Minny dance; Minny "would turn round & round as quick as she could go & then her hair would seem like a burning bush." Anny describes her own position as an observer and a recorder of life—as a mature author examining her past and creating art out of her life.

Unlike the 1864 journal, the 1878 journal is consciously planned and executed. The writing is smoother, and the feelings are more refined and artfully conceived. Despite this deceptive outer crust, the underlayers of the journal are meaningful and substantial. The journal is remarkable for its presentation of a woman who, though happy, still needs to justify herself to her dead sister and father. Able at last to cope with her guilt, Anny enters into a new life; the 1878 journal is a fitting epilogue to the old.

JOURNAL

Ray/Morgan
MA 4500[1]

Part I

The first time I saw y.^r Mommee she was all wrapped in flannel & lying on our old nurses[2] knee. My nurse said Come here Missy & look at y.^r little sister. And I said but I cant see her Brodie & Brodie said look at her kicking her little feet. Then I can remember her as a little baby with a long green veil because her eyes used to be sore We were in Ireland up on a hill — There were sloping fields leading to a great wide river & ships were floating, & in one of the fields some beautiful buttercups were growing. & somehow I used to run away by myself & play with some other little children in the field & a kind old gentleman used to come up with his pockets full of apples. One day the nurse let me tie the babys green veil on my hat & as I ran along it floated beautifully in the air. Your Grandpapa was quite young in those days[3] & in great trouble but he always laughed & made the best of his great deep sorrow The next thing[4] I can remember is being in the dark in a diligence & the baby[5] was crying & I began to cry & my Father struck a light to cheer me up. There was a sick man in the corner moaning & then the dawn came My Papa has told me since that it was a most weary terrible night Then we got to Paris to our Grandmama & Grandpapa & to a young lady with long black hair we called Aunt Mary.[6] They all lived in an old house w^h has long since been pulled down nr. the Arc[7] My Grandmama was quite young too & very beautiful & tall & kind We called her Grannie & her mother[8] also came to live with us & we called her Grandmama. She had a brown face & bright dark eyes I used to go out walking with my little sister who still wore her green veil & who used to wake me up at night & in the morning by crying piteously. Our Papa went away & we stayed with our Grandmothers. Grannie was very kind & Grandmama was very unkind & always scolded me but she could not help loving the poor darling little baby. One night I dreamt somebody had cut the

197

babys two little feet off & I scrambled out of bed & went to look at her & O I was so glad to see her warm & sound asleep. I had never loved her till then but then I loved her. We went into the country that year & we used to spend the day in a big forest under the trees & pick tiny little blue deep flowers that I made into wreaths & y.^r Mommee used to wear a tiny little pink frock. One day when we had just done some luncheon someone said look look at Baby, & baby was beginning to walk & holding on to the chairs. I was very naughty that day & I had refused to say grace, but my Grannie was so pleased with Baby for beginning to walk that I was forgiven I used to be naughty every day like naughty Lucy.[9] Once I picked some cherries off a tree once I kicked a gentleman's legs once I was shut up in a cubboard. I also ran away three times

Margie & Annies mama[10] was a little girl in those days but she was much older than I & their Uncle George[11] was a baby & they were all in this country place. They lived in a delightful old house with a round hole in the wall through w^h I could climb backwards & forwards. There was also a boy called Frank Hankey[12] who used to twist my arm round & round. One summers day a little girl in the house died & all the little children came dressed in white and carried her away. When we went back to Paris our Grannie bought a nice little green cart for Minnie to go out in. Sometimes as a great treat I was allowed to get in too. We used to have big bits of bread given to us & a penny each & our nurse used to drag us to a little shop where they sold milk & we used to breakfast in the little shop & then go on to a green shady terrace & spend long mornings out of doors. Minnie drank her milk but never would eat much She used to run away from the table & sometimes my Grannie used to give her her dinner under the table. She never liked Rhubarb or vegetables or puddings Our good old Brodie had gone away to England & was living with M.^r & Mrs Darwin[13] who had a little girl of my own age called Annie too. We had a new nurse a funny little short long nosed punch like woman called Justine[14] who was very very fond of y.^r Mommee & took great care of her. Our Aunt Mary was married by this time & we were all living in the Champs Elysées in a big house called the Maison Valin. One day Aunt Mary went to India, but about a week after she left our Grandmama told us to go upstairs one morning & when we went up with the maid she took us into a room we had never seen before & there was a little boy in his bath. It was our little cousin, Aunt Mary's little boy[15] who had fallen ill on the way to Marseilles & been sent back to live with us. We were so enchanted we thought he would melt away & become a dream. Our Papa used to come & see us from time to time & I thought he was Jesus Christ. Once he went to Jerusalem[16] & when he came back he had funny little mustachios & y.r Mommee cried & would only kiss him through a newspaper so he went into his room & shaved them off & came out quite smoothe & gave her a kiss.[17] I liked seeing him shave very much he used to go so quick & so straight. Sometimes when he was dressing & we were there he would tear out long paper pictures with little pigs all trotting after one another. We always went away in the summer. One year we went to Montmorency where I was very unhappy & naughty & shut up in my room for a long time & I was whipped   Another year we went to Chaudfontaine[18] in Belgium & then y.r Mommee was a little girl about four years old. She & I used to dance together & little Charles Carmichael used to sit & kick on the floor. One day Grannie told me a great secret. We were to go over to England to pay our Papa a visit and all night long we were sick in a ship & in the morning it was England & we went to a dear little village called Fareham n.r Southampton to an old aunt[19] in an old house with blue china pots & old pictures. One of them was the gentleman in the red coat[20] that poppee[21] will show you   He was our Grannie's papa & the husband of the old brown lady[22] & he was the brother of Aunt Becher with whom we went to stay. It was very rainy weather when we were at Fareham & our Grannie bought us each a little pair of pattens. There was a little girl there of my own age called Mariana & her Aunt Miss Pooke & Mommee went to see some of the old ladies & I went to see some of the others & then we paid a visit to some friends in a country home[23] on a hill & we put on our best india frocks & blue sashes every day   Magdalene[24] will show you the picture of M.rs Barlow[25] the lady with whom we stayed.

Then we went to London[26]   Our Father was living in London[27] in chambers opposite S.t James Palace[28] & he came to meet us at the station & immediately gave us each 2 wax dolls. & at breakfast he gave us bigger helps of jam than we had ever had in our lives & after breakfast he took us to feed the ducks in S.t James Park, & then he bought us picture books the Arabian Nights & Grimms Fairy Tales & then he took us to a diorama & to the Colosseum.[29] I thought he would spend all the money he had in the world when I saw how much he had to pay for us. One day he took us in our flapping straw hats to see Aunt JOB who was quite a young lady with curls & who gave us a book

I cannot remember going back to Paris, but I think I then went to do my lessons every morning with a little girl called Laura Colmache & Mommee & I used to go & play round & round the statues in the Tuileries in the afternoon & then Aunt Mary[30] came back fm. India & in the summer we all went to Normandy. And I used to read the books Papa had bought us, at my bed room window & look out & see all the Normandy men & women dancing on the green.

And Mommee liked finding pretty little shells & sea-weeds & we made friends with a little boy called O'Farrell & his sister Fanny[31] & we used to dig deep holes in the sand & line them with oyster shells & sit in them & look at the sea.[32]

One of the nicest things that ever happened to us when we were children at Paris was the arrival of a huge parcel, w^h my Grannie cut open and inside there were piles & piles of the most beautiful delightful wonderful fairy tale books all painted with pictures — I thought they would never come to an end but alas! in a week we had read them all. They were called the Felix Summerly series & on the first page was written — To my three daughters Letetia Henrietta & Mary I dedicate these volumes.[33] I used to think that they must be the happiest little girls in the world but I never thought we should ever know them.

We had some other books — The one about little Willy & his Mama was y.^r Mommees favourite Years afterwards she found it in a shop & asked me to buy it for Margie & Annie & now it is you who read out of it

There were a great many nice little french books, too that I used to read & read our kind cousin Charlotte Ritchie used to give them to us, Chanoine Schmidt & l'Ami des Enfants, & the Journal des desmoiselles.[34] Our Grandpapa who we used to call GP used to wear a short cloak he called a poncho & a straw hat & to buy Almanachs full of pictures w^h he gave us to play with. He was a dear old man & we always thought it a treat to be with him. He was quite bald with kind blue eyes & he had a room full of chemical experiments barrels of beer, bottles, boots, old German dictionaries & medical works[35]

Our Mama was ill & she used to live with a Doctor in a big house with a great garden full of little paths & we used to go & spend the day with her & run after her down the long slopes of the garden.[36] She was quite young with beautiful red-golden hair, one day when we came we found her sitting on the terrace with all her hair tumbling about her shoulders & somebody combing it out. Then the Doctor said it was better we should not go & see her anymore & we came away to England to live with our Papa.³⁷ He lived in an old brown house in³⁸ Young Street Kensington opposite to the house where Richmond & I are going to live.³⁹

We came one evening in the autumn. There were raging fires lighted & volumes of punch were put out on the round drawingroom table & also beautiful red silk books that I was never tired of reading afterwards when I had had time to value it all. Upstairs was a dear little room with two little beds & some pictures. One was of a good boy doing a sum & another of a sleepy boy yawning on his way to bed, & then over the drawers hung Daniel O'Connel⁴⁰ who used to make the most horrible faces at us.⁴¹ Your Mommee was six & she had dear little feet & such pretty blue eyes & long curls & she used to play by herself at all sorts of little games — How bitterly she cried when our Grannie went away & left us. An old friend called Bess came to take care of us.⁴² I think I must have been a very discontented child for it seems to me now that I was always in disgrace & that Bess used to call me a Viper But with our Papa we were always happy & we used to go into his room & see him every morning before he got up, & our Grannie taught us to love him with all our hearts After Bess went away we had a pretty young governess called Miss Drury. We used to go out to childrens parties in white muslin frocks, to Mr. Dickens & Mr. Macreadys.⁴³ One day our Papa told us to put on our hats & we walked with him up Kensington gravel pits to a house where we found a gentleman⁴⁴ at breakfast with a tea pot at wʰ he was looking. He told our Papa that this was a tea-pot he had had made himself, & he said his children would be home next day & that we must come & see them & that their names were Letitia Henrietta & Mary They were the very same little girls I had thought about so much at Paris Your Mamma used to be always happy in the garden feeding the cats digging deep holes wʰ she meant to reach the centre of the earth. She had a doll she loved dearly with long eyelashes & a wax neck, she used to like dressing up too very much & we used to put on some spangled veils out of an old trunk & a Turkish dressinggown our Papa had brought back & sometimes he used to call us to sit for the pictures of Vanity Fair⁴⁵ One day we were the two naughty children rolling over & over on the ground, & there is a little picture of yʳ Mommee sitting building cards upon a little three legged stool our Grannie had given us⁴⁶

One day we could not find your Mommee anywhere — not in the house not in the garden My Papa was dreadfully frightened & thought somebody had stolen her.[47] He called for his horse & he galopped away to the park & I cried & the governess was so frightened she began to pack her box for fear our Papa should send her to prison, & at last I went up to our little bed room because I was so miserable, & I heard a little voice out of the cubboard w^h said Ainy! Ainy![48] — it was your own Mommee who peeped out & she said she had hidden herself for fun, & then when Papa called & everybody looked for her she was afraid to come out.

Besides Mrs Brookfield we had another great friend. Lady Cole she is now, the mother of Tishy Hennie & Mary — We used to go to tea there once a week & play in the garden with the children & pretend we were Kings & Queens & fairies & all sorts of things. We used to act a great deal & at Christmas we used to get up little plays: & we used to walk out in Kensington Gardens together On May day we went off into the lanes & gathered may, all that part of our lives I have written about in Old Kensington —

About twice a year we used to go over to Paris to see our Grannie. She was beautiful & good & she loved my papa tenderly but she used to make him unhappy by her reproofs & she always treated him as if he was a little boy Then he would get indignant & my Grannie used to cry & Minnie & I did not know what to think or to do My brown Grandmama died when I was about twelve & Mommee was nine.[49] Mommee slept in her room & in the night she heard poor Grandmama moaning & she got up & took her some water, & poor Grandmama began to cry & blessed her & thanked her & next day we went to spend the day with Laura Colmache & when we came back our[50] Grannie told us that poor Grandmama was dead. Minnie was very sorry for she had always been fond of her & Mommee & I lived with y^r Grandpapa who used to write like poppee in his study He used to breakfast with us when he was well, but the days he was ill, & that was a great many days I am sorry to say he had his breakfast upstairs in his room & we used to go in & pour out his tea & look at his dear face.

He had such a kind face with grey hair all waving & brown eyes like Richmonds[51] Mommee was very like him She had a wide open look w^h brought him back to me & thin blue veins across her temples like his. On Sunday mornings we had no lessons & we used to sit with him in his study & help him with his wood blocks. We used to rub them out & very soon he began to make use of us as his secretaries & to dictate his books to us.

My mama was ill[52] & away & my Papa was very lonely at times for we were only little girls after all & we could not quite understand all that he thought & felt but a great deal we could understand & we liked nothing so much as when he talked to us & told us all that he was doing. Aunt Job was a dear kind beautiful young Lady then & our Papa used to go & see her & talk to her & we too used to go & spend long days with her. This we liked almost better than anything else. She used to tell us stories & lend us books & one day she told me she came in & saw y^r Mommee peeping over the great stair case & — throwing her shoe at the housemaid whom we did not like We had a maid called Eliza Jordan who used to be very kind to us & of whom we were very fond, but we could not bear the manservant whose name was Samuel James.[53] He was very clever & very fond of Papa & he was always thinking what he could do for him, & Mommee & I were afraid that Papa would like him better than us. Were not we silly little girls? We had a governess called Miss Alexander[54] whose father & mother lived in an old house at Twickenham & when our Papa used to go away for a little Miss Alexander used to take us to her home take us to her home [sic]. In 1848 there was a revolution in France & people were afraid that in England too all sorts of terrible things w^d happen. The gentlemen all became policemen to keep order & we looked out of window & saw our papa cross the street & go past the house w^h Richmond & I are going to live in & he stopped at the Greyhound[55] & went in & when he came out he was carrying a great purple staff with a lion & unicorn painted on it.

That evening we were sent to Chapel House Twickenham[56] to Miss Alexanders home It was a beautiful old house with an oak staircase & a great many nice little wooden rooms there was a carved Bishop on the stair case with his hands out & a great many little girls a pretty one called Vittoria, a curly headed girl called Kathleen, a little dark eyed girl called Josephine they all came to look at us & we were all told to go to bed in our clothes because a chalk cross had been found marked upon the door. I believe one of the boys of the house had done it but we all hoped it was the revolution coming to set us on fire. It was very uncomfortable sleeping in our clothes & we were very glad to go to bed really the next night when the danger was supposed to be over.[57]

Part 2

We went to pay a second visit to the Alexanders in the course of the summer. They had left Chapel House & moved into a smaller one and M.ʳ & M.ʳˢ Tennyson[58] had come to live with the carved Bishop Our papa rode over one summers evening to say goodbye to us he carried a little basket of cakes before him, on his brown cob, he told us he was going to Germany next day. I cried & cried & made Minnie cry too & Mrs. Alexander was very angry with us. I dont know why we were so unhappy there I think I was out of temper & jealous & suspicious Minnie was very happy & one day Henry Alexander said to me as we were all sitting in the garden What a pretty little girl your sister is: & I looked at her & thought why what a pretty little girl she is Miss Alexander our governess was engaged to be married & we were very much left to our own devices, we played in the garden took long walks squabbled & made it up with the other children Sometimes we used to cut ferns in Windsor Park & one fact is very vividly impressed upon my mind wʰ is that the Alexanders being a Norfolk family had pudding before their meat.

One happy happy morning our maid Eliza Jordan appeared to fetch us home again. Papa was back in his study — oh how happy we were. I think it was this summer[59] soon after Grannie came to us that we went to Wales with our Grannie & GP to a little seaside place near Caernarven[60] called Langharne — This was a great era in our lives. We were all night in a steamer & GP covered us with his 'poncho.' The end of the journey was very adventurous, we missed the 2nd steamer & we were nearly wrecked in a little open boat coming by some cross way among the rocks When we got to Longharne we found some of Grannies old Fareham friends living at the Rectory, & what was most thrilling of all, was a big volume of Martin Chuzzlewit wʰ I used to go & read there every day. M.ʳ Dickens himself had sent it to a Lady from Langharne who wrote to him for his autograph

Then we went to a nice little day school with a long garden sloping to the sea. It used to be so pretty when school was over to come along by the cliff & to look out across the bay wide & sweet & fresh with the evening light upon it — There were some friendly girls there. Harriet who lent me novels Lavinia the half pay Captains daughter who could repeat Milton, the Misses Myers[61] grandest of all from Tenby whose papa with his own hand pulled down the blinds of every window in the house on Sunday. The surly music master Mr Ticher^{62} the kind little governess, they were all delightfully interesting Y^r mama made friends Miss Isabella Myers while I & Miss Fanny the elder exchanged confidences One day Grannie was crying, & then she & GP told us that our Papa was very very ill^{63} & we all travelled back across the country We came to Breknoch on the day of a great national fast for the cholera I think, & when we came to Gloucester & then Grannie hurried on & GP & Minnie & I followed the next day. On our way back we came to a station called Minniken Station

Dear Papa was better but so thin & weak & with great eyes when we came home. He was sitting up in his bedroom in the big chair We were just allowed to see him for a few minutes then he went to Brighton He didnt know how anxious & unhappy we were I cannot remember what happened for a long time after this, Miss Trulock came to be our daily governess & we went to Southampton on a visit to Mrs Fanshawe Rosa Fanshawe was my age, & we had acted charades together at Mrs Brookfields & raced about the house — We also acted with the Coles little plays as well as charades

Your Mommee always said that she was sure she had been an actress at some time or other & that she could remember the great dark theatre empty, while she rehearsed to it in a white dress She acted better than any of us. She never seemed to do loud things or stamp or shout but she would say a little word or move a hand & somehow it meant more than all the rest of us together. When she was about eleven & I about fourteen our Papa took us abroad & we went for a long long journey to Antwerp to Germany & the Rhine We met Mr. Kingsley^{64} on board the Rhine steamer in a garibaldi hat & many more people than I can remember. We went to Vienna & to Venice & to Milan & we lost our shoes & our shifts & our collars & I think we came home with very little besides a chessboard in our trunk. But it was all so lovely & so wonderful the things we didnt lose were the pictures & the places I can see them now after all these long years & years when I look for them. the austrians were in Italy then, & I remember their white uniforms & their lovely music & I can remember your grandpapa standing before the great picture of the Virgin in Venice & stamping on the ground because it was so beautiful, & then when we came to Dresden, there was another Virgin with her little boy in her arms. Sometimes I think of your Mommee looking like one of these beautiful good Virgins. With her sweet eyes & peaceful wondering face — only she was funnier & cleverer than any of them, & made little jokes [65] She was thirteen & I was sixteen when we went to Paris one autumn with Papa & from Paris to Rome where we spent the winter.[66] It seemed all golden like the great picture at Venice when we landed at Civita Vecchia, I have never been there again nor to Pisa but I daresay it all looks just the same blue sky & beggars in the sun & shadows & lovely old sloping ruins & arched palaces. As we got to Rome it was evening & papa said Look out there is St Peters. & we looked out & a great dark <u>living</u> sort of dome seemed to hunch up its shoulders as we drove under the stars, then a sentry stopped us & then we rattled along the streets to our hotel in the Condotti It had yellow paper on the walls & next morning when I looked out I saw a bandit & an Italian woman with a red boddice & white sleeves walk by the window & all the bells were jangling Our Father took a lodging in a great Palazzo & hired an old cook called Octavia & Papas servant Charles [67] waited upon us & used to fetch us from the tea parties & friends houses who asked us the two people we liked best in Rome were Mrs Browning & Mrs Sartoris Walter Scotts son in law Mr Lockhart [68] was there & next to them Mary Brotherton [69] & a kind Mr Creyke & M^r McBean [70] too was very kind & lent me all Bulwers novels & a great many of Disrealis & in the lodging shelf was a library where I read the Sorrows of Werther Your Mommee & I used to write for y^r grandpapa sometimes,[71] & it was here at Rome when we gave a childrens party that he drew us all the funny pretty pictures for the Rose & the Ring My Miss Meme knows Mr Bulbo & prince Giglio & Mrs Gruffanuff. All the little children for whom he first drew the pictures are grown up married people now & Pen Browning [72] can make pictures for himself.

Our Papa was very ill in Rome [73] & then we went to Naples & one evening we were out late in a beautiful sunset & the next day I awoke with a sore throat & a headache & all day long it got worse & worse & the Doctor came & said it was Scarlatina, & Mommee jumped up in the night & gave me water. Nobody was such a good nurse as Mommee. Her little hands always seemed to send pain away — once when her little kitten was ill she stroked it quite well, & once she kept a little fly in a dolls tea pot for two days with roseleaves We told her it was dead, but she w^d not hear of it the second day she took up the lid to put some sugar crumbs in, & out flew the little fly. We were ill some weeks at Naples,[74] but after our throats were better we liked lying in bed & looking out of window at the chiaja⁷⁵ & all the long strings of carriages & listening to the singing of the musicians Every night a man used to come & tinkle a guitar & sing Ah! li voglio ben assai wʰ means something like I hope you are very well⁷⁶ — When we were better we went out for a drive in the beautiful streaming light to a blue [?] grotto & then we went on board a ship & sailed back to Marsailles & saw Corsica in the distance & then we came to Paris to our Grannie again and stayed with her But everybody else ran away from us. When we got back to London all yͬ Mommees pretty curls fell off & one day our Papa took her to Mͬ Trufitts⁷⁷ & had her head shaved, I think I cried. She thought it great fun & used to take off her wig & pop her dear little bald head into the room thro' the door One day she dressed herself up like a little Turk with a turban I was very easily alarmed for I screamed loudly & didnt know her a bit I thought she was Prince Cameralzeaman⁷⁸ out of the arabian nights Our Papa took a pretty old country house at Boulogne that autumn & we went to stay there with our Grannie⁷⁹ All the place was full of soldiers, we had a long garden & from the wall at the end we could see them living in their tents cooking their pots dancing & singing Mͬ Dickens was at Boulogne that year whose books Mommee read so often when she was a little girl

When our Papa went to America we went to live in Paris⁸⁰ with our Grannie, & all our life at that time was a little bit like the Story of Elizabeth wʰ perhaps will amuse you to read some day yͬ Mommee told me to write it & said all our life just then would make such a good book — But this was long after & I hope you wont think that Mommee & I were ever quite so naughty as Elizabeth used to be We did lessons, & music with our friends the Colmaches & never went to the play & once a week we went to a french class at Mͬ Monods to prepare for confirmation⁸¹ A very celebrated man called M. Guizot⁸² used to sit in a corner & Mͬ Monod used to come in, and look at us & begin his lectures They were very beautiful & good & he used to call us his children & tell us to be good & unselfish & to be brave & humble He thought a great many things wrong wʰ our own Papa thought right & a great many things right that our Papa thought untrue: but he was a good man & did his duty & when he preached to us, it was not what he said but his whole heart & life that seemed to reach us.⁸³ The girls used to sob & shake & I am sure we did (only we wanted) to tell him that we thought there was no harm in being happy & laughing & in being interested in plays & stories, & that our Papa said this world was as much God's world as that other world for which Mr Monod wanted us to live alone He was very pale with dark cloudy hair & he had kind dark eyes I think except my own Papa nobody ever talked to me as he did, for tho' I disagreed with him I could feel how good he was & how he was trying to be as good as he probably could and I think that is religion, to be true & good & that is why I love your poppee because he is sincere & so thank God is my Richmond who married me when I was so ill & old & unhappy & who has not loved me a bit the less for that & so was Mommee & so is y.^r Godmama[84] & if my Meme lives to be a woman & to marry, it must be somebody good who speaks the truth & who tries to help others But Mommee & dear Godmama will arrange what is best if I am not there to have a voice in the matter It was a very hot summer & we went to a funny little country house of my Grandmamas at Mennecy near Corbeil where we used to eat grapes & make friends with the neighbours[85] & walk by the Canals of an evening. In the day time it was too hot to go out.

There was M. le Maire who used to come in & squint & sing till one couldnt help laughing & the paper manufacturer & a lovely romantic Mme Nassuet who used to sing Kradugah! ma bien aiméééééé & so did Pauline Colmache who used to teach us Italian under the vines, & there was the young lady up at the castle, very fat who drank beer & held her tumbler between her knees One thing made us both very miserable at this time w^h was that our Grannie was so unhappy because we said we were sort of Unitarians.

The first time out Papa came back from America[86] he sent a telegram 'Come home all well' & Grannie & Minnie & I packed up & started off that very day O how happy we were. He was out for he did not expect us and we went to bed & I remember it seemed as if the bed was flying in the air & then we heard him & jumped out of bed & rushed down in our dressing gowns — and there he was. He himself quite safe

I must get my dates into order for I find I cannot quite remember when everything happened[87]

The Crimea was the autumn after our winter[88] in Rome & then Margie & Annie's Mama had come to live with us in Onslow Sq. She & I used to read the horrible papers with the dreadful lists of wounded &

of killed — I remember the foggy Sunday when Balaclava was fought[89] People were coming & going & full of excitement

It must have been the following[90] summer that the still more wretched news of the Indian Mutiny came to us in beautiful sunshiny weather. We spent a great deal of time with the Coles this year, they too lived in Onslow Sq & we used to play a sort of lawn tennis in the pretty gardens of Gore House[91] where the Horticultural Brick[92] horrors now stand   In 1856[93] about the 10th of October Papa who had been coming & going & lecturing in England & Scotland sailed for America a second time.[94] That was a heartache worse than the first time, for he had never been well since that Roman fever & I was old eno' to be anxious now

We all breakfasted together one morning & he read prayers & his voice broke & he went quite away, as I thought without saying goodbye, & I remember standing still & hearing his voice say 'poor Nan!' & long after when he died & when My darling your Mommee died I heard his voice saying poor Nan[95] but now I think we shall all be together again some day, & if it is not God's will, at least it has once been his will to make us all, & when I think of them & of Richmond & of you my dearest children[96] I don't know how to thank God

All that winter in Paris[97] seemed a very eventful grown up one — Grannie was very lame after her horrid accident[98] & I read a letter from her to my papa telling him how when there was a crowd Minnie came & stood between her & the people to protect her against them. I used to treat Minnie as if she was a very little girl always but one day she looked at me & said You dont suppose Ainy that I dont know all the things you think tho you dont say them   One night I was ill in horrible pain & she came & put her arms round me & all the pain went away & I fell asleep   Amy lived with us in Paris in a pretty little apartment next door to our Grannies, & our maid Eliza Jordan waited on us & we used to do a great many amusing things & give tea parties to Gussie & Blanchie & Pinky who were such dear little girls.[99]

We used to go to dine with Auntie Charlotte & Jane[100] & to look at the Pictures in the Louvre & to tea at Mrs Sartoris' who now lived at Paris in a beautiful old house in the Rue Royale   She used to have music there & pink lamps & beautiful ladies came & grand looking gentlemen & of an evening she used to sing, most wonderfully & the house seemed all full of light & music & quite different from our dear old Grannies sleeping apartment with the two candles & the tea & the peat stove. One day I went to dine with Mrs Sartoris and after dinner she took me to the play & while the play was acting she said look & there in a box was a lady with coal black hair & a hard red face & a tight black silk dress & a cameo brooch. "That is George Sand my child" Said Mrs Sartoris [101] — Your Mommee read George Sands life, it was almost the last book she ever read & she admired it & many of her books almost more than any others: and I am very glad to have seen her once tho I did not think she looked very nice or at all like her beautiful thoughts.

Mrs Browning [102] was also in Paris this winter, in a little warm sunny shabby happy apartment with a wood fire always burning and a big sofa where she sate, & wrote her books out of her tiny inkstand in her beautiful delicate handwriting. Mr Browning used to come in & talk & Pen was a little boy with long curls & some of the gentlemen from Mrs Sartoris used to come in & sit round the fire. Mr Browning said that he & Mrs Browning always wrote poetry every morning till 2 or 3 o'clock. That was the year when I first remember hearing about Richmond in India [103] Guzzie & Pinkie Nely Blanchie were little bits of girls living with dear Auntie Charlotte & Janie & Felicie their Grandmama had died when we were in Rome, & they will tell you about y.^r Mommee & how she could draw for them & tell them stories, & she could always remember things, what had happened what people had said nobody can ever remember for me as she used to do because we had lived just the same life together like the married & even then we were not much parted. One day our Papa came back from America & we sat expecting him in the twilight, & we heard the tinkle of the door bell. My heart beat so I couldn't move & then the bell rang again, & then we rushed to open it We went back & lived in London [104] after this & after a time Grannie went to pay some visits & we used to go to parties & to dine out & people used to come & dine with us & then Papa took a house in Kensington & finding it w^d not do, as it was he had it knocked down & a new one built. [105] It took a long time & we used to think of little else from morning to night. It was a beautiful airy house with windows over looking the garden & at last — it was finished, & fires were lighted in all the rooms & then we thought we should like to give a housewarming & to act a play that our Father had written. [106] We had made great friends with a young man called Herman Merivale & he kept us up to the idea & so did his sisters, & we acted & rehearsed & acted & it was very great fun & excitement The night of the first rehearsal I remember so well, the great new house full of shadows & corners the people coming & going the unaccustomed doors & arches & passages, it seemed too delightful to think that we were really & truly going to live in this beautiful place & be young ladies & have fun & society & see life. Our life had been very quiet always[107] for papa was often ill & we could not have many people to the house. We had a great many pets, a dear dear little dog called Brownie We used to sit in the balcony of an evening & talk to the Marochettis. & I had begun to write a good deal — It was when we were leaving Onslow Sq. that I began Elizabeth & scrawled away in the window to the sound of the Church bells that used to fill the green drawingroom — The back room was almost the nicest for it had an avenue of trees at the back. Minnie y.^{r} Mommee said write about our life at Paris Annie (as I have already told you) & so I wrote my first novel as hard as I could write on all sorts of untidy scraps of paper & then I stuffed it away & did not think any more of it, in the great events of the play & the move and so the wonderful night came & your Mommee acted so wonderfully that people could hardly believe it was her. She acted the part of an old lady so that I hardly knew her & then she acted a sweet young peasant in a white cap & she looked quite lovely all of a sudden.

Even now after years & years people talk about her acting at that time. She could do things suddenly all unexpectedly — On this occasion she arranged her own dress & managed it all quite alone Margie's Mama[108] arranged the play & all the things that were wanted & I rec^d the company & ordered the supper. In a little green book in my room w^h I will keep for you my Meme you will find the play bill & the Epilogue and all the names of the people who acted in the W–(Em)–Ty House[109] theatricals. I remember writing to ask Godmama whom I had never seen then but she w^d not come.

I think this was the year of the Exhibition[110] & Gussie & Blanchie came to stay with us after their papa died[111] & so did their mama who was very very sad & pale & changed & then Tishy & Gerald & Richmond[112] came & I remember it tho' Richmond doesn't & then Margie & Annies papa proposed to Amy & first she said no & then she said yes. I had never thought about it but y^r Mommee did & wanted it very much & one day dear Amy was married & went away to India. All of a sudden y^r Mama had become quite grown up & so pretty & beautiful that people hardly recognized her. That was the first year we went to live in Palace Green. She went to the Exhibition one day & looked at a statue & changed her hair. She turned it up in pretty loose wavy loops instead of the little tight plats she had always worn & her cheeks became pink and I felt very proud of her. Then after a little while she began to droop somehow — I could not think of what was amiss, & I begged our Papa to let her go away to Scotland & the kind Lows[113] asked her to go with them You will like to read some of her dear funny letters.[114] That was when she was photographed knitting her stocking. Cousin Emmy[115] came to stay with me while she was away. & y.ʳ

The[116] first break that came in our home was when our kind old Grandpapa died. Y.ʳ Mommee, & Margies & Annies Mama & I were all in Wales one autumn, & our Papa was abroad & we had not heard from him for sometimes tho we knew that he was ill When one day about 3 o'c. in the afternoon I saw a little telegraph boy coming along the path that led to the door — I thought it was bad news of my Papa & I hardly could open the paper But the telegram was from Grannie in Scotland dear kind old GP had died quite suddenly. & so we we packed up & set off that evening. It was a long long tiring journey & we were very sad & still very frightened about our Father & when we got to Ayr it was the next evening very late & we went to a house & someone said Go quietly to bed, all is at peace here & your Grandmama is in bed Good night Good night & then we went to the inn still very frightened & tired out & we said our name was Thackeray & we wanted some rooms & the waiter said There is a gentleman of that name in bed upstairs. He arrived today and then we rushed into Papas room & there he was quite well & sound asleep.

Next day dear GP was buried & the sun shone & we came away & Grannie came with us & lived in Onslow Sq.[117] I can remember her walking holding Papas arm She looked so tall & beautiful in her black & he too looked so big & so noble taking care of her[118]

I[119] was 9 & Mommee was 6 when we came to live in Young Street with our Papa. It was winter-time & a nice fire was burning in the drawingroom & all the Punch books were out upon the table & someday you must come over the old house & see the room, Mommee lived in I think she liked the garden best of all. She used to dance about on the little green lawn & her long thick curls used to shine so, that I used to look out of window at them sometimes she would turn round & round as quick as she could go & then her hair would seem like a burning bush.

7

1879–1900

INTRODUCTION

I have home and children and family and blessings innumerable, but I never leave off thinking of the past.[1]

URING the period 1879–1900 Anne Thackeray Ritchie confirmed the reputation she had established during the 1860s and 1870s. She published six books, including the best of her novels, *Mrs. Dymond*. But the majority of her publications were reminiscences of the past, and portraits of people she had known in her youth. She brought to this work a double vision: her youthful memories and her mature insights. In regard to her father, her work reached its zenith with the publication of the biographical introductions to the thirteen volumes of the *Works of William Makepeace Thackeray*. But Anny did not dwell in the past. Her letters from this period show her sustaining old friendships and winning the affection and admiration of new acquaintances, including that of Henry James.

On a personal level, Anny delighted in her family, especially in her two children. Like Thackeray, Anny was extremely fond of children. Embracing motherhood wholeheartedly, she filled her letters with loving references to her daughter and her son. It was preordained that her son would be named William Thackeray Denis. He was the completion of her father's arrested *Denis Duval*. When Billy was a year old she wrote that "Billy opened his eyes and laughed and looked like his Grandfather for a moment . . . like a shadow in the past."[2] Later, when Billy was at Sedburgh, "she was struck . . . by how he looked like Papa [Thackeray] with high shoulders and well set up."[3] Just as she had tried to read Thackeray into Richmond Ritchie when she married him, so now she saw her father in her son. In 1880, a year after her son's birth, Anny wrote to a childhood friend, "I daresay you may have heard of me & of my deep blessings coming after so much sorrow."[4]

Anny completed the last of her novels during this time of happiness. *Mrs. Dymond* was published in 1885. Of all her fiction, *Mrs. Dymond* is the most sound structurally. It is a well-made story, with a solid plotline, the most adult and psychologically convincing of her fiction, and especially interesting because its subject matter shows a striking development.

Similar in structure to *The Village on the Cliff*, *Mrs. Dymond* veers from the sentimental ending of *The Village* to narrate the awakening of its heroine. Not a story of female emancipation, it is a tale of a Victorian woman with an overwhelming desire to change her life. Poor little Catherine of *The Village* embraces the role of guilty widow of an elderly husband she never loved. Susanna (Mrs. Dymond), on the other hand, sheds her widow's weeds to accept the love of a young and spirited man. Catherine remains the more than human Victorian heroine, altruistic to the end; Susanna leaves behind altruism, passivity, and the stereotype of the quiescent widow. That she finds happiness in a second marriage is not a new theme in Anny's fiction; *To Esther* and *Miss Angel* both end in happy second marriages. *Mrs. Dymond* is revolutionary because the hero holds the heroine in his arms and each feels a sexual attraction for the other. In stark contrast, Colonel Dymond's proposal of marriage is quiet, inhibited, and bloodless. Like a well-brought-up Victorian young woman, Susy is helpless. She marries her "good friend" because she and her family need someone to care for them. Throughout her marriage to the Colonel, Susy tries to live up to her conception of what he wants in a wife:

> She was not insincere, but she was not outspoken; she did not say all she felt, she put a force and a constraint upon herself, crushed her own natural instincts, lived as she thought he expected her to live, was silent where she could not agree, obliged herself to think as he did, and suffered under this mental suicide.[5]

Never subjected to "mental suicide" of her own, Anny endowed her heroine with a sensibility to save herself. She marries a second time for love. The emotion of a young woman who finds herself in love for the first time rings true to human nature.

To introduce her novel *Mrs. Dymond,* Anny quotes the opening three lines of Shakespeare's Sonnet CVII:

> Not mine own fears, nor the prophetic soul
> Of the wide world dreaming on things to come,
> Can yet the lease of my true love control.

On the dedication page of *Mrs. Dymond* a triangle appears with the letters R, h, and d at its angles. For Anny, the love of her husband and her children (*R*ichmond, *H*ester, and William *D*enis) was the secret that made life worth living. This "secret"—that love is best—her heroine embraces in the end. "True love" will not be controlled and Susy no longer tries to do so.

At the beginning of *Vanity Fair* Thackeray assumes the persona of "the Manager of the Performance" of a vast puppet show. At the end, he returns, elegantly, to his opening metaphor and admonishes, "Come, children, let us shut up the box and the puppets, for our play is played out."[6] The panoramic view of the world of *Vanity Fair* affords Thackeray the opportunity to be its ringmaster, its manager—sophisticated, knowledgeable, and psychologically astute.

Anny begins *Mrs. Dymond* with a chess game:

> Before the game of chess begins to be played, the heroes and heroines of the coming catastrophe are to be seen in orderly array. There is nothing to tell in which direction the fortunes of the board will drift. . . . And so in story telling, when the performance begins, the characters are to be seen, quietly drawn up in their places, and calmly resting before the battle. (5)

Thackeray enters the world of *Vanity Fair* as its manager, its puller of strings, its energizer; Anny compares her storytelling to a game of chess, one in which she is the observer, not a participant. Yet, she is as intensely involved in the lives of her characters as Thackeray is. She never uses her chess metaphor again; her novel ends with a cautionary French nursery rhyme:

> Promenons-nous dans les bois
> Pendant que le loup n'y est pas,

sing the little voices, taking up in their turn that song of childhood and innocent joy which reaches from generation to generation, which no sorrow, no disaster, will ever silence while this world rolls on. (274)

The children may walk in the woods—but only when the wolf is not there; yet there is hope in "the joy which reaches from generation to generation." For Thackeray, the husband of an insane wife, the world was not a playground. For Anny, the world had at last divulged its possibilities to her. After much sorrow, her husband and her children—her new "blessings"—reassured her that the world could be, at times, a place where "le loup n'y est pas."

Richmond Ritchie always enjoyed the companionship of beautiful, energetic women. Ironically, it was Anny herself who sent her husband to help the woman to whom he later lost his heart. Long a friend of Anny's, Lionel Tennyson, the poet's second son, was taken ill in India. Returning to England, he died at sea on 20 April 1886. His beautiful young widow was distraught, and Anny asked Richmond to help Eleanor Tennyson with her affairs.

Afflicted with sciatica, Anny went to Aix-les-Bains for the baths. Richmond was thirty-two years old and handsome; Anny was forty-nine and ill. Eleanor Tennyson was in need not only of counseling but of a man. Inevitably, she and Richmond fell in love. When he confessed to his wife, she sent him off to Brighton to decide which of the two women he wanted—Eleanor Tennyson or Anne Ritchie. Given the society in which they lived, he had little choice. Divorce was almost impossible and his position at the India Office was at risk. Within two days Anny received a postcard addressed "Dearest wife";[7] he had chosen Anne Ritchie.

The relationship between Mary and Michael Marney in *Mrs. Dymond* leads one to believe that Anny had a great understanding and a special empathy for loving older wives and wayward younger husbands. However, the novel was published in 1885; Richmond Ritchie became involved with Eleanor Tennyson in 1886. Anny may have already sensed that Richmond was susceptible to the charms of other women. Her acute, insightful delineation of the relationship between Mary and Michael Marney supports this assumption. While Thackeray avenged himself on Mrs. Brookfield by changing their relationship into one in which Lady Castlewood is older than Esmond, and in love with him long before he loves her,[8] Anny modeled the Marneys on her own circumstances, an older wife in love with a younger, handsome husband. That Marney was a womanizer may have been part of the pattern of Anny's own marriage, or of her unconscious fears.

Richmond Ritchie's personality is elusive. A great deal can be inferred from Anny's letters to him and from the people who became his friends. What is revealing about the family, and in particular, about

Richmond Ritchie, is that his private family name is Wizz. With this nickname, the weight, the seriousness, of the India Office slip from his shoulders. At what was he a wizard? The lighter side of his nature is confirmed by Anny in her letter to Mrs. Savile Clarke (Letter 82) in which she describes her husband's reaction to the performance of *The Rose and the Ring*. Not only did Wizz attend a children's play (albeit based on a story by his father-in-law), but he "began breakfast this morning with the ode to Kedgeree." This lends credence to an elegiac eulogy of Richmond Ritchie.

> But for all his accessibility and genial humour at the Office, he was a most formidable person—six foot three inches tall and heavily built, with a glance at once humorous, sardonic, and shattering, a rich voice, sober but expressive gestures, and sharp and mordant wit ready to flay the self-complacent and blast the sentimental.[9]

This picture is quite different from Henry James's description of the "infantile husband" of Miss Thackeray.

Certainly Richmond was successful in the India Office and knighted for his work there. But he seemed to live on the periphery of Anny's life. Perhaps because of their estrangements, they went their separate ways. Never a typical Victorian housewife, Anny filled her days with writing. They both loved and enjoyed music, but aside from this shared experience, they seemed to have little in common. Emulating Thackeray in his frenetic traveling, Anny ranged over England and the Continent. When she was stricken with sciatica, she sought spas, hoping for a cure.

With her need for movement, and Richmond Ritchie's position, which kept him tied to a desk in London, the only solution for her was to go off on her own. Her husband's preferences were not hers. He liked to fish, to play golf, and to take long walks. He preferred quiet and solitude after his hectic days of government business. She preferred people and socializing after a day of writing in solitude. Although he may have been beguiled by her accomplishments and worldliness when he married her, living with a legend and "a woman of genius" was, no doubt, trying for the introverted Richmond Ritchie. On the surface it may have appeared to him as if his wife had no need of him. The women to whom he was attracted were young, beautiful, and in need of him. Although Richmond's love for his wife faltered, his devotion to his home and to his children did not.

Richmond and Anny may have been an ill-assorted couple; they had their problems, but in the balance, their marriage worked.

Like Thackeray before her, Anny (and Richmond as well) anchored their lives in their family. Born in India and sent to relatives in England at an early age, Thackeray and Richmond shared a common heritage of displacement, while Anny herself lost her home at the same early age owing to her mother's insanity. For all three, home and family were of inordinate importance. Anny and Richmond were purposeful people, dedicated to the jobs they had chosen. Husband and wife worked hard; they needed the money to support the extravagance of their Thackerayan way of life.

After Thackeray's death, Anny took over many of his responsibilities, one of which was the care of Isabella. Not only did she visit her mother but she later brought her children with her. Whether it was Anny's own need for a feeling of continuity, or whether she wanted Isabella to remain part of her family, Hester and Billy knew their grandmother, went to her funeral, and "were very sad, poor darlings, and cried and cried."[10]

Anny's letters to family members reveal different aspects of her life. In Anny's three letters to Isabella in the last years of her life, mother and daughter reveal reversed roles, Anny writing to her mother as though she were a bright ten year old. In a letter from Aix-les-Bains, Anny enclosed a picture postcard "to show you the way people come home from the baths here" (Letter 74). In Letter 84 Anny described her garden and the children playing in it, drawing a sketch of them. The tone of all three letters is lighthearted, even when she or her children are ill. Isabella must be shielded from all unpleasantness and only "[t]he air [which] is delicious sleepy soothing fattening" (Letter 85), or similar topics are discussed.

Lovingly, Anny signs the letters with the childhood nickname "Nanny." This is the person Isabella knows, not Mrs. Richmond Ritchie. Perhaps, too, Anny wanted to be Nanny again, if only briefly for Isabella. When Isabella died in 1894 Anny wrote: "My dearest mother did not suffer; . . . Dear Mama, so silent, so undemanding, so loving, so contented. . . . I shall miss her day after day. . . . my kind, sweet, patient mother."[11] To the sorrow she felt for Thackeray's loneliness, the sadness of Isabella's life was added. Her own hostility mitigated, Anny acknowledged the tragedy that was her mother's. Isabella's family had been broken up by her insanity, but she survived for fifty years. If Thackeray died a weary, sickened man at fifty-two, Isabella, barely having lived, died in her seventies, isolated from her family.

By the time William Ritchie entered Trinity College he was her "Bill of Bills" (Letters 92, 94, 98). In describing a letter from Colonel Richmond Webb to his son in college, which she intended to use in her biographical introductions, she wrote to William that "it says all the things one <u>feels</u> now my beloved Bill tho' parents don't say them so much" (Letter 90). In his explicit statement of his feeling for his son, Webb's Polonius-like instructions are yet sincere and loving. Not reticent about her feelings, Anny nevertheless used Webb's letter of a parent writing to a son newly launched in college to express her love for William.

By discussing her work freely, she made it part of the fabric of her life; she lived the time she was writing about by incorporating it into everything she did, even in her correspondence. In other letters to William there are overt declarations of love, concern, and caring. For example: "After all Mothers & sons are more made up of all the things they dont say than the things they do say & you know all the things I think & feel & wish for my darling boy" (Letter 93). And, "Beloved I havent written much but I constantly pay you little inside visits" (Letter 94). Even though the connection between mother and son was extraordinarily close, this did not preclude good family relationships all around. Anny had a genius for friendship and a vast capacity for love.

Always the letters, particularly those to William, speak of a closely knit family. Hester advises her mother to send Billy more money at college (Letter 90); Anny has received "a telegram from y^r Father . . . & a delightful long letter from Hester" (Letter 90); Wizz said your river expedition put him in mind of his own youth & expeditions" (Letter 89). Anny never woos one family member at the expense of another. Essentially Anny's letters to Billy are those of a loving mother to her son. They are informative, warm, and reassuring, bringing home a little closer. Written during 1898–99, they reveal the pattern of her life. She entertained, she traveled, and she was finishing the biographical introductions to Thackeray's *Works*. Despite all these activities, she was plagued by illness. In a footnote to a published letter which Anny wrote in 1898, Hester added, "My mother's letters give no impression of the constant ill health from which she suffered; she never dwelt upon this, not did she allow it to interfere with the ordinary course of her life."[12] "[T]he ordinary course of her life" was not that of a sixty-year-old, ailing, Victorian woman.

Anny was not an ordinary woman. She was the famous daughter of a famous father. Her correspondents were attached to her for many different reasons, among them her generosity. Occupied as she was, Anny nevertheless answered even strangers. One of the reasons that Thackeray's manuscripts were cannibalized was Anny's generosity in sending pieces of his handwritten work to readers who made the request. Later on, she would learn to refuse.

In Letter 67 she solicited a review in the *Saturday Review* for an unknown poet. She asked another friend to permit "a very nice little millionaire called Carnegie [who] . . . is the owner of a great iron foundry in America" to call on her (Letter 72). In both of these requests—the review for the unknown poet and the interview with the nice little millionaire—Anny asked favors for each of them with the same sense of generosity, without any consideration of how important the person was. As openhanded as Thackeray, like him also she was generous of her own spirit.

Many people were drawn to Anny because she was exceptional. Letter 77 is of particular interest because the recipient was Elizabeth Robins (1862–1952). Born in Kentucky, she was an actress, novelist, and active feminist. Twenty-five years younger than Anny, Robins became her friend. Although the letter has little value in itself, it is extraordinary when considered in the light of the friendship between these two very different women. And yet, they had a great deal in common. Both lost their mothers to insanity; both worked and earned their own livings; both felt that women were the equals of men. Strong, assertive, and productive, they flouted the stereotype of the dependent Victorian lady.

Even in her business letters, Anny's unique qualities are apparent. She researched whatever she was writing about by going, wherever possible, directly to the source. For example, she queried Octavia Hill about her business relationship with Ruskin (Letter 73). Her dealings with her publishers were friendly, but she asked for what she wanted without equivocation or hesitation, executing all of her own business arrangements. In Letters 84 and 85 she put forth her demands to Savile Clarke for the copyright to *The Rose and the Ring*. In Letter 70 to Mr. Payn, the new editor of the *Cornhill,* she discussed her ongoing series in an informal manner, but on her terms. In Letter 69 she greeted Baron von Tauchnitz as a friend, which no doubt he was. These are really quasi-business letters; Anny was always herself, charming and effectual.

Anny's charm was not always appreciated immediately. It is hard to fix the date of the beginning of her friendship with Henry James; it is simple to trace the rising line of his admiration, respect, and finally his love for her. In 1869 James wrote to his sister, "(I forgot to say just now by the way, *apropos* of the Stephens, that Miss Thackeray is absent on the Continent—... else I should have seen her)."[13] From being an aside in a parenthetical phrase, Anny works her personal magic and, despite his reservations, James capitulates to her real worth. In 1877 he wrote:

> I lunched yesterday with poor Leslie Stephen, whom, however, rendered more inarticulate than ever by his wife's death, I find an impossible companion.... I had but a glimpse of Miss Thackeray, who has likewise been greatly knocked up by her sister's death, and is ill and little visible. She inspired me with a kindly feeling. (II, 101)

In the next year, after Anny's marriage, James's kind feeling appears to be sorely taxed. He wrote:

> Present were poor Miss Thackeray and her juvenile husband (one Ritchie) —the latter even out-silencing Stephen: and Miss T. herself the very foolishest talker (as well as most perfectly amiable, and plainest, woman) I have lately encountered. Compared with her conversation, *Miss Angel* is Baconian! (II, 157)

In a stunningly Jamesian sentence he destroys at once both Anny and her novel. She further outraged James's sensibilities by going to a dinner party while she was visibly pregnant:

> I went in with poor Miss Thackeray—further advanced toward confinement (though I believe it has not yet come off) than I have ever seen a lady at a dinner party. This is a thoroughly good, gentle creature; but exquisitely irrational. But I believe she is very happy with her infantile husband Richmond Ritchie. (II, 160)

Though pregnant, Anny is still "poor Miss Thackeray"; however, her "infantile husband" is now acknowledged by his full name. In the following year, 1879, James expanded on both Anny's faults and her virtues:

I took in the *ci-devant*[14] Miss Thackeray, with whom I had already considerable acquaintance, and in whose extreme good nature and erratic spontaneity I find something lovable and even touching. She has the minimum of common sense, but quite the maximum of good-feeling. . . . Miss Thackeray is at any rate very happy and satisfied in her queer little marriage. Her husband is, superficially, an ill-mannered and taciturn youth; but he improves on acquaintance.[15]

Again in 1879 James referred to "a dinner party given by the Thackeray-Ritchies" and to Richmond Ritchie as "Miss Thackeray's boy-husband."[16] Although he cannot manage, as yet, to call them "The Ritchies," he does acknowledge that there is a connection between them—referring to them as "the Thackeray-Ritchies."

As James grew fonder of Anny, his view of Richmond mellowed as well. However, in his references to the Ritchies early in their friendship, James drew a caricature of the couple. With distaste, he protested Anny's marriage, and in a footnote added to her letter to him, he mocked her (Letter 66). James sent her letter on for someone else to read with the following notations: "(Could anything be More Miss Thackerayan?) Please destroy." If Anny's letter in its artlessness, love of nature, and concern for friends appears typically Miss Thackerayan, then James's addition to it is typically Jamesian in its sense of superiority and ambiguity. By asking for the letter to be destroyed, he (supposedly) covered his tracks.

By 1895 James's attitude toward her had changed. He addressed her as "Mrs. Ritchie" (Letter 88); and by 1897, she became "My dear Anne Ritchie."[17] In Letter 88 he accepted a dinner invitation graciously and offered her seats for his short-lived play *Guy Domville*. By 1900 James addressed her as "Dearest Anne Ritchie!" (Letter 96). He is playful, charming, and thoroughly at ease in his role as friend of the family. His attitude to Richmond Ritchie is one of complete acceptance. That Anny considered James her friend is apparent in a letter she wrote describing a visit to the home of Leslie Stephen and his second wife:

> Last night we dined at Leslie and Julia's. . . . I felt as sad and strange as I always do at first, but I made a push and got happy and joking with Henry James, who devotedly jumped into the cab with us, and drove back half-way to Putney, for the sake of a little more talk.[18]

However foolish Anny's dinner party conversation appeared to James at first, he was beginning to understand and appreciate the woman herself.

At the beginning of their friendship, James considered Anny an exotic creature with her enthusiasm, her spontaneity, and her superficial vagueness. In time, James held to much the same view of her as Leslie Stephen expressed in the *Mausoleum Book*.

> She generally came to sound conclusions. . . . she had really sound abilities. . . . Her mind was a little too active in jumping from one topic to another. . . . But she was exceedingly popular and everyone who could appreciate kindness and sympathy and simplicity combined with real brilliancy sought for her company. (14–15)

Stephen's accolade of "real brilliancy" is praise indeed; of whatever the brilliancy consisted, James also recognized it, and for her depiction of the home of a French Protestant minister in *The Story of Elizabeth*, he referred to her as "a woman of genius."[19] He wrote:

> Above all, however, she was blessed with the faculty which when you give it an inch takes an ell, . . . The power to guess the unseen from the seen, to trace the implication of things, to judge the whole piece by the pattern, the condition of feeling life in general so completely that you are well on your way to knowing any particular corner of it. (389)

The friendship between Anne Ritchie and Henry James deepened, and continued until his death.

Once Anny acquired friends, she had the art of keeping them. Anny's friendship with Browning was ongoing. Her letters to him disclose the informality of their relationship and her willingness to ask favors of him. In the habit of being indulged by Thackeray, she acted in like manner with Browning. In Letter 79, she struck a more personal note: "I cannot help writing just this one more word which is dear Friend. thankyou for your goodness." There is no hint of what Browning's benevolence consisted, yet the note conveys honest emotion.

In a letter to Browning's sister, Anny asked for biographical information on Elizabeth Barrett Browning for her article about the poet. She also inquired as to "where I may send you the proofs of my little paper" (Letter 71). With sensitivity and delicacy she made her request, not of Browning himself, but of his sister. Modest about her work,[20] Anny referred to this article for the *Dictionary of National Biography* as "my little paper" and revealed with good humor Leslie Stephen's treatment of it.

> I sent it to Leslie who has sent me my shorn lamb without any tempered winds but I see that for a Dictionary it is necessary to be ruthless. . . . Leslie

was very compunctious about the shearing & said it was a relief to him that I should be able to use what I had written elsewhere. (Letter 71)

Anny desired to employ all her "little rigmarolles which are at least genuine and mean the loving & grateful remembrance of some thirty years." Her reminiscences gave Anny an opportunity to use all of her memories.

As her life with her husband became difficult, Anny sought refuge in memories of her father and of their shared past. The past acted as a restorative for her. She found steadfastness in Thackeray, both in his relationship with Isabella and in his love for Anny herself. Just as she had never disappointed Thackeray, so he had never disappointed her. Her biographical introductions were an escape from her unhappiness and at the same time the tribute of her love for her father. Through her work on the introductions and the production of Thackeray's *The Rose and the Ring,* the past became part of the present.

In her recitation of quotidian events Anny unpretentiously discussed her work. In one letter she wrote, "I am putting in little farewell notes to the Edition — . . . an american paper says it has been such a success that all the other authors daughters are writing notes & introductions."[21] For someone who dashed off letters to friends on the front of apothecary statements (Letter 68), and who composed her work on any paper available, she was meticulous in her editing. In a letter to her editor, she enclosed the original manuscript of Thackeray's lecture on Swift, explaining that it was "partly in my Fathers writing (about 25 p. & partly in mine as a girl) — you will see his corrections here & there" (Letter 87). Correspondence for her biographical introductions of Thackeray's *Works* illustrates the minute discussions (including punctuation marks) which she carried on with the editor.

The biographical introductions are important for several reasons. In the 1890s, Anny's reminiscential writing reached its highest level of artistry. The introductions were preceded in 1894 by *Chapters from Some Memoirs,* and *Records of Tennyson, Ruskin, and Robert and Elizabeth Browning* (1892). Anny's memories are insightful, brooding, and sharp. Yet, she remains tender and tolerant. If she peruses the past through rose-colored glasses, she is never myopic.

As Anny matured, her reminiscences took on greater authority and more depth. She held to a double perspective—that of the child she was in the past as well as that of the woman she was in the present. Because she looked at her childhood through the eyes of an honest and sensitive adult, her writing is never sentimental or banal. In *Chapters,* she wrote: "my memory is a sort of Witches' Caldron, from which rise one by one these figures of the past. . . . Now perhaps looking back, one can tell their worth better than at the time" (54). As an adult she could evaluate people and events, but she never dismissed her childhood feelings as foolish or inappropriate for the time. Her remarkable memory, combined with her novelist's eye and ear, gave her introductions and all her reminiscent writing endearing and enduring qualities.

Another and equally important reason for the popularity of the introductions was their wealth of unpublished Thackeray correspondence and drawings. Scrupulously, Anny had followed her father's dictum that she not participate in any biography about him. Following no chronological sequence, she wrote, as she called them, "notes and introductions,"[22] to each of the volumes. Making use of Thackeray's letters, journals, drawings, and her own diaries as well as the correspondence from friends and relatives, she fortified her actual memories. This episodic mode was particularly well suited to her talents.

She brought fresh insight into Thackeray's method of creation and illuminated not only his work habits but his meaning as well. By describing his personal life at the time of a particular work, she shed light on his feelings and his state of mind. She uncovered motives and identified causes; Thackeray was humanized.

These introductions helped to put her life with Thackeray into perspective for her. She had been examining and analyzing this past since Thackeray's death. In *Chapters,* she wrote:

> There is often a great deal more of the past in the future than there was in the past itself at the time. We go back to meet our old selves, more tolerant, forgiving our own mistakes, understanding it all better, appreciating its simple joys and realities. (191)

When still "a hobbledehoy," she spent time with Mrs. Kemble in Rome. Later Anny wrote, "I only half understood her; but when I, too, was an elder woman the scales fell from my eyes" (197). Each time she discussed her childhood, she faced the demons that haunted her. In her fiction, she reshuffled her early life, sifted through her experiences, sometimes knowingly, and often unconsciously, for the solid facts of her work.

Comprising thirteen individual essays, *Chapters from Some Memoirs* forms a loosely connected, episodic autobiography of her childhood and adolescence. The first essay, "My Poet," begins: "My father lived in good company, so that even as children we must have seen a good many poets and remarkable people, though we were not always conscious of our privileges" (1). As friends of her father, Tennyson and Browning did not gain the stature of poets for her until she was older. In "Tout Chemin" she describes a trip through France:

> I can still see in a sort of mental picture a barge piled with great golden onions floating along one of the quays, guided by a lonely woman in blue rags with a coloured kerchief on her head. There goes the Lady of Shalot said my father; and when we looked at him rather puzzled, for we knew nothing of onions and very little of Tennyson in those days, he explained that a shalot was a species of onion, and after a moment's reflection we took in his little joke, feeling that nobody ever thought of such droll things as he did. (174–75; see also Letter 30)

Anny's first knowledge of a poet came when she was twelve. She went out on a cold, rainy Paris night with her grandmother to meet Jasmin, a poet whom she had dreamed about in her French class back in London. When he was pointed out to her, she was horrified.

> For suddenly, just under the swinging chandelier, I see a head, like the figure-head of a ship—a jolly, red, shiny, weather-beaten face, with large, round, prominent features, ornamented with little pomatumy wisps of hair, and a massive torso clothed in a magnificent frilled shirt over a pink lining . . . I falter, gazing at Punchinello, high-shouldered, good-humoured! (10)

Her youthful vision of a poet shattered, she tried to hide her disappointment from her grandmother: "I can't help laughing even now as I conjure up the absurd little dream of the past and the bitterness of that childish disappointment. . . . Why, I had been in a world of poets!" (12) She has no scorn for her twelve-year-old immaturity; amused by the child she was, at the same time she understands the bitterness, and feels compassion for her younger self.

This double vision recurs in "My Musician." Again in Paris, this time she was taken by a friend of her grandmother to bring a basket of provisions to an ailing musician. Thanking them, he began to play the piano.

> then the music began, and the room was filled with continuous sound, . . . The lady sat absorbed and listening and as I looked at her I saw tears in her eyes—great clear tears rolling down her cheeks, while the music poured on and on. I can't, alas, recall that music! I would give anything to remem-

ber it now; but the truth is, I was so interested in the people that I scarcely listened. (26)

The novelist in Anny observed the scene; she paid little attention to the music. With adult regret she reveals that as they drove away her grandmother's friend admonished her, "Never forget that you have heard Chopin play" (27). At the time, the scene meant only that she had accompanied an old lady of whom she was afraid on an errand of mercy. Now she responds to the pathos of the dying Chopin, beholden to charity for survival. She regrets her own naïveté and ignorance. Just as she had missed Thackeray's pun on the Lady of Shalot, so she failed to hear Chopin's music.

> Things certainly strike children oddly, . . . They are so busy in early life with all that is going on on every side, that one person or another person, the visitor in the drawing-room, the tortoise-shell cat on the garden wall, the cook's little boy who has come in to partake of cold pudding, all seem very nearly as important one as the other. (1)

Exploring her feelings of long ago she accounts for them, and accepts her lack of perception.

In addition to the momentous events of her life, she described the intimate life of her family. Private views of Thackeray abound. Getting into a small boat in Genoa, they are being rowed out to board their ship, when the Italian sailors stop rowing. They demand more money than the agreed upon price and refuse to move.

> Then the steamer sent up two more rockets, which rose through the twilight, bidding us hurry; and then suddenly my father rose up in the stern of the boat where he was sitting, and, standing tall and erect and in an anger such as I had never seen him in before or after in all my life, he shouted out in loud and indignant English, D——n you, go on! a simple malediction which carried more force than all the Italian polysyllables and expostulations of our companions. (180–81)

Filled with realistic details, these essays show a tolerant understanding for the child she was. All of her life she examined not only her own actions but those of the people around her. She viewed events as a writer, even before she had become one. Trying to decipher her own feelings, she analyzed the traumatic events in her life. Like a narrative, *Chapters* embodies motive, action, reaction. The book was an immediate success and like the biographical introductions is important for a better understanding of both Thackerays—father and daughter.

In the biographical introductions Anny wrote, "But I think the realities, and even many of the disappointments of life have been better than ever were the childish dreams of those early days."[23] At the same time that Anny enjoyed what she could of the present, she savored her past. The period 1879–1900 provided Anny with a wide field on which to consolidate her gains and accept her losses, and to shape, to a great extent, her own fortunes.

LETTERS 66–98

To Henry James

Letter 66
Harvard

The Clough's Nest/Lynton/North Devon/Tuesday [1879]¹

Dear Mr. James

Richmond says you are in London to w^h lovely spot I hope very soon to be returning & Blanche Cornish² says How delightful it would be of you if you would come & see us here for a few days before I leave. Do think of it. It is most lovely country thym. blown & burning to purple & honeysuckle with sea gulls & Exmoor for a background & now that the weather is fine the steamer brings you straight under our great cliff

As I walk along I persistently long for my dear Mrs. Satoris to have looked at it all, You would understand what I mean if you saw the place Even before the sad sad news came to me she was constantly in my mind here.

Do think of it if it is at all possible & if the house full of children & babies doesnt frighten you We should be so very glad — & Hester³ is looking so splendid she is worth coming to see in her country cheeks

Yours Sincerely
Anne Ritchie

(Could anything be More Miss Thackerayan?) H.J.[4]
Please destroy
both of them.[5]

To Mr. Walter[1]

Letter 67
Fales

27, Young Street
Kensington Square, W.
Sunday [c. 1880–81]

Dear M.ʳ Walter

I wonder if you could do me a real kindness — An American friend of mine, Virginia Vaughan[2] by name has written a book called "The New Era"[3] — a sort of philosophical poem abt a new world & angels & liberty There is a great deal that is very good in it — Do you think you could be so very kind as to help her to a review not a complimentary but a real review in the Saturday.[4] She is publishing it at her own expense & modestly hopes that if she is reviewed her next book may be taken by a publisher.

If it could be possible I should think it very kind of you but I know how difficult things are — With my love to y.ʳ wife.

Yours sincerely
Anne Ritchie

She has had Reviews in strange papers wʰ she sends me did you ever hear of Fact?[5]

To W. W. F. Synge

Letter 68
Fales

Dear London[1]   Xmas   1881
M — Synge Esq   27 Young St
            Dʳ to F. Wright
            Chemist & Dentist
               High Street
                  Kensington. W.

May 25   Draught   8
   27   Sedative Mixture   1.6
                                   2.2

Sorry am I to read on so unpleasant a missive in return for you [*sic*] kind delightful Xs gifts w.h are the joy of the children M.rs Bob² came looking realy very Hennee to see us just as I was starting for the station — I might have stayed & talked to her for I missed my train

We spent Sunday with Darwin to our great pride & delight

Much love as usual f.rm

Y.r aff
ATR

M.rs Bob was so nice & pretty & most beautifully dressed.

To Baron Von Tauchnitz¹

Letter 69
Fales
65.6.6-6. 2288

New Years day 1882
27. Young Street
Kensington

Dear Baron I must write & thankyou for your kind & delightful present. Oh! that I had known & had taken my best pen when I last wrote to you   I value the book very much & wish you very cordially — & gratefuly too — a happy New Year (w.h must please include your family as well as for yourself) & believe me always

Yours very truly
Anne Ritchie

To James Payn¹

Letter 70
Fales

Moray Lodge
Kew Gardens Road
March 8 [1883]²

Dear M.r Payn

Thankyou for your very kind letter which has set me speculating — are you going to make some eventful phoenix change in the beloved old CHM³

I shall go on with my story⁴ & send it in — It may run longer than

I meant to three parts or even four but I write so badly that I never can quite tell. I daresay you will be able kindly to make arrangements for it & also for one more Literary lady to make up my volume

Yours very truly
Anne Ritchie

To Miss Browning

Letter 71　　　　　　　　　　　　　　　　Wimbledon
Yale　　　　　　　　　　　　　　　　　　Sunday
　　　　　　　　　　　　　　　　　　　　13 9 1885[1]

My dear Miss Browning

I was so glad to hear from Mrs Corkran that you were well — both of you — & that Pen was to join you somewhere in some calm holiday place. We are just packing up to leave Wimbledon where we have all revived after our trying experiences of the spring and early summer. I want you please dear Miss Browning to help me once more and I know you will forgive me for asking you to take the trouble of writing me a letter to tell me where I may send you the proofs of my little paper. I sent it to Leslie who has sent me my shorn lamb without any tempered winds but I see that for a Dictionary it is necessary to be ruthless.[2] I have a hope that I shall be able to reprint my article somewhere with all my little rigmarolles which are at least genuine and mean the loving & grateful remembrance of some thirty years. Leslie was very compunctious about the shearing & said it was a relief to him that I should be able to use what I had written elsewhere. I want you also please to be so good as to send me Mrs Brownings birthday and the day in June when you lost her.

I have jsut [*sic*] finished my story[3] which is a load off my mind & we are now going away for a little holliday beginning with the Lockers — the Lampsons[4] as they have now to be called but first we shall be at
Mrs Ritchies
Southmead
Wimbledon Park
till the 23d & after that any letter directed to 36ᵃ Rosary Gardens will

reach us. I hope we may have a few days at Paris in 8ᵇʳ & hear everybody talk french again. Pinkie has been in Cottonnightcap Country⁵ tell Mʳ Browning & also in Switzerland with Mʳˢ Kemble who is come back — people seem to wake up one by one out of their summer rest The Lionel Tennysons⁶ are in town preparing for India I am taking the children up to see those dear little boys next week.

How thankful I was to hear better news of poor Claire Milsand Please give my love to Pen & his Father & I'm always

Your affectionate
Anne Ritchie

The children are playing cricket with their father. My boy is really a very fair bat already — Hester has got a jackdaw & 2 doves & has been promised a little dog — the jackdaw seems to me almost like a 3ᵈ child

To Mary Thackeray[1]

Letter 72
Fales

27, Heath St
Saturday
[Before 1886]

My dear Mary

I want you & yʳ Mother to be so very kind as to forgive the liberty I have taken in telling an American — a very nice little millionaire called Carnegie[2] whom I met at dinner that I thought I might write & ask you to be so good as to let him call.

He had corresponded with Lᵈ Northesk[3] & is the owner of a great iron foundry in America. He has a mother to whom he is devoted & he crosses the ocean about twice a year. He was so interested & pleased & anxious to make your acquaintance that I felt sure you would forgive the coolness of my proceeding — Being an American you will not be ridden by a [word illegible] acquaintance — & indeed I liked the little man very much indeed. He knows Mʳ Matt. Arnold.[4]

Your affectionate
Anne Ritchie

I was so sorry to fail that Thursday I have been behaving quite <u>horribly</u> lately jumbling all my engagements & tho' I realy do try to keep them & <u>want</u> to I seem to miss trains loose my way & jumble everything more & more everyday. I do hope my brain isnt [?] softening

To Octavia Hill[1]

Letter 73	Southmead
Princeton	Wimbledon Park
AM17414	Friday
	[c. 1886–87]

Dear Miss Hill

I am trying to write a short article about Ruskin[2] & I have a very great favour to ask of you. I know it was by you & through you that he was able to help so many people. I have a feeling that his example might be more widely followed by less emotional people who have money & taste without genius to battle with & its consequent overwhelming & passing impressionability A very short sentence such as "this society is now entirely carried on by Miss Hill" — or something to that effect w^d describe the present state of things without going into any details.

I hope what I ask isnt impertinent. what he did materially & what the results were, it would give a certain <u>heart</u> to the more pictoreal aspect of this Power for good & for mighty complexity

I remember years ago once asking you something on the subject & your kindness not objecting to my doing so. I had refused two or three times to attempt the article but now for various reasons I have agreed (& indeed it is my duty) to try & write it I have a sort of feeling that you would not mind my mentioning the[3] useful & all-important fact of y^r mutual work & I cant help feeling that if I might say <u>something</u> of this my article might be more like the reality than if I only <u>wrote</u> it out of books & reviews & pictures. Knowing you to be <u>yourself</u> I am not afraid of asking, even tho it may not be possible or easy for you to agree to my request. But it seems to me that if you would give me even two or three sentences just to the point saying what you originally said to him, when you began to reform the dwellings

Forgive me if I shouldnt have written!

Do you ever hear from the Schuylers⁴ now & do you go on — I'm sure you do — thinking of dear Jeanie Senior⁵ as often as I do

> Yours sincerely & respectfully.
> Anne Ritchie

We now live here together.

From Mrs Ritchie daughter of Thackeray⁶

To Isabella Thackeray

Letter 74
Ray/Morgan

Hotel des Thermes
Aix les Bains
France
Friday Ev^g
[Postmark: 4 Sept. 1886]

My darling Mammy.¹ I was so glad to get your letter to day, & I was just going to send you the enclosed photograph to show you the way people come home from the baths here. You are wrapped up in a blanket & carried right off by two porters who bring you up to your very bedroom. I came here for the waters² (How I wish Mrs Thompson³ could come too & be cured, but she must try Ramsgate⁴ which is so much nearer at hand) & I shall be going home in a fortnight or so — I thought coming off very dreadful but it has been much nicer than I expected, & thank God I have had nothing but good news from Richmond & the children. Wasnt it a pity he couldnt come any bit of the way with me — I luckily found a friend on the road so that I have not been at all lonely. I am in a pleasant little hotel where they give one the most delicious things for dinner I have a pretty room with a lovely view & I pay 10/ everyday for everything. When I came Princess Louise⁵ was down stairs but she is now gone.

> Goodbye my dearest Mammy
> My love to Mrs Thompson.
> Ever your loving Nanny

To Austin Dobson[1]

Letter 75
U. of London
MS 810/III/154

27 Young Street
Kensington Sq. W
1. Heathfield Gardens[2]
Hampstead. June 11 [1887]

Dear Sir   How can I thankyou? — Your most beautiful & touching dedication[3] went to my heart & I can only tell you that I am grateful indeed. As I read your words about my Father I remembered how sympathy such as yours would have cheered & gladdened him & what extraordinary pleasure he always felt in the things which made us to whom he was so tender, happy — & so in all ways & times this most tenderly written & most kindly felt dedication which you have sent us would have made him glad I think.

I need not tell you how proudly I shall put by the lovely, dear little book to show our children some day, when they are old enough to understand how much their parents prize it.

Perhaps some day you would come & see us here, or in London where I should like to show you some of my Fathers drawings & the only remnant of his home that is now left.

And once more thankyou from yours most faithfully — most gratefully

Anne Ritchie

To Robert Browning

Letter 76
Yale

5 Sunnyside
Wimbledon
15 2 8[1]

My dear M! Browning

I am always asking favours of you! Shall you be at the Athenaeum on Monday — Would you kindly help Frank Cornish[2] of Eton to get in — I daresay they have already asked you & if so please forgive my troublesomeness but it is always good for ones soul to say howdydo to an old friend. — And I hope you wont mind.

We are here for 6 months & enjoy the birds & actually meeting red breasts & goats & nice fresh things — my Valentine to the children has been a pair of Pigeons

With my love to dear Miss Browning

Yours ever dear
Mr Browning
Anne Ritchie

To Elizabeth Robins[1]

Letter 77
Fales

Friday.
Kingsley Lodge,
Lingfield Road,
Wimbledon.
[1889–98][2]

My dear

I hope you remember your kind promise to come next Sunday to lunch & tea. The Darwins[3] are coming to meet you who have long wished to know you & I have asked Grace[4] & I send you a train paper — Do come by the early train if you can manage it & have a calm sit with me in the arbour before lunch

Y.^{rs} affect^{ly}
Anne Ritchie

How are you & have you had any more silver tea pots?

To Miss Browning

Letter 78
Fales

Kingsley Lodge,
Lingfield Road,
Wimbledon
[Postmark: My 29, 89]

My dear Miss Browning

I write this in case I dont find you to ask Mr Browning thro your kind intercession for I dont want to bore him when he is busy or harassed if he (who has already written Bily's[1] name) would now be so very very dear & kind as to write

Hester Helena Makepeace Ritchie
& <u>his own name</u> & 1st of June 1889 into the first page of this book for her birthday. We are going to get the whole set bound for her with the later ones, & she reproached me one day for having asked Mr Browning for Billys name only, & I promised when her birth day came I would come begging once more & I know you will forgive me. We are all very happily established in our little Villa & my blessed health really does seem to be returning at last, after a horrid winter & I do hope you you are both well & I love you very much & am your & Mr Brownings grateful & troublesome & always

        Affectionate
        Anne Ritchie

P.S.
 I started with this but I was prevented coming & I now post it & hope to come & fetch the book late on Wednesday or Thursday
 Am I grasping Even if I am I think you will forgive me

To Robert Browning

Letter 79   Kingsley
Yale   Monday
                22 7 1889[1]

My dear Mr Browning
 I cannot help writing just this one more word which is dear Friend. thankyou for your goodness Indeed I can appreciate it — & your letters which are just like you both

           Ever always
           Your affectionate
           Anne Ritchie

To Savile Clarke[1]

Letter 80
Fales

Kingsley Lodge,
Lingfield Road
Wimbledon.
[c. September 1890][2]
Monday.

Dear M.ʳ Savile Clarke

I am so much interested to hear from one or two of my friends that they have heard with interest of the forthcoming matinées — the one special friend I consulted says that as possessor of the copyright of the story wʰ furnishes the staple of the entertainment I ought to receive about 3/per cent of the gross receipts — or say £3 for every performance I suppose that during the run of any successful piece a good deal more than £100 is taken on average & that £3 a performance would be less than 3/p/c. I am of course ignorant on all these matters but I suppose all payments would be made by the manager of the theatre

Will there be one comprehensive contract to cover all parties interested ie. yourself, & M.ʳ Slaughter[3] for the music and myself, or will there be a separate agreement in each case? Meanwhile quite apart from the advantage to us wʰ a success wᵈ be — I can only tell you again how glad & delighted I shall be for every possible reason, if as I hope & believe your delightful enterprise is a real success. I remember how happy we used to be — when we were sure when things went well — Please remember me to M.ʳˢ Clarke & yʳ daughters

& believe me

Yʳˢ very truly
Anne Ritchie

To Savile Clarke

Letter 81
Fales

Kingsley Lodge
Lingfield Road
Wimbledon.
October 1.ˢᵗ [1890]

Dear M.ʳ Clarke

I was not able to write to you last night wʰ I am sorry for & I am anxious not to keep you waiting any longer than I can help. Of course having written you a business letter I am only obliged to you for sending me a direct business answer, & why should we be ashamed of writing business to one another.

As regards Mess.rs Smith and Elder[1] you are perfectly right in saying that the copyright is theirs, but as I told you they told me it was to be mine for this occasion & that I was to make my own bargain, so that for all practical present purposes, I am the owner of the copyright: when our present discussion is settled I undertake that there will be no difficulty about a formal letter from Mess.rs Smith & Elder   As to the terms, my letter was founded on the best advice I could get, but I quite admit I had no grounds on which to form any opinion of any kind   The question seems to be one of the division of author's profits between you & M.r Slaughter on the one hand, who furnish the piece & the music & me on the other as representing my Father who furnishes the characters & the frame-work of the plot. It would not I think be difficult for me to make up my mind, if I knew what sort of proportion of the 1 p/c you mention bears to the total amount to be paid for authors property, but I can quite understand that it may not be possible for you to state this and there may be a thousand good reason why in such cases Managerial Agreements must be kept private, in which case please dismiss my suggestion that I should see the agreement with the Manager without ceremony. The only other suggestion I can make is that instead of the percentage there should be a fixed payment for every performance which certainly would be a simpler plan.

You will think me I am afraid terribly business like, but as I said before why should we not write plainly for I am certainly not afraid of quarrelling with you & I sincerely hope you feel the same about me & believe me

Sincerely yours
Anne Ritchie

To Mrs. Savile Clarke

Letter 82
Fales

Kingsley Lodge,
Lingfield Road,
Wimbledon.
[21 December 1890][1]
Sunday

Dear Mrs Savile Clarke

I am still laughing, and clapping in spirit, & enjoying the remembrance of our happy expedition to Fairy Land last night! — How charming it all was, how pretty how harmonious — I do think Mr Clarke has seized hold of the Fairys own Blackstick & worked his delightful skills with it — though I must confess that we have untied the Rose & the Ring today & put them into water up to their chins, so as to keep your kind token as long as possible.

My husbands only suggestion w^h I do think might be effective is that Rosalba should come on in chains at the end of the 2^d act (as she does in the Lion picture), it w^d give more prominence to Giglios happy arrival in time to deliver her f^m the Lions.

How droll the two monks are — we have been raging we are, we are, we are — ever since & my husband began breakfast this morning with the ode to Kedgeree[2] I have written to Mr George Smith with Mr Ambrents[3] message about a new cheap edition for the bookstalls, & how I do wish he had been there to see our dear story come to life — Bulbo is quite admirable & Gruffanuff and Giglio whom I had not expected to admire was as good as possible, but that little creature with her little song was altogether pathetic & pretty. My children are both in love with her. I have kept my boy in bed all day today, but is much better & I am so glad he sh^d have seen the first play of his Grandpapas on such a happy first occasion. I hope you got home not too tired & chilled The young ladies are sure to have brightened the way for you.

Believe me yours Sincerely with all best X^s wishes
Anne Ritchie

To Charlotte Yonge[1]

Letter 83
Fales

Wedy [1891][2]
Kingsley Lodge,
Lingfield Road,
Wimbledon.

My dear Miss Yonge

    I read 'that stick'[3] last night before going to bed & then to my great pleasure found it was the January No. of the Monthly packet[4] that I had stolen from a friends house at Brighton, so that I could get some more chapters at once & then I found my little girl asleep upstairs with the Daisy Chain[5] by her bed side & I then began to think how often I too had had it by my bedside, & then what a pity — oh! what a pity it is that <u>we</u> are all growing old who have had such happy happy times with one another. (I am taking it for granted that an author w^d enjoy having made any reader as happy as you have made me in years gone & present too — for indeed <u>that stick</u> seemed to me as good & fresh & interesting as ever) — And then I thought time was passing & I should so like to say howdydo to so old a friend & to tell you once more how very real & delightful a bit of the holiday of my life is <u>yours</u> Another thing in the number touched me inexpressibly — dear dear poor Mrs Oliphants story[6] which <u>cut</u> one somehow knowing how it was written. I had a very sweet note from her as she was starting from Davos[7] — She had liked Sir Walters Diary[8] w^h I sent her to read & she had been ill she said — I have not heard any more for some weeks — We are still here at Wimbledon where the children thrive — & I should like to show you my daughter & my boy some day; — if ever we spend a night at Winchester again I shall think you will let me bring them We go on living here the children & my husband like it & I keep well & sit about more or less whereas in London I turn into nothing but a pillow & a bolster & night light Please forgive one for writing this hap-hazard letter, it is not from undue familiarity but the outcome of 52 years or shall I say 42 years — of the affectionate appreciation & sympathy of yours with real affection

                                  Anne Ritchie

To Isabella Thackeray

Letter 84
Ray/Morgan

Saturday
Kingsley Lodge,
Lingfield Road,
Wimbledon.
{Postmark: AP 12/91}

My darling mama

I have been doing something very nice. We had a dreary gap in the hedge at one end of the garden & two bushes running into one another at the other end & I have just given a man 6^s to carry the box bush from the place where it wasnt wanted to the place where it <u>was</u> wanted & the moment the job was finished down came a nice shower of rain. We have been having our lawn seen to, it had got into such a horrid muddy condition & all the poor borders had turned to slimy dirt but it is all greatly improved the last few days & the crocusses we planted in the autumn have come up very well indeed. Most of the laurel bushes have been killed this winter & we have also cut down a fusty old tree in front of the dining room window.

these children are all in the window painting <u>in oil</u> — We gave Billy some for his last birthday but he rather groans over them & says he likes to squirt them & not to paint. A friend reminded me yesterday that when he was a baby he came to see her garden & said Billy may pick de fowers not de pretty <u>rainbows</u> meaning the geraniums which stood in long rows & the daisies in the grass

Tell Mrs Thompson that I am only waiting to hear f^m Mr Fladgate to write to her I went there to try & hurry matters but nothing seems to have happened

Your loving loving Nanny

To Isabella Thackeray

Letter 85
Ray/Morgan

Talland House
St Ives
Cornwall
[Postmark: Ap 6/93]

My darling Mama.

You will like to hear that we are here all safe & that the change has already done Billy good He looks different & better & less transparent.

We got down very comfortably on the whole & found a beautiful bay & a lighthouse waiting & better still & a nice comfortable house with beds made & fires lighted The air is delicious <u>sleepy</u> soothing fattening just what we all need, & the town is so amusing & lively it is almost like a little foreign town Mrs Leslie Stephen[1] has arranged everything most beautifully for us

How glad I shall be of a line to tell me how you are & how Mrs Thompson is! — how I wish I had a nice delicious place to send you to like this one, where you could throw off y.^r horrid influenza — for Influenza I do believe yours has been. Your cough y.^r tongue & all about you were so <u>exactly</u> like Bills attack

I have some writing to do so I mustnt write any more but I just have left off a minute to send my hug & my love to my Mama.

Mrs Thackeray[2] came to see us looking quite radiant but I didnt ask about her new husband. Bless you. I asked a friend to choose you a <u>chair</u>. I'm afraid you will detest that red dressing gown but it seemed <u>warm</u> and loos [*sic*].

To Mr. Skeffington[1]

Letter 86
Fales

Aug. 13. [93][2]
Marlboro' House
<u>Cromer</u>

Dear M.^r[3]

I am interested to hear that <u>you</u> are the purchaser of Philip after all — I meant to have had it put up to auction & then when Mr Bain[4] told me there was a purchaser I thought I would settle the matter & have done with it — I am sure I have no more mss of Philip & as M.[5] Walker did the drawings I have no sketches that I know of. When I get home I will look & see if there are any rough suggestions by my Father — but I dont think so. The proof sheets come to nothing at all — just one or two of the Virginians — which I am going to bind up with the mss & keep.

I wont forget if ever I think of selling Boudin[6] to write to you — I thought of it abt Philip but having given it to M.[r] Bain I determined to leave the matter for his decision

Believe me
Yours truly
Anne Ritchie

To ?

Letter 87
Berg

The End House
Berkeley Place,
Wimbledon
[c. 1894–98][1]

Dear[2]

I am so sorry I am not yet ready to come down — Here is the lecture on Swift[3] — partly in my Fathers writing (about 25 p. & partly in mine as a girl) — you will see his corrections here & there. If M.[r] Pearson[4] w.[d] like to change anything will he please do so — Even the Rose and the Ring I sometimes wish back again![5]

With kind wishes for y.[r] journey
believe me Truly yrs

Anne Ritchie

Would you please take the Hoggarty[6] picture (It is one of his very best I think) a maid will bring you string & paper

From Henry James to ATR

Letter 88
Harvard

Tuesday
34, De Vere Garden S.W.
[1895]¹

Dear Mrs. Ritchie.

You wrote me a benevolent note some time ago which I have too much delayed to thank you for. I have been immersed in correspondence—that is flooded with letters, for the last 15 days—& have left my old friends confidently alone for the sake,—as it were—of my new, who have <u>most</u> made me nervous.—Should you care to see, some afternoon, my little play at the St. James's?² I say afternoon, because I haven't the assurance to suggest to you an evening struggle. Would <u>next Saturday</u> afternoon p.m.—i.e. afternoon—be possible to you if <u>I</u> should send you 2 or 3 seats—or a box? I will do this with joy if I hear from you affirmatively.—And about my coming out to you some evening, as I so much desire to do. Would either Monday, Tuesday or Wednesday of next week suit you—at 7.30—or the hour you may be so good as to designate I shall be delighted to come; & I am yours forever

<u>Henry James</u>

To William Ritchie

Letter 89
U. of London
MS797/I/5832

Seven o clock Sunday
116. Marine Parade¹
[1898]

My darling Bill Annie is just gone & the post is just gone & the sun is set, but it has been a most amusing day First we went to Roedean² for Annie to see the school & the Lawrences³ that was a sort of heaven — Then we went & had tea in a Metropole Limbo⁴ — I never saw anything so horrible & yet so amusing. It looked like all the Theatres boiled into one with the villains standing twirling their wicked mustacheos by every pillar & doorway & in every arm chair a sprawling millionaire: & Ladies my gracious! what ladies! Gamblers with lofty plumes & spangles Italian desperadoes flashing under sorts of helmets & curls & then icy snakey ladies wriggling — I had never seen anything more out of the common than a clergyman there before but this was the most sur-

 prising assemblage. Annie & I sat transfixed I wonder if anybody took us for gamblers our tea was very nasty but cheap at a shilling. I then came back in Lady Louises Loders[5] chair, & finally dispatched Nancy in a street fly to the station. She said she wished for you last Sunday when they had Uncle Leslie & Henry Sidgwick.[6] She said fortunately Albert[7] is very deaf & everybody shouted & Leslie could hear quite well

She is staying with her Papa till they go. Her papa is bringing out a book,[8] but nobody is ever to know what it is called. Reginald is to publish it. Codgie[9] has decided in favour of my favourite lodging — a large square Harrogate[10] like horror but cheap & well drained & our address will be Holmrook/Tunbridge Wells. I shall first think of the Trinity Raven & then of a rook, but Holm is beyond me I think it the most difficult word in the English Language to remember. I shall have a solitary week w{h} I am not sorry for, & on Friday I shall take leave of Mrs Brown.[11] Her family have come down for the day & make a most tremendous noise, & smoke in the drawingroom &tc. They have a dashing friend who has a Pullman car return ticket. The rabbit is to have a treat before we leave & go to the Devils Dyke[12] & I am going round to take leave of all my old ladies. We asked for Uncle Willie & Artie[13] at the Metropole today but they hadnt come so I had to sit in the porch without him Send me back her nice letter. Im sure he practices drawing those plaid trowsers

Goodnight my darling boy. Wizz[14] said your river expedition put him in mind of his own youth & expeditions.

Goodnight mon cher fils bienaimé

To William Ritchie

Letter 90   October 14, 1898
U. of London
MS 797/I/5830

My dearest darling Bill

My first letter must be for you & I had almost dated it f{m} Trinity College for I certainly have been there this morning tho it is only 7 o'c or so — Are you awake & unpacking — Did you arrive pretty early last night & dine in hall? I had a telegram from yʳ Father saying he was going to Paris & a delightful long letter from Hester about linen, dressing cases & packing telling me all the things I wanted to know. She says I am to send you some more money Let me know if this isnt enough by an odd chance I dived into a mass of papers last night & pulled out a most charming letter from Colonel Richmond Webb to his son who was just going to College. You will see it in the Edition[1] it says all the things one <u>feels</u> now my beloved Bill tho' parents don't say them so much & then other things belonging to the times "Learn to wield your sword and your pen" is one thing the Colonel recommends & then (not very complimentary) "I must dispose somehow of <u>all</u> your sisters & you & I and Mama will spend the winter in London"[2] — One sister must have gone to India & become yʳ great great grandmama

Tell Hugo[3] with my love I am expecting his mother to lunch today which is very delightful — We have got a pheasant & some grapes in her honour Codgie & Char[4] come on Monday & Miss Anderson[5] stays til Thursday if there is room, but the Lodgers seem unending. my good little Bessie[6] is going today She weeps because of her departing nurse & says wont <u>I</u> be her nurse. I go on enjoying the nice top room. Minnie[7] & Miss A are both on this floor — the Doctor has sold his horses whereat he is very jubilant — I never saw anything at the circus like the jumps & bumps of a horse I met on the common he went up right into the air the rider sat like a cucumber quite cool & firm. Darling boy write as soon as ever you can are your rooms tolerable can you keep yʳ window open — Im so glad the linen was all right

            Yʳ loving loving
            Mama

I'm pretty well.

To William Ritchie

Letter 91
U. of London
MS 797/I/5833

Thursday/Brighton
[c. Feb. 1899]

My Bill I went for the books yesterday after one of my tiresome cracks. I looked at them yesterday eve they are perfectly delightful I think — & I shall pack them and send them off tomorrow after I have shown them to Arty I hope he is coming to lunch, but I am not sure. Uncle Willy I have seen a good deal He has been most charming & kind. He talks more interestingly than almost anybody I know when he will talk once in a hundred years or so like an aloe[1] He has gone into Herbert Spencer[2] — who luckily for me called but left word he wouldnt come in & couldnt unbutton his coat so that he was not able to leave a card — This amused Uncle Willy who began lecturing me abt his books. He says he writes extraordinarily eloquently & conclusively but he sometimes starts on quite wrong premises w^h if they were true w^d be most convincing. He advises me to read Sociology.

Tell me when you write if you have the 2^d blue bound volume of Lamb's letters[3] I will send the 1st w^h is here (moping alone) with the Bewick[4] but the other may be in London. I blush for the way I have written y^r name I took immense pains & it looks like a cooks handwriting

If Arthur comes I shall take him — or them — to lunch at the Crescent as it will be more cheerful than the little back dining room here. In after years I believe he will be General Sir Arthur Field Marshal Lord Ritchie of Lexham but it is horrid seeing him go. He certainly ought to be all those things even if he isnt. W^h is better still than getting them when you dont deserve them

Y^r loving loving loving platitudinizing Mama

To William Ritchie

Letter 92
U. of London
MS 797/I/5834

Thursday
[c. Feb. 1899]

My Bill of Bills

I was just sending this idiotic picture off when Arty & Uncle Willy drove up in an open fly It was very very nice having him to lunch dear boy. Uncle Willy looked on. We went to the Hotel & I boldly ordered half a bottle of Champagne Roederer & a nice pudding & then (I confess it was Uncle Willys suggestion) beckoned the waiter & bought a cigar. Im so glad you can get away Satdy.

I'm afraid Wizz will be gone if he comes to T.W[1] but that you must settle It makes one very choky & cheerful too to see Arty he looks happy & well & is so dear.

I saw Uncle Willy walking away taking his arm & felt very near crying.

Mr Wright[2] has bought him a parting present an abomination like a watch hung to a massive chain it is a case for sovereigns I can hardly imagine any thing more useless. It holds 5 w^h w^d go into a waistcoat pocket & take up about as much room as a bun. As Arty gets 5/2 a day it will take some time to fill. I went to the Metropole & sat in state in the gorgeous halls between Uncle Willy & Master Arty

Good night my dearest son
God bless thee.

To William Ritchie

Letter 93
U. of London
MS/797/I/5838

Holmerook T Wells
[c. 17 Mar. 1899]

My Darling Bill this will come on y^r real birthday with Godbless you from your Mama

We are posting 2 buttonholes. You are to wear one & put the other in water Catena Something from America is the orchid. It is worth £10 a root. O joyful joy to think of seeing you on Tuesday Codge is coming back that day   Arthur does not yet know if it is Wednesday or Wednesday week he sails

We are wishing you luck and wondering about y.^{r} Ex.^{m} All the amusing things I can imagine perfectly the instructive things are much less easy to think of. I am plodding on thro' the Oxford book of the Colleges w.^{h} is really very interesting tho immensely long & I find there was a time when Trinity looked down upon Balliol. The master of B. finding his yg men didnt get on called them together & warned them against that hellish liquor cald ale; but immediately after Dr Bathhurst, of Trinity[1] who was Vice Chancellor having given leave to drink it the old master said he w.^{d} also give leave soe that now they might be sots by authoritie   with this choice anecdote I shall finish my birthday letter. After all Mothers & sons are more made up of all the things they dont say than the things they do say & you know all the things I think & feel & wish for my darling boy. I am just going to write to Mrs Hart.[2] I shall tell her that she mustnt keep anything for you & Hester but that you w.^{d} write if you found you could go for Hester thinks it w.^{d} be a long way   Adieu mon cher cher cher fils. Ta Maman

To William Ritchie

Letter 94
U. of London
MS/797/I/5841

9.15 a m Diningroom
clock goes
tick tock
[before Oct. 1899][1]

My Bill of Bills   Codge has gone off to ride on Wimbledon Common. She got very yellow & lost her appetite & instead of a doctor I said I would giver her £2 worth of rides so she went yesterday & came back blooming   (She did look so beautiful going off to dine at the Lawrences) & she is gone today to ride & I am up early expecting Wizz & I have been reading of the triumphs of Kruger[2]   If I were the 'Gov' I should give him an enthusiastic Reception over here too too & have done with it. Why dont they make him transparencies & Knight him & a crown of honor & send him about his stupid old business

Beloved I havent written much but I constantly pay you little inside visits. I devotedly went off to call on Miss Johnson in y.^{r} honour

Mr J. was <u>extremely</u> angry with us because some formality about

Arthur Shawe hadnt be [*sic*] carried out. I had been begging y.^r Papa to do it for years but he didn't believe me till this most alarming letter arrived. However it is all right & Miss J. is coming to lunch & Mr C. P. Johnson³ I trust is forgiving   I had a most interesting visit from Edward Morice⁴ who is, it turns out, the bosom friend of Mr Merivale & f^m him he had heard of our vague plans. He says if you will go & see him some time when you are up or down (w. is it — he will tell you every detail so that you should be able to judge. He says he was most miserable when he first left Oxford & went into the business & hated it for some years. Now, (I happened to ask him if he would leave it if he could   he says that he has had a fortune left him, & <u>could</u> retire but that he is going on & that is the best answer to my question

He says if the Johnson is a real offer you <u>couldnt</u> have a better opening but that without some such chance he would not have advised you to take it up as he is convinced the civil service w^d suit you better in every way.

Perhaps if you take a pretty good degree & if you go hard to Scoones when you leave Oxford you may after all get into the C S⁵   You c^d always go back to the Solicitorship if you didnt like it. If you get in — ever so low — you can be <u>fished up</u> remember.

Here comes the CB⁶   He has been writing a most diplomatic kind <u>clever</u> letter about some office business   I feel quite elated over it.

We are going to have a dinner party on Thursday

Mom	Wizz
Codge	Alfred Tennyson unknown gent
Mag	Mr Pelham
Imogen	George Booth
Nem	Alick

wish you were going to be the U. G.⁷

Bless thee
Thy Mama

Letters

To William Ritchie

Letter 95
U. of London
MS 797/I/5844

Saturday. Rain cats dogs &ct
[c. 1900]

My Bill of Bills. I hope you have recovered from y[r] fightings. What a nuisance that Trinity didn't win, but you have won so much that it makes it less monotonous, I prefer monotony however when things go right. It is still raining & we are going to drive to Scotland Yard to ask for H's umbrella. I am rather collapsy a mixture of Aunt Blanche & the concert proved too much for my digestion & I retired all yesterday & still feel rather squeamish: however a drive will get me up & Codge will be glad to recover her parapluie. Everyone ought to have 2 umbrellas one in each hand such weather as this —

Wizz has started for Kidbrooke[1] on Monday with exquisitely packed luggage. I have had rather fun with the Dicys[2] writing them a papyrus letter of thanks w[h] was approved of [*word illegible*] also I sent a copy of Cranford.[3] There sits Codgie bolt upright & sound asleep in her chair —

Lunch is over — She has had her Italian lesson — poor Will Royse[4] said the weather was repulsive & revolting I dont know if he wasnt even too damp to weep over Dante today h-ache & all I took a note to Desmond MacCarthy[5] to ask him to lunch tomorrow to meet Hester Adeline[6] Charles W[m] & M[r] and M[rs] Simon[7] — you know him I think f[m] Baliol, but D. M. is going to Cambridge to the Greek play. He lives in a nice little house with a charming old mother Char is now quite established with pictures & visitors Aunt Nelly is home P.[8] came yesterday

We are going to have a concert alas before y[r] return for M[r] McInnes[9] leaves on the 10th or 11 & our concert is to be the 7 also a dinner party to w[h] we are going to ask young M[r] Pelham Codge is producing various balls for you & her when you come back with a different disease I blush for my stupid letter & feel as if nothing ever happened worth writing or ever would happen, except in the papers — The Pollocks[10] were giving a quiet little luncheon party when a friend came in saying "I'm sure you wont mind my having brought the Chinese Ambassador" & a little old horrible man with a pigtail walked in He tells them he is sure to be executed on his return for his English tendencies so if the English cut him & the Chinese execute him he wont have a very good time I went to the old Simons. He asked abt you very kindly but he was very dull & depressed Boo is always drunk now w. adds to the dear old peoples melancholy happily Max[11] is established to keep his eye upon her

Bless you my dearest darling How we do still enjoy our luncheon & our tea. That was so comfortable. This sofa that I am lying on is as comfortable as yours only you arnt here but when you come it will be delightful & you shall make tea for w^h you have a special gift — Bless you again

We have been asked to the Darwin wedding

Codge still sounder asleep

From Henry James to ATR

Letter 96
Harvard

Reform Club
Pall Mall, S. W.
January
4th
1900

Dearest Anne Ritchie!

Your kind letter is a great balm—for I did wander forth yesterday into the fog & the dim distances, broken & desperate. Mary[1] was so invidious—that was the cruel thing. She so freely admitted you were at home—"but she's engaged with a Gentleman!"—much italicized. Dear Leslie is a gentleman if there ever was one,—but he's a a gentleman whom—well, whom, also, I should have been delighted to see. But all's well that end's well & I congratulate you on your gallant little Sentinel. If ever need be, she will perish at her post. On Friday next 11th at 8, I will dine with great joy! I'm so sorry you've had the trouble of a letter—which as I told Mademoiselle, was exactly what I wished to save you. "Yes, Sir," she slowly [?], heartedly replied—but closing the bright portal a little further.—I rejoice Richmond finds fine weather at

Rye,[2] & wish I could have helped him to other things. But I fled the other day, incapable after too long a continuity, incapable of another hour of it. May Brighton be blest to you.

Yours always Henry James

To William Ritchie

Letter 97
U. of London
MS 797/I/5840

[Carte Postale, postmarked Paris and Oxford Fe 20/00}[1]
S.[t] Romain. Monday

My Bill — We did wait for you & Wizz all yesterday. This morning is calm grey rainy grave & businesslike Codge is out taking a walk & I am looking out of window & neatly dressed there I looked for company

for you That is the shoemaker opposite on steps in the street dusting the walls in front of his house & his shop with a feather broom in the rain. There is a cook carrying home all the dinner in a big basket — then 2 policemen I cant draw them with hoods & military shako[2] The wind & rain make people bend. The heroic Codge is facing it all in her waterproof & little fur cap We are preparing for our journey tonight — Yesterday we enjoyed our place immensely — Everybody was noble but they did do it so well so pat, so alltogether, just like a fine bit of music. After the play we had tea at the fashionable tea-rooms americans with such hats & pearls & furs — hardly any English except a couple of weedy widows who seem to be having a good time I'll write a letter f[m] Chateau Rendel dont forget Chateau de Thorene [?] (Rene) Cannes France Then Pension Bellini Lungarno Florence Bless you f[m] y.[r] Mama Codge is quite well & so am I

To William Ritchie

Letter 98
U. of London
MS 797/I/5842

6 Embankment Gardens/Saturday
[late fall, 1900]

My Bill of Bills of Bills

It is agreeable to reflect that I shan't write next Saturday & now when we make plans we say O but Billy will be here & then we grin. I am going to call on the lovely Miss Opp[1] to invite her to lunch on Sunday, to meet You

This is rather Satanday than Saturday — moisty chilly foggy crawly grubby revolting & when I think of Brighton it seems a blaze of light, joys, jews, waves clouds & gleams along the horizon.

I came back in tearing condition for the dinner — Has Hester described it? M.r Pelham is as nice as a young man can be & wants to come & meet you. & talk things over. I said dont get into fistycuffs for he thinks of nothing but Baliol except for football. He said earnestly "Trinity is very good indeed you know & when I went to Cambridge they were speaking of a match between the two Trinities & with the greatest respect of our Trinity." Then we had Mag who was so pretty & nice & helped to do the table & M.r Thompson[2] who has a passion for Egyptology so I trotted out M.r Grefell[3] & the papyrus — Nem Alick & the Booths came. Poor poor George is so ill still. I do feel so sorry for him he had a dull evening between Nem & Mag Not so Imogen the sprightly one who sat between Wizz & M.r Pelham & looked very nice. So did Codge. I didnt look nice but I talked 19 to the dozen & made myself most agreeable & everybody murmured thanks when they went away for their delightful eveg. Codge had made a mistake & only ordered eno' vol-au-vent for one side of the table so ½ the people had a delicious dinner the other half had to put up with a hasty mince up; but that didnt matter in the least.

Here comes poor Codgie f.m the bank. She says it is horrid out of doors & neuralgic as well.

My darling Boy what more shall I tell you? — Hervey Fisher[4] is all but well. They are going to Lymington for the winter to escape Brighton fierceness. Claude Montefiore[5] came in while I was there, also looking the picture of health & jollity Wizz lives on bread & milk but

 he is quite well. I steadily eat my dinner with Codge & Wizz looking on I feel just like an Ogress — but I cannot help it, & I shall trust you to keep me company & set the fashion of eating again. Pinkie is coming tonight — last night Hester went to an Eve^g in Airlie w. is more crammed with choice objects than ever Olivia is very nice & Eleanor[6] in an exquisite hat feathers Now I will post this with my blessing I have come out in the C. H. M.[7]

8

1901–1919

INTRODUCTION

Who says, 'Youth's a stuff will not endure?' It lasts as long as we do, and is older than age. For those moments of eager life, of seeing and being, come back to us, and we babble of green fields and live among them to the very end.[1]

WRITTEN six weeks before she died, these lines embody the principles by which Anne Thackeray Ritchie lived her old age. Anny rejected the concept of *carpe diem* expressed by Feste the clown, but paralleled her experience with that of Falstaff.[2] In one of her essays Anny made a similar statement in response to her account of having seen John Lockhart being taken for a drive by Mrs. Sartoris. As an elderly woman she reacts to this youthful memory: "The clown says that youth is a stuff that won't endure. But moments of youth last as long as we do ourselves, and we babble of green fields to the last."[3] Anny believed that the past remains a constant part of one's life. From her past, from her life with her father and sister, she drew strength.

Anny kept the past alive both in her letters and in her writings. The letters of this period indicate that Anny maintained a steady relationship with her old friends like Henry James, Lisa Robins, and Maude Morrison Frank. During this time Anny was saddened by the deaths of numerous friends. Written in October of 1910, Letter 104 shows the effect of the death of William James on his brother, who was already suffering from a deep depression. In answer to Anny's repeated letters to him, Henry James submits the following explanation for his "poor acknowledgement":

> The reason is that for more than a year — all through my miserable illness of so many months — the days were almost heavier with rue than I could bear, & that of late, since my beloved Brother's death, I have sat stricken & in great darkness. (Letter 104)

According to Leon Edel, James's depression did not abate until the spring of 1911 when he returned to London.[4] Nevertheless, this letter to Anny has glints of the Jamesian wit. He describes America as "this prodigious & unspeakable & unlikeable country (one may love it, from the old customary superstition, but like it never!)." Although he borders on being effusive (he calls her "Dearest old Friend," "dear éprouvée & generous & exquisite friend"), the letter is genuine and heartfelt: "I yearn over you meanwhile & greet Richmond & your children ever so faithfully — & am yours, my dear Anne Ritchie, ever & so affectionately always."

Anny's letter to Henry James is playful and intimate. She addresses him as "Dear Henry Jaques." In Letter 108, written soon after Richmond's death, Anny confirms her intimacy with James. Despite its inauspicious beginning, their friendship had meaning for them both.

Anny's friendship with Leonard Woolf developed from her family ties to his wife. Anny's letters to him are poignant and compassionate. She asks for the return of a book she has lent to Virginia in hopes that "it might have . . . [a] peaceful soporific effect upon her — ! — would you — if she does not want it — send it back to me & forgive my boring you" (Letter 106); she wonders if they "w^d like the little Porch for a few weeks" (Letter 107). Concerned about Virginia's mental condition, she inquires as well about her work. They are the letters of an old woman, saddened by her niece's ill health, wanting to help, but powerless to do so. Her signature, "Yours auntfully," is both witty and wistful (Letter 106).

Still receiving correspondence from strangers about Thackeray, she responded. Even as late as 1913 she received requests for her own autograph — because she was Thackeray's daughter. Yet in some ways she and Richmond Ritchie had changed places. His position in the India Office was powerful and he was in demand socially. No longer the silent "infantile husband" of Miss Thackeray, but Sir Richmond Ritchie, he had made a place and a name for himself. Assured of his contribution to the India Office, he spoke of it with a proprietary conviction. Knighted in 1907, he carried the honor with dignity.

In the early letters of this period Anny continued to communicate with great authority, vitality, assurance. Despite tragedies, illness, and age, she had the ability to spring back and enjoy life. In a manuscript notebook, under the heading "Notes of Happy Things," she wrote between 1902 and 1905, "my message is nearly over now, but I mean to enjoy old age as much as I can. . . . I still love my own life and the lives of others very much indeed."[5]

Her greatest personal sorrow was the death in 1912 of Richmond Ritchie. Because she was so much older than he was, she had expected that she would predecease him. However, suffering from overwork and Ménière's disease, he died of complications. Days after his death she wrote to Henry James: "Your true note sounds thro my heart. . . . We are doing our poor best and thanking God for what has been & will not cease to have been" (Letter 108). Throughout her correspondence she makes frequent and loving references to Richmond. Upon being presented with her portrait, she wrote, "Naturally enough my first thought was how pleased Richmond would have been."[6] After the outbreak of World War I, her thoughts centered on him: "I long for Richmond every hour, and feel if he were only here."[7] All unhappiness of the past is forgiven; she remembers only Richmond's good qualities: his intelligence, his companionship, and finally his love. Seventy-five at Richmond's death, Anny finally accepted her old age. And she continued to work at several personally important projects.

Between 1894 and 1898 Anny had created introductions for thirteen volumes of her father's works which were published by Smith, Elder.[8] Swinburne commented on these introductions in the *Quarterly Review*:

> To the exquisite genius, the tender devotion, the faultless taste and the unfailing tact of his daughter, we owe the most perfect memorial ever raised to the fame and to the character of any great writer on record by any editor or commentator or writer of prefaces or preludes to his work.[9]

A second edition was conceived by Reginald Smith but never developed. The Centenary Edition, in twenty-six volumes, was planned to tie in with the anniversary of Thackeray's birth in 1911 and began to appear in 1910.

Her correspondence with Mr. Williams, the editor of her Centenary introductions to Thackeray's *Works,* is self-assured but never dogmatic. Aided by Hester, she was diligent in asserting the facts as she remembered them. In Letter 105 she corrected the date of her "little drawing [which] was later than 54. I had given my Father a certain dressing gown with my first earnings w^{h} he is wearing." Not satisfied with merely compiling another set of introductions, she assiduously followed up all particulars (Letter 102). With her usual modesty, she acknowledged suggestions made to her by Richmond and Hester (Letters 101, 102). Not above recognizing the value of someone else's ideas, she wrote:

> One thing I do think we might with advantage borrow from the various Melville Editions — printing the yellow facsimiles to each novel in turn. It gives a certain character to the books to appear with their old dress & habit. (Letter 102)

The facsimiles of the title pages were included and add greatly to the flavor of the edition.

Anny expanded her original biographical introductions for the Centenary Edition by inserting more sketches, portraits, unpublished letters, and journal entries. The latter introductions are more anecdotal than the earlier ones. They serve the same purpose of humanizing Thackeray and elucidating his work. MacKay has stated in her introduction to a recently republished edition of the introductions that "[b]y writing Thackeray's biography, [Anny] reconstructed herself as a fellow artist."[10] At the same time that Anny created her father's biography, she fashioned her own biography, and saw herself in juxtaposition to her father.

In 1914, just before the war, John Singer Sargent drew Anny's portrait. Given to her by her friends, it delighted her: "It really is an enchanting picture. . . . I feel quite shy before my portrait, it is so human, and I feel so like it, yet more grim, alas!"[11] Included in the 137 friends who subscribed to it were J. M. Barrie, Arnold Bennett, Rhoda Broughton, Henry James, and even Pierpont Morgan. Edmund Gosse's description of the portrait should be cited:

> Here Mr. Sargent, with his wonderful discernment of character, gives us a commentary on Lady Ritchie's nature, . . . The pure full arch of the forehead, the smiling eyes, by turns so keen and so vague, the sensitive and mobile mouth, all combine to render that look of exquisite and humorous sensibility, that quaint refinement which were native to the charming original.[12]

Just as her portrait remains to show us what she looked like, so her books remain to illustrate her writing ability and her unique habit of mind. *Blackstick Papers* (1908) and *From the Porch* (1913) are collections of articles and a short story, all previously published. After editing and revising them, she wrote, "My printed page has done very well, and is going into a second edition. I liked putting the scraps together, rewriting some of them and thinking of the beloved past. It seems so great a boon to live back again."[13]

Ramblings into the past, these articles are filled, nevertheless, with vitality, humor, and insights. Named for Thackeray's good fairy in *The Rose and the Ring*, *Blackstick Papers* contains, as Anny explains, "certain things in which she was interested—old books, young people, schools of practical instruction, rings, roses, sentimental affairs, etc., etc."[14] Anny discusses the education and condition of women, poets, musicians, writers, Paris in the spring, and a scene that caught her eye:

> Look at the greengrocer's man washing his carrots which flash with colour in the slanting sun rays, while the owner of the shop, sitting on a straw chair with an ink-bottle carefully adjusted into a sack of potatoes, is writing his accounts in a book. (154)

In a piece on "Jacob Omnium" (Matthew James Higgins) Anny writes with true Thackerayan humor:

> Carlyle called my father a Cornish giant once, and Mr. Higgins he dubbed Eupeptic giant. Not being eupeptic himself, grim Thomas seemed to disapprove of tall men and of many other obvious and inevitable facts. (182)

From the Porch contains thirteen articles divided into three sections: "Divagations," Monographs," and "Reminiscences." This book, too, has scattered throughout it flashes of perception, now rather simply and unself-consciously placed, such as, "What we human beings seek for in life, is life, and we instinctively turn to it."[15]

From Friend to Friend (1919), edited by Anny's sister-in-law Emily Ritchie, is a collection of six essays and a short story, all previously published, and two unpublished letters of Thackeray's. According to Emily Ritchie, one of the essays, "In a French Village," contains the last words Anny ever wrote for publication.[16] This slight piece is evidence that, however diminished, Anny's power to describe a scene was still in force. She depicts a French village celebration for the war heroes of the Franco-Prussian War. Later, in 1918, at Freshwater, she added the words, "This was written in August, 1913. Was it some presentiment which so impressed us as we stood by during the village-gathering, of the far more terrible war which was to over-shadow the old one?" (121) After the armistice of World War I, Anny added a letter written to her by her grandson James Ritchie describing London on that fateful day. The juxtaposition of the two—the small French village and the great city of London—both in the throes of celebrating the cessation of war, is a telling stroke, yet marred with sadness and irony. Each festivity commemorated the end of war. Anny witnessed the celebration for the end of the Franco-Prussian War and now her grandson is witnessing the rejoicing for the end of a world war. In France and in England, indeed all over the world, cessation of hostilities is commemorated, and yet, wars continue. James wrote, "One felt that the dark cloud that had been hanging over us for four years had been suddenly cleared away, thank God, and we have all emerged, sadder and wiser" (123). Emily Ritchie adds that Anny "wished [James's letter] printed as a fitting conclusion" to her essay.[17]

The later letters of this group show a gradual decline of Anny's powers, but never a complete loss. More strikingly, an increase of weariness, which she tried to dispel with her usual buoyancy, becomes apparent. Occasionally this despondency surfaces in a single telling sentence in her letters. For example, "I do hope you will both come in happier times" (Letter 109); "But we have had sad news of our own from the front & we are only cheering up again" (Letter 111). Yet she never loses her felicity with words. She thanks a friend for a letter: "It picked me up & patted me on the back & shook me by the hand & said old friend old friend, so sweetly & caressingly that I dont know how to thank you" (Letter 112). In 1915 she wrote with a sense of playfulness:

> Everything is so sad and unnatural that to fly away into one's youth and the youth of one's friends and companions is the best calmer and comforter. I wish you could get younger and younger, and I too! and that one could go off via childhood again.[18]

Despite the plague of increasing illness and advanced years, she remained optimistic and enthusiastic, her imagination always spinning tales of happier times. On a visit to London at the start of 1917, she tries still to maintain an optimistic and happy demeanor, but the strain of the war and of her age wears through: "It is a good thing one is nearing the end at last, for life is too overpowering for this tired mortal coil" (Letter 112). But with characteristic resilience she still brings humor to the situation. She continues, "I hope I shall be two or three young cheerful capable people in my next life."

During the war she wrote articles, raising money for the refugees and for the wives of service men. Thanking an American friend for her contribution, she wrote:

> The best anodyne to worry & anxiety is trying to help a little & I am thankful that there are certainly things old people can do. . . . It gives one a reason for going on still, but O how one prays for an end to all this. (Letter 110)

First through the death of her favorite nephew, Arthur Ritchie, and later through the bombing of her home in London, she felt the reality of war. In Letter 111 she wrote from the Porch, her home on the Isle of Wight, outlining the reasons for removing from London:

> With my bronchitis it is such a problem keeping quiet enough & keeping the house warm eno' that it seems easier to spend the winter here where we can get wood to eke out the coal & where there is plenty to interest us & occupy us.

The society at Freshwater still centered around Farringford, now occupied by the new Lord Tennyson as by his father before him, who was a close friend of Anny's as his father had been.[19]

Anny spent the last two years of her life there, writing to friends and relatives, and enjoying visits from her family, particularly from her grandchildren.

> You may imagine how happy we are to have them here neatly packed in the little Porch. . . . We are beautifully decorated with loops of mistleto & ivy berries. The Soldiers attracted by the magnificence of our porch garlands all came to sing glees to us last night. I wish you could have heard James & the little girls singing Good King Wencelas & marching round the room as they sang. (Letter 114)

As Henry James noted, Anny was "an infatuated grandmother" (Letter 104). Her last available letter is a picture postcard, almost illegible, of one line, to her granddaughter Catherine: "I am sitting up & send my love / Grandmama" (Letter 115). Written shortly before her death, it illustrates Anny's insistence on keeping in touch with her grandchildren, on participating in life, through the one medium which never failed her—writing. Anny died, following a brief illness, on 26 February 1919.

All her life Anny had no head for numbers, lost track of dates, and often seemed to act in a vague and disorganized manner. Her writing sometimes bore these marks—not in their composition but in their manuscript form. Establishment mores bored her; there was no room in them for her fancy. In a book of memoirs George Smith wrote:

> [Anny's] "copy" for her books was a medley of pieces of paper of all shapes and sizes, written here and there and fastened together with a needle and thread: an expressive symbol of her somewhat vagrant genius. . . . [She was] a woman of genius—with many of the characteristics—and some of the limitations, of a woman of genius.[20]

Eccentric and genius, both implied in Smith's summary, are the characteristics most frequently used to describe Anny. In different ways they are both appropriate and both incomplete. Anny was unique as a personality and as a writer. No one who was muddleheaded could have written twenty-one books, countless introductions, and innumerable articles. The proper daughter of a Victorian household, she nevertheless found ways to be herself—an original. Thackeray gave her the courage to stand alone. When he said, "I am afraid she will grow up to be a man of genius," he was able to foretell that she would move contrary to the mainstream of women of her time. Outwardly she conformed to Victorian mores; when they did not suit her, she forgot the numbers or dates, blamed it on faulty memory. As she got older, Anny sometimes neglected the distinctions of the present because she spent so much time in the past. In this way, she did as she liked without flouting society, and for it she was labeled eccentric and patronized and indulged by a male-oriented world. Being a lady bred, she was never abrasive, but softly achieved her purpose. Her vagueness and disorganization were not studied effects; they were unimportant details about which she chose not to concern herself. Just as there was a hard core of reality underneath her most frothy writing, so there was a pith and marrow of great strength within Anny herself.

Many of Anne Thackeray Ritchie's critics have been unable properly to value her writing because they adored the woman, and because of this, they did not deal seriously with the artist. In addition, the myths that engulfed her—Thackeray's daughter, vague and disordered, a Victorian dinosaur, a social butterfly—all contributed to obscuring her writing. Beguiled by the surface ease with which she wrote, and her casual and modest acceptance of her own work, they looked no further. They have qualified their praise by comparing her to Thackeray, or pointing out that her métier was not fiction but prose, or not prose but letters. Critics have gushed over her as well—for all the wrong reasons. Her writing was wholesome; it was full of "Matthew Arnold's hackneyed catchword . . . 'Sweetness and light.' "[21]

Critics commonly compared her, unfavorably, with Jane Austen. Leslie Stephen did this in his estimation of her writing which he placed in an entry under her husband's name in the *Dictionary of National Biography*. In his *Mausoleum Book* he decries her eccentric method of composition:

> [Anny] showed more perception and humour, more delicate and tender and beautiful emotion, than would have made the fortune of a dozen novelists, had she had her faculties more in hand. Had she, for example, as I often thought, had any share of Miss Austen's gift for clearness, proportion and neatness, her books would have been much better and incomparably more successful. . . . She wrote fragments as thoughts struck her and pinned them (with literal not metaphorical pins) at odd parts of her MS. . . . I remember how old Trollope (who was free from *that* fault!) and G. Smith and I used to entreat for a little more orderly arrangement of her plots, the relationship of her characters and so forth. (14)

That Anny could not or would not learn to write like Jane Austen was a subject of grave concern to Leslie Stephen. Perhaps Anny was not capable of changing; more likely, she chose not to do so. Whatever the reason, Anny did not become a pallid copy of Jane Austen. As Virginia Woolf pointed out, Anny remained true to her own vision. Stephen seems not to recognize that the source of Anny's eccentricity was also the source of her special strengths.

In 1897 Leslie Stephen wrote, "If anybody compared our letters they would say that it was like a dove talking to a gorilla."[22] Slippery to explicate, the metaphor of the dove was used again by Edmund Gosse. When "A Discourse on Modern Sibyls" was published in the *Cornhill,* Gosse wrote to congratulate Anny, "You are yourself the one authentic Sibyl left, with your delicate wavering style that is like shot silk . . . George Eliot is satin, Mrs. Gaskell is velvet, but you are the dove's neck."[23] From her own day onward, readers of Anne Thackeray Ritchie have been surprised at how good her writing really is.

In Virginia Woolf's second novel, *Night and Day* (1919), the character of Mrs. Hilbery is based on Lady Ritchie. Discussing her novel, Woolf wrote to Vanessa Bell, "My only triumph [in *Night and Day*] is that the Ritchies are furious with me for Mrs. Hilbery."[24] And again, "I think the most interesting character is evidently [Mrs. Hilbery] who is made exactly like Lady Ritchie down to every detail apparently. Everyone will know who it is of course."[25] In the novel Mrs. Hilbery is writing the biography of her famous poet father. As the mother of the heroine, Mrs. Hilbery brings the two lovers together. Mrs. Hilbery ascertains that her daughter Katherine and Ralph love each other, and acts as the *deus ex machina* to furnish the novel's happy conclusion. Traveling to the unfashionable side of London, Mrs. Hilbery brings back the hesitant Ralph in a trip with many diversions. As with Anny, her eccentricities lead to an unexpected truth.

Virginia Woolf's portrayal of Anny as Mrs. Hilbery is of course an equivocal one. As Gordon Ray sums it up:

> Though there is more than a touch of animus in Virginia Woolf's picture of Lady Ritchie as Mrs. Hilbery struggling helplessly with her poet-father's biography in Chapter 3 of *Night and Day*, the episode is not altogether without warrant.[26]

Virginia Woolf leads one to believe that Mrs. Hilbery will continue to bumble along, collecting material for, but never finishing her father's biography. Anny completed two sets of biographical introductions for Thackeray's *Works*. In many places Mrs. Hilbery is a caricature of Anny; but Woolf also appreciates her strong points:

> Ideas came to her chiefly when she was in motion. She liked to perambulate the room with a duster in her hand, . . . musing and romancing as she did so. Suddenly the right phrase or the penetrating point of view would suggest itself, and she would drop her duster and write ecstatically for a few breathless moments. . . . And yet they were so brilliant these paragraphs, so nobly phrased, so lightning-like in their illumination, that the dead seemed to crowd the very room.[27]

Woolf repeatedly endows Mrs. Hilbery with a certain magnificence, and then, through caricature and parody, undercuts her portrait. For example, after extolling her writing skills, Woolf adds, "many of these [paragraphs], it is true, were unfinished, and resembled triumphal arches standing upon one leg, but as Mrs. Hilbery observed, they could be patched up in ten minutes, if she gave her mind to it" (42). In a review of *Night and Day*, Ford Madox Ford described Virginia Woolf's attitude toward the Hilberys and their class: "You find it difficult to know whether she approves of them or whether—as is probably the case—she isn't mocking at them tenderly."[28] Ford is correct in finding Virginia Woolf's feeling for Anny ambivalent. In a letter to Vanessa Bell, Woolf wrote:

> And I've just done Aunt Anny, on a really liberal scale. Yes, since I wrote last she has died. . . . I suppose my feeling for her is half moonshine; or rather half reflected from other feelings. Father cared for her; she goes down the last, almost, of that old 19th Century Hyde Park Gate world. . . . For myself, though, she need have had no anxieties on this head, since I admired her sincerely.[29]

If Aunt Anny had not been a Victorian, she would have fared better in the hands of the younger novelist. Woolf's own hostility for that Hyde Park Gate crowd found its target in Lady Ritchie as Mrs. Hilbery.

Yet Woolf could see beneath the tea-party manners to the strength and uniqueness of the "ancient voyager" and "magician" (483, 485) when she assessed her as a writer. In a review entitled "The Enchanted Organ," Virginia Woolf discusses a book of newly published letters of Anne Ritchie. She was, recognized Woolf, "always escaping from the Victorian gloom and dancing to the strains of her own enchanted organ."[30] In this essay, written five years after Anne Ritchie's death, and therefore with more dispassion and distance than the one written directly after her death, Woolf paid general tribute to her aunt's abilities as a writer:

> But if her random ways were charming, who, on the other hand, could be more practical, or see things when she liked more precisely as they were. . . . Her most typical and, indeed, inimitable sentences rope together a handful of swiftly gathered opposites. To embrace oddities and produce a charming, laughing harmony from incongruities was her genius in life and letters. . . . She was a mistress of phrases which exalt and define and set people in the midst of a comedy. . . . And the music to which she dances, frail and fantastic, but true and distinct, will sound on outside our formidable residences when all the brass bands of literature have (let us hope) blared themselves to perdition. (836)

Even in the *Times Literary Supplement* article to which Woolf refers in her letter to her sister, published shortly after Anny's death, Woolf pays tribute to Anny the writer on "a really liberal scale." Three times she uses the word "genius": "a writer of genius," "Lady Ritchie's genius," and "whimsical and capricious genius."[31] The ending, sentimental and florid, is not characteristic of Woolf; Anny herself would have laughed at it. Yet within the body of the article Woolf says much that is valid and laudatory:

> While none of her novels can be called a masterpiece, each one is indisputably the work of a writer of genius.

She was completely and transparently faithful to her vision. In other words she was a true artist.

With all her power of creating an atmosphere of tremulous shadows and opal tinted lights, with all her delight in the idyllic and the rapturous, the shapes of things are quite hard underneath and have, indeed, some surprisingly sharp edges.

In her task . . . of recording the great and small figures of her own past . . . the whimsical and capricious genius has its scope unfettered and exquisitely inspired. . . . she invented an art of her own. . . . But her skill in suggesting the mood, the spirit, the look of places and people defies any attempt to explain it. (123)

Although not actually related by blood, Anne Ritchie and Virginia Woolf remain linked, and their relationship has attracted the attention of a number of critics.[32] Talented, individualistic, and honest, both writers shared a common heritage. Despite their great difference, both in temperament and in achievement, they admired and respected each other. One of the differences between them was that Anny never used Virginia Woolf, or anyone else, as the model for a caricature. And Woolf also owed more to Anny than she ever admitted or recognized. As Winifred Gérin sees it:

[T]hey had in common the poet's vision, the capacity to see. It was Virginia's recognition of this hidden power in her aunt that made her perhaps take stock so closely of her every variation of mood. And Anny was unwittingly setting her an example as the eminent writer she herself intended to be. (242)

In 1952 a *Times Literary Supplement* article stated that "no enthusiast has as yet thought to establish a cult of Anne Thackeray Ritchie" despite the fact that "to-day she is forgotten."[33] The critic pleaded for Anny to "speak for herself" in her own letters and reminiscences. Yet, this writer, sympathetic as he was to her, nevertheless added that "though she may have earned no permanent place in the history of English literature, yet [she] escapes oblivion by virtue of her unquenchable kindliness and charm" (92). Perhaps Anny's misfortune was that she was too "eupeptic," too good-natured, to be seriously considered by some critics, who could essentially dismiss her in this way with praise for her "kindliness and charm." Unlike the Brontës, Anny's life allowed no legend of possibilities cut off by personal tragedy; unlike George Eliot, Anny did not occupy an intellectual throne that could add status to her position as a novelist; unlike Woolf herself, she did not see her art as the fragile exercise of genius. She wrote easily and naturally, every day until she died, and without the fuss attendant upon it by those who perceived writing as a God-given vocation. It was what her father had done—and it was what she did.

In contemporary criticism, most writing has explored Anny's relationship with her father.[34] Even Winifred Gérin, Anny's first biographer, came to her in a convoluted and secondhand fashion. Gérin wanted to write about Thackeray, but, in her own words, "It would have been presumptuous to write about just Thackeray after Ray's book."[35] She turned, instead, to Anny and traced the relationship between father and daughter. Appreciative of her writing, and sympathetic to her life, Gérin nevertheless depicts Anny essentially as Thackeray's daughter. Gérin writes of their relationship: "Anne Thackeray's love for her father was of the essence of her life. She was more his child by inheritance of mind and spirit than most children are to their parents" (268). Certainly Thackeray was the most important factor in her life; but more than that, Anny partook of the essence of his life. As Leonard Woolf wrote, "Aunt Anny was a rare instance of the child of a man of genius inheriting some of that genius."[36]

In critical reviews and personal memoirs about Anne Thackeray Ritchie, the one word that keeps recurring is: genius. This cannot all be ascribed to excessive Victorian civility. In defining the parameters of the novel, Henry James refers to Anny as "a woman of genius." Against all things Victorian, Virginia Woolf nevertheless used the word genius for her aunt Anny.

Thackeray's daughter Anny, the writer Miss Thackeray, and Sir Richmond Ritchie's wife Lady Ritchie, all elicited hyperbole from friends, relatives, and critics alike. With a tremendous capacity to love and be loved, Anne Thackeray Ritchie kept her old friends and made new ones all her life. Prickly only enough to give her conversational zest, she was tolerant and broad-minded. Enthusiastic, ebullient, and optimistic despite all the tragedies in her life, she inherited, from Thackeray, the ability to know and insist on reality. Like him, she disliked humbug, and was not hesitant in ferreting it out. Her optimism stemmed from her genuine love of people and their possibility for good. Being her father's daughter, she perceived that reality carried with it evil, but never conceded the world to the cynics. Like Thackeray, she was a moral writer, but she also understood that human nature was frail, that no one was all evil, and that fate could deal sudden or secret blows to the just or unjust. She embraced the world—with its misfortunes—and looked for its happiness, indeed made it, where she could. "I do thank God," she wrote, "that life is not only bad and hard, but strong and kind and enduring."[37]

LETTERS 99–115

To Henry James

Letter 99
Harvard
(392)

Friday [c. 1901–12]¹
109, St George's Square, S.W.

Dear Henry Jaques I had a delightful account from Miss Askwith² of the medieval apparition of the men of mark of today — marching right out of the temp Edwards & Henrys with dignified robes & impassive mien & being cheered by the young men of today — I cannot find it in the Times³ & I do hope I am giving you the proper title

and I find I do take an interest & a very warm one in <u>my</u> own interest in honouring of my friends — however old friend I am! — & Im y^r affect

AIR

I went to the Irish play last night — did I take an interest I wonder? —

To "Dear Madam"

Letter 100
Princeton
AM21903

109 St George's Square, S.W.
May 30 1904

Dear Madam

I am sure you will understand when I tell you that although I should like to do as you request, & send you, what I am sure you w^d value — , I have so little left of my Father's mss — & I still — after 40 years — get so many letters about it that I am obliged to my great regret to make a rule to refuse any but old friends and relations. It seems very churlish but I have no other way to preserve something for my children

Believe me
Faithfully y^{rs}
<u>Anne Ritchie</u>

To W. J. Williams[1]

Letter 101
Princeton
AM 15626

109 St George's Square, S.W.
[19 May 1906][2]

Dear Mr Williams

My daughter has read marked & is delighted with the introductions. She has made one or two excellent suggestions — once I had repeated myself —

another page she wants me to keep back out of the Newcomes for the final volumes for w^h we shall want material Having quoted Miss Hennell it was rather long to again quote Mr Elwin[3]

I am returning the mss of the Lectures on the Eng: Humourists & the IV Georges (withdrawing pp. 12 & 24 about Charity Humour w^h comes in later on) the Newcomes (withdrawing p 45 . 46 — a portion of 47, & page 48 & Christmas books

Y^{rs} sincerely
Anne Ritchie

To W. J. Williams

Letter 102
Princeton
AM 15626

Swannington House
18 Sept [1910][1]
Leicester

Dear Mr Williams

Here are the two portraits I wrote of. I think they are both very good — better than some of those we selected. I should much like to come again with my daughter & look at our collection when we return on the 1st of 8^{br}[2] Will the 4th or 5th suit you to see us?

I am writing to Cambridge & also to Mr Lambert.[3] I was busy & accidentally prevented from doing so yesterday — & I have not yet had time to go thro' the proofs but I send you certain passages from the Introductions w^h my husband wrote down for the 26th Volume w^h I think might follow the preface in Italics & w^h I think express all that Mr Reginald Smith[4] wished said. It seemed to me better than anything I could write & they — as you suggested — follow admirably upon the preceding sentences. The rest of the Introduction will remain for V. 26.

One thing I do think we might with advantage borrow from the various Melville Editions — printing the yellow facsimiles to each novel in turn.[5] It gives a certain character to the books to appear with their old dress & habit.

I have been reading & comparing, & I am glad to have another fortnight here to get on & to compare the lists & proofs you kindly send me with what material we have

Can you remember what happened about the quotation from Elwin[6] — I think we rec.d permission to quote from it at the time

I will write no more now as I wish to catch this post.
With thanks

Yours very truly
A Ritchie

To W. J. Williams

Letter 103   Sep 20/10[1]
Princeton
AM/ 5626

Do you like 'Centenary' in inverted commas.

The Centenary Biographical Edition. — seems to me to be much more dignified unquestioning & <u>English</u>. America uses inverted commas more than we do.

2). Would you place the picture as I have not got it here.

3) p 18. Kindly alter this page

AIR

From Henry James to ATR

Letter 104   [30 Oct 1910][1]
Harvard

Dearest old Friend.

I have to thank you for the most generous & repeated bounties, renewed signs of tenderness & fidelity of remembrance by which I have been greatly touched & yet this poor acknowledgement is shamefully belated & weak. The reason is that for more than a year—all through my miserable illness of so many months — the days were almost heavier with rue than I could bear, & that of late, since my beloved Brother's death,[2] I have sat stricken & in great darkness. It has all together meant a great deal of blackness, for the worst of my illness was a hideously cruel & melancholic nervous crisis — following on a primary damnable disorder. Then came this tragic climax of my loss of my wonderful & admirable brother the most valued & cherished, & pre-eminent presence in my life. However, that is what it is — such ordeals are what it is — to have a life; as no one knows in this prodigious & unspeakable & unlikeable country (one may love it, from the old customary superstition, but like it never!) but the end of that will come, & when I return to dear old England (which I both love and like!) I shall be more in London (which I really adore) than the recent years have allowed & then I shall come & show you a hundred yards of the silver cord all shining & straight & strong. Meanwhile the company of this one handful of the only near relatives I have left in the world infinitely sustains & consoles me — for the reason that they happen to be each & all valuable & charming, which is an extraordinary piece of good fortune to their aged & doting & dazzled relative. It's the next thing to being, like you, an infatuated grandmother — which would have been, better than you, dear éprouvée[3] & generous & exquisite friend. I have seen you far too little for far too long — & yet you have always let me feel that no thread of our particular old silver cord of friendship was the least bit loosed. I am spending 3 or 4 — 4 or 5, or even more — months with my sister in law & my singularly interesting & delightful nephews & niece.[4] I feel, my real vocation. I yearn over you meanwhile & greet Richmond & your children ever so faithfully — & am yours, my dear Anne Ritchie, ever & so affectionately always

Henry James

Cambridge
Mass. U. S. A.
Oct: 30: 1910

To W. J. Williams

Letter 105
Princeton
AM15626

109, St George's Square, S.W.
Sp 30/11[1]

Dear Mr Williams

I see my little drawing was later than 54. I had given my Father a certain dressing gown with my first earnings w^h he is wearing The facsimile page is all right & out of the big 4 George Note book but it evidently concerns early times — Put it into 25 if you think it easy

I see I made a slip of grammar in that last little note

Will you kindly have it re-typed

Y^{rs} in haste
AIR

To Leonard Woolf[1]

Letter 106
Berg

9 St Leonards Terrace
Chelsea
June 1 [c. 1912–16][2]

Dear Leonard. I wonder if you would do me a kindness — one gets little <u>fads</u> as one grows old — I find one of mine is to read myself to sleep over certain books w^h send me off peacefully. I despatched one of these to dear Ginia[3] — C Leslies Life & letters[4] thinking it might have the same peaceful soporific effect upon her — ! — Would you — if she does not want it — send it back to me & forgive my boring you — I find that I miss it & I cant get another copy easily

But what I want still more is a good account of her & news of her. Are you coming to London at all — Is she pretty well — Is V's new book[5] out are you ever this way. I went to Gordon Square w^h seemed full of workingmen then I wrote to Nessa,[6] but I have not heard from her & now I shall cast this upon the waters for I do want to hear something of you all

Yours auntfully
<u>Anne Ritchie</u>

I am here till Sat^{dy} next.

To Leonard Woolf

Letter 107
Berg

9, St Leonard's Terrace,
Chelsea, S.W.
July 9 [c. 1912–16]

Dear Leonard

I am beginning to think I sh^d so much like a note from you about dear Ginia if you w^d kindly write here or to Kilmonan Freshwater Bay IW,[1] where I am going for a final week end to be with the children I wonder whether some day you & she w^d like the little Porch for a few weeks Molly McCarthy is there. You have to take a maid for they are difficult to gather on the island That is the only impediment

With my love to V

    Yours ever & looking forward to the new book
    Anne Ritchie

To Henry James

Letter 108
Harvard
(393)

[Oct. 23] [1912][1]

Your true note sounds thro my heart.
Thank you dear old friend

    Yr
    AIR

Be well get well We are doing our poor best and thanking God for what has been & will not cease to have been.

To Maude Frank[1] and Sister

Letter 109
Columbia

9, St Leonard's Terrace
Chelsea, S.W.
Aug 21 [1914]

Dear Maude Franks

Here is a little scrap of my Father's mss — I wonder if you will think it as interesting as I do — It is f.^m the Newcomes where the Colonel goes to ask Barnes for Ethel for Clive & you see a little drawing underneath[2] I found it by chance & it is worth about £4 or £5

I am just leaving home please <u>register</u> & return it to me if for any reason you do not care to keep it. It has been printed from, for the printers name is there You & Miss Schodle[3] have been so kind to us, that before going I tried to do as you wished & looked for something you might like <u>This framed</u> I think w^d be a memento you might value — I would gladly keep it and indeed I should like to give it you but I have promised my children to keep from giving without consulting them. & they are both away & not well[4]

It is a very sad solemn time for us. One can only thank God for the courage & goodness of the brave allies— & those the Germans driven to war by their officers their officers ache ones heart. May God grant peace.

I do hope you will both come in happier times & go on being our friends

In future I shall only think of you as my Fathers friend and appreciator & ours & with all love & good wishes to you both think of me dear Miss Franks[5]

To Maude Frank and Sister

Letter 110
Columbia

London 21 Jan [1915]
9, St Leonard's Terrace,
Chelsea, S.W.

Dear Miss Franks What a kind friend What kind friends you are. I dont think I can do better than send £4 to the enclosed fund for which we are working hard. I am getting a letter into the London Times.[1] I have had to copy it out & I[2] send you — gratefully indeed the original draft.

The rest of the money will be so very very useful for a wives club which is being started to keep the poor souls from brooding alone — or worse still in Public houses — The friendly (American Lady) groaned out to my daughter "The wooden chairs alone are over £5 — Now they will be less thanks to you.

The best anodyne to worry & anxiety is trying to help a little & I am thankful that there are certain things old people can do, remember reach to out of the past [?]. It gives one a reason for going on still, but O how one prays for an end to all this how one feels sympathy how one shrinks from cold & critical works & feelings such as one comes across not from ones Friends in America but from ones non-friends who dont know us & who — thank goodness we dont know or understand.

Yours gratefully
A I Ritchie

To Elizabeth Robins

Letter 111   Aug 7 [The Porch, Freshwater, c. 1916]¹
Fales

My dear Lisa Robins (tho' I know yours is now another name)² I only know the old one & gratefully realise that you are giving dear dear Florence³ help & strength. And what a kind letter you write & what a mountain of work she has been climbing with her wondrous spirit & organising power. Beloved woman she must now organise her own life w^h is so big & full of gifts for other people & with so many sick people wanting her health, that she must indeed take care of it. I am interested & amused to hear today of my little grand-nephew — a charming little Charles Villiers — doing his reading every day in her french book and getting on so admirably. Pinkie says he speaks quite charmingly. We have had our dear little creatures here & are expecting James & Linny⁴ before we go. We are told we can sell our house easily in 8^{br} or Nov & so we want a week or two more in London for ourselves. With my bronchitis it is such a problem keeping quiet enough & keeping the the house warm eno' that it seems easier to spend the winter here where we can get wood to eke out the coal & where there is plenty to interest us & occupy us. Lord Tennysons marriage makes everything much less sad somehow for all of us who care for him & one can speak <u>out loud</u> at Farringford again. All last year this Lady Tennyson who loved Audrey Tennyson[5] had been running the hospital & then to everyones relief Ld Tennyson & she eloped. But we have had sad news of our own from the front & we are only cheering up again.[6] Old friends & those who have shared our troubles in the past & helped us, cannot be replaced. Again thankyou for writing & do <u>come</u> someday if you are in town in September or 8^{br}

Yours with affectionate greetings
AIR

Mrs Ernest Richmond[7] & her children came to tea last night & to a bonfire in our orchard   The little boy was up the trees in a minute like a bird & all the little Tennysons toddled up with sticks & dry leaves   The eldest is 4

To Lady Georgina Pollock

Letter 112
Fales

Sesame Club,
29, Dover Street,
Piccadilly W.
<u>Monday. 1 Jan (1917)</u>

I wish you a loving New Year dearest Lady Georgie & thank you for your dear warming words! — Who ever wrote so kind a letter — It picked me up & patted me on the back & shook me by the hand & said old friend old friend so sweetly & <u>caressingly</u> that I dont know how to thank you. I feel proud that you & Sir Phil sh^d have read what I <u>loved</u> to write: and how it interests me to think of such dear past neighbours as you & Sir Edward in our street. it will always seem quite different to me now that you have graced it. Hester & I have both come <u>here</u> to lunch & for a <u>change</u> after this grim Xmas of fire & flurry   I hoped Claire w^d have come with Peggy next Saturday (I had sent her a message) but I hear she is going to <u>you</u>. Oddly eno I had been telling Margie Peggys[1] mother what a real friend & playfellow I always felt you to be & y^r dear letter came in just after. I shall tie it up for my sweet little granddaughters to see & I am going to them for January & if Billy has to be in town he will stay with Hester during much of the time. It is a good thing one is nearing the end at last, for life is too overpowering for this tired mortal coil — I hope I shall be two or three young cheerful capable people in my next life & O how one has enjoyed things here & thanked God for them — tho not half eno'

"Le meilleur de tout et un ancien ami"[2]

That was not Ruskin but Victor Hugo I never saw

Dearest <u>amie</u> y^r grateful with love to you all

AIR

To Sir Algernon West[1]

Letter 113
Fales

The Porch,
Freshwater Bay,
Isle of Wight
Monday
20 Aug 1917.

Dear Sir Algernon

<u>How</u> I enjoyed y.^r charming book[2] — So many many names & people I remember they all come & go in turn before me & how graciously you evoke them all — & I hear them talk once more

This tiny scrap of my Father's is all I can send alas — only a bit of paper w^h he tried his pen There is a pencil on the back of a fading old lady & her knitting The picture I thought of, is <u>ugly</u> & not like him somehow — (a number of his best drawings went down in the American Steamer the Lusitania)[3] Yes I have enjoyed the city & the men & the women & thankyou so much. I only saw Ld Randolph Churchill[4] in that sort of attitude windmilling at Mr Gladstone with a box between them[5] on w^h he banged as he scolded I was furious for I adored M.^r G in those days — Now you have made me care for him again by your warm hearted & beautiful tribute & for Ld Randolph too!

Yesterday Lady Gore came to tea to meet the elite of FW[6] at the Albion where Hester & I sometimes give modest entertainments. Sir

Francis had gone to the golph course. Another Sir Francis — Elliot[7] f^m Athens came with Mr Elliot who interested me & Mrs Boyle & I wish you had been there

Yours sincerely
Anne Ritchie

To Mrs. Charles Booth[1]

Letter 114	THE PORCH,/FRESHWATER BAY,/
U. of London	ISLE OF WIGHT.
MS797/I/5845	Christmas Day [1918][2]

My dearest Mrs Booth

Yesterday came your welcome beloved gift — O how much I like to have it from you & I am reading it with more interest than I can well express — every word means so much just as his life means so very <u>very</u> much. and you have told the story[3] so simply so convincingly. I have finished the first half — my eyes dont hold out for more than a little. I am grateful for the good print & the fine style which makes reading easy (Another friend has written a book of which I have to read & re-read each sentence)

I like the pictures very much I feel what it must have cost you to write down all that you give as well as all that you <u>keep</u>. But the life will make his dear presence more & more real & vivid to his grandchildren as it does even to those who remember him & knew what he was.

You may imagine how happy we are to have them here neatly packed into the little Porch. Meg kept in bed yesterday she was so tired & she has the little spare room to rest in & the others are at Mrs Downers[4] with windows to the sea & the downs. They arrived wonderfully fresh we thought; we can <u>just</u> get 8 into the room in which we dine We are beautifully decorated with loops of mistleto & ivy berries. The Soldiers attracted by the magnificence of our porch garlands all came to sing glees to us last night. I wish you could have heard James & the little girls singing Good King Wencelas & marching round the room as they sang. Billy is taking them off to church this morning. It is a dear old church but such a long way off — a mile at least — It used to seem nothing at all We are all going to tea with Mrs Alfred Tennyson and tomorrow we are going to Farringford

I send you my love & my loving thanks dear dear old friend and I am your faithful and affectionate

<u>Anne Ritchie</u>

Meg <u>is</u> a letter & tells me about all your varied & <u>most</u> interesting changes & hopes — Dear Dodo What a blessing one <u>longs</u> for, for her

To Catherine Ritchie[1]

Letter 115
U. of London
MS 797/I/5846 [Postmark: 24 Fe./19][2]

Miss Catherine Ritchie/The Old Vicarage/Ware/Hert

The Porch

I am sitting up & send my love

Grandmama

Appendix
Chronological Summary of Letters
1846–1919

Abbreviations: C-S for Carmichael-Smyth
ATR for Anne Thackeray Ritchie (including the time when she was Anne Isabella Thackeray)
HMT for Harriet Marian Thackeray

No.	Date	Depository	Writer	Addressee
		1846		
1.	[27 Nov.]	Ray/Morgan	Mrs. C-S	ATR and HMT
2.	26 Nov.	Ray/Morgan	ATR	Mrs. C-S
3.	5 Dec.	Ray/Morgan	ATR	Mr. and Mrs. C-S
4.	26 Dec.	Ray/Morgan	ATR	Mrs. C-S
		1847		
5.	14 Jan.	Ray/Morgan	ATR	Mr. and Mrs. C-S
6.	26 Feb.	Ray/Morgan	ATR	Mrs. C-S
7.	[April]	Ray/Morgan	ATR	Mrs. C-S
8.	[April]	Ray/Morgan	ATR	Mrs. C-S
9.	[July]	Ray/Morgan	ATR	Mrs. C-S
10.	[July]	Ray/Morgan	ATR	Mrs. C-S
		1850–1851		
11.	[c. 1850–51]	Ray/Morgan	ATR's verse	Amy Crowe
		1852		
12.	[2 Dec.]	Ray/Morgan	ATR	Laetitia Cole

No.	Date	Depository	Writer	Addressee
		1853		
13.	[12 Jan.]	Ray/Morgan	HMT	Thackeray
		1854		
14.	June	Fales	ATR	W. W. F. Synge
		1855		
15.	18 Feb.	Berg	ATR	Susan Scott
16.	[6 March]	Ray/Morgan	Mrs. C-S	ATR
17.	[before 9 June]	Ray/Morgan	ATR	Mrs. Fanshawe
		1856		
18.	[16 Aug.]	Ray/Morgan	ATR	Mrs. C-S
19.	[22 Aug.]	Ray/Morgan	ATR	Amy Crowe
20.	[10 Sept.]	Ray/Morgan	ATR	Amy Crowe
21.	[26 Oct.]	Ray/Morgan	ATR and HMT	Amy Crowe
22.	[after 21 Nov.]	Ray/Morgan	ATR	Amy Crowe
23.	28 Nov.	Ray/Morgan	ATR	Amy Crowe
		1857		
24.	[late Aug./ early Sept.]	Ray/Morgan	ATR	Mrs. Stoddart
		1858		
25.	[before 10 April]	Ray/Morgan	ATR	?
26.	[late Dec.]	Ray/Morgan	ATR	Amy Crowe
		1859		
27.	[before 6 Mar.]	Ray/Morgan	ATR	Mr. and Mrs. Cole
28.	6 Mar.	Fales	ATR	W. W. F. Synge
29.	27 Aug.	Fales	ATR	W. W. F. Synge
30.	[16 Sept.]	Ray/Morgan	ATR	Amy Crowe
		1860		
31.	5 Feb.	Fales	ATR	Mrs. Synge

No.	Date	Depository	Writer	Addressee

1861

32.	[1861]	Harvard	HMT	Mrs. C-S

1862

33.	1862	Ray/Morgan	HMT	ATR
34.	[15 Sept.]	Ray/Morgan	ATR	Amy Crowe

1863

35.	22 Jan.	Fales	ATR	Mrs. Synge
36.	[6 May]	Ray/Morgan	ATR	Amy Thackeray
37.	[19 July]	Fales	ATR	W. W. F. Synge
38.	[Sept.]	Ray/Morgan	HMT	Thackeray
39.	[Sept.]	Ray/Morgan	HMT	ATR
40.	[Sept.]	Ray/Morgan	HMT	ATR

1864

41.	[1864]	Huntington	ATR	Lady Stanley
42.	[1864]	Ray/Morgan	ATR	Mrs. Cole
43.	[1864]	Ray/Morgan	ATR	Mrs. Cole
44.	[1864]	Ray/Morgan	ATR	Mrs. Cole
45.	[19 May]	Ray/Morgan	ATR	Jane Shawe
46.	20 May	Fales	ATR	Mr. and Mrs. Synge
47.	2 Nov.	Huntington	ATR	Miss Boyle
48.	28 Dec.	Fales	ATR	Mrs. Synge

1865

49.	[c. 1865]	Columbia	ATR	Mrs. Baxter
50.	9 June	Ray/Morgan	ATR	Prayer

1867

51.	[1867]	Fales	ATR	W. W. F. Synge
52.	23 Oct.	Fales	ATR and Leslie Stephen	W. W. F. Synge

1868

53.	[July]	Columbia	ATR	Mrs. Baxter

1870

54.	[1870]	Columbia	ATR	Lucy Baxter

288   APPENDIX

No.	Date	Depository	Writer	Addressee
		1871		
55.	[c. spring or summer]	British Lib.	ATR	Memorandum
		1872		
56.	[1872]	Princeton	ATR	George Leslie
57.	17 Aug.	Columbia	ATR	Mrs. Baxter
		1873		
58.	3 Dec.	Yale	ATR	Robert Browning
		1874		
59.	1 Jan.	Ray/Morgan	Leslie Stephen	ATR
60.	29 Jan.	Baylor	Robert Browning	ATR
61.	4 Dec.	Baylor	Robert Browning	ATR
		1875		
62.	[Dec.]	Columbia	ATR	Mrs. Baxter
		1876		
63.	17 Oct.	Berg	ATR	George Eliot
		1877		
64.	[1877]	Fales	ATR	W. W. F. Synge
65.	[May]	Fales	ATR	Henrietta Synge
		1879		
66.	[1879]	Harvard	ATR	Henry James
		1880		
67.	[c. 1880–81]	Fales	ATR	Mr. Walter
		1881		
68.	25 Dec.	Fales	ATR	W. W. F. Synge

No.	Date	Depository	Writer	Addressee
		1882		
69.	1 Jan.	Fales	ATR	Baron von Tauchnitz
		1883		
70.	8 March	Fales	ATR	James Payn
		1885		
71.	13 Sept.	Yale	ATR	Miss Browning
72.	[before 1886]	Fales	ATR	Mary Thackeray
		1886		
73.	[c. 1886–87]	Princeton	ATR	Octavia Hill
74.	[4 Sept.]	Ray/Morgan	ATR	Isabella Thackeray
		1887		
75.	[11 June]	U. of London	ATR	Austin Dobson
		1888		
76.	[15 Feb.]	Yale	ATR	Robert Browning
		1889		
77.	[c. 1889–98]	Fales	ATR	Elizabeth Robins
78.	[29 May]	Fales	ATR	Miss Browning
79.	[22 July]	Yale	ATR	Robert Browning
		1890		
80.	[Sept.]	Fales	ATR	Savile Clark
81.	[1 Oct.]	Fales	ATR	Savile Clark
82.	[21 Dec.]	Fales	ATR	Mrs. S. Clark
		1891		
83.	[1891]	Fales	ATR	Charlotte Yonge
84.	[12 April]	Ray/Morgan	ATR	Isabella Thackeray
		1893		
85.	[7 April]	Ray/Morgan	ATR	Isabella Thackeray
86.	13 Aug.	Fales	ATR	Mr. Skeffington

No.	Date	Depository	Writer	Addressee
		1894		
87.	[c. 1894–98]	Berg	ATR	?
		1895		
88.	[1895]	Harvard	Henry James	ATR
		1898		
89.	[1898]	U. of London	ATR	Wm. Ritchie
90.	14 Oct.	U. of London	ATR	Wm. Ritchie
		1899		
91.	[c. Feb.]	U. of London	ATR	Wm. Ritchie
92.	[c. Feb.]	U. of London	ATR	Wm. Ritchie
93.	[c. 17 Mar.]	U. of London	ATR	Wm. Ritchie
94.	[before Oct.]	U. of London	ATR	Wm. Ritchie
		1900		
95.	[c. 1900]	U. of London	ATR	Wm. Ritchie
96.	4 Jan.	Harvard	Henry James	ATR
97.	[20 Feb.]	U. of London	ATR	Wm. Ritchie
98.	[late fall]	U. of London	ATR	Wm. Ritchie
		1901		
99.	[c. 1901–12]	Harvard	ATR	Henry James
		1904		
100.	30 May	Princeton	ATR	Dear Madam
		1906		
101.	19 May	Princeton	ATR	Mr. Williams
		1910		
102.	18 Sept.	Princeton	ATR	Mr. Williams
103.	20 Sept.	Princeton	ATR	Mr. Williams
104.	30 Oct.	Harvard	Henry James	ATR

APPENDIX 291

No.	Date	Depository	Writer	Addressee
		1911		
105.	30 Sept.	Princeton	ATR	Mr. Williams
		1912		
106.	[c. 1912–16]	Berg	ATR	Leonard Woolf
107.	[c. 1912–16]	Berg	ATR	Leonard Woolf
108.	23 Oct.	Harvard	ATR	Henry James
		1914		
109.	21 Aug.	Columbia	ATR	Maude Frank and Sister
		1915		
110.	21 Jan.	Columbia	ATR	Maude Frank and Sister
		c. 1916		
111.	7 Aug.	Fales	ATR	Elizabeth Robins
		1917		
112.	1 Jan.	Fales	ATR	Lady Georgina Pollock
113.	20 Aug.	Fales	ATR	Sir Algernon West
		1918		
114.	25 Dec.	U. of London	ATR	Mrs. Booth
		1919		
115.	24 Feb.	U. of London	ATR	Catherine Ritchie

Abbreviations

BOOKS BY ANNE THACKERAY RITCHIE

Blackstick	*Blackstick Papers.* London: Smith, Elder, & Co., 1908.
Bluebeard's Key	*Bluebeard's Keys and Other Stories.* London: Smith, Elder, & Co., 1874.
Chapters	*Chapters from Some Memoirs.* London: Macmillan & Co., 1894.
Da Capo	*Da Capo and Other Tales.* Leipzig: Bernhard Tauchnitz, 1880.
Divagations	*Miss Williamson's Divagations.* London: Smith, Elder, & Co., 1881.
Elizabeth	*The Story of Elizabeth.* London: Smith, Elder, & Co., 1863.
Esther	*To Esther and Other Sketches.* London: Smith, Elder, & Co., 1869.
Five Old Friends	*Five Old Friends and a Young Prince.* London: Smith, Elder, & Co., 1868.
Friend	*From Friend to Friend.* London: Smith, Elder, & Co., 1919.
Island	*From an Island and Some Essays.* Leipzig: Bernhard Tauchnitz, 1877.
Porch	*From the Porch.* London: Smith, Elder, & Co., 1913.
Records	*Records of Tennyson, Ruskin, and Browning.* London: Macmillan & Co., 1892.
Sibyls	*A Book of Sibyls.* London: Blackwood & Sons, 1883.
Toilers and Spinsters	*Toilers and Spinsters and Other Essays.* London: Smith, Elder & Co., 1874.
Village	*The Village on the Cliff.* London: Smith, Elder, & Co., 1867.

OTHER BOOKS CITED

Adversity	Gordon N. Ray, *Thackeray: The Uses of Adversity, 1811–1846*. New York: McGraw-Hill Book Co., 1955.
Bio. Intro.	Biographical Introductions to *The Works of William Makepeace Thackeray*. Biographical Edition. 13 vols. London: Smith, Elder, & Co., 1898–99.
Cent. Intro.	Biographical Introductions to *The Works of William Makepeace Thackeray*. Centenary Edition. 26 vols. London: Smith, Elder, & Co., 1910–11.
Gérin	Winifred Gérin. *Anne Thackeray Ritchie: A Biography*. Oxford: Oxford University Press, 1981.
Letters	*The Letters and Private Papers of William Makepeace Thackeray*. 4 vols. Ed. Gordon N. Ray. Cambridge: Harvard University Press, 1946.
Stephen	Leslie Stephen. *Sir Leslie Stephen's Mausoleum Book*. Oxford: Clarendon Press, 1977.
Thackeray and His Daughter	*Thackeray and His Daughter: The Letters and Journals of Anne Thackeray Ritchie, with Many Letters of William Makepeace Thackeray*. Ed. Hester Thackeray Ritchie. New York: Harper & Brothers, 1924.
Thackeray's Daughter	Hester Thackeray Fuller and Violet Hammersley, compilers. *Thackeray's Daughter: Some Recollections of Anne Thackeray Ritchie*. Dublin: Euphorion Books, 1951.
Wisdom	Gordon N. Ray, *Thackeray: The Age of Wisdom, 1847–1863*. New York: McGraw-Hill Book Co., 1958.

Notes

PREFACE

1. *Letters,* II, 240. Also see *Letters,* II, 292.
2. *Thackeray's Daughter,* 119.
3. Gérin, 257, quoted from George Smith's "Recollections."
4. Stephen, xxiv–xxv, also xxiii, and 12.
5. *Adversity,* 6, quoted from *Thackeray and His Daughter,* 262.
6. "The Art of Fiction," *Partial Portraits* (1884; reprinted Ann Arbor: Univ. of Michigan Press, 1970, 388–89). See below, chap. 7.
7. *Times Literary Supplement,* 6 March 1919, 123. See below, chap. 8.
8. *Thackeray and His Daughter,* 128, n. 1.
9. *Letters,* III, 30; in a letter from Edward FitzGerald.
10. *Red Cotton Night-Cap Country.*
11. In a letter to Anny which ends in a verse to her, Stevenson wrote, "All your craft is magic and mystery in my matter-of-fact eyes; but the result is indeed exquisite," *Thackeray's Daughter,* 10.
12. See below, chap. 5.
13. This work publishes a selection of the very large number of Ritchie letters still unpublished. Letters have been chosen to represent all periods of her life with a relatively large concentration from the Ray collection. The two journals form the focal point of this work. A large number of diaries of the time from 1859 to 1903 (with a hiatus between 1862 and 1864) and other journals from 1859 to 1903 (Ritchie's own chronological reworkings from diaries) are in a private collection. In addition there is material at the University of London Library not yet catalogued and made available to scholars. Some of these diaries and journals have been excerpted and published by Hester Ritchie, Gordon Ray, and Winifred Gérin. [Editors' note.]

CHRONOLOGY

1. Date given as 1816 in *Letters* and Gérin; 1818 in *Thackeray's Daughter;* 1820 in *Adversity.*
2. Date given as 28 May by Stephen.
3. Month given as January by Stephen.
4. Name given as William Makepeace Thackeray by Gérin; William Thackeray Denis in *Thackeray's Daughter.*

CHAPTER 1

INTRODUCTION

1. *Letters*, I, 318, n. 22.
2. On 22–30 October 1833, Thackeray wrote: "I want to settle . . . to marry . . . rising early, & walking in the Park with Mrs T. & the children." The letter contains a sketch of a giant, rotund Thackeray and his future wife—petite and crinolined—with children and nurse. *Letters*, I, 268.
3. Carlyle described Thackeray at this time as "a half-monstrous Cornish giant, kind of painter, Cambridge man, and Paris newspaper correspondent, who is now writing for his life in London." Charles Townsend Copeland, ed., *Letters of Thomas Carlyle to His Youngest Sister* (Boston, 1899) 86, quoted in *Letters*, I, 347, n. 27.
4. Using letters of Thackeray and of Isabella, 1840–44, Dr. Cobb described Isabella's illness: "The diagnosis is schizophrenia, of a type that often begins with depression and ideas of unworthiness a few weeks after childbirth. Some of these patients get well spontaneously. . . . Others seem to drift into a permanent state of apathy and live the rest of their lives in an unreal world of fantasy, with gradual mental deterioration. Such was the fate of Mrs. Thackeray. Stanley Cobb, M.D." *Letters*, I, 520. "The Psychiatric Case History of Isabella Shawe Thackeray."
5. *Adversity*, 250. Quoted from *Letters*, II, 429.
6. "Mr. Brown's Letters to a Young Man about Town," *Punch*, 7 July 1849.
7. *Letters*, I, 460.
8. *Letters*, II, 796.
9. Edward FitzGerald to Thackeray, April 1852. *Letters*, III, 30.
10. *Adversity*, 281.
11. *Letters*, II, 125.
12. *Letters*, II, 240.
13. Bio. Intro., IV, xxx–xxi. Cent. Intro., VI, xxvii.
14. *Letters*, II, 382.
15. *Letters*, II, 291.
16. *Letters*, II, 240.
17. *Letters*, II, 286, 292.
18. *Letters*, II, 335.
19. *Letters*, II, 379.
20. *Letters*, II, 788–89.
21. *Letters*, II, 545.
22. Henrietta Corkran, "A Child's Recollection of William Makepeace Thackeray," *Temple Bar* 81 (October 1887), 240, quoted in *Wisdom*, 339.
23. *Letters*, II, 788–89.

24. *Letters*, II, 231.
25. Gordon N. Ray, *The Buried Life: A Study of the Relation between Thackeray's Fiction and His Personal Life* (Cambridge: Harvard Univ. Press, 1952), 85–95.
26. *Letters*, II, 400.
27. Chapter 3, Letter 28, below.

LETTER 1

1. GP was Thackeray's stepfather, Major Henry Carmichael-Smyth (1780–1861).
2. Granmama or GM was Mrs. Harriet Butler (c. 1770–1847), Mrs. Carmichael-Smyth's mother. *Letters*, I, cv.
3. Bess Hamerton, an Irish protégée of Mrs. Carmichael-Smyth's. The children's governess until 1847, when Thackeray realized, "Anny & Bess do not go on well together. The child is the woman's superior in every respect." *Letters*, II, 285.
4. Probably Flora Colmache. Laura, Flora, and Pauline were daughters of Mrs. Carmichael-Smyth's friend, a journalist in Paris.
5. Aunt Becher, Anne Becher, Thackeray's great-aunt. *Letters*, I, 4, n. 7.
6. "Mrs. Dance (d. 1854) was the former Mrs. Ralph Ingilby. . . . She married Charles Dance (1794–1863), the dramatist, in 1840." *Letters*, II, 286, n. 47.
7. Maria Hamerton, Bess's sister.
8. Thackeray's cook.
9. Grannie was Thackeray's mother, Mrs. Carmichael-Smyth, the former Anne Becher (1792–1864). *Letters*, IV, Genealogy 53.
10. Not identified.

LETTER 2

1. Not identified.
2. Her spelling for Scott's *The Lay of the Last Minstrel* (1805).
3. Thackeray's butler and valet.
4. A piece of needlework (similar to that worked by children today called a "horse-rein").

LETTER 3

1. Thackeray's cousin. *Letters*, IV, G 48.
2. Jane Townley Pryme (1788–1871).
3. Madame Tussaud's Waxworks, established in London in 1802.
4. Mr. and Mrs. Eyre Crowe (1799–1868) were friends of Thackeray's in Paris. He was Paris correspondent for the *Morning Chronicle*. Their children were Eyre, Joseph, Eugenie Marie, Edward, Amy (Marianne), and George.

5. *Swiss Family Robinson* by Johann Rudolf Wyss (1781–1830), published Zurich 1812–13 and in an English translation a year later.
6. Eyewash.
7. A piece of needlework.
8. Thackeray's maid of all work.
9. Ephesians 6.11. "Put on the whole armour of God, that ye may be able to stand against the wiles of the devil."
10. "Thank your grandmother for me and tell her that I hope she'll be happy for me and my little girl."
11. Aunt Becher.
12. Possibly Thackeray's friend who in 1839 was "delighted with Anny." *Letters*, I, 400.
13. Probably Susan Scott, daughter of Thackeray's friend Rev. Alexander John Scott.
14. A line of squiggles follows, as though Minny tried to write her name.
15. See Letter 1, above.
16. Not identified, probably a member of the Colmache family.

LETTER 4

1. An early example of Anny's editing: "in plenty" is inserted above the line.
2. Wife of the Rev. Charles S. Fanshawe, Perpetual Curate of Holy Trinity Church, Southampton. *Letters*, II, 276, n. 32.
3. Henry Cole (1808–82), later (1875) K.C.B.; painter, engraver, writer, friend of Thackeray's. His daughters were Laetitia or Tishy, Henrietta or Henny, and Mary. *Letters*, I, cxvii–cxx.
4. Anny seems to intend a bonbon; a *bonbonnière* is a candy store or dish.
5. Marianne Shakespear, who married Colonel Archibald Irvine in 1835, Thackeray's cousin. *Letters*, IV, G 88.
6. Low: Augusta Ludlow Shakespear, Thackeray's cousin, married General Sir John Low in 1829. *Letters*, IV, G 81.
7. Miss Waddell and her mother, acquaintances of Thackeray and his mother.
8. Mme. Auber, the widow of the composer, a friend of Mrs. Carmichael-Smyth's.
9. Not identified.

LETTER 5

1. The letter reads "1846," but this is a mistake since Anny and Minny did not come to live with Thackeray until October 1846.
2. "it seems to me" is inserted above the line. An example of Anny's

search for the accurate phrase. Further example of this is "but" crossed out after "very hard."

3. "The Miss Thackerays present their compliments to Mrs. Smithe and hope they will have the pleasure of seeing her next spring." The Smith family is mentioned in *Blackstick*, pp. 114–29.

4. Her signature is printed.

LETTER 6

1. Reads "1846"; should be 1847. The postmark is 3 March 1847.
2. I.e., in a game of blind man's bluff.
3. Goldbeater's skin: a prepared animal membrane employed to separate the leaves of gold foil; used to cover wounds. OED.
4. "Frederick Hervey Foster Quin (1799–1878), M.D., the first homeopathic physician to practice in England." *Letters*, I, 400–401, n. 54.
5. Wife of Thackeray's friend Rev. Alexander John Scott (1805–1866), Presbyterian minister and professor of English literature. *Letters*, II, 282, n. 42.
6. Not identified.
7. March 1847.
8. Parts Five and Six of Dicken's *Dombey and Son*. Repeating the conversation between Florence and her father, Anny reports the dramatic highlights and the skeleton of the plot.
9. Carmichael.
10. One of Mrs. Carmichael-Smyth's Parisian friends. *Letters*, I, 442.
11. The home of Lord and Lady Holland. She was the former Saba Smith. He was Henry Edward Fox (1802–59), fourth Baron Holland. *Letters*, II, 335, n. 6.
12. The following note from Bess is written across the first page of the letter.
13. William Makepeace Thackeray first used the name Michael Angelo Titmarsh for an article on painting exhibitions for *Fraser's Magazine* in June 1838. "At first, like Yellowplush, a figure of fun . . . Michael Angelo Titmarsh gradually came more and more to resemble Thackeray himself, until by the middle 1840s he was practically Thackeray's alter ego." *Adversity*, 198.

LETTER 7

1. Employed in 1847 as a governess.
2. Not identified.
3. Negro minstrels from America, extremely popular in England. *Times*, 4 April 1847, 3, col. 2.
4. Playbill.

LETTER 8

1. The new House of Lords was completed in April of 1847.
2. "THE FEMALE AMERICAN SERENADERS—Messrs. D'Almaine and Co., Soho-Square, have the honour to announce that they are the proprietors of all the music sung by the Female American Serenaders, . . . The songs are illustrated by exquisitely illuminated portraits of the ladies." *Times,* 20 April 1847, 1, col. 3.
3. Major Carmichael-Smyth's younger brother Charles (1790–1870) married Martha Graham. They had three children: Charles Henry Edward, called "Chéri" or "Che" here (1842–95), Rose Gordon, and Florence Graham (d. 1873). *Letters,* I, cx.
4. Mary Carmichael.
5. Flower on a currant plant.
6. The nurse who cared for Anny and Minny and later Isabella. She was a "sturdy young nurse." *Adversity,* 202.
7. Arthur Shawe, older brother of Isabella.

LETTER 9

1. Not identified.
2. I Samuel 15.22–26.
3. Morning glories.
4. Edward Talbot Thackeray (b. 1836), a cousin of William Makepeace Thackeray, "for whom Thackeray secured a cadetship at Addiscombe through Sir John Cam Hobhouse. He had a distinguished career in the Indian army, receiving the Victoria Cross in 1857, and in 1862 married Amy Crowe." *Letters,* II, 707, n. 163.
5. *Noel and Chapsall:* a French reader.
6. Sir Walter Scott, *The Tales of a Grandfather* (1828–31).
7. Not identified.

LETTER 10

1. I Kings 1–11.
2. *Vanity Fair,* chapter 35. First edition, 319, shows Thackeray's sketch of Major SugarPlum, Amelia, and Georgie as described by Anny. Her résumé of the plot covers numbers 9 and 10, August and September 1847. In the Bio. Intro. to *Vanity Fair,* Anny wrote, "I also remember making one of a group composed of the aforesaid Eugénie, representing Amelia after the battle of Waterloo, with a sofa cushion for an infant; a tall chair stood in the place of Dobbin who brings the little horse for his godson to play with" (xxxi). The scene originally described by Anny as taking place in Normandy happens, according to Thackeray, in England. Since Eugenie Crowe portrayed Amelia, Anny must have stood in for the little French girl.

3. There is a small hole in the paper.
4. Possibly the children of Marianne Shakespear and Major Irvine. *Letters*, IV, G 88, 89.
5. A scarf covering the neck and shoulders, usually having the ends hanging down in front.

LETTER 11

1. Amy Marianne Crowe (1831–65), later to marry Edward Thackeray.
2. In Anny's adult handwriting with no misspellings. The verse was written before the Crowes moved out of Hampstead in 1851.

Written across the top of the paper are the words: "Old letters to A.M.A.C. from A. & M."

3. Tennyson, "Locksley Hall" (1842). "Oh my cousin, shallow-hearted! O my Amy, mine no more!" *Poems of Tennyson* (Boston: Houghton Mifflin, 1958), 105.
4. Anny's initials to her father's nom de plume.

CHAPTER 2

INTRODUCTION

1. Examples of Thackeray's feelings: "I find I'm constantly talking of dying somehow—but hope to wait time enough to see the poor wife and children provided"; "[I] think decidedly I'm not for this world very long—dont care much to stay, as soon as Anny and Minny are comfortably settled." *Letters*, III, 154, 379.
2. *The Buried Life*, 122–23.
3. William Wetmore Story (1819–95), Boston lawyer and poet, came to Rome in 1847 to study sculpting. Thackeray wrote *The Rose and the Ring* for his daughter Edith. *Letters*, III, 330–31, n. 260.
4. *Letters*, III, 52.
5. *Letters*, III, 81.
6. *Letters*, III, 57, 81, 93.
7. *Letters*, III, 86.
8. *Letters*, III, 93, 96. Thackeray's teachings found ready ground in Anny, who wrote in her diary "Perhaps these times appear differently to me, to what they do to every other mind? Perhaps Minny sees the trees blue not green, and Amy thinks them red." *Thackeray and His Daughter*, 69.
9. *Letters*, III, 141.
10. On her father's remarriage, Amy found herself in need of a home, which Thackeray provided.
11. When she was older, Anny wrote, "It almost seems to me now that all the rest of my life dates in some measure from those old Roman days." *Thackeray's Daughter*, 72.

12. *Thackeray's Daughter*, 84.
13. *Letters*, IV, 63.
14. Edmund Yates (1831–94) "composed for No. 2 [of *Town Talk* of which he was the editor] a very impertinent and unfriendly sketch of Thackeray." *Dictionary of National Biography*. Thackeray retaliated by characterizing "young Grubstreet, who corresponds with three penny papers and describes the persons and conversations of gentlemen whom he meets at his 'clubs.'" *The Virginians*, chapter 35.
15. "On March 11 [Yates] wrote to a friend: 'By a series of Jew-lawyer-like tricks, . . . the Committee of the Garrick have got the best of me.'" *Letters*, IV, 131, n.13.
16. That this long continued to be a volatile issue is clear in Edgar Johnson's *Charles Dickens: His Tragedy and Triumph*, rev. and abr. (New York: Viking, 1977). In a later article than Johnson's first edition, "Dickens versus Thackeray: The Garrick Club Affair," *PMLA* 69 (September 1954), 815–32, Gordon N. Ray outlined the underlying causes of the quarrel between Thackeray and Dickens and the reasons that led to their estrangement. Johnson acknowledged that in Yates's original attack "[t]here was, indeed, cause for offence" (468). Johnson nevertheless still states that "[n]ot until a few days before Thackeray's death in 1863 did he and Dickens ever speak to each other again" (472), with no mention of the fact that it was Thackeray who extended his hand first to Dickens at the Athenaeum Club (*Wisdom*, 404). Fred Kaplan, in *Dickens: A Biography* (New York: William Morrow, 1988), refers to this event as "a mostly perfunctory reconciliation" (453). Carol Hanbery MacKay describes Anny's warm correspondence with Yates some forty years later in "'Only Connect': The Multiple Roles of Anne Thackeray Ritchie," *Library Chronicle of the University of Texas*, n.s., no. 30 (1985): 95.
17. *Thackeray's Daughter*, 67.
18. *Letters*, III, 255.
19. *Letters*, III, 618.
20. *Letters*, III, 4, 61, 222.
21. *Letters*, IV, 55–56.
22. In 1856 Thackeray wrote, "Her drawing is very good in spite of what the Master may say—much better than mine at her age, and so is her writing too." *Letters*, III, 544.
23. *Letters*, IV, 75.
24. *Letters*, IV, 88. Note "my" underlined by Thackeray.
25. *Letters*, IV, 109.
26. *Wisdom*, 352.
27. *Letters*, III, 251, 152.
28. *Letters*, III, 238, 251. Mr. Turveydrop, the Professor of Deportment in *Bleak House*, lived on questionable past glories and the hard work of his

son and daughter-in-law. Not serious about living off his daughter's possible earnings, Thackeray could be doubting his own powers.
29. *Thackeray's Daughter*, 87.
30. *Letters*, III, 138.
31. *Letters*, III, 140.

LETTER 12

1. In the letter, Anny writes, "Yesterday :N: was declared Emperor." Napoleon III was crowned emperor on 1 December 1852.
2. Alice Jane Trulock: A governess of the Thackerays.
3. Rose Cole: born 21 July 1852. Supplement to the *Times*, 3 August 1852, 9, col. 1.
4. During the summers Anny frequently went with her grandparents to their property in Mennecy, near Paris, a former hunting lodge of Henry IV's.
5. See n. 1, above.
6. See *Letters*, III, 106, for Thackeray's first letter from America to his daughters.
7. Henny [Henrietta] and Mary Cole, Laetitia's sisters.
8. Sir Thomas Erskine Perry (1806–82), who had given up an Indian judgeship and returned to England in 1852. *Letters*, III, 81.
9. Turnabouts: merry-go-rounds.
10. End of letter missing.

LETTER 13

1. The cake was sent from London to Anny and Minny by Thackeray's friend Mrs. Procter. *Chapters*, p. 170.
2. Not identified.
3. Probably Thackeray's cousin Sarah Eliza Donnithorne, called Selina. *Letters*, IV, G 90.
4. Not identified.
5. Mr. and Mrs. John Frazer Corkran and five children were among Thackeray's closest friends in Paris. His daughter Henrietta published her impression of Thackeray in *Celebrities and I*. *Letters*, II, 140, n. 8.
6. Sally (Sarah) Baxter, daughter of Thackeray's newfound New York friends. Minny's jealousy here is in reply to Thackeray's description of Sally in his letter to his mother 20 December 1852, "I have been actually in love for 3 days with a pretty wild girl of 19." *Letters*, II, 149.
7. The Reverend Henry Whitney Bellows (1814–82), pastor of the First Unitarian Church of New York, where Thackeray delivered one of his lectures. *Letters*, III, 122, n. 181.
8. Charlotte Sarah Thackeray (1786–1854). *Letters*, IV, G 57.

LETTER 14

1. William Webb Follett Synge (1826–91), member of the Foreign Office, contributor to *Punch,* and friend of Thackeray's. *Letters,* III, 210, n. 89.
2. Sarah Grey: the Thackerays' cook, more frequently spelled Gray; Eliza Jordon: the Thackerays' maid; Charles Pearman: Thackeray's valet.
3. Robert Follett Synge (1835–1920). The "Bobby Mistletoe" of "Round about the Christmas Tree."
4. This sentence is written in a different hand.

LETTER 15

1. Dated in pencil in a different hand.
2. John Alexander Scott (1846–94), son of Rev. Scott. *Letters,* III, 97.
3. The custom was to shave the head of patients ill with diseases that registered high fevers, such as scarletina, from which Minny was recuperating.
4. Crimean War.
5. 36, Onslow Square, Brompton, where Thackeray lived from 1854 to 1862 in an elegant stuccoed house built in 1846.
6. Amy Crowe.

LETTER 16

1. Célestine Doudet was governess to the five daughters of an English widower, Dr. James L. Marsden. Opening a small school in Paris, Doudet accepted the Marsden girls as her first pupils. Charged with starving the girls, beating them, locking them in closets, and using mechanical devices to stop suspected masturbation, Doudet was tried for murder in Paris after one of the Marsden girls died there suddenly. Cleared of the murder charge, Doudet received five years for maltreating the other Marsden girls. Thackeray wrote to his mother on 22 April, "What a fiend! I wish she could be locked up in that closet where she kept the poor girls." *Letters,* III, 439. Mary S. Hartman, *Victorian Murderesses* (New York: Schocken Books, 1977), 85–129.
2. Nicolas I (1796–1855), the Iron Tsar of Russia, died 2 March 1855.
3. An acquaintance of Thackeray and his family, residing in Paris. *Letters,* III, 668.
4. At the Doudet trial, the remaining Marsden children testified on behalf of their governess even though they had suffered the same punishments as their dead sister. This behavior is consistent with that of abused children.
5. John Allen (1810–86), distinguished theologian; friend of Thackeray's since their Trinity days; possible model for Dobbin in *Vanity Fair.* He and his wife were friends of the Thackerays when they were "on the fringes of the literary world." *Adversity,* 206.
6. Probably the German violinist, Friedrich Hermann (1828–1907).

7. Possibly a member of the family of Prince Adam Czartoryski, an exiled Polish statesman, who lived in France from 1831 to 1861.
8. Not identified.
9. Not identified.
10. Probably the Faubourg St. Germain, an aristocratic quarter of Paris.
11. Sarah Kemble Siddons (1775–1831), tragic actress.
12. Not identified.
13. Not identified.
14. Not identified.
15. Probably Elizabeth Cleghorn Gaskell (1810–65), novelist and biographer of Charlotte Brontë.
16. Not identified.
17. Eyre Crowe (b. 1824), painter, Thackeray's amanuensis for *Esmond* and secretary on his trip to the United States in 1853. *Letters*, I, cxix–cxx.

LETTER 17

1. Written shortly before Anny's birthday on the 9th of June and before Thackeray's second trip to America, 13 October 1855.
2. In a letter to John Forster 3 June 1855, Thackeray wrote, "I'm constantly unwell." *Letters*, III, 453. The Thackerays left for Paris 16 June 1855. *Letters*, III, 457.
3. The Fanshawes lived in Southampton.
4. Not identified.
5. Not identified.
6. Mrs. Fanshawe was one of Anny's many surrogate "aunts."
7. Mary Holmes, a Catholic convert, whom Thackeray had known when he was a boy in Devon, wrote to him in 1852, asking for his help. He hired her as a music teacher for his daughters, cautioning her not to proselytize.
8. During Thackeray's first absence in America, Anny and Minny followed a *cours* of religion with Pasteur Monod. This time, Thackeray bypassed Monod by providing for secular instruction in literature and music for his daughters.
9. "Flummery" was a favorite word with Thackeray. For example, see *Letters*, I, 465.
10. In "A Journal written by Anny at the age of seventeen," she records, "Tuesday. I got a letter from Mrs. Fanshawe; I think I will copy it out and keep it for ever, in case I am in want of advice. June 9th, 1855. And now my birthday has come round again and I have been determining to spend my eighteenth better than my seventeenth year, and to be less sentimental, more cheerful and honest and charitable." *Thackeray and His Daughter*, 71.
11. Harriet Martineau (1802–76), writer and abolitionist. In her novel

Deerbrook (London: Edward Moxon, 1839, 3 vols.) two young women discuss employment opportunities: Maria says, "Do not think dear, of earning money. You are doing all you ought in saving it." Margaret responds, "I must think about it, because earning is so much nobler and more effectual than saving" (III, 168).

12. Dr. William Bullar, "a Southampton physician who experimented with anesthetics." *Letters*, II, 271, n. 27.

13. Rosa "Totty" Fanshawe, Mrs. Fanshawe's daughter.

LETTER 18

1. This letter was written at the start of the Thackerays' trip abroad, 14 August–7 October. *Letters*, II, 686. Anny and Minny are staying in Paris with Charlotte Ritchie.

2. Resort in W. Germany with mineral springs and mud baths.

3. Lady Elizabeth Elgin (d. 1860), a patron of the "Holy Catholic Apostolic Church," founded by Edward Irving in 1832. *Letters*, II, 749, n. 42.

4. Eugenie Crowe married Robert Wynne in 1850. *Letters*, I, cxviii.

5. Lady Elizabeth Mary Carnegie (1798?–1886), married (1825) Frederic Rennell Thackeray (1775–1860), Thackeray's distant cousin. On 11 October 1855, Thackeray refused an invitation to visit Lady Elizabeth but asked to come the following summer. This is most likely the visit that Anny describes to her grandmother. *Letters*, III, 478.

6. Not identified.

7. Knight of the Garter.

8. Anny originally wrote "pew-te-full" then crossed out "te," editing her pun.

9. Albert Edward, prince of Wales (1841–1910).

10. Henry Davison (1805?–1860), an old friend of Thackeray's to whom he dedicated *The Virginians*. *Letters*, II, 370, n. 86.

11. Not identified.

12. Uncle Charles Carmichael.

13. Probably George Wood of Edinburgh, music seller, who made the arrangements for Thackeray's lectures. *Letters*, II, 805, n. 125.

14. Entry in Thackeray's diary for 10 August 1856 reads, "ill with spasms in the evening w^h began to yield about 3." *Letters*, III, 686.

15. 36, Onslow Square.

16. Thackeray refers to Thomas Fraser as his mother's favorite; he was one of Thackeray's oldest Parisian friends, the "laughing Tom" of "The Ballad of Bouillabaisse," and Paris correspondent of the *Morning Chronicle* from 1835 to 1855. *Letters*, II, 140, n. 6; IV, 79.

17. Not identified.

18. About this projected new book, Ray writes that Thackeray "soon abandoned this scheme." *Wisdom*, 387. See also *Letters*, III, 619, n. 126.

LETTER 19

1. The Thackerays stayed at the Hotel des Pays Bas in Spa, 19–24 August 1856. *Letters,* II, 686. Friday fell on the 22nd.
2. "I have only a little to tell you."
3. Cockney for "author."
4. Not identified.
5. Alphonse de Lamartine (1790–1869). Many of Lamartine's works were available at this time. However, because of his financial difficulties, in early 1856 Lamartine began a monthly periodical, *Le Cours familier de littérature,* available by subscription. In 1858 Thackeray was part of a London committee to promote subscriptions in Britain. Membership included Sir Robert Peel, Sir Edward Bulwer-Lytton, R. Monckton Milnes, and Charles Dickens. William Fortescue, *Alphonse de Lamartine: A Political Biography* (New York: St. Martin's Press, 1983), 264–66.
6. Possibly rest in peace.
7. Not identified.
8. Edward Robert Bulwer-Lytton (1831–91), statesman and poet, son of the novelist, viceroy of India, 1876–80; ambassador to France, 1887–91.
9. Possibly the former Helena Saville Faucit (1817–98), actress, and Theodore Martin (1816–1909), writer, married in 1851. They were neighbors when the Thackerays lived in Onslow Square. *Letters,* IV, 121–22, n. 77.
10. "Having said this."

LETTER 20

1. Abbreviation for September, the seventh month in the early Roman calendar.
2. A servant.
3. *Rez-de-chaussée.*
4. Although there is no mention of this "brown young lady" in Thackeray's correspondence at this time, she could be his Indian niece by his half-sister, Mrs. Blechynden.
5. Aunt Ritchie's devoted maid. Gérin, 245.
6. Not identified.
7. Not identified.
8. Not identified.
9. Augusta Trimmer married (1844) Thackeray's cousin William Ritchie; Mrs. Trimmer was Ritchie's mother-in-law. *Letters,* G VI.
10. "Together."
11. Robert Browning (1782–1866), father of the poet.
12. Lady Louisa de Rothschild (1821–1910), Thackeray had met her on a Rhine river steamer in 1848.
13. At Aix-la-Chapelle Thackeray learned of the death of the wife of Major Robert Carmichael-Smyth, Major Henry's younger brother. Thinking

his parents might need him, Thackeray went to Paris immediately, only to find that they had not returned from their holiday. *Letters,* III, 616.

14. Not identified.
15. Not identified.
16. "We are not to go to Scotland with our father."
17. Thackeray's cousin Jane Ritchie (1822?–1865). *Letters,* IV, G 111.

LETTER 21

1. The start of the letter is missing. The beginning of the existing letter is written by Anny; then Minny continues, ending with her sign; Anny closes the letter.
2. Probably the daughter of Dr. and Mrs. Joseph Douglas. *Letters,* III, 638, n. 159.
3. Possibly a reference to the scenic production by Charles Kean that opened at the Princess Theatre, London, 25 October 1856. William Winter, *Shakespeare on the Stage,* 3rd series (New York: Benjamin Blom, 1916), 250–253.
4. Anny and Minny had to forego their trip to Scotland with Thackeray in order to nurse Mrs. Carmichael-Smyth. *Letters,* III, 625.
5. A pulsatory swelling on the fore part of the elbow joint.
6. Anny breaks off; new handwriting, smaller, tighter.
7. There is a discrepancy between the pulse, which is normal, and the blood pressure, which is extremely low.
8. Not identified.
9. Letters written horizontally, turned, and then written across vertically.
10. A servant with the Thackerays until 1858. *Letters,* IV, 82.
11. Not identified.
12. Not identified.
13. Thackeray's cousins Charlotte and Jane Ritchie. *Letters,* IV, G 110, 111.
14. In a letter describing Anny and Minny, Thackeray writes, "the girls are behaving like trumps." *Letters,* III, 628. An example of Anny using the same word as Thackeray.

LETTER 22

1. In a letter to Anny and Minny dated 18–21 November, Thackeray describes his visit to Captain Hankey on 15 November 1856. *Letters,* III, 634, 687. Therefore, Anny's letter to Amy in which she tells her friend all about Thackeray's visit to Captain Hankey would have had to be written after 21 November.
2. Onslow Square.
3. Home of Captain Hankey. *Letters,* III, 687.
4. Probably a maid.

5. Lecture on George IV.
6. Albert Richard Smith (1816–60), *The Adventures of Mr. Ledbury and His Friend Jack Johnson* (London: R. Bentley, 1847).
7. Young boys who cleaned boots at inns.
8. Cockney pronunciation, omitting *h*s.
9. Probably a reference to Thackeray's "Mrs. Perkins's Ball," in which the Mulligan of Ballymulligan is featured.
10. An example of Anny's editing: the phrase "every minute or two" was inserted above the line.
11. The Normandy coast near Le Havre-de-Grâce was popular among landscape painters, including Isabey, Diaz, Daubigny, Corot, Troyon, Courbet, Boudin, and Monet.
12. Col. and Mrs. Charles Carmichael.
13. No signature but in Anny's handwriting.
14. Note added by Minny on front page, no signature, but her mark.

LETTER 23

1. The postmark of November is stamped on the stationery. November is the ninth month in the early Roman calendar.
2. Not identified.
3. Thackeray's friend Henry Davison was appointed puisne judge of the Supreme Court of Madras, 16 March 1857; knighted 23 November 1856. *Letters*, III, 637, n. 157.
4. Thackeray's cousin William Ritchie (1817–62) was made advocate general of Calcutta in 1855, for which he earned £15,000 per year. It was Ritchie's son Richmond whom Anny later married. *Letters*, I, clx.
5. Possibly a relative of the Carmichael-Smyths', as the major's sister married a Dr. Alexander Monroe in 1800.
6. Perhaps the daughter of Thackeray's old friend the Rev. James White. *Letters*, III, 17.
7. A highly evangelical clergyman, "not [a man] to be liked." *Letters*, I, 429, 432.
8. Not identified.
9. Henrietta Cole.
10. Lectures on *The Four Georges*, which Thackeray was writing at this time.
11. Peter Cunningham (1816–69), author of *A Handbook for London, Past and Present* (1849).
12. Kate Dickens married Charles Allston Collins (Wilkie's brother) on 17 July 1860.
13. No signature but in Anny's handwriting.

LETTER 24

1. Possibly the wife of Thackeray's friend William Wellwood Stoddart. John Blackwood said to Thackeray of her, "She's such a dear creature." *Letters*, III, 647.
2. Thackeray returned from Germany 13 September 1857. *Letters*, IV, 53.
3. The first number of *The Virginians* appeared in November 1857.
4. Thackeray was an unsuccessful candidate for Parliament from Oxford in July 1857, a personally expensive venture in Victorian England. *Wisdom*, 268–71.

LETTER 25

1. Charles Pearman left Thackeray's service 10 April 1858. *Letters*, IV, 80.
2. Beginning and ending of letter missing but in Anny's handwriting.
3. John Thaddeus Delane (1817–79), editor of the *Times* from 1841 to 1877; friend of Thackeray's.
4. *The Virginians*.
5. Sims was hired as a temporary coachman and remained as butler after Charles left.
6. Like her heroine in *Old Kensington*, Anny has her district for social work.
7. See 1864–65 Journal, below.
8. Not identified.
9. The ending is missing.

LETTER 26

1. Not identified.
2. Thackeray spent parts of December and January at the Bristol Hotel in Paris.
3. Plum.
4. Not identified.
5. The cook and housemaid for the Thackerays.
6. Probably John Blake Dillon (1814–66), a leader of the Young Ireland rebellion of 1848. *Letters*, III, 228, n. 108.
7. Not identified.
8. Wife of the Italian sculptor Baron Carlo Marochetti (1805–67). They were Thackeray's neighbors in Onslow Square, and he executed the bust of Thackeray in Westminster Abbey. *Letters*, III, 388.
9. Not identified.
10. Perhaps the maid whose departure Thackeray sweetened. *Letters*, III, 209.
11. The Yates affair, in which Edmund Yates was asked to resign from the Garrick Club on Thackeray's charges that Yates had used privileged con-

versations overheard at the Club to malign Thackeray in print. Dickens took Yates's part against Thackeray. *Wisdom*, 404.

12. In *Wisdom*, Ray footnotes this phrase as follows: "The words 'manly service' perhaps caught Anny's attention because they echo the unfortunate phrase about 'the manly consideration towards Mrs. Dickens which I owe to my wife' that Dickens had used in his notorious 'violated letter' to Arthur Smith of 25 May 1858." *Wisdom*, 478, n. 46.

13. Ellen Ternan was the actress with whom Dickens set up house after he left his wife. Dickens's oldest son, Charles Culliford Boz, remained with his mother. Kaplan gives no corroboration to this rumored meeting.

14. When Charlotte Brontë dedicated the second edition of *Jane Eyre* to Thackeray, without knowing about his domestic situation, scandalmongers said that a discarded governess had based the novel on Thackeray and his mad wife.

15. Francis Fladgate (1799–1892), barrister friend of Thackeray's, member of Garrick Club. *Letters*, II, 343, n. 20.

16. No signature but in Anny's handwriting.

CHAPTER 3

INTRODUCTION

1. Thackeray wrote, "Anny's style is admirable and Smith and Elder are in raptures about it. But she is very modest." *Letters*, IV, 271–72.

2. One of the many times Thackeray wrote of death he said, "I dont feel much care about dying." *Letters*, IV, 279.

3. Priscilla Metcalf, an architectural historian, quotes Thackeray when she describes the house as "THE REDDEST HOUSE IN ALL THE TOWN": "The first deliberately 'Queen Anne' house . . . for all the visual awareness of its artist-author, has for us a rather Second Empire look. It was a literary idea in more ways than one, and perhaps influential as such." "Postscript on Thackeray's House," *Journal of Society of Architectural Historians*, 28 January 1969, 123. *Letters*, IV, 236.

4. Diary, 1859–62, private collection.

5. Other visits included one to the Milnes, where Anny met Swinburne for the first time, when he shocked and delighted her with a reading of "Les Noyades." *Letters*, IV, 285.

6. *Letters*, IV, 230.

7. *Letters*, IV, 291.

8. *Letters*, IV, 81.

9. Thackeray wrote of a friend's wife that she was a "pretty nice amiable milksop Amelia sort of wife." *Letters*, II, 383.

10. *Letters*, III, 626.

11. *Letters*, III, 613.
12. *Letters*, IV, 230.
13. Thackeray suspected the cause of his daughter's discontent: "They are both of them beginning to bewail their Virginity in the mountains." *Letters*, IV, 272.
14. *Letters*, IV, 230.
15. *Chapters*, 3.
16. *Thackeray's Daughter*, 87–88.
17. *Thackeray's Daughter*, 88.
18. "Little Scholars," *Toilers and Spinsters*, 102.
19. Like most articles, Anny's piece was published anonymously in the *Cornhill. Letters*, IV, 185.
20. In *Victims of Convention* Jeanne Kennard concludes that most Victorian novels suffer from a "convention of two suitors." If the heroine chooses the right one, she manifests maturity, which "consists of adjusting oneself to the real world." Her happiness depends not on herself but on the man she marries. In Anny's novels her plots revolve around two women, although in the end the heroine chooses the "right" suitor. (Hamden, Conn.: Archon Books, [1978], 10–14).
21. Anon. review of "Story of Elizabeth," *Athenaeum* 41 (25 April 1863), 552–53.
22. *Elizabeth*, 6.
23. *The George Eliot Letters*, 9 vols., ed. Gordon S. Haight (New Haven: Yale Univ. Press, 1954–79), IV, 209.
24. *George Eliot Letters*, IV, 209.
25. *George Eliot Letters*, VI, 123.
26. "Out of the World," *To Esther* (London: Smith, Elder, & Co., 1876), 93.
27. Charles Dickens, "In Memoriam," *Cornhill*, reprinted in Richard Henry Stoddard, ed., *Anecdote Biographies of Thackeray and Dickens* (New York: Scribner, Armstrom, & Co., 1875), 190.

LETTER 27

1. In Letter 28 below, dated 6 March [1859], Anny writes "Our Coles came back from Rome . . ."
2. Laetitia Cole.
3. Hyde Park Gardens.
4. Probably the son of Thackeray's friend John Livingston Craigie, F.R.C.S. *Letters*, IV, 397, n. 15.
5. Not identified.
6. Edmund Thackeray.
7. Wife of Thackeray's friend (1805–60), editor. *Letters*, I, 455, n. 88.

8. Mary Cole.
9. Not identified.
10. An order of contemplative nuns founded at Assisi, Italy, in 1212.
11. Quarreling sisters in *Philip*.
12. Wife of Thackeray's Cambridge friend William Henry Brookfield. Jane Octavia Elton Brookfield (1821–96) was an intimate of Thackeray's from 1848 to 1851. *Letters*, I, xcv–c.
13. Lady Dorothy Nevill (1826–1913), author of several volumes of reminiscences.
14. Daughter (b. 1850) of Reverend William Henry and Jane Octavia Brookfield.
15. Charles Bagot Cayley, or George John Cayley, both friends of Thackeray's.
16. Henry Cole was involved in the manufacturing of household articles such as pottery, porcelains, cutlery, etc.; John Bell was one of his designers. Henry Cole, *Fifty Years of Public Work* (London: George Bell & Sons, 1884), II, 178–93.
17. Woolwich was noted for its arsenal and the royal military academy.

LETTER 28

1. At the time, Yates was suing both Thackeray and the club. Explaining that the expense of bringing a case against the Garrick Club and Thackeray was too costly, Yates wrote, "My only resource . . . has been the publication of a pamphlet," namely, *Mr. Thackeray, Mr. Yates, and the Garrick Club Affair: The Correspondence and the Facts. Letters*, IV, 131, n. 13.
2. Synge was in the Foreign Office, stationed in Central America.
3. Gilbert Synge.
4. Oatlands Park Hotel.
5. Mrs. Russell Sturgis, wife of the owner of the house in which the ball took place.
6. Mr. and Mrs. James Russell and daughter Katie. He was a banker friend of Thackeray's. Gérin, 109, n. 7.
7. John Crawfurd (1783–1868), distinguished Indian civil servant and geographer. Thackeray wrote 2 May 1861, a John Crawfurd "is going to marry Miss Ford (30000f)." *Letters*, IV, 173, n. 2; 233.
8. Not identified.
9. John Sturgis; probably the daughter of Sir Thomas Erskine Perry (1806–82), brother of Kate Perry; mentioned by Thackeray, "gave the Lectures in a present to Loo Perry on the 1st of June her birthday." *Letters*, III, 81, 276.
10. Mr. Felix, Harry, May, and Miss Gordon not identified.
11. Edward Bruce Hamley (1824–93), later K.C.B. (1882), lieutenant

general in the Crimean War. *Letters,* III, 633, n. 105; possibly the Mr. Alexander whom Thackeray recommended to Gladstone in 1863. *Letters,* IV, 290; Mrs. Julia: not identified.

12. The officer in charge or officer commanding.

13. Arthur Prinsep, son of Henry Thoby Prinsep (1793–1878) and Sarah Pattle, friends of Thackeray's. *Letters,* I, 189, n. 23.

14. Charles Stuart Aubrey Abbott (1834–82), later (1870) third Baron Tenterden. Permanent under-secretary for Foreign Affairs. *Letters,* IV, 233, n. 29; Jane Perry Elliot (d. 1859), and her elder sister Kate Perry were friends of Thackeray's.

15. Not identified.

16. On 4 December 1858 Thackeray wrote that Arthur Shawe "informs me that he is about to be arrested for a bill of 235£—w^h I shall end by paying. Isn't it jolly?" *Letters,* IV, 121. Mr. Isaacs was a moneylender.

17. On 4 February 1863 Thackeray describes L. Fardel, who "when he lived with me was a very honest sober & respectable man . . ." *Letters,* IV, 281.

LETTER 29

1. *The Virginians.*

2. *The Saturday Review.* Anny's prediction was correct. In the phrase of Merle Moubray Bevington, Thackeray was "damned with faint praise" in the issue of 19 November 1859. *The Saturday Review, 1855–1868* (New York: Columbia Univ. Press, 1941), 171.

3. Not identified.

4. The ending is missing.

LETTER 30

1. The year, omitted by Anny, is 1859, because she describes the itinerary taken by the Thackerays in 1859. However, in September 1859 Thursday fell on the 15th, but this would be in line with Anny's admission that Thursday is the 16th "more or less."

2. Boulogne.

3. Jardin des Plantes.

4. Small boots.

5. "Are there perfectly preserved cadavers, sir?"

6. Nectarines.

7. In later years Anny confessed that at the time Thackeray made this pun, he had to explain it to his daughters, since they were not as yet familiar with Tennyson's poem. *Chapters,* 208.

8. "Some milk, sugar, bread and butter, please." "We have no milk, miss." "Oh! no matter." "We have no butter miss. It's not good in this country."

9. "France is declaring war because England continues to keep and protect the rascals that wanted to attack our Emperor. Sir, France is indignant. Sir, France will make you pay for your obstinancy with every drop of your blood."
10. "Here's the fourth station."
11. "Do you want some licorice, my son."
12. "I bet that he's the cousin, I bet that it's his hat in that carriage." "They are our parents who have come to pick us up in their very own carriage."
13. Not identified.
14. Cole.
15. "Here you are given drink and food, & drink and food."
16. Anny's initials are written with a flourish.

LETTER 31

1. Anny's godson.
2. Miss Russell came to dinner at the Thackerays' on 5 May 1861. *Letters,* IV, 397.
3. Home of Russell Sturgis, friend of Thackeray's, "a Merchant Prince," "who has a palace of a house near London." *Letters,* IV, 63; III, 653.
4. In Coire.
5. Victorian medicine prescribed a shorn head to combat high fever.
6. Probably the children of Mrs. White.
7. Not identified.
8. Possibly the daughter of Samuel Warren. *Letters,* IV, 365.
9. Lecture tours.
10. Not identified.
11. Lord Kilmarnock: Probably a descendant of William Boyd (1704–46), fourth earl of Kilmarnock. The family was noted for its antagonism to the English. The conflict, possibly concerning Don Pacifico, whom Lord Palmerston supported against the foreign oppression, did not lead to a change in government. Palmerston had formed a Whig administration in 1859 that endured until 1865.

LETTER 32

1. Date probably 1861. This letter is written on black-bordered stationery; there is no mention of Major Carmichael-Smyth, who died 9 September 1861.
2. Home of Anthony Trollope.
3. "John Gilpin": ballad by William Cowper, 1782. In 1831, FitzGerald wrote to Thackeray, "I am glad you have taken to Cowper." *Letters,* I, 166. Thackeray quotes several times from Cowper's poems, for example: *Letters,* I, 241, 420. Either he transmitted his early fondness for Cowper to Minny, or

she had access to the eighteenth-century poet's work through his volume in her father's library.
4. Not identified.
5. Aunt Mary and Uncle Charles.

LETTER 33

1. Tennyson lived at Farringford, near Mrs. Cameron in Freshwater, where Anny was visiting. In her memoir of Tennyson, Anny wrote:

> One autumn, when everything seemed happy at home, Mrs. Cameron took me with her to Freshwater for a few delightful weeks, and then, for the first time, I lived with them all, . . . in her ivy-grown house near the gates of Farringford. For the first time I stayed in the island, . . . and walked with Tennyson along High Down, treading the turf, listening to his talk, while the gulls came sideways, the poet's cloak flapped time to the gusts of the west wind. (*Records of Tennyson, Ruskin, and Browning*, 41–42)

2. Possibly the children of Marianne Shakespear and Major Irvine. *Letters*, IV, G 88, 89.
3. Mrs. Fanny Kemble (1809–93), actress, Shakespearian reader. Anny wrote about her in *Friend*.
4. Not identified.
5. Not identified.
6. Julia Margaret Prattle Cameron (1815–79), photographer. Anny wrote about her in *Chapters*.
7. Not identified.
8. Thackeray's "dainty little Italian greyhound." *Wisdom*, 359.

LETTER 34

1. Anny's letter is written over the following note:

> Palace Green,
> Kensington, W.
> Would Messrs. Jackson and Graham please send somebody to see to the kitchen chimney at Mr. Thackerays — The clamps [?] and the water still come oozing through the wall.

2. Jackson and Graham, contractors for Thackeray's house at 2, Palace Green, Kensington. *Letters*, IV, 397, n. 19.
3. Edward Thackeray, Amy Crowe's fiancé; Eugenie Wynne, Amy Crowe's sister, whom she was visiting in Wales.
4. Not identified.
5. Perhaps a reference to the man Charles Carmichael-Smyth had been taken to for medical treatment in 1842. *Letters*, II, 46.
6. Herman and Miss Terry not identified.

7. William George Prescott (1800–1865), a wealthy banker. *Letters*, III, 674, n. 12.

LETTER 35

1. Son of Mr. and Mrs. Synge.
2. Anny was not being melodramatic; many English men and women never returned from India, as indeed Amy did not.
3. Charles Albert Fechter (1824–79), noted English actor.
4. *The Duke's Motto* also known as *The Duke's Daughter* or *The Hunchback of Paris*, a melodrama, written by John Brougham (1814–80), first produced in London on 10 January 1863. Allardyce Nicoll, *Nineteenth-Century Drama, 1850–1900* (New York: Columbia Univ. Press, 1946), V, 280.
5. Lord Dundreary, an indolent English lord in Tom Taylor's comedy *The American Cousin*, made famous by the comedian Edward Askew Sothern (1862–81), who was a dinner guest at Thackeray's home on Sunday, 18 January 1863. *The American Cousin* received lasting recognition as the play Lincoln was seeing the night he was assassinated. *Letters*, IV, 408.
6. Not identified.
7. Thackeray's diary for 1863 does not list the visit to the Trollopes; it does list their trip to the Rothschilds on 26 January. *Letters*, IV, 408.
8. Colonel James Montgomery Caulfield, F.R.G.S., and his wife, friends of Thackeray's in the last years of his life. *Letters*, IV, 252.
9. A member of Chapman and Hall, one of Thackeray's publishers.
10. George Smith (1824–1901), publisher and friend of Thackeray's. *Letters*, I, clxvi–clxviii.
11. *Denis Duval*.
12. A drawing has been deliberately cut off the bottom of the page.
13. Mary Elizabeth Braddon (1837–1915), wrote *Lady Audley's Secret* (1862), *Aurora Floyd* (1862), *Eleanor's Victory* (1863), among eighty novels.
14. Julian Henry Charles Fane (1827–70), fourth son of the eleventh earl of Westmorland; friend of Thackeray's.
15. Possibly the son of Sir James Robert Carmichael (1817–83), second baronet, who dropped the Smyth from his surname; friend of Thackeray's.
16. Not identified.
17. Not identified.
18. Sister of Mrs. Elliot and Sir Thomas Erskine Perry.
19. Possibly a daughter of Herman Merivale.

LETTER 36

1. Anny tells Amy that the Thackerays are dining at their archbishop's that evening. In Thackeray's diary for 1863, he records "Archbishop of Y" for

May 6. Ray identifies him as William A. Thomson. *Letters*, IV, 411, n. 18; 285, n. 8.
  2. Amy lived in Fort William, Calcutta.
  3. Not identified.
  4. Thackeray's diary for 1 May reads "H. Wilson." *Letters*, IV, 411.
  5. Adelaide Kemble Sartoris (1814?–79), English soprano; the Kemble "Thackeray liked best"; also a favorite of Anny's, who wrote a memoir of her, published later in *Friend. Letters*, I, cxliv.
  6. Julia Cameron.
  7. Not identified.
  8. Possibly Samuel Rogers, friend of Thackeray's.
  9. Not identified.
  10. South Kensington Museum.
  11. Royal.
  12. Not identified.
  13. Dined at Thackeray's on 16 May 1862 and 29 April 1863. *Letters*, IV, 400, 411.
  14. Not identified.
  15. Possibly a member of the family of John Sterling (1806–44).
  16. Thackeray's diary for 3 May 1863 reads, "Leech at Richmond." The John Leeches lived in Richmond at the time. *Letters*, IV, 411.
  17. Morgan John O'Connell (1811–75), one of Thackeray's closest friends in middle and later life. *Letters*, II, 362, n. 55.
  18. Probably Charles Collins; M is Minny.
  19. Wife of Russell Gurney (1804–78), Recorder of the City of London from 1856 to 1878; friend of Thackeray's. *Letters*, IV, 402, n. 19.
  20. "Out of the World," *Cornhill*, September–October 1863, but with its title changed.
  21. The art show Anny referred to here is the exhibition at the Royal Academy that opened on 2 May 1863 and was reviewed in the *Times*, 2 May 1863, 11.
  22. The *Times* reviewer describes Eyre Crowe's painting: "In passing a look should be taken, till the longer examination they deserve can be given, . . . at Mr. E. Crowe's 'Brick-court' (797) outside of Dr. Goldsmith's staircase, on the morning of his death, with the outcasts and vagrants whom the doctor's ungrudging and undistinguishing charity used to relieve, gathered together to lament their kindly benefactor." *Times*, 2 May 1863, 11. In 1862 Crowe had exhibited "Defoe in the Pillory."
  23. Valentine Cameron Prinsep was the son of Adelaide Prinsep, the model for his painting. The painting bore the motto from "Christabel," "whispering tongues can poison truth." The reviewer comments on "a want of beauty in the lady—inexcusable to those who know his model—." *Times*, 2 May 1863, 11.

24. The Millais painting that Anny and the reviewer were so fond of is "My First Sermon." The "listening eyes" of the little girl which so captivated Anny are described in the *Times* as "reverent eyes fixed upon the preacher."

Since Anny did not care for this picture, she did not bother remembering its correct title, which was "The Wolf's Den."

This painting is "from Keats's poem of the 'Eve of St. Agnes,' where Madeline [is] undressing in her moonlit chamber." What took the reviewer an entire paragraph to describe, Anny does in three adjectives, "weird, & odd & silvery." *Times*, 2 May 1863, 11.

25. The *Times* reviewer is in agreement with Anny about "King of Hearts," and despite the dictum of the crowd that "Dr. Lushington" is very fine, the reviewer and Anny dislike the painting. *Times*, 2 May 1863, 11.

26. Walker's "Lost Path," the reviewer finds "another cruel piece of bad hanging." *Times*, 2 May 1863, 11.

27. Charles Freak lived at 55, Onslow Square. *Letters*, IV, 35, n. 45. Thackeray spelled the name as Anny did, with a final "e." *Letters*, IV, 35.

28. Not identified.

29. Not identified.

30. See Julia Sterling.

31. The word "very" is crossed out.

32. Presumably one of the Thackeray's maid servants; Sophia Weston of *Tom Jones*.

33. Not identified.

34. Onslow Square.

35. Augusta Small Twyford dined with the Thackerays on 26 April 1863. *Letters*, IV, 410, n. 16.

36. Colonel Edward Bruce Hamley (1824–93), later K.C.B. *Letters*, III, 633.

37. *At Odds* (1863), a novel by Baroness Tautphoeus (1807–93), an Irish novelist (Jemima Montgomery) who wrote of German life; and Thomas Carlyle, *History of Friedrich II of Prussia: Called Frederick the Great* (1858–65).

38. Selina Shakespear, Thackeray's cousin; Hyde Park.

39. Sir James Colvile (1810–80), returned to England after a distinguished career as an Indian judge. *Letters*, IV, 409, n. 9; Arthur William Buller (1808–69), later K.C.B. Queen's Advocate in Ceylon; judge in Calcutta; returned to London in 1858, where he became M.P. for Devonport and Liskeard; friend of Thackeray's.

40. Not identified.

41. Richard Monckton Milnes (Lord Houghton) (1809–85), friend of Thackeray's; "Lt.-Col. Edward Harris Greathed (1812–1881), later (1865) K.C.B. and a General," *Letters*, IV, 411, n. 19; Colonel Sir Thomas St. Vincent Hope Cochrane Troubridge (1815–67); and Louisa Jane Gurney (d. 1867). *Letters*, IV, 395, n. 3.

The dinner party Anny describes here was held on 14 May 1863 for eighteen people: "2 Troubridges. Col. Greathed 2 Milnes 2 Lows Heatly. Baring Ld Stanley. 3 Selves. Venables. 2 Thackerays. Ellison. Lady Cullum." Thackeray's diary for 1863, *Letters,* IV, 411.

42. Probably a child of Thackeray's friends the writer Bryan Waller Procter, to whom *Vanity Fair* is dedicated, and his wife. *Letters,* I, cliv.

43. Manson Craigie.

44. Not identified.

45. Anny uses the word "fetch" to mean the ghost of a living person which appears as an omen of that person's death.

46. Charlotte and Alan not identified.

47. John Hungerford Pollen, Fellow of Merton College until 1852, when he seceded to Rome, *Letters,* III, 102, n. 145; probably Richard Doyle (1824–83), artist, illustrator of *The Newcomes;* the Smiths are not identified.

48. John Leech (1817–64), atttended Charterhouse with Thackeray, cartoonist at *Punch,* close friend of Thackeray and his family. *Chapters,* 93–100.

49. Robert Gregory Creyke, whom Thackeray called "my disciple." Thackeray's mother was responsible for manufacturing "an affair" between Creyke and Anny. *Letters,* IV, 84; III, 524, 613.

50. Probably wife of Henry John Temple Palmerston (1784–1865), English statesman and prime minister.

51. Prince of Wales.

LETTER 37

1. Morgan John O'Connell (1811–75), one of Thackeray's closest friends in middle and later life. *Letters,* II, 362, n. 55.

2. Herman Merivale (1806–74), barrister, writer, and friend of Thackeray and Mrs. Merivale.

3. A road and trade center in northeast Assam, India.

4. Sir Aukland Colvin (1838–1908), English administrator in India civil service (1858–78).

5. Not identified.

6. Not identified.

7. Hannah More Macaulay (d. 1873), married Sir Charles Edward Trevelyan in 1834. *Letters,* III, 68, n. 95.

8. Lou Perry.

9. Not identified.

10. Not identified.

11. Not identified.

12. *Austin Elliot* (1863), by Henry Kingsley.

13. *The Duke's Motto,* an adaption of Paul Feval's play *Le Bossu.*

14. Tom Taylor (1817–80), dramatist and art critic; editor of *Punch* 1874–80; wrote *The Ticket-of-Leave Man,* first produced in London in May of 1863.

15. Gounod's *Faust* premiered in London on 11 June 1863.
16. Not identified.
17. Swedish singer (1820–87).
18. Alexander William Kinglake (1809–91), historian; wrote *Eothen*, Eastern travel book, 1844; *Invasion of the Crimea*, 1863–87; M.P. for Bridgewater 1857–68; friend of Thackeray's. *Letters*, I, 195.
19. Paul Belloni Du Chaillu, born in Paris in 1835; African explorer and writer.
20. In 1863 the fighting in the American Civil War was particularly fierce. Thackeray's American friendships made them all anxious about the war's outcome.
21. Samuel Lucas, minor Victorian journalist (1818–68), literary reviewer for the *Times*. *Letters*, IV, 170, n. 91.

LETTER 38

1. Clatto: Country home of General Sir John Low (1788–1880) and his wife, Augusta Shakespear Low (Thackeray's cousin). *Letters*, IV, G IV.
2. Not identified.
3. On 23 September 1863 Thackeray wrote to Dr. John Brown, "I am very glad you like my little Min. . . . when she has done with the Lows, I think she ought to come back to her Papa and sister." *Letters*, IV, 291.
4. Perhaps a member of the family of Susan Edmonstone Ferrier (1782–1854), novelist, friend of Scott's.
5. Blackwood (1818–79), a friend of Thackeray's since 1839. "In 1845 Blackwood succeeded his eldest brother as editor of *Blackwood's Magazine* and settled in Edinburgh." *Letters*, III, 406, n. 128.
6. Not identified.
7. In her review in *Blackwood's Edinburgh Magazine*, Oliphant comments that "the faculty which can execute a series of little pictures so vivid and so lifelike, and which has the courage to utter, so singular a disclosure of the secrets which lie within that mist of virginal sanctity and supposed angelhood in which the heart of a pretty girl is veiled from close inspection, is one of no small power and promise" (94, August 1863, 178). Anny, in 1897, recounted, "It was Mrs. Oliphant who bestowed on me my first review when I was twenty-three. It was summertime and I opened *Blackwood*, and my father beamed with satisfaction." *Thackeray and His Daughter*, 261.
8. "Dr. John Brown (1810–1882), a Scottish physician who devoted his leisure to letters." Author of *Horae Subsecivae* (Edinburgh, 1858–82). Ray writes of the relationship between Brown and Thackeray, "Each saw in the other what he might himself have been: Brown was a Thackeray of modest talent playing out his destiny in the retirement of a provincial city, Thackeray a Brown whose genius had given him a splendid role in the great world." *Letters*, I, c–cii.

LETTER 39

1. Minny's acquaintances not identified.
2. John Ruskin (1819–1900), married Euphemia Chalmers Gray in 1848. The marriage was never consummated. When John Everett Millais went to Scotland with the Ruskins, Millais used Effie as a model. In 1854 she left Ruskin and received a nullification of their marriage. The next year she and Millais were married.
3. George Gray of Bowerswell, Perth, a friend of Ruskin's father and a writer to *The Signet*, a legal appointment.
4. Not identified.
5. Not identified.
6. The wife of Thackeray's friend Nassau William Senior (1790–1864), economist and writer. *Letters*, III, 277, n. 180.

LETTER 40

1. Eugenia Crowe Wynne.
2. Both Thackeray and Anny wanted Minny to return home; Dr. Brown wanted her to stay.
3. Not identified.
4. Ending missing.

CHAPTER 4

INTRODUCTION

1. This journal has an impressive leather binding and lock. It may well have been purchased by Anny for the purpose of writing her thoughts about her recently deceased father. The first page of the journal is dated "January 28. 1864."
2. See chapter 3 for an analysis of Horatia.
3. Thackeray's diaries are published in Ray's *Letters*. Anny's journals for 1863–64 and 1878 are in the Ray collection of the Morgan Library. The diaries to which she referred while writing her journals are in a private collection.
4. *Letters*, IV, 299.
5. *Wisdom*, 423.
6. Katherine C. Hill-Miller has suggested that Anny saw herself as both her father's son and his daughter. "In her early years Anne Thackeray showed all the energy and aspiration of a first-born son determined to follow in his father's footsteps; as her life wore on, she became more and more the dutiful daughter, devoted to recapturing her happy youth in her father's home." "'The Skies and Trees of the Past': Anne Thackeray Ritchie and William Makepeace Thackeray," in *Daughters and Fathers*, ed. Lynda E. Boose and Betty S. Flowers (Baltimore: Johns Hopkins Univ. Press, 1989), 363.

7. Two entries in Anny's 1859–62 diary read:

January 22, 1863. Just been to see Amy & Edward off. I remember her back getting into the cab in the mist . . . Knocked at Papa's door He wouldn't let me in

23 Ill — took a walk.

Was Anny's undefined illness caused by her belief that Thackeray was angry with her?

8. *Vanity Fair*, 661.
9. *The Virginians*, 34.
10. *Letters*, IV, 298–99.
11. Diary of Anne Thackeray.
12. *Thackeray and His Daughter*, 133–35; *Thackeray's Daughter*, 98–100.
13. Diary of 20 August, *Wisdom*, 423.
14. Diary of 9 September, *Wisdom*, 423.
15. *Letters*, IV, 304.
16. *Letters*, IV, 303.
17. Throughout the journal Anny made choices. Most of what she wrote depended on her memory, but it was Anny who selected the episodes, many of which are suggestive of sexual imagery. Climbing a mountain can be construed as a symbol of sex; her father, a man of experience, would naturally be able to go on while she would be left behind. However, the incest taboo, even in a dream, is operative here. The reference to Mr. Longman may indicate that the dream establishes Anny's vocation.
18. Diary.

1864–1865 JOURNAL

1. The 1864–65 journal is bound in black leather, and closes with a brass clasp (patent: S Mordan & Co London). According to a sticker on the inside front cover it was purchased from W & A Webster, Booksellers and Stationers, 60, Piccadilly. The journal measures 8½ by 6 inches. It is 1 inch thick, exclusive of the ⅛ inch binding. The pages, which are white and lined with light blue, are edged with a blue, red, and yellow feather design. Anny wrote on twenty pages of the journal; approximately forty are left blank.

2. This verse, written in Anny's hand, appears on the first page of the journal. Anny refers to the verse in the Biographical Introductions, but seems not to remember the author's name: " 'Good Will' was the name some one gave him in some verses written after his death" (Vol. 13, xxiii).

The date and name are written on the first page of the journal; the text begins on a separate sheet.

3. Anny originally wrote, "Sometimes he used to smile & say Godblesh you an' he will."

4. Amy Crowe married Edward Talbot Thackeray on 6 December 1862 and was no longer in need of Thackeray's gift.

5. This, indeed, is what happened, because Thackeray died without signing his will.

6. Thackeray dined with "Norman" on 5 May 1863, and with "two Normans" (of the banking family) on 14 October 1863. *Letters*, IV, 411, 414.

7. The 1851 Crystal Palace Exhibition in Kensington necessitated many new roads.

8. Silver threepences.

9. The Arians of the fourth century distinguished between God the Father and Jesus Christ by identifying the latter as a changeable creature and therefore subordinate and inferior.

10. Anny uses this scene in *Old Kensington*, 450–61.

11. Herman Merivale, Jr., barrister and writer, son of Thackeray's close friend Herman Merivale. With Frank Marzials, he wrote *The Life of William Makepeace Thackeray* (London, 1891).

12. Sir William Wellesley Knighton, second baronet (1811–85), keeper of George IV's privy purse, married Clementina Jameson in 1838. *Letters*, IV, 267, n. 25; the Thackerays visited Richard Monckton Milnes (Lord Houghton) at Fryston Hall in Yorkshire on 6–13 April 1863. *Letters*, IV, 285.

13. Since the Thackerays were living with Thackeray's mother when Anny was born, Isabella was put under the care of her mother-in-law's homeopathic doctor.

14. Charles Allston Collins (1828–73), brother of Wilkie, painter, writer. In 1860, he married Dickens's daughter Kate; John Livingstone Craigie, F.R.C.S., dined with Thackeray on 5 May 1861, *Letters*, IV, 397. Robert Curzon (1810–73) (fourteenth baron Zouche), attended Charterhouse with Thackeray; a writer of travel books. *Letters*, IV, 410.

15. Charles Bagot Cayley dined with the Thackerays on 29 March 1863. *Letters*, IV, 410.

16. Possibly the masthead of the newspaper the *Realm*.

17. Charles Robert Leslie's family. Leslie (1798–1859), R.A., Thackeray's friend. Born in America of English parents, Leslie came to England to study art.

18. Probably Kate Collins.

19. In Bio. Intro. XII, xiv, Anny writes, "Milton's Sonnet to Shakespeare in Johnson's poets was one of the last things he ever read."

20. Anny wrote in 1861 of "a pretty little maid called Fanny who is literary and quotes the Cornhill Magazine." *Letters*, IV, 230.

21. Daughter of Thackeray's friend Sir Henry Davison. *Letters*, II, 370, n. 86.

22. A servant.

23. Most likely a reference to Thomas Longman (1804–79), English publisher and partner in the firm established by his father.

24. A page and a half left blank in the manuscript.

25. Thackeray's diary reads, "June 9, 1863. Dined with girls at Star & Garter."
26. The words "us three" have been crossed out.
27. The entry in Thackeray's diary for 10 June 1863 reads "Clifford. Trafalgar." *Letters*, IV, 412. Charles Cavendish Clifford (1821–95), later (1892) fourth baronet, private secretary to Lord Palmerston, M.P. Isle of Wight and Newport. *Letters*, III, 316, n. 238.
28. Thackeray's entry for 15 June 1863 reads, "Lady Troubridge Mr Roderick Murchison." *Letters*, IV, 412. Lady Troubridge was the wife of Colonel Sir Thomas St. Vincent Hope Cochrane Troubridge (1815–67). *Letters*, IV, 395, n. 3. Sir Roderick Impey Murchison (1792–1871), later (1866) first baronet, a distinguished geologist. *Letters*, IV, 391, n. 7.
29. Thackeray's diary for 17 June 1863 reads, "Mr Grant Duff." Mountstuart Elphinstone Grant Duff (1829–1906), later G.C.S.I., politician and colonial administrator. *Letters*, IV, 412, n. 24.
30. The words "The little Ritchies were with us" have been crossed out, probably by Anny after her marriage so as not to draw attention to the difference in age between her and her husband.
31. Thackeray's diary for 19 June 1863 reads, "Mr Walter 7.30 M^r & Miss Donne." John Walter (1818–94), proprietor of the *Times;* Rev. William Bodham Donne and daughter. *Letters*, IV, 412, n. 26. Donne (1807–82), a direct descendant of John Donne, contributed to periodicals and was Examiner of Plays in the Lord Chamberlain's office. *Letters*, I, 346, n. 25.
32. Before marrying Thackeray's mother in India, Thackeray's father had kept a native mistress. Their daughter married and became Mrs. Blechynden. Richmond Thackeray left both Mrs. Blechynden and her mother an allowance. When Mrs. Blechynden's daughter came to Europe, Thackeray entertained her, but was happy to see his "black niece" leave. *Letters*, I, cxiii, n. 63; II, 367.
33. John Leech (1817–64), attended Charterhouse with Thackeray, artist, *Punch*'s first cartoonist. Charles Allston Collins. Charles Neate (1806–79), Fellow of Oriel College, M.P. for Oxford 1863–68; when he was unseated for bribery, Thackeray stood in his place at a second election. *Letters*, II, 457–58, n. 228.
34. Professor Richard Owen (1804–92), later (1884) K.C.B., eminent naturalist. Dined with Thackeray 26 July 1863. *Letters*, IV, 413. The old Dean of St. Paul was Henry Hart Milman (1791–1868), historian and professor of poetry at Oxford, known for his unconventional views. Robert Bell (1800–1867), journalist-writer, friend of Thackeray's in his last years. *Letters*, IV, 232.
35. JOB was Jane Octavia Brookfield; Marianne Irvine, Thackeray's cousin, the former Marianne Shakespear; Emmy, another name for Amy Crowe; Kate Collins; Tishy Cole (Laetitia), daughter of Henry Cole. Thackeray wrote, "I think I shall marry Tishy Cole." *Letters*, III, 77. Mrs. Whitmore

dined with the Thackerays on 26 September 1862. *Letters*, IV, 404. Mrs. Jackson was the wife of Rev. John Jackson (1811–85), rector of St. James, bishop of Lincoln, bishop of London. *Letters*, II, 439, n. 197.

36. Adelaide Procter (1825–64), daughter of Thackeray's close friends Bryan Waller Procter (1787–1874) and Anne Skepper Procter (1799–1888). Kate Perry lived with her sister Jane, who married Thomas Frederick Elliot (1808–80). She and the Elliots became Thackeray's close friends. Mrs. Elliot died 4 January 1859, and Miss Perry at the end of the century. *Letters*, I, cxxv–cxxvi. Mrs. Mansfield had dinner with the Thackerays 4 December 1863. *Letters*, IV, 414. Mrs. Stephenson had dinner with Thackeray on 6 November 1863. *Letters*, IV, 414. In his diary of 1844 Thackeray records meeting Capt. Vivian at the Hotel des Bains in Ostend on 24 May. *Letters*, II, 145. Mrs. Denman was the wife of the Honourable Richard Denman (1814–87), third son of first baron Denman. *Letters*, IV, 392, 408. The Denmans were friends of the Thackerays in Rome in 1853. *Wisdom*, 226.

37. "You are repeating yourself my dear."

38. The Thackerays visited Sir William and Lady Knighton at Blendworth 29 July 1863. *Letters*, IV, 288.

39. The word "now" has been crossed out.

40. " 'We had a friend, a faithful and loving-hearted Scotch nurse, called Jesse Brodie, who rather than quit my father in his troubles at that time, broke off her own marriage, so she told me shyly, long years after.' " Bio. Intro., V, xiii. This episode is described also in the 1878 journal, with the notable difference that in the later journal Thackeray "struck a light to cheer [Anny] up." Anny described the trip again in Cent. Intro., VI, xxvi–xxviii.

41. Henry Thoby Prinsep (1793–1878), a wealthy Indian merchant; after his return to England in 1843, he and his wife lived at Little Holland House. George Frederic Watts (1817–1904), celebrated painter, lived with the Prinseps at Little Holland House. He painted portraits of Anny and Minny.

42. Jane Thackeray (1838–39), Thackeray's second daughter, died before she was a year old.

43. *The History of Henry Esmond* (1852).

44. Captain Costigan, a disreputable and engaging Irishman created by Thackeray in *Pendennis* (1850).

45. James Hannay (1827–73), after five years in the Royal Navy, became a journalist. Hannay wrote *Brief Memoir: Studies on Thackeray* (London, 1869).

46. In a letter, Agnes de Severne's mother writes about her newborn child, "I had her christened Agnes, and I was christened Agnes too. Think of my being christened at twenty-two! Agnes the First, and Agnes the Second." *Works*, XII, *Denis Duval*, II. Agnes the daughter, who was Thackeray's heroine, was born on 25 November 1768; therefore, his references to St. Agnes would probably allude to:

St. Agnes of Rome martyred c. 258?; patron saint of young girls and of gardeners. "On the eve of her day [January 21] many kinds of divination are practiced in England by virgins to discover their future husbands."

Agnes of Montepulciano, b. 1268. At the age of nine, joined a sisterhood; later abbess at Montepulciano of a Dominican convent. Died 1317.

Keats in "The Eve of St. Agnes" (1819) and Tennyson in "St. Agnes' Eve" (1834) referred to St. Agnes of Rome. Rt. Rev. F. G. Holweck, *A Biographical Dictionary of the Saints* (London, 1924), 33–34.

47. Thackeray drew on his memory of Isabella for his depiction of "the poor crazy lady" in *Denis Duval*.

48. Ray reads "pushed" for my reading of "pulled." *Adversity*, 254. Pulled perhaps suggests a double, suicide and infanticide, impulse.

49. Thackeray uses this incident in *Denis Duval*, chapter 4, but Denis the young hero rescues the infant Agnes.

50. Virginia Garden and her husband lived in Russell Square. *Letters*, II, 602, n. 186.

51. Not identified.

52. Like Victorian young ladies of the upper middle class (with social consciousnesses and Evangelical backgrounds), both Anny and her heroine of *Old Kensington* were volunteers at workhouses.

53. John Forster (1812–76), chief critic of *The Examiner;* friend of Thackeray's despite quarrels until the Yates affair, when Forster sided with Dickens. *Letters*, I, cxxxiii–cxxxvii.

54. Amy and Edward Thackeray left for India on 29 January 1863.

55. Thomas Phinn (1814–66), a barrister and politician who dined with Thackeray on 21 January 1863.

56. Needlework done by Victorian ladies.

57. The Garrick Club.

58. Henry James Byron, popular playwright of the 1860s.

59. *Miriam's Crime,* drama by Henry Thorton Craven.

60. Servant of Thackeray's.

61. An example of Anny's imaginative memory. Psalm 59.6 reads: "They return at evening; they make a noise like a dog, and go round the city."

62. Son of Dean Milman.

63. Probably the son of Charles Heath (1785–1848), engraver, promoter of annual and keepsake books; friend of Thackeray's. *Letters*, IV, 287.

64. The Procters, the Coles, the Crowes, all lived in Hampstead. This may be a reference to Mrs. Crowe, who died in 1853.

65. Possibly a piece of velvet with which Thackeray cleaned his eyeglasses.

66. Frederick Mullett Evans (d. 1870), of the publishing firm of Bradbury & Evans.

67. The word "white" has been crossed out.
68. In 1849.
69. A page and a half left blank in manuscript.
70. Mrs. Carmichael-Smyth died 18 December 1864.
71. The night Thackeray died at Palace Green.
72. As a young girl, Mrs. Carmichael-Smyth had been the belle of Bath. She traveled to India, and there met and married Richmond Thackeray. After his death, she married Major Carmichael-Smyth, her former suitor.
73. *The Christian Year* by John Keble (1792–1866), first published 1827. Written by the Oxford clergyman of the Established Church, the book contains religious verse for Sundays and special holidays. Although Mrs. Carmichael-Smyth was Evangelical, she read Keble.
74. William George Prescott (1800–1865), banker. *Letters*, III, 674, n. 12. Admiral Robert Fitzroy (1805–65), author with Darwin of the *Narrative of the Surveying Voyages of H.M. Ships Adventure and Beagle*, and captain of the ship during Darwin's voyages. *Letters*, IV, 290, n. 18.
75. Stephen Edmond Spring-Rice (1814–65), deputy chairman of the Board of Customs. *Letters*, II, 481, n. 283.
76. Thackeray attended Cambridge, February 1829–June 1830. William Whewell (1794–1866), distinguished scientist and philosopher, a Fellow, later the Master, of Trinity College, 1817–41; Thackeray's tutor. *Letters*, I, 30.
77. Edward FitzGerald (1809–83), English poet and translator.
78. Psalm 51.1. Again Anny's text differs slightly. The Psalm reads:

> Have mercy on me, O God,
>   according to they steadfast love;
>   according to thy abundant mercy
>   blot out my transgressions.

LETTER 41

1. Henrietta Marie Dillon-Lee (1808–96), married Edward Stanley (1802–69), later (1850) Baron Stanley of Alderley Park. *Letters*, I, clxviii–clxx.

LETTER 42

1. Anny, Minny, Mrs. Carmichael-Smyth, and two maids.

LETTER 43

1. Anny, Minny, and Mrs. Carmichael-Smyth visited the Ritchies in Henbury in February. Huntington ms 15265, Anny to W. C. Macready, 21 February 1864.

LETTER 44

1. Sir J. W. Lubbock and Company of 11, Mansion House Street, Thackeray's bankers. *Letters,* I, 187, n. 14.
2. The words, "I don't know w^h, They are Grannies I do believe" have been crossed out.

LETTER 45

1. Sister of Isabella Shawe Thackeray.
2. Not identified.
3. The Royal Literary Fund Dinner was held on 18 May 1864. The prince of Wales called Thackeray "a distinguished man of letters whose loss must be deeply deplored in all literary circles. . . . I allude to him not so much on account of his works, . . . but because he was an active member of your committee, and always ready to open his purse for the relief of literary men struggling with difficulties. (Hear, hear.)" *Times,* 19 May 1864, 9.
4. Philip-Henry Stanhope (1805–75), styled Lord Mahon (1855), fifth earl of Stanhope, author of many historical works. *Letters,* II, 664, n. 69.
5. Lord John Russell, foreign secretary in Lord Palmerston's second cabinet. *Letters,* IV, 233, n. 31.
6. Jane Shawe was unmarried.
7. Frederick William Robertson (1816–53), clergyman with a famous ministry in Brighton.
8. "Beloved, if God so loved us we ought also to love one another." 1 John 4. 11.
9. A notation next to this question leads to the poem, as though the poem is a response to the question. The poem does not appear to be in Anny's hand. Thackeray wrote of Uncle Arthur Shawe's wife, "I become dumb in her presence as in some other people's: and yet I like her very much and esteem her sincerely." *Letters,* III, 415.

LETTER 46

1. The words "& then" have been crossed out.
2. Like Thackeray, Anny feared there was too much of Isabella (and perhaps a threat of madness) in Minny.
3. See *Letters,* IV, 301, letter from Anny to Mrs. Baxter, 24 October 1864, in which she describes the transaction in detail.
4. Bobbie Synge.

LETTER 47

1. Perhaps a daughter of Richard Edmund St. Lawrence Boyle (1829–1904), ninth earl of Cork and Orrery, friend of Thackeray's. *Letters,* IV, 390, n. 3.

2. John Leech, a close friend of Thackeray's, died on 2 November 1864.
3. The word "sister" is probably intended.

LETTER 48

1. Bobbie Synge was sent to Charterhouse, for which Thackeray recommended him. *Letters*, IV, 200, n. 54.
2. Hawaiian Islands, originally named the Sandwich Islands by Capt. Cook.
3. Queen Liliuokalani of the Sandwich Islands.
4. Gilbert Synge, Anny's godson.
5. Amy Crowe Thackeray.

LETTER 49

1. Anna Smith Strong Baxter (1798–1885), wife of George Baxter (1801–85), warehouse owner of New York City, and their children (Sarah Strong [Sally] [1833–62]; George [183?–80]; Lucy [1836–1922]; Wyllys Pomeroy [1839–72]; George Strong [1845–1928]); close friends of Thackeray's. He visited them on both of his trips to America and corresponded with Mrs. Baxter. *Letters*, I, lxxxvii–xc; Ann Fripp Hampton, ed., *A Divided Heart: Letters of Sally Baxter Hampton, 1853–1862* (Spartanburg, S.C.: Reprint Co., 1980), xix–xx.
2. Date should read 1866, since this is well after the death of Mrs. Carmichael-Smyth.
3. This trip did not materialize, but Lucy did visit Anny in 1892.
4. The last "very" is underlined four times; the others, twice.
5. Daughter of Amy and Edward Thackeray. She, and her sister Annie, came to live with Anny when their mother died.

LETTER 50

1. "Aet.": an abbreviation for the Latin *aetatis*, meaning of age, aged. Compare this prayer to Thackeray's, written after the madness of Isabella. *Letters*, II, 30–31.
2. What follows was written in a different ink at a later time—1875.
3. Minny's husband, Leslie Stephen (1832–1904).
4. Minny's daughter, Laura Stephen (1870–1945).
5. Annie and Margie Thackeray.
6. Anny's husband, Richmond Ritchie, and his sister Emily.

CHAPTER 5

INTRODUCTION

1. ALS Columbia, 3 March [1866], to Mrs. George Baxter.
2. Tennyson's black cloak hangs in a showcase in a back room at Far-

ringford, now an inn with a cigarette vending machine and a pin-ball game in its foyer. The downs and the sea are, however, still unspoiled.

3. *Thackeray and His Daughter*, 141.
4. *Thackeray and His Daughter*, 143.
5. *The George Eliot Letters*, ed. Gordon S. Haight, 9 vols. (New Haven: Yale Univ. Press, 1954–79), V, 96.
6. *Records*, 152.
7. Carol Hanbery MacKay, Critical Introduction to *The Two Thackerays: Anne Thackeray Ritchie's Centenary Biographical Introduction to the Works of William Makepeace Thackeray*, 2 vols. (New York: AMS Press, 1988), discusses similarities in the works of Thackeray and Ritchie.
8. Katherine C. Hill-Miller sees Ritchie exploring two themes in her fiction, "the necessity of breaking free of dependence on a paternal figure and the conflict between the conventional and the unconventional woman." " 'The Skies and Trees of the Past': Anne Thackeray Ritchie and William Makepeace Thackeray," *Daughters and Fathers*, 361–83.
9. *Vanity Fair*, Bio. ed., II, 408, 426.
10. Germaine Greer, *The Obstacle Race: The Fortunes of Women Painters and Their Work* (New York: Farrar Straus Giroux, 1979), 91.
11. Anthony Trollope, *An Autobiography* (London: Oxford Univ. Press, 1974), 221.
12. Leslie Stephen, in the *Mausoleum Book,* describes how his brother, Fitzjames Stephen, compared Anny to Austen in a review of one of Anny's stories in 1867. Leslie Stephen also compared Ritchie's artistic creativity with that of Austen in his *Dictionary of National Biography* (London: Smith, Elder & Co., 1903).
13. "Silly Novels by Lady Novelists," *Essays of George Eliot,* ed. Thomas Pinney (New York: Columbia Univ. Press, 1963), 324. (Originally published in the *Westminster Review* 66 [October 1856], 442–61.)
14. *Cornhill* 3, no. 15 (March 1861), 318–31.
15. "Doubtful privilege": ever since Thackeray's defeat when he ran for M.P. from Oxford, Anny took a skeptical view of the value of the vote.
16. The similarity between Ritchie's "Toilers and Spinsters" and Woolf's *A Room of One's Own* has been commented on by Elizabeth French Boyd, *Bloomsbury Heritage: Their Mothers and Their Aunts* (London: Hamish Hamilton, 1976), and by Carol Hanbery MacKay in the Critical Introduction to *The Two Thackerays*.
17. "Adieu," *The Collected Poems of Thomas and Jane Welsh Carlyle,* ed. Rodger L. Tarr and Fleming McClelland (Greenwood, Fla.: Penkevill Pub. Co., 1986), 52–53.
18. *Thackeray and His Daughter*, 181.
19. Stephen, 45.
20. Also noted by Gérin, 188.

21. *Thackeray's Daughter*, 150.
22. Gérin, 185.
23. *Thackeray and His Daughter*, 192.

LETTER 51

1. W. W. F. Synge.
2. Henrietta Synge, daughter of W. W. F. Synge.

LETTER 52

1. Abbreviation for October, the eighth month in the early Roman calendar.

LETTER 53

1. The Stephens traveled in America during the summer and fall of 1868.
2. Thomas Gold Appleton (1812–84), brother-in-law of Longfellow, friend of Thackeray's, writer, painter. *Letters*, IV, 164.
3. Not identified.
4. Thackeray had dined at Longfellow's house in 1855, and had written, "He is a kindly pleasant gentleman, has pretty children. I liked him." *Letters*, III, 514.

LETTER 54

1. Thomas Hughes (1822–96), author of *Tom Brown's School Days*, county court judge.
2. Brother of Thomas Hughes, proposed to Anny but was refused.
3. Henry Bingham Mildmay (1828–1905), a young Englishman who had met Thackeray in London. When Mildmay visited Thackeray at the Clarendon Hotel in New York in November 1852, he brought along Mr. Baxter to meet Thackeray. Thus Thackeray's friendship with the Baxters resulted from this meeting. Mildmay was a rejected suitor of Sally Baxter. *Letters*, I, lxxxvii.
4. The words "for I dont mean that I mind being But" are crossed out.
5. The former Mary Elizabeth A'Court-Repington (1822–1911), a famous beauty who married the statesman Sidney Herbert (1810–61), later (1861) first Baron Herbert of Lea, in 1846. *Letters*, II, 481, n. 282.
6. Not identified.
7. *To Esther*, 1869.
8. The former Fanny Kemble (1809–93). After an American tour in 1832, she became Mrs. Pierce Butler and her friendship with Thackeray dwindled. *Letters*, I, cxliii–cxliv.
9. Line or lines cut off as explained in the postscript.

LETTER 55

1. Torquay is a seaside resort in southwest England known for its mild climate.

2. In her "Jane Austen," Anny writes, "Once she lived for some months in Hans Place, nursing a brother through an illness." *Sibyls*, 225. Note Annie's last sentence below. These pages are probably notes for "Jane Austen," *Cornhill Magazine* 24 (August 1871), 158–74, republished in *A Book of Sibyls: Mrs Barbauld, Mrs Opie, Miss Edgeworth, Miss Austen*, 1883.

3. Jane Austen has written to her sister on 6 November 1813, "—By the bye, as I must leave off being young, I find many Douceurs in being a sort of Chaperon for I am put on the Sofa near the Fire & can drink as much wine as I like." Letter 91 of *Jane Austen's Letters to Her Sister Cassandra and Others*, ed. R. W. Chapman, 2nd ed. (London: Oxford Univ. Press, 1952), 370.

4. Jane Austen.

5. Esther and Lucien de Rubempré in Balzac's *Splendeurs et misères des courtisanes*.

6. Gabrielle Emile Le Tonnelier De Breteuil du Chatelet (1706–49), mathematician, physicist, philosopher, mistress of Voltaire.

7. Aspasia was an Ionian courtesan who settled in Athens in the fifth century, B.C.E. She became Pericles' mistress because as a foreigner she could not marry. She held an important place in the intellectual society of the time.

8. Richard Whately (1787–1863), archbishop of Dublin, wrote an unsigned review of *Northanger Abbey* and *Persuasion* in *Quarterly Review* 24 (January 1821), 352–76.

9. Ritchie has substituted the word "authors" for the original "authoresses." Otherwise, she has deleted a few phrases, but retained the sense of Whately's remarks.

10. Jane Austen's description of Mrs. Musgrove as she mourns over the death of her son to Captain Wentworth. *Persuasion* in *The Complete Works of Jane Austen* (New York: Modern Library, n.d. [1818]), chapter 8, 1250.

LETTER 56

1. *Old Kensington* mentioned in this letter was published in 1872.

2. George Dunlop Leslie, born 1835. Son and pupil of C. R. Leslie; elected to the Royal Academy 1876, noted Victorian painter.

3. *Old Kensington*, chapter 10, 81. Leslie did not follow Anny's suggestion. A mature Dolly in the foreground holds a stick, while Henley, dark-haired and elegant, stands far off in the background. There is no snow in evidence. *Cornhill Magazine* 25 (May 1872), 513.

LETTER 57

1. Family bathing resort in northwest France.
2. Not identified.
3. Mrs. Baxter's son Wyllys died in 1872.
4. Two lines crossed out by Anny.
5. Later, Anny will find a resemblance to Thackeray in her own son.

LETTER 58

1. Date probably added by Browning. Thackeray became intimate with the Brownings in 1853. Anny knew him more closely as an old man when he lived with his sister in London. Gérin, 225–26.
2. Unlike *The Ring and the Book,* which was based on an old trial, *Red Cotton Night-Cap Country* was based on a case at law in which some of the participants were still alive. Browning had to make certain the names, dates, and places were changed to suit the heirs.
3. J. A. Milsand, French critic and friend of Browning's, praised in *Red Cotton Night-Cap Country.*

LETTER 59

1. Stephen's mother died 27 February 1875. Leslie Stephen, *The Life of Sir James Fitzjames Stephen* (London: Smith, Elder & Co., 1895), 301.
2. Meme(e): a nickname for Laura Stephen.

LETTER 60

1. Shelley, "Adonais," stanza LV.

LETTER 61

1. Browning's sister, Sarianna Browning, who lived with him after Elizabeth's death.

LETTER 63

1. Anny and Leslie Stephen moved into 11, Hyde Park Gate South in the late summer of 1876.
2. *Daniel Deronda* (1876).
3. George Henry Lewes (1817–78), English writer on philosophy and other subjects. He separated from his wife and cohabited in great respectability with the novelist.

LETTER 64

1. According to Leslie Stephen's account in the *Mausoleum Book,* Anny and Richmond were engaged in January of 1877. John W. Bicknell, however, questions the accuracy of this date (letter to the editors).
2. Lady Maria is a character in Thackeray's *The Virginians;* Lady Esmond, Esmond, and Beatrix are characters in his *Henry Esmond.* Anny is being modest here; both women are older than their love interest, but Lady Esmond is a paragon and Lady Maria's affection is never reciprocated.
3. The word "approved" has been crossed out and "agreed" substituted.

LETTER 65

1. Anny and Richmond were married on 2 August 1877.
2. W. W. F. Synge, Henrietta's father.

CHAPTER 6

INTRODUCTION

1. Stephen, 19.
2. Gérin, 165.
3. *Letters,* I, 520. More recent discussions have also disagreed over the nature of Isabella's and Laura's illnesses.
4. *Thackeray and His Daughter,* 147.
5. *Thackeray and His Daughter,* 146–48.
6. Diary, 8 February 1862.

1878 JOURNAL

1. The 1878 journal consists of 28 large sheets of paper, each folded to make 4 pages. Two types of paper were used: some pages measure 4½ by 7 1/16 inches, some measure 4 3/8 by 7 1/8 inches. The pages have been numbered in pencil in the upper right-hand corner. Numbers 1 through 22 have a small hole near the top left corner as if they had once been held together in some way.

The loose leaves of the journal have been inserted inside an envelope and marked with this description, evidently written by a bookseller in preparation for sale: "Very Precious. / M.S. A.I.R.'s recollections, of her Father and of her sister. / Written 1878. / Some 30 sheets (usually four sides to the sheet) covering the years 1840 to 1862. The final sheets seem to be missing. Evidently written for Laura Stephen, when she was a little girl." Another sheet states: "AIR / autobiography / of her life / with WMT. / Aunt Minny. / Written by A.I.R. in 1878." This introductory material, typed on a separate sheet from Anny's manuscript, refers to "Aunt Minny" and consequently would appear to be the work of Anny's daughter, Hester Ritchie, who published works about her mother.

2. Dates and other information have been inserted above the lines of the manuscript. As far as one can tell from the handwriting, the notes would appear to have been added by Anny at a later time, using pencil or a different ink. These additions will be indicated in the notes and prefaced by the words "Inserted note."

Inserted note: (1840).

3. Inserted note: (1840–41).
4. Inserted note: (His wifes illness).
5. Inserted note: (from Boulogne to Paris).
6. Mary ("Polly") Graham (1815–71), Mrs. Carmichael-Smyth's niece, lived with her from 1826. In 1841, Mary married Major Carmichael-Smyth's younger brother Colonel Charles Montauban Carmichael (1790–1870).
7. The Carmichael-Smyth house was on "the Avenue Sainte-Marie [which] led from the Faubourg du Roule to the Arc de Triomphe." *Thackeray's Daughter*, 29.

Inserted note: de Triomphe.

8. Inserted note: (Mrs Butler).
9. Not identified.
10. Margaret (Margie) and Anne (Annie) Thackeray were the daughters of Amy Crowe and Edward Talbot Thackeray.
11. George Crowe, born 1841. The Crowes lived at 5, rue du 29 Juillet, St. Germain, until 1842, when they moved to St. Cloud. *Letters*, I, cxvii–cxx.
12. Frank was the son of William Hankey, a friend of Thackeray's. See Thackeray's diary for 1844, *Letters*, II, 139; also *Letters*, III, 77, 687.
13. Charles Robert Darwin (1809–82), the famous theorist of evolution.
14. Not identified.
15. Charles or "Cheri" Carmichael.
16. Inserted note: 1845.
17. Anny describes this episode in Bio. Intro., V, xlii; in Cent. Intro., VI, xvi.
18. Anny discusses these holidays in Bio. Intro., V, xxxiv, calling Chaudfontaine an "Arcadian sort of country." Also discussed in Cent. Intro., VI, xxxi–xxxii.
19. Inserted notes: Miss Becher [*initials illegible*]. In Bio. Intro., VIII, xiii–xiv, Anny describes Miss Becher, her home and Fareham, as a "Miss Austen-like village."
20. John Harmon Becher (1764–1800?), Miss Becher's brother. *Adversity*, 305.
21. Leslie Stephen.
22. Inserted note: (Mrs Butler. See her letters.
23. Inserted note: Mrs. Barlow.
24. Brookfield.
25. Not identified.

NOTES TO PAGES 199–201   337

26. This trip took place in June 1845. *Adversity*, 305.
27. Inserted note: 1845?
28. From April 1845 to June 1846, Thackeray lived at 88, St. James Street. *Adversity*, 280.
29. The Diorama and the Colosseum were "entertainment palaces" built in Regent's Park. John Timbs, *Curiosities of London*, 2nd ed. (London: John Camden Hotten, 1867), 307–8, 280–82.
30. Carmichael.
31. Not identified.
32. Inserted note: in Beaujon.
33. Children's books written by Sir Henry Cole under the pseudonym of Felix Summerly.
34. Chanoine Johann Christopher Schmid (1768–1854), German Roman Catholic priest, schoolmaster, and prolific writer of stories for children. Arnaud Berquin (1749–91), published *L'Ami des enfans*, moral stories for children in twenty-four volumes, 1782–83. The *Journal des Desmoiselles* was a Parisian fashion magazine published from 1833 to 1896.
35. Anny uses this description of Major Carmichael-Smyth in the fictional depiction of a granduncle in "Across the Peat-Fields," *Divagations*, 143–244.
36. Isabella was living at this time at the Maison de Santé, Ivry. *Adversity*, 260–61.
37. Inserted note: 1846 [?].
38. Inserted note: 13.
39. Anny and Richmond moved into 27, Young Street across the street from number 13, in May 1878.
40. Daniel O'Connell, called The Liberator (1775–1847), Irish nationalist, statesman, and orator.
41. Among the pictures in Anny's and Minny's bedroom were "Thorwaldsen prints, Hunt's delightful sleepy boy yawning at us over the chimneypiece, all of which [Thackeray] had caused to be put up; and the picture of himself as a child he had hung up with his own hands." *Thackeray's Daughter*, 44.
42. Bess Hamerton, a friend of Mrs. Carmichael-Smyth's, was unsuitable as a governess and Thackeray soon dismissed her. *Letters*, II, 284–86.
43. William Charles Macready (1793–1873), actor-manager.
44. Inserted note: Sir Henry Cole.
Cole also designed china, executed at the Minton Potteries, under his nom de plume of Felix Summerly. *Fifty Years of Public Work*, 2 vols. (London: George Bell, 1884), I, 104–5.
45. In Bio. Intro., I, xxi, Anny describes how she and Minny often posed for Thackeray's sketches.
46. The sketch of "the two naughty children" appears in chapter 10 in

Vanity Fair, first edition. The sketch of Minny "building cards" is an endpiece for chapter 7, 64. *Vanity Fair* (London: Bradbury & Evans, 1848).

47. On 14 June 1849, Thackeray wrote, "Minny [gave] me a fine fright previously by hiding herself in the closet, and leaving me to imagine that the little rogue had gone out into the street and lost herself there." *Letters*, II, 551.

48. "Ainy . . . (as she always call me)." Letter 45 above.

49. Mrs. Butler died in Paris on 1 November 1847; Anny was ten years old and Minny seven.

50. Inserted note: 1849?

51. Anny imagined more of a physical resemblance between Richmond Thackeray Ritchie and Thackeray than actually existed. From a comparison of photographs, all that appears valid is that both men were tall.

52. Inserted note: (about 1849).

53. The best of Thackeray's servants, with him until the summer of 1852. He wrote letters to the newspapers signing his name "Jeames de la Pluche." *Letters*, II, 647, n. 33.

54. An example of Anny correcting her memory. "Our governess was now called Miss Trulock" is crossed out. Miss Alexander was her governess from November 1847 to August 1848; Miss Trulock from April 1850 to June 1852. Miss Alexander was the daughter of Captain Alexander with whom Anny and Minny once stayed. Thackeray wrote of her, "Poor Alexander must go: she is not clever enough for Anny." *Letters*, II, 382.

55. The Greyhound was an inn.

56. Chapel House, Montpelier Row, Twickenham, was soon to become the Tennysons' home, 11 March 1851 to November 1853. Sir Charles Tennyson, *Alfred Tennyson* (New York: Macmillan Co., 1949), 259–61.

57. These words have been crossed out: "In a month or two we went to France to."

58. Inserted note: (who went in Dec. 50 or 1851).

59. Inserted note: (No. it was in 1849 [?]).

60. An old walled seaport in northwest Wales.

61. Not identified.

62. Not identified.

63. Inserted note: Sept. 1849?

Thackeray nearly died of cholera in September 1849 and was nursed by Mrs. Brookfield. His mother arrived from Wales on 17 October when Thackeray was convalescing, the major and Thackeray's daughters arriving a few days later. *Wisdom*, 87–88.

64. Charles Kingsley (1819–75), novelist and muscular Christian. For a further discussion of this crossing, see *Chapters*, 103–7; also *Thackeray's Daughter*, 64–67.

65. These words have been crossed out: "There is a little Virgin—funny St John of Helbeins."

66. Inserted note: (1853–54).
67. Charles Pearman.
68. John Gibson Lockhart (1794–1854), writer, son-in-law, and biographer of Scott. *Thackeray and His Daughter*, 60.
69. Mrs. Brotherton (Mary or Maria) knew Thackeray from his Larkbeare days. She and her husband lived in Rome in the 1850s. *Adversity*, 102–3.
70. Alexander Macbean was British consul at Leghorn, Italy, when Thackeray met him in 1845. *Letters*, II, 187.
71. Inserted note: (The Newcomes).
This sentence seems to have been added at a later date as it is written in different ink.
72. Robert Weidemann Browning (1849–1912), known as Penini or Pen, son of the poets, English genre painter and sculptor.
73. Thackeray was ill with Roman fever (malaria).
74. Anny and Minny were ill with scarlatina 1–16 March 1854. *Letters*, III, 352.
75. "Chiaja": meaning not known.
76. A possible explanation is that wandering serenaders composed lyrics to sing under the balcony of affluent tourists hoping for some coins.
77. The firm of Frances Truefitt, a barber who opened shop in 1805, is mentioned in Thackeray's *The Four Georges* as wigmaker to George IV.
78. Prince Camaralzaman, whose name means "Moon of the Century," was an unusually handsome youth.
79. Thackeray rented the Chateau Brécquerecque near Boulogne, where his daughters and the Carmichael-Smyths lived from 26 June to September 1854. Dickens and his family lived nearby and "there were frequent exchanges of hospitality." *Wisdom*, 234.
80. Inserted note: (autumn 1856).
81. Inserted note: Jan 1865.
For the disagreement between Thackeray and his mother over the religious education of his daughters, see *Letters*, III, 168–70; and Anny's letters describing the *cours* to her father, *Letters*, III, 137–39. Anny's time sequence jumps back to 1852–53 here. Although Thackeray and his mother did have genuine religious differences, she also wanted to wrest authority from Thackeray and wield power over her granddaughters. Adolphe Monod (1802–56), French Protestant minister, preacher at the Oratoire, Paris. Later Anny referred to Monod as "the St. Paul of my own time." *Chapters*, 148.
82. François Pierre Guillame Guizot (1787–1874), French historian and statesman.
83. Inserted note: (1854) see letter to L Cole, Jan 1855.
This letter has not been published.
84. Mommee refers to Laura's stepmother; Laura's godmother was Dalsy Huth, probably the nickname of a daughter of Augusta Louisa Sophia Huth

and Henry Huth (1815–78). The Huths purchased Palace Green after the death of Thackeray.

85. These words have been crossed out, "I think this was the summer after the crimea but I." Anny describes this house in north-central France in her essay "In Villeggiatura," *Chapters*.

86. Inserted note: (1853).

87. These words have been crossed out: "Papa went to America the second time in 1856."

88. Inserted note: (1854).

89. Inserted note: (Oct. 25 1854).

90. Inserted note: (not till 1857).

91. In an 1859 letter Anny wrote: "Have you any fancy for playing at trap bat & ball? We have got a trap club in Gore house Garden w^h is very pleasant. . . . The subs.[cription] is sixpence for the season so that its not a ruinous affair." U. of London, A.L. 294/2.

92. Inserted note: (near Albert Hall & [*two words illegible*]).

Albert Hall now covers the site of Gore House, once the salon of the countess of Blessington.

93. Inserted note: (should be 1854).

94. Thackeray sailed for America the second time on 10 October 1855.

95. Anny wrote, "Just a week before Christmas a thief got into our house & stole all my pretty trinkets that [Thackeray] had given me at one time or another When Papa came home & said 'Poor Nan' I remember thinking it was worth losing them for him to look so kind." *Letters,* IV, 303.

96. Margie and Annie Thackeray.

97. Inserted note: (1854–55).

98. In a letter dated 20–23 September 1858, Thackeray writes that his mother "has broken a bone in the hip somewhere and is to be lame for life." *Letters,* IV, 113.

99. The three Ritchie sisters who later became Anny's sisters-in-law: Gussie or Augusta, Blanchie or Blanche, and Pinkie or Emily.

100. Thackeray's cousins, the Ritchies.

101. In "Mrs. Sartoris," *Friend,* 64–65, Anny elaborates on this episode of seeing the celebrated French novelist.

102. "Whether at Florence, at Rome, at Paris, or in London, she seemed to carry her own atmosphere always, something serious, motherly, absolutely artless, and yet impassioned, noble, and sincere." *Chapters,* 162.

103. Richmond Ritchie came to England in 1859. Anny first heard about him from his older sisters who were living in Paris.

104. Inserted note: (1855).

105. Inserted note: (Palace Green 1862).

106. *The Wolves and the Lamb* was performed at Palace Green, 24–25 March 1862.

107. Inserted note: in Onslow Square.
108. Inserted note: (Amy Crowe).
109. "Thackeray had printed a playbill which began with a characteristically primitive pun ('W. Empty House Theatricals')." *Wisdom*, 396.
110. Inserted note: (1862).
111. William Ritchie died 22 March 1862. *Letters*, IV, 261, n. 13.
112. The Ritchie children.
113. General Sir John Low (1788–1880), married Augusta Ludlow Shakespear (Thackeray's cousin) in 1829. He retired from the India service to his estate of Clatto at Cupar, Fife. *Letters*, IV, G 81–82.
114. See Minny's letters from Scotland, chapter 3.
115. Emmy Irvine, daughter of Thackeray's cousin Marianne Shakespear Irvine.
116. The manuscript begins a new page.
117. Inserted note: (must have been before 1862).
118. These words have been crossed out: "With his silver hair & bright looks."
119. Inserted note: an extra page — repetition [?] except for Minny dancing.

All of the pages of the journal have been numbered, but not by Anny. This final sheet has been variously numbered for inclusion within the pages of the journal. Most likely Anny wrote it at a later date, intending to include it in the journal if she were to have it bound or published.

CHAPTER 7

INTRODUCTION

1. "To Mrs. Gerald Ritchie," [1885], *Thackeray and His Daughter*, 208.
2. *Thackeray and His Daughter*, 240.
3. Anne Thackeray Ritchie's Journal, 1895, quoted in Gérin, 244.
4. MS Fales [1881], "to Gertrude?"
5. *Mrs. Dymond: A Novel*, Harper's Hand Series, 18 December 1885 (New York: Harper & Brothers, 1885), book II, chapter 11, 124.
6. *Vanity Fair*, Bio. ed., II, 431.
7. Gérin, 215.
8. See Gordon N. Ray, *The Buried Life*.
9. Philip Leigh-Smith, *Record of an Ascent: A Memoir of Sir Richmond Thackeray Ritchie* (London: Dillon's Univ. Bookshop, 1961), 33. From the India Office Library and Records, IOR:MSS.EUR.C.342 Ritchie Papers comes the following description: "Richmond Ritchie was Permanent Under Secretary, a civil servant of immense power, very tall, very funny in a dry way and easily irritated. . . . [he] understood genius—he had married one—."
10. *Thackeray and His Daughter*, 240.

11. *Thackeray and His Daughter,* 240–41.
12. *Thackeray and His Daughter,* 266, n. 1.
13. Leon Edel, ed., *Henry James Letters,* 4 vols. (Cambridge: Belknap Press at Harvard Univ. Press, 1974–84), I, 91.
14. In additon to its usual meaning of "former," *ci-devant* acquired the meaning "aristocrat," from the time of the French Revolution. Here, James uses the phrase in both its meanings: the former Miss Thackeray as well as the daughter of the Royal Literary House of Thackeray. In a letter dated 25 March 1913, he refers to Anny as "the Princess Royal." Percy Lubbock, ed., *Letters of Henry James,* 2 vols. (London: Macmillan's, 1920), II, 304.
15. *Letters of Henry James,* II, 209.
16. *Letters of Henry James,* II, 211.
17. Gérin, 285.
18. *Thackeray and His Daughter,* 211.
19. "The Art of Fiction," *Partial Portraits* (1884; reprint, Ann Arbor Paperbacks, Univ. of Michigan Press, 1970), 388.
20. With amusement and a sense of proportion, Anny views the success of *Divagations.* "Everybody is asking me to dinner and begging for copies. They did not think there was so much life left in me!" *Thackeray and His Daughter,* 197.
21. MS I/5836, U. of London [1898].
22. MS I/5836, U. of London [1898].
23. Bio. Intro., XI, xlvii.

LETTER 66

1. Mrs. Sartoris died in 1879.
2. Richmond Ritchie's sister. She wrote "Moral Conflicts and Religious Beliefs," reprinted in *Thackeray: Interviews and Recollections,* ed. Philip Collins, 2 vols. (New York: St. Martin's Press, 1983), II, 193–201.
3. Anny and Richmond's daughter, Hester Helen Ritchie, b. 1878.
4. Note added by Henry James to the bottom of the second page of the letter.
5. In James's handwriting at the top of the first page. Whoever received this letter (and another) did not heed James's instructions.

LETTER 67

1. Possibly John Walter (1818–94), proprietor of the *Times. Letters,* IV, 412, n. 26.
2. Virginia Vaughan (18?–1913), American journalist, translator, and poet.
3. "The New Era: A Dramatic Poem" (1880), a philosophical poem about a new world and angels and liberty. Vaughan's next poem, "Orpheus

and the Sirens: A Drama in Lyrics," was published by Chapman and Hall, London, in 1882.

4. Probably the *Saturday Review*.

5. *Facts* (1882–87), an American monthly by L. L. Whitlock, Boston, devoted to supernatural experiences.

LETTER 68

1. Letters and numbers underlined are part of the pharmacy bill which Anny has used for stationery.

2. Mrs. Robert Synge.

LETTER 69

1. Envelope attached addressed to "Baron von Tauchnitz, Leipzig, Germany;" stamp dated "Ja 2, 82." Von Tauchnitz was Anny's continental publisher.

LETTER 70

1. James Payn (1830–98), novelist, editor of the *Cornhill*, 1883–96.

2. Envelope dated "Jy 9 1884" attached mistakenly to this letter. Date should read 1883 because Payn became editor of the *Cornhill* in 1883.

3. *Cornhill Magazine*.

4. *A Book of Sybils* (1883) was composed of essays first published in the *Cornhill*.

LETTER 71

1. Although the letter is dated "Sunday" by Anny, it bears the date also of "13 9 1885," probably when it was received by Browning, which fell on a Wednesday.

2. *Dictionary of National Biography*. Anny later republished this material in her essay on both the Brownings, in *Records*.

3. "Mrs. Dymond," *Macmillan's Magazine,* March–December 1885.

4. Frederick Locker-Lampson (1821–95), poet, admiralty clerk, friend of Thackeray's. Took the additional name of Lampson when he married his second wife, Hannah Jane Lampson. *Letters,* IV, 221, n. 13.

5. See chapter 5, Letter 58.

6. The poet's second son. He died returning to England 20 April 1886.

LETTER 72

1. Possibly Mary Elizabeth Thackeray, daughter of Frederic Rennel Thackeray (1775–1860), who married Lady Elizabeth Mary Carnegie (1798?–1886). *Letters,* IV, G 18. Anny speaks of Mary's mother, who is still alive and a

Carnegie, which might be of particular interest to Andrew Carnegie in "tuft hunting."

2. Andrew Carnegie (1835–1919), American steel magnate, writer, and philanthropist.

3. Probably a descendant of Lord Northesk (1758–1831), William Carnegie, the seventh earl of Northesk, commander in chief of the Navy.

4. Matthew Arnold was introduced to Carnegie in 1883 at a London dinner party. When Arnold visited America in 1883 Carnegie met him at the dock and escorted him around New York.

LETTER 73

1. Octavia Hill (1838–1912), pioneer in housing reform for the working classes and poor in London; with Ruskin's help remodeled houses in London.

2. Anny's article on Ruskin was written in 1887 for *Macmillans* and published in *Harper's Magazine* in 1890.

3. The words "to the world" have been crossed out.

4. Louisa Lee Schuyler (1837–1926), American social worker. In 1875, while president of the State Charity Aid Association, she collected five of Hill's magazine articles and brought them out in America.

5. Jeanie Senior (d. 1877), wife of Nassau Senior, sister of Thomas Hughes. Anny wrote about her in "In My Lady's Chamber," *Porch*.

6. This note is made in pencil in a different handwriting.

LETTER 74

1. Thackeray addressed his mother as "Mammy" in many of his letters.

2. Anny was suffering from sciatica.

3. Mrs. Thompson took care of Isabella.

4. A popular seaside resort seventy miles east southeast of London. In her youth Queen Victoria resided in Ramsgate.

5. Princess Louise, born 1848, sixth child of Victoria. Anny describes how Princess Louise sent for her and took her for a drive, stopping off at a peasant's house, where the princess stirred the potatoes while Anny watched. "I thought to myself," Anny continues, "this is a fairy tale, a real cottage, and a real Princess stirring potatoes and *me* looking on. *Thackeray and His Daughter*, 212–13.

LETTER 75

1. Henry Austin Dobson (1840–1921), poet, man of letters, member of the Board of Trade.

2. Envelope postmarked: "Hampstead Ju 12 87." The stationery is engraved with the Kensington address; the Heathfield address is handwritten.

3. Dobson may have sent Anny a copy of *Richard Steele* (1886), in which Dobson speaks highly of Thackeray's portrait of Steele.

LETTER 76

1. Date added, probably by Browning.
2. Husband of Ritchie's sister Blanche; vice-provost of Eton.

LETTER 77

1. (Lisa) Elizabeth Robins (1862–1952), an American actress and writer, arrived in London in the 1880s.
2. The Ritchies lived at Kingsley Lodge from 1889 to 1898.
3. Sir Francis Darwin (1848–1925), third son of Charles, botanist at Cambridge, knighted in 1913.
4. Not identified.

LETTER 78

1. Anny's son, William Thackeray Denis Ritchie, b. 1880.

LETTER 79

1. Date added, probably by Browning.

PORTRAIT SKETCH

This portrait is with the Ritchie collection at Yale, but it is not connected to any single letter.

LETTER 80

1. Henry Savile Clark (1841–93), minor playwright, theatrical entrepreneur, drama critic.
2. The play under discussion, a dramatization with music of Thackeray's *The Rose and the Ring,* opened at the Prince of Wales's Theatre on 20 December 1890, for "great and small children," with a "chorus (including children) of 150 voices." *Times,* 20 Dec. 1890, 8.
3. A. Walter Slaughter, English light opera composer and conductor.

LETTER 81

1. After her father's death, Anny sold Smith and Elder the copyright for her father's *Works. Letters,* I, clxviii.

LETTER 82

1. The play opened on 20 December 1890.
2. Kedgeree is an Indian dish of rice, lentils, onions, eggs, and spice, as well as an English dish of cold fish, boiled rice, and eggs. Undoubtedly this is a number from the play.
3. Not identified.

LETTER 83

1. Charlotte Mary Yonge (1823–1901), popular novelist (*The Heir of Redcliffe*, 1853), a follower of Keble.
2. The letter must have been written in 1891, as the January number of *The Monthly Packet* is the one Anny discusses. This, however, makes her reference to fifty-two years at the end obscure. Perhaps she intends that she has been cognizant of the world for fifty-two years and of Yonge for forty-two.
3. Yonge's novel *That Stick* (Macmillan, 1892) was serialized beginning with the January 1891 issue of the *Monthly Packet*.
4. *Monthly Packet*: periodical started in 1851 with Charlotte Yonge as its first editor, "to imbue young people especially women" with the spirit of the Oxford movement.
5. *The Daisy Chain* (1856) by Yonge.
6. "New Year's Day," published in the January 1891 issue of the *Monthly Packet*, concerns people making restitution for their errors and a mother's sorrow for her missing firstborn son. Oliphant's eldest son died in November 1890.
7. A health resort in southeast Switzerland.
8. *The Journal of Sir Walter Scott*, 2 vols. (Edinburgh: David Douglas, 1890).

LETTER 85

1. After Minny's death, Stephen married Mrs. Julia Jackson Duckworth, widow of Herbert Duckworth.
2. Not identified.

LETTER 86

1. Not identified.
2. The year has been added in a different ink.
3. The name "Skeffington" has been crossed out.
4. Not identified.
5. Frederick Walker (1840–75), artist, engraver, illustrator. *Letters*, IV, 219–20. In July of 1862 Thackeray wrote, "I wrote Finis to Philip. . . . Young Walker who is twenty does twice as well." *Letters*, IV, 270.

6. *The Heroic Adventures of M. Boudin* is "one of the many sequences of comic drawings which William Makepeace Thackeray drew for the amusement of himself and his friends." A facsimile of the original manuscript was published by Syracuse University Library Associates, Syracuse, 1980, with an introduction by Gordon N. Ray.

LETTER 87

1. Written to the editor of the Bio. Intro. The date, therefore, is c. 1894–98.
2. The name has been crossed out.
3. *The English Humourists of the Eighteenth Century* (1851).
4. Not identified.
5. The sheets of *The Rose and the Ring* were mounted and bound by Sir Theodore Martin in 1865–66. This album was acquired by Major William Harrison Lambert in 1896. It is now in the Pierpont Morgan Library, New York.
6. Probably an illustration by Thackeray for *The History of Samuel Titmarsh and the Great Hoggarty Diamond* (1841).

LETTER 88

1. The play mentioned in the letter opened in 1895.
2. *Guy Domville* (London, 1895). "The hostility of the audience on opening night caused James to abandon his early theatrical aspirations." J. Don Vann, ed., *Critics on Henry James* (London: George Allen & Unwin, 1974), 8.

LETTER 89

1. A central street in Brighton, above the retaining wall facing the English channel.
2. Famous girls' school founded in 1885 in Brighton.
3. Probably an exhibition of paintings by the English portrait painter Sir Thomas Lawrence (1769–1830).
4. The Metropole Hotel was built in 1890. The architecture was associated with the smartness and vulgarity of some of its patrons.
5. Possibly the wife of Gerald Loder, Liberal M.P. for Brighton and a leader of Brighton society.
6. Leslie Stephen; Henry Sidgwick (1838–1900), philosopher, professor at Trinity College, Cambridge.
7. Not identified.
8. Sir Edward Thackeray's *Biographical Notices of Officers of the Royal (Bengal) Engineers* (London: Smith, Elder, 1900).
9. Char is Charlotte Cornish, Richmond Ritchie's niece.

10. A health resort with over eighty mineral springs thirteen miles north of Leeds.
11. Not identified.
12. A deep and narrow combe in the Downs near Brighton.
13. William Ritchie, Richmond's brother, and his son Arthur.
14. Family name for Richmond Ritchie.

LETTER 90

1. Colonel Webb's letter to his son, 25 August 1765, which Anny uses in the Bio. Intro., XIII, xxxix–xl.
2. Anny quotes from memory. The lines read: "Make yourself master of your pen and your sword, . . . I must now busy myself with putting all your sisters out, and Mama and you and I spend the winter in London." Bio. Intro., XIII, xl.
3. Not identified.
4. Codge or Codgie was a family name for Hester. *Letters*, III, 435–36, n. 44.
5. Not identified.
6. Not identified.
7. Not identified.

LETTER 91

1. There was a mistaken popular theory that the American aloe plant did not flower but once in a hundred years.
2. Herbert Spencer (1820–1903), English philosopher, founder of the system which he called synthetic philosophy.
3. Possibly a reference to Alfred Ainger, ed., *The Letters of Charles Lamb: Newly Arranged, with Additions*, 2 vols. (London: Macmillan, 1888).
4. Thomas Bewick (1753–1828), English designer and engraver on wood. In "Concerning Thomas Bewick," *Blackstick Papers*, Anny recounts that Austin Dobson's book, *Thomas Bewick and His Pupils* (London: Chatto & Widmus, 1884), led her to Bewick's *Memoir*, published posthumously in 1862.

LETTER 92

1. Tunbridge Wells: an inland spa, well known to Thackeray.
2. Not identified.

LETTER 93

1. Ralph Bathurst (1620–1704), dean of Wells and president of Trinity College, Oxford.
2. Née Lawrence, married the headmaster of Sedburgh School, which William Ritchie attended.

LETTER 94

1. Date of letter is before October 1899, when war broke out with the Boers.
2. Stephanus Johannes Paulus Kruger (1825–1904), a leader of the Boer Rebellion, and president of the Transvaal.
3. C. P. Johnson, eminent solicitor, godfather of Belinda Ritchie. Thackeray's first bibliographer.
4. Not identified.
5. Civil Service. Entrance, for the most part, was by a competitive examination. Scoones was a London crammer.
6. Probably Companion to the Order of Bath, an honor that preceded Ritchie's being knighted in 1907.
7. Mag Cornish; Imogen Booth; Nem and Alec Smith. U. G. may refer to the Uninvited Guest after a play by Tristan Bernard (1866–1947), or to the unknown gentleman coming with Tennyson.

LETTER 95

1. A section of southeast London, primarily an agricultural community.
2. Edward Dicey (1832–1911), English journalist and historian, author of *England and Egypt* (1881).
3. In 1891 Anny wrote an introduction for Elizabeth Cleghorn Gaskell's *Cranford* (1853), a novel of English village life in the second quarter of the nineteenth century.
4. Not identified.
5. Sir Charles Otto Desmond MacCarthy (1877–1952), literary and dramatic critic, knighted in 1951, married in 1906 Mary Warre-Cornish, Richmond's niece.
6. Adeline Ritchie married Charles Thackeray, her cousin.
7. Charles Wm and the Simons not identified.
8. Aunt Nelly was Richmond Ritchie's sister Elinor, who married Herbert Paul.
9. Probably J. Campbell McInnes, English baritone.
10. Lady Georgina Harriet Pollock (d. 1937) and Sir Frederick Pollock (1845–1937), third baronet, distinguished jurist and legal writer, eldest son of Sir William Frederick, grandson of Sir Jonathan Frederick, friend of Thackeray's, Sir Edward was fourth baronet and Lady Georgina's son. *Letters*, II, 207, n. 31.
11. Boo and Max not identified.

LETTER 96

1. Lady Ritchie's maid.
2. Town southeast of London where James lived at Lamb House, 1898–1916. Possibly James lent his house to Ritchie.

LETTER 97

1. 20 February 1900.
2. A stiff, cylindrical military dress hat with a metal plate in front, a short visor, and a plume.

LETTER 98

1. Not identified.
2. Henry Francis Herbert Thompson (second baronet) (1859–1944), noted Egyptologist.
3. Bernard P. Grenfell (1869–1926), English classical scholar and archaeologist. Grenfell, Hunt, and Hogarth were sent to Egypt by the Egypt Exploration Society in 1895 with the specific purpose of finding papyri.
4. Possibly the husband of Olivia Fisher; see n. 6.
5. Claude Joseph Goldsmid Montefiore (1858–1938), Jewish biblical scholar and philanthropist.
6. Airlie Gardens was the home of the Freshfields; Olivia Fisher, née Freshfields; Eleanor Clough, née Freshfield.
7. *Cornhill Magazine* published Anny's "Blackstick Papers," December 1900–June 1907.

CHAPTER 8

INTRODUCTION

1. *Thackeray and His Daughter*, 328.
2. *Twelfth Night* II.iii.50, and *Henry V* II.iii.11.
3. "A Roman Christmas-Time," *Friend*.
4. Edel, ed., *Henry James Letters*, IV, 364–65.
5. *Thackeray and His Daughter*, 284.
6. *Thackeray and His Daughter*, 306.
7. *Thackeray and His Daughter*, 310.
8. Discussed by Gérin, 231–52.
9. *Quarterly Review*, July 1902, 39.
10. *The Two Thackerays*, xxxvii.
11. *Thackeray and His Daughter*, 307. This drawing is reproduced in *Thackeray and His Daughter*, as well as on the cover of Gérin.
12. Edmund Gosse, *Books on the Table* (London: Heineman, 1921), 293.
13. *Thackeray and His Daughter*, 303.
14. *Blackstick Papers*, 1.
15. *Porch*, 86.
16. *Friend*, 121.
17. James Ritchie was killed in World War II at the age of thirty-three.
18. *Thackeray and His Daughter*, 313.

19. "Hallam Lord Tennyson sent to cover [Anny's] coffin the splendid cream-coloured pall embroidered with roses, which had served for the Poet." *Thackeray's Daughter*, 178.

20. Gérin, 257, quoted from George Smith, *Recollections*.

21. Howard Strugis, "Anne Isabella Thackeray," *Cornhill Magazine* 48 (November 1919), 449.

22. *Thackeray's Daughter*, 159.

23. Gérin, 271.

24. *The Letters of Virginia Woolf*, ed. Nigel Nicolson and Joanne Trautmann, 6 vols. (New York: Harcourt Brace Jovanovich, 1976), II, 474.

25. *Letters of Virginia Woolf*, II, 407.

26. *Adversity*, 7.

27. Virginia Woolf, *Night and Day* (London: Hogarth Press, 1966), 40–41.

28. "Review" in *Picadilly Review*, 23 October 1919, 6, in Robin Majumdar and Allen McLauren, eds. *Virginia Woolf: The Critical Heritage* (London: Routledge & Kegan Paul, 1975), 74.

29. Anne Olivier Bell, ed., *The Diary of Virginia Woolf* (New York: Harcourt Brace Jovanovich, 1977), I, 247. The article referred to by Woolf appeared in the *Times Literary Supplement*, 6 March 1919, 123.

30. "The Enchanted Organ," *The Nation & The Athenaeum*, 15 March 1924, 836.

31. *Times Literary Supplement*, 6 March 1919, 123.

32. In *The Forgotten Ring & Other Essays* (London: Constable, 1960), 216, Derek Hudson wrote that Anny's novels "are . . . full of felicities of phrases and impressionist touches that look forward to Virginia Woolf." Joanne P. Zuckerman, "Anne Thackeray Ritchie as the Model for Mrs. Hilbery in Virginia Woolf's *Night and Day*," *Virginia Woolf Quarterly* 1, no. 3 (Spring 1973), 32–46, and Carol Hanbery MacKay in the Critical Introduction to *The Two Thackerays* and in "The Thackeray Connection: Virginia Woolf's Aunt Anny," *Virginia Woolf and Bloomsbury: A Centenary Celebration*, ed. Jane Marcus (Bloomington: Indiana Univ. Press, 1987), 68–95, have also written on the interrelationship of Woolf and Ritchie.

33. Barbara Dunlap considers Ritchie's importance to the development of the modern novel in "Anne Thackeray Ritchie," in *Victorian Novelists after 1895*, ed. Ira B. Nadel and William E. Fredeman, *Dictionary of Literary Biography*, vol. 18 (Detroit: Gale Research, 1983), 251–57: "The line of descent from James to Virginia Woolf has been traced more than once in studies of the modern novel; the student of these two seminal figures clearly should not overlook the work of Virginia Woolf's 'Aunt Anny' and Henry James' 'intimately associated old friend,' Anne Thackeray Ritchie" (256–57).

34. Carol Hanbery MacKay in "Biography as Reflected Autobiography: The Self-Creation of Anne Thackeray Ritchie," in *Revealing Lives: Autobiography, Biography, and Gender*, ed. Susan Groag Bell and Marilyn Yalom

(Albany: State Univ. of New York Press, 1990), as well as other studies, and Katherine C. Hill-Miller in "'The Skies and Trees of the Past': Anne Thackeray Ritchie and William Makepeace Thackeray," in *Daughters and Fathers,* have investigated Ritchie's relationship with her father.

35. Conversation with Winifred Gérin, London, 17 August 1980.
36. Leonard Woolf, *Beginning Again* (New York: Harcourt Brace & World, Inc., 1963), 70–71.
37. *Thackeray and His Daughter,* 275.

LETTER 99

1. The Ritchies lived at 109, St. George's Square from 1901 to 1912.
2. Possibly a member of Prime Minister Asquith's family, with whom James was friendly.
3. Leon Edel appears to have located notice of this event, "in which James presided at a French lecture, by André Beaunier. The visitor spoke on Madame Récamier." *The Life of Henry James,* 2 vols. (New York: Penguin Books, 1977), II, 678.

LETTER 101

1. W. J. Williams worked for Smith, Elder from 1888 to 1915. "[H]e had the privilege of assisting Lady Ritchie in organising the Thackeray Centenary celebrations" as well as being her editor for the Introductions. Leonard Huxley, *The House of Smith, Elder* (London: priv. print., 1923), 248.
2. A different hand has written across the top of this letter, "Left by Miss Hester Ritchie May 19/06." Anny worked from 1905 to 1907 on what was to be called the Standard Edition of Thackeray's works. The project was abandoned because of the defection of the third contracting party. Gérin, 263–64.
3. Sara Hennell (1812–99), writer on theological speculation, *Thoughts in Aid of Faith* (1860), a friend of George Eliot's; Whitwell Elwin (1816–1900), country rector, editor of the *Quarterly Review* from 1853 to 1860, friend of Thackeray's.

LETTER 102

1. Date has been added in another hand.
2. 8br: Abbreviation for October.
3. William Harrison Lambert (1842–1912), American collector of Lincoln and Thackeray literature and manuscripts.
4. George Smith's son-in-law and successor. Gérin, 253.
5. The Centenary Edition was published with yellow facsimiles of the title pages.
6. Anny wrote, "It is impossible to resist quoting at length from Canon

Elwin's essays on Thackeray, so instinctively does he strike the note that is wanted to elucidate the story of his old friend's early life." Cent. Intro., I, xx.

LETTER 103

1. Date has been added in another hand.

LETTER 104

1. Address and date at end of letter.
2. William James (1842–1910), philosopher.
3. "Unfortunate."
4. For a short time after his brother's death, James remained at his brother's summer house in Chocorua, New Hampshire, with his sister-in-law, Alice; his nephews, Henry James III and William James, Jr.; and his niece, Margaret Mary.

LETTER 105

1. Date has been added in another hand.

LETTER 106

1. Leonard Sidney Woolf (1880–1969), English writer, historian, and political essayist. He and Virginia Stephen married in 1912.
2. Lady Ritchie lived at 9, St. Leonard's Terrace from 1912 to 1916.
3. Virginia Woolf (1882–1941).
4. Charles Robert Leslie (1794–1859), painter and writer, son of American painter Robert, friend of Thackeray's. *The Life and Times of Sir Joshua Reynolds* begun by Leslie was completed by Taylor in 1865.
5. Virginia Woolf had finished *The Voyage Out* in 1913, but it was not published until 1915. Quentin Bell, *Virginia Woolf: A Biography,* 2 vols. (New York: Harcourt Brace Jovanovich, 1972).
6. Vanessa Stephen Bell (1879–1961), m. 1907, painter and woman of letters.

LETTER 107

1. Isle of Wight.

LETTER 108

1. Month and day are written on letter in brackets in another hand. This note, in a large scrawl, was written on black-bordered stationery, shortly after Richmond's death on 12 October 1912.

LETTER 109

1. Maude Morrison Frank (1870–1956), born New York; author of English textbooks, plays, articles. Anny is writing to Maude Frank and her sister, hence "Franks."
2. Chapter 51.
3. Not identified.
4. The thought of this paragraph seems confused.
5. No signature.

LETTER 110

1. Anny's letter, an appeal on behalf of the French Wounded Emergency Fund, appeared in the *Times* on 25 January 1915.
2. The following words have been crossed out: "dont think I can do better than."

LETTER 111

1. Anny retired to her home The Porch, in Freshwater, Isle of Wight, in 1916.
2. Robins had married in the 1880s, but never assumed her husband's name. Anny must be referring to a role she played.
3. Not identified
4. Charles Villiers, son of Beatrice Paul and grandson of Elinor Ritchie and Herbert Paul; James and Belinda Ritchie, Anny's grandchildren.
5. Audrey Boyle married Hallam Tennyson, the poet's older son in 1884. After she died, he remarried.
6. Anny refers to a favorite nephew, Arthur Ritchie, who was killed in battle in 1916.
7. Not identified.

LETTER 112

1. Margie Peggy is Anny's daughter-in-law.
2. "Best of all is an old friend." "Et" should be "est." Quotation not identified.

LETTER 113

1. Sir Algernon Edward West (1832–1921), chairman of the Inland Review Board.
2. *Recollections, 1832 to 1886* (1899).
3. Reproduced sketch by Thackeray. Lusitania: British passenger vessel sunk 7 May 1915 by a German submarine.
4. Lord Randolph Churchill (1849–95), English politician, father of Winston Churchill.

5. In the House of Commons.
6. Freshwater.
7. Elliots and Mrs. Boyle not identified.

LETTER 114

1. Mary Booth was the wife of Charles Booth (1840–1916), philanthropist, parents of Margaret, called Meg (b. 1879), who married William Ritchie.
2. [1918] has been added to the letter either by Anny or a later hand.
3. *Charles Booth: A Memoir* (London: MacMillan, 1918).
4. Not identified.

LETTER 115

1. Addressed to the youngest child (b. 1911) of Billy and Meg Ritchie; sister of Belinda and James.
2. Postcard with picture of Freshwater Bay Bathing Beach.

Works by Anne Thackeray Ritchie, 1860–1920

ABBREVIATIONS

(*L.*)   Published about one month later in *Littell's Living Age,* Boston.
(*H.*)   Published about one month later in *Harper's New Monthly Magazine,* European edition.
(*C.*)   Published about one month later in *The Critic,* New York.
(*T.*)   Published also in Leipzig by Bernhard Tauchnitz.
(*H.B.*) Published also in New York by Harper & Brothers.

Periodical and newspaper entries for Ritchie will also be found in books named in parentheses.

CHRONOLOGICAL LIST OF WORKS

BOOKS

The Story of Elizabeth. London: Smith, Elder, & Co., 1863. (Novel) (*T.*)
The Village on the Cliff. London: Smith, Elder, & Co., 1867. (Novel) (*T.*)
Five Old Friends and a Young Prince. London: Smith, Elder, & Co., 1868. (Short stories) (*T.*) [Published as *Fairy Tales for Grown Folks.* Boston: Loring, n.d.]
To Esther and Other Sketches. London: Smith, Elder, & Co., 1869. (Short stories)
Old Kensington. London: Smith, Elder, & Co., 1873. (Novel) (*T.*)
Toilers and Spinsters and Other Essays. London: Smith, Elder, & Co., 1874. (Essays)
Bluebeard's Keys and Other Stories. London: Smith, Elder, & Co., 1874. (Short stories) (*T.*)
Miss Angel. London: Smith, Elder, & Co., 1875. (Novel) (*T.*)
From an Island and Some Essays. Leipzig: Bernhard Tauchnitz, 1877. (A story and essays) (Boston: Loring, n.d.) [The story appeared previously in *Story of Elizabeth* and eleven of the twelve essays in *Toilers and Spinsters.*]
Da Capo and Other Tales. Leipzig: Bernhard Tauchnitz, 1880. (Short stories)
Madame de Sévigné. London: Blackwood & Sons, 1881. (Biography)
Miss Williamson's Divagations. London: Smith, Elder, & Co., 1881. (Six short stories, four published in *Da Capo and Other Tales.*)

A Book of Sibyls. London: Blackwood & Sons, 1883. (Essays)
Miss Angel and Fulham Lawn. London: Smith, Elder, & Co., 1884. (Rpt. of *Miss Angel,* with addition of *Fulham Lawn.*)
Mrs. Dymond. London: Smith, Elder, & Co., 1885. (Novel)
Records of Tennyson, Ruskin, and Browning. London: Macmillan & Co., 1892. (Reminiscences) (H.B.)
Lord Amherst and the British Advance Eastwards to Burma. Oxford: Clarendon Press, 1894. (Biography, written with Richardson Evans.)
Chapters from Some Memoirs. London: Macmillan & Co., 1894. (Memoirs, title changed to *Chapters from Some Unwritten Memoirs* in Harper edition.) (H.B.; T.)
Blackstick Papers. London: Smith, Elder, & Co., 1908. (Essays) (New York: G. P. Putnam's Sons, 1908.)
From the Porch. London: Smith, Elder, & Co., 1913. (Essays)
From Friend to Friend. London: Smith, Elder & Co., 1919. (Essays, published posthumously) (New York: E. P. Dutton, 1920.)

MAJOR INTRODUCTIONS, PREFACES, REMINISCENCES, BIOGRAPHICAL ESSAYS, IN WORKS BY OTHER AUTHORS

Introduction to *The Orphan of Pimlico* by W. M. Thackeray. London: Smith, Elder, & Co., 1876.
Memorial preface to *Poems & Music* by Anne Evans. London: Kegan Paul & Co., 1880.
"Elizabeth Barrett Browning." *Dictionary of National Biography* (1886).
Preface to *Cranford* by Elizabeth C. Gaskell. London: Macmillan & Co., 1891.
Introduction to *The Fairy Tales of Madame d'Aulnoy.* London: Lawrence & Bullen, 1892.
"Reminiscences." *Lord Tennyson and His Friends: A Collection of Photographs* by Julia Margaret Cameron and H. H. Cameron. London: T. Fisher Unwin, 1893. (New York: Macmillan & Co., 1893.)
Introduction to *Our Village* by Mary R. Mitford. London: Macmillan & Co., 1893.
Introductions to the following works by Maria Edgeworth. London: Macmillan & Co.:

Castle Rackrent and The Absentee. 1895.
Ormond. 1895.
Popular Tales. 1895.
Helen. 1896.
Belinda. 1896.
The Parents' Assistant. 1897.

"Reminiscence." *Life and Letters of Frederick Walker,* edited by John G. Marks. London: Smith, Elder, & Co., 1896.
Biographical introductions to *The Works of William Makepeace Thackeray.* "Biographical Edition." 13 vols. London: Smith, Elder, & Co., 1898–99.
"Some Recollections of Millais." *Life and Letters of Sir John Millais,* edited by John Guille Millais. Vol. II. London: Smith, Elder, & Co., 1899.
Preface to *A Week in a French Country House,* by Adelaide Sartoris. London: Smith, Elder, & Co., 1902.
"Recollections of G. J. Cayley." *The Bridle Roads of Spain,* by G. J. Cayley. London: T. Fisher Unwin, 1908.
Biographical introductions to *The Works of William Makepeace Thackeray.* "Centenary Edition." 26 vols. London: Smith, Elder, & Co., 1910–11.
Introduction to *W. M. Thackeray and Edward FitzGerald: A Literary Friendship. Unpublished Letters and Verses by W. M. Thackeray.* London: privately printed by Clement Shorter, 1916.

SELECTED PERIODICAL AND NEWSPAPER PUBLICATIONS

"Little Scholars." *Cornhill Magazine* 1 (May 1860), 549–59. (*Toilers and Spinsters.*)
"How I Quitted Naples." *Cornhill Magazine* 2 (Aug. 1860), 192–210.
"Toilers and Spinsters." *Cornhill Magazine* 3 (March 1861), 318–31. (*Toilers and Spinsters.*) (*Island.*)
"To Esther." Part I, *Cornhill Magazine* 5 (Jan. 1862), 43–51; Part II, *Cornhill Magazine* 13 (Feb. 1865), 228–56. (*Esther.*)
"A House in Westminster." *Cornhill Magazine* 6 (Aug. 1862), 258–68.
"The Story of Elizabeth." *Cornhill Magazine:*

> Part I. 6 (Sept. 1862), 330–45.
> Part II. 6 (Oct. 1862), 490–511.
> Part III. 6 (Nov. 1862), 623–39.
> Part IV. 6 (Dec. 1862), 814–29.
> Part V. 7 (Jan. 1863), 104–19.
> (*Elizabeth.*)

"Out of the World." *Cornhill Magazine,* Part I, 8 (Sept. 1863), 366–84; Part II, 8 (Oct. 1863), 449–65. (*L.*) (*Esther.*)
"The End of a Long Day's Work." *Cornhill Magazine* 10 (Aug. 1864), 253–56.
"A Country Sunday." *Pall Mall Gazette,* 18 March 1865, 10–11. (*Toilers and Spinsters.*) (*Island.*) [Original article signed "H.M." but attribution doubtful; may be Harriet Marian Thackeray's.]
"Five O'Clock Tea." *Pall Mall Gazette,* 22 March 1865, 10. (*Toilers and Spinsters.*) (*Island.*)

"A Book of Photographs." *Pall Mall Gazette,* 10 April 1865, 10–11. (*Toilers and Spinsters.*)

"An Easter Holiday." *Pall Mall Gazette,* 2 May 1865, 10–11. (*Toilers and Spinsters.*) (*Island.*)

"Heroines and Their Grandmothers." *Cornhill Magazine* 11 (May 1865), 630–40. (*Toilers and Spinsters.*) (*Island.*)

"Making Merry." *Cornhill Magazine* 12 (Nov. 1865), 547–54. (*Esther.*)

"The Sleeping Beauty in the Wood." *Cornhill Magazine* 13 (May 1866), 556–66. (*L.*) (*Five Old Friends.*)

"Cinderella." *Cornhill Magazine* 13 (June 1866), 721–42. (*L.*) (*Five Old Friends.*)

"The Village on the Cliff." *Cornhill Magazine:*

Part I. 14 (July 1866), 1–27.
Part II. 14 (Aug. 1866), 129–51.
Part III. 14 (Sept. 1866), 358–84.
Part IV. 14 (Oct. 1866), 487–512.
Part V. 14 (Nov. 1866), 513–35.
Part VI. 14 (Dec. 1866), 641–65.
Part VII. 15 (Jan. 1867), 75–91.
Part VIII. 15 (Feb. 1867), 242–56.
(*The Village.*)

"Beauty and the Beast." *Cornhill Magazine* 15 (June 1867), 676–709. (*Five Old Friends.*)

"Little Red Riding Hood." *Cornhill Magazine* 16 (Oct. 1867), 440–73. (*L.*) (*Five Old Friends.*)

"Jack the Giant Killer." *Cornhill Magazine,* Part I, 16 (Nov. 1867), 589–608; Part II, 16 (Dec. 1867), 589–608; Part III, 17 (Jan. 1868), 1–29. (*L.*) (*Five Old Friends.*)

"A Sad Hour." *Cornhill Magazine* 17 (March 1868), 357–69. (*L.*) (*Five Old Friends.*)

"Out of the Silence." *Cornhill Magazine* 17 (May 1868), 573–77. (*L.*) (*Toilers and Spinsters.*) (*Island.*)

"A City of Refuge." *Cornhill Magazine* 17 (June 1868), 735–44. (*Toilers and Spinsters.*)

"From an Island." *Cornhill Magazine:*

Part I. 18 (Nov. 1868), 610–25.
Part II. 18 (Dec. 1868), 739–60.
Part III. 19 (Jan. 1869), 62–78.
(*L.*) (*Elizabeth.*) (*Island.*)

"Chirping Crickets." *Cornhill Magazine* 19 (Feb. 1869), 235–42. (Title changed to "Newport Market" in *Toilers and Spinsters.*)

"Rome in the Holy Week." *Pall Mall Gazette,* Letter I, 6 April 1869, 11; Letter II, 7 April 1869, 11. (*Toilers and Spinsters.*)

"Sola." *Cornhill Magazine,* Part I, 20 (July 1869), 102–28; Part II, 20 (Aug. 1869), 215–35. (*Esther.*)

"Moretti's Campanula." *Cornhill Magazine* 20 (Dec. 1869), 687–721. (*L.*) (*Esther.*)

"Two Ladies—Two Hours." *Cornhill Magazine* 21 (April 1870), 435–59. (*L.*) (Title changed to "Two Hours" in *Elizabeth.*)

"Fulham Lawn." *Cornhill Magazine* 22 (July 1870), 62–86. (*Miss Angel.*)

"Little Paupers." *Cornhill Magazine* 22 (Sept. 1870), 372–84. (*Toilers and Spinsters.*)

"Bluebeard's Keys." *Cornhill Magazine,* Part I, 23 (Feb. 1871), 192–220; Part II, 23 (June 1871), 688–709. (*Bluebeard's Keys.*)

"Jane Austen." *Cornhill Magazine* 24 (Aug. 1871), 158–74. (*L.*) (*Toilers and Spinsters.*) (Enlarged in *A Book of Sibyls.*) (*Island.*)

"Riquet à la Houppe." *Cornhill Magazine,* Part I, 25 (Jan. 1872), 45–59; Part II, 25 (Feb. 1872), 177–95. (*L.*) (*Bluebeard's Keys.*)

"Old Kensington." *Cornhill Magazine:*

> Part I. 25 (April 1872), 385–407
> Part II. 25 (May 1872), 513–38.
> Part III. 25 (June 1872), 641–61.
> Part IV. 25 (July 1872), 1–20.
> Part V. 25 (Aug. 1872), 129–54.
> Part VI. 25 (Sept. 1872), 257–78.
> Part VII. 25 (Oct. 1872), 385–406.
> Part VIII. 25 (Nov. 1872), 513–33.
> Part IX. 25 (Dec. 1872), 641–61.
> Part X. 27 (Jan. 1873), 1–28.
> Part XI. 27 (Feb. 1873), 129–50.
> Part XII. 27 (March 1873), 257–80.
> Part XIII. 27 (April 1873), 385–408.
> (*H.*) (*Old Kensington.*)

"In Friendship." *Cornhill Magazine* 27 (June 1873), 666–70. (*Toilers and Spinsters.*) (*Island.*)

"Jack and the Beanstalk." *Cornhill Magazine* 28 (Sept. 1873), 311–34; 28 (Oct. 1873), 431–56. (*L.*) (*Bluebeard's Keys.*)

"Sir Edwin Landseer." *Cornhill Magazine* 29 (Jan. 1874), 81–100. (*Toilers and Spinsters.*) (*Island.*)

"The White Cat." *Cornhill Magazine* 29 (April 1874), 424–56. (*L.*) (*Bluebeard's Keys.*)

"Arachne in Sloane Street." *Cornhill Magazine* 29 (May 1874), 571–76. (*Toilers and Spinsters.*)

"Maids-of-all-Work and Blue Books." *Cornhill Magazine* 30 (Sept. 1874), 281–96. (*Toilers and Spinsters.*) (*Island.*)

"Miss Angel." *Cornhill Magazine:*

Part I. 31 (Jan. 1875), 1–23.
Part II. 31 (Feb. 1875), 231–56.
Part III. 31 (March 1875), 257–80.
Part IV. 31 (April 1875), 489–512.
Part V. 31 (May 1875), 513–34.
Part VI. 31 (June 1875), 737–60.
(*L.*) (*Miss Angel.*) (*Miss Angel and Fulham Lawn.*)

"Mr. Campbell's Pupils." *Cornhill Magazine* 33 (March 1876), 349–57.

"Across the Peat-Fields." *Cornhill Magazine,* Part I, 34 (Oct. 1876), 489–512; Part II, 34 (Nov. 1876), 570–94. (*Divagations.*)

"Da Capo." *Cornhill Magazine,* Part I, 36 (Dec. 1877), 641–60; Part II, 37 (Jan. 1878), 1–24. (*L.*) (*H.*) (*Divagations.*)

"Miss Morier's Visions." *Cornhill Magazine* 39 (Feb. 1879), 173–83. (*Divagations.*)

"Susanna: An Introduction." *Cornhill Magazine,* Part I, 39 (May 1879), 613–40; Part II, 39 (June 1879), 641–62. (*Mrs. Dymond,* Book I.)

"Fina's Aunt." *Cornhill Magazine,* Part I, 42 (Dec. 1880), 641–61; Part II, 43 (Jan. 1881), 65–89. (*Divagations.*)

"Mrs. Barbauld." *Cornhill Magazine* 44 (Nov. 1881), 581–603. (*Sibyls.*)

"Upstairs and Downstairs." *Cornhill Magazine* 45 (March 1882), 334–47. (Pamphlet for Council of the Metropolitan Assoc. for Befriending Young Servants.) (*Porch.*)

"Miss Edgeworth." *Cornhill Magazine,* Part I, 46 (Oct. 1882), 404–26; Part II, 46 (Nov. 1882), 526–45. (*Sibyls.*)

"Mrs. Opie." *Cornhill Magazine,* n.s., 1 (Oct. 1883), 357–82. (*Sibyls.*)

"Alfred Tennyson." *Harper's New Monthly Magazine* 7 (Dec. 1883), 20–41. (*Records.*)

"Mrs. Dymond." *Macmillan's Magazine:*

Part I. 51 (March 1885), 321–35.
Part II. 51 (April 1885), 401–19.
Part III. 51 (May 1885), 1–15.
Part IV. 51 (June 1885), 81–95.
Part V. 51 (July 1885), 173–87.
Part VI. 51 (Aug. 1885), 241–53.
Part VII. 52 (Sept. 1885), 321–32.
Part VIII. 52 (Oct. 1885), 455–72.

Part IX. 53 (Nov. 1885), 63–74.
Part X. 53 (Dec. 1885), 141–52.
(L.) (*Mrs. Dymond,* Books II, III, IV.)

"Mrs. John Taylor of Norwich." *Macmillan's Magazine* 55 (Dec. 1886), 106–15. (*Porch.*)
"Pensioners in the Tower Hamlets." *Cornhill Magazine,* n.s., 8 (April 1887), 369–76. (Printed twice as a pamphlet.)
"Madame de Sévigné's Grandmother." *The Woman's World,* edited by Oscar Wilde. London: Cassell's, 1888, 11–16. (Title changed to "Sainte Jeanne Francoise de Chantal" in *Porch.*)
"The Boyhood of Thackeray." *St. Nicholas* 17 (Dec. 1889), 105.
"John Ruskin: An Essay." *Harper's New Monthly Magazine* 80 (March 1890), 578–603. (*Records.*)
"Chapters from an Unwritten Memoir." *Macmillan's Magazine:*

Part I. "My Poet." 62 (July 1890), 189–92.
Part II. "My Musician." 62 (Aug. 1890), 252–56.
Part III. "My Professor of History." 63 (Dec. 1890), 112–18.
Part IV. "My Witches' Caldron." 63 (Feb. 1891), 249–53.
Part V. "My Witches' Caldron," Part II. 63 (April 1891), 424–53.
Part VI. "My Witches' Caldron," Part III. 66 (May 1892), 17–22.
Part VII. "My Witches' Caldron," Part IV. 66 (Aug. 1892), 265–70.
Part VIII. "My Witches' Caldron," Part V. 66 (Sept. 1892), 344–49.
Part IX. "Mrs. Kemble." 68 (July 1893), 190–96.
Part X. "At Mennecy." 69 (April 1894), 443–50.
Part XI. "In Italy." 70 (Oct. 1894), 429–34.
(L.) (*Chapters.*)

"Thackeray and His Biographers." *Illustrated London News* 98 (20 June 1891), 811.
"Robert and Elizabeth Barrett Browning." *Harper's New Monthly Magazine* 84 (May 1892), 832–55. (*Records.*)
"Comment on 'Lord Bateman': A Ballad Attributed to Thackeray." *Harper's New Monthly Magazine* 86 (Dec. 1892), 124–29.
"Of Thomas Bewick." *Macmillan's Magazine* 67 (Jan. 1893), 236–40. (*Blackstick.*)
"Dwellers in Arcady: Angelica Kauffman." *Macmillan's Magazine* 68 (Sept. 1893), 353–56. (L.)
"Willie." *Illustrated London News* 103 (28 Oct. 1893), 537–39; 103 (4 Nov. 1893), 569–71. (Title and character's name changed to "Binnie" in *Friend.*)
"The First Number of 'The Cornhill'." *Cornhill Magazine,* n.s., 1 (July 1896), 1–16. (*Porch.*)
"Blackstick Papers." *Cornhill Magazine:*

1. "Introduction: Haydn." O.s., 82, 9 (Dec. 1900), 721–27.
2. "Felicia Felix." N.s., 10 (Jan. 1901), 37–42.
3. "St. Andrews." N.s., 10 (Feb. 1901), 148–54.
4. "Concerning Joseph Joachim." N.s., 10 (April 1901), 433–42.
5. "Egeria in Brighton." N.s., 10 (June 1901), 722–29.
6. "Nohant in 1874." N.s., 11 (Oct. 1901), 433–46.
7. "Links with the Past." N.s., 15 (Nov. 1903), 604–11.
8. "No. 8." N.s., 16 (Jan. 1904), 54–62.
9. "Paris, Prisms and Primitifs." N.s., 17 (July 1904), 43–55.
10. "Jacob Omnium." N.s., 18 (Jan. 1905), 1–13.
11. "Mrs. Gaskell." N.s., 21 (Dec. 1906), 757–67.
12. "Mabys." N.s., 22 (June 1907), 761–74.

(C.) (*Blackstick*.)

"Concerning Tourgénieff." *New Quarterly* 1 (March 1908), 183–94. (*Blackstick*.)
"Quills from the Swan of Lichfield." *Cornhill Magazine*, n.s., 27 (Nov. 1909), 607–27. (*Porch*.)
"The First Editor: And the Founder." *Cornhill Magazine*, n.s., 28 (Jan. 1910), 1–5. (*Porch*.)
"Charles Dickens as I Remember Him." *Pall Mall Magazine* 49 (March 1912), 300–309. (*Porch*.)
"Alfred Stevens." *Contemporary Review* 101 (April 1912), 487–92. (*Porch*.)
"A Discourse on Modern Sibyls." *Cornhill Magazine* 34 (March 1913), 309–20. (*Porch*.)
"L'Art d'être Grandpère." *Cornhill Magazine*, n.s., 35 (July 1913), 21–32. (*Porch*.)
"Morland at Freshwater Bay." *The Sphere* 54, 710 (30 Aug. 1913), 242. (*Porch*.)
"In a French Village." *The Sphere* 55, 716 (11 Oct. 1913), 40. (*Friend*.)
"A Roman Christmas-Time." *The Sphere* 55, 726 (20 Dec. 1913), 300. (*Friend*.)
"Present Tapestries and Far-off 'Bells and Pomegranates'." *The Sphere* 57, 755 (11 July 1914), 44. (*Friend*.)
"A Frenchwoman's Letter Bag." Edited with Hester Ritchie. *Cornhill Magazine*, n.s., 39 (Oct. 1915), 449–55.
"From Friend to Friend." *Cornhill Magazine*, n.s., 41 (July 1916), 21–43. (*Friend*.)
"Seagulls and White Coiffes at Chelsea." *The Spectator* 117 (26 Aug. 1916), 232.
"An American Lady." *The Spectator* 119 (25 Aug. 1917), 185–86.
"Two Letters to a Painter from W. M. Thackeray." *Cornhill Magazine*, n.s., 43 (Dec. 1917), 571–76. (*Friend*.)

Index

Abbott, Charles, 74, 314n
Alexander, Miss (governess), 203, 204, 338n
Allen, John, 41–42, 304n
Anslie, Mr., 65, 72, 127
Appleton, Thomas Gold, 174, 332n
Athenaeum Club, 67, 134, 136, 137, 236
Auber, Mme. Esprit, 16, 19, 298n
Austen, Jane, 177–78, 266, 331n

Bathurst, Ralph, 251, 348n
Baxter, Anna Smith Strong (Mrs. George), 112, 330n. Letters to: 151–52, 179–80, 183–84
Baxter, Lucy, 39, 151, 174, 330n. Letter to: 175–77
Baxter, Sally, 39, 303n, 332n
Becher, Aunt, 14, 22, 297n
Bell, Robert, 129, 325n
Bell, Vanessa Stephen, 276, 353n
Bellows, Rev. Henry, 39, 303n
Bess. *See* Hamerton, Bess
Beyne, Mrs. (WMT's cousin), 13, 297n
Blackwood, 95, 321n
Blechynden, Mrs. (Bletchenden), 128, 325n
Booth, Mrs. Charles, 355n. Letter to: 282–83
Boyle, Miss (daughter of Richard?), 329n. Letter to: 148–49
Braddon, Mary, 86–87, 317n
Bréquerecque, Chateau (Boulogne), 28, 207, 339n
Brodie, Jesse, 22, 86, 130, 300n, 326n
Brontë, Charlotte, 311n
Brookfield, Jane Octavia Elton (JOB), 7–8, 199, 203, 313n; and ATR, 72, 142, 143; and WMT, 27, 109, 124, 129, 169–70; —, memories of, 132, 133
Brookfield, Magdalene, 7, 72, 313n
Brotherton, Mrs. Mary (Maria), 206, 339n
Brown, John, 61, 95, 97, 321n
Brownie (WMT's dog), 86, 90, 137, 145, 211
Browning, Elizabeth Barrett, 158, 206, 210, 223–24
Browning, Robert, 158, 181, 210, 237–38; *Red Cotton Night-Cap Country*, 158, 181, 334n. Letters to: 181, 236–37, 238. Letters from: 183
Browning, Robert (father of the poet), 48, 307n
Browning, Robert W. (Pen), 158, 206, 210, 339n
Browning, Sarianna, 183, 334n. Letters to: 232–33, 237–38
Bullar, Dr. William, 44, 306n
Buller, Sir Arthur, 91, 319n
Bulwer-Lytton, Edward, 47, 307n
Butler, Mrs. Harriet (Grandmama, GM), 5, 11, 25, 197, 202, 297n, 338n

Cameron, Julia, 83, 111, 176, 316n
Carlyle, Thomas, 262
Carmichael-Smyth, Anne (Grannie) (ATR's grandmother, Mrs. C-S), 2, 4, 30–31, 202, 297n, 328n; and ATR, 13, 52, 114–15, 120, 142; death of, 138–39, 149; health of, 30–31, 50–51, 57, 73; and WMT, 60, 126. Letters to: 13, 13–15, 15–16, 16–17, 18–19, 20, 21–22, 22–24, 24–25, 44–46, 82–83

365

INDEX

Carmichael-Smyth, Anne (*continued*) (from HMT). Letters from: 11–12, 41–42

Carmichael-Smyth, Charles, 21, 45, 300n

Carmichael-Smyth, Major Henry (GP) (ATR's stepgrandfather), 2, 4, 11, 200, 212, 297n. Letter to: 13–15

Carmichael-Smyth, Robert, 48, 307–8n

Carnegie, Andrew, 233, 344n

Caulfield, Mr. and Mrs. James, 86, 317n

Cayley, Charles, 124, 324n

Charles. *See* Pearman, Charles

Chave, Mr. (clergyman), 53, 309n

Che, Chéri. *See* Carmichael-Smyth, Charles

Churchill, Lord Randolph, 281, 354n

Clarke, Savile, 345n. Letters to: 239, 239–40

Clarke, Mrs. Savile. Letter to: 241

Clifford, Charles, 127, 325n

Cole, Henrietta, 54

Cole, Henry (Coal) (Felix Summerly), 71, 74, 90, 125, 200, 201, 205, 298n, 313n, 337n. Letter to: 71–73

Cole, Mrs. Henry, 15, 74, 202, 205. Letters to: 71–73, 141–42, 142, 143

Cole, Laetitia, 53, 71, 93, 129, 141, 325n. Letter to: 37–38

Cole, Mary, 71, 141

Collins, Mr. and Mrs. Charles Allson (the former Kate Dickens), 28, 54, 111, 124, 125, 129, 309n, 324n

Colmache family, 12, 14, 15, 16, 297n

Colvile, Sir James, 91, 319n

Corkran family, 39, 42, 50, 303n

Cornhill Magazine, 59, 65–66, 68–69, 82, 231

Cornish, Frank and Blanche, 229, 236, 253, 342n, 345n

Cowper, John, 82, 315–16n

Craigie family, 71, 124, 312n, 324n

Crawfurd, John, 74, 76, 313n

Creyke, Robert, 92, 206, 320n

Crimean War, 40–41, 208–9

Crowe, Amy (later Mrs. Edward Thackeray), 31, 62–63, 75, 81, 85, 93, 129, 150, 301n, 323n. Letters to: 26, 46–47, 47–49, 49–50 (from ATR and HMT), 50–53, 53–54, 56–58, 76–80, 84–85, 87–92

Crowe, Eyre, 89, 305n, 318n

Crowe family, 14, 15, 18, 44, 297n, 306n, 336n

Cunningham, Peter, 54, 309n

Curzon. *See* Kurzon, Robert

Dance, Mr. and Mrs. Charles, 1, 12, 14, 297n

Darwin, Sir Charles, 231, 237, 336n

Darwin, Sir Francis, 237, 345n

Davison, Sir Henry, 53, 306n, 309n

Davison, Miss (daughter of Sir Henry), 125, 127, 324n

de Lamartine, Alphonse, 47, 307n

Delane, John, 55, 310n

Denman, Mrs. Richard, 129, 326n

de Rothschild, Lady Louisa, 48, 307n

Dicey, Edward, 253, 349n

Dickens, Charles, 34, 52, 58, 70, 201, 204, 207, 302n, 311n

Dickens, Kate. *See* Collins, Mr. and Mrs. Charles Allson

Dobson, Austin, 344n, 345n. Letter to: 236

Donne, Rev. William, 127, 325n

Doudet, Célestine, 31, 41, 42, 304n

Drury, Miss (governess), 20, 23, 25, 201, 299n

Duckworth, Julia (Mrs. Leslie Stephen), 244, 346n

Duff, Elphinstone Grant, 127, 325n

Duke's Motto, The, 85–86, 317n, 320n

Dundreary, Lord (Edward Askew), 86, 317n

Edward. *See* Thackeray, Edward

Elgin, Lady Elizabeth, 44–45, 306n

Eliot, George, 69, 170, 171. Letter to: 184–85

Eliza (servant), 50, 51, 57, 308n

Elliot, Jane, 74, 314n
Elwin, Whitwell, 352n, 352–53n
Emma (servant), 57, 310n
Ervings. *See* Irvine family
Evans, Frederick, 137, 327n

Fane, Julian, 87, 317n
Fanshawe, Mrs. Charles, 15, 205, 298n, 305n, 306n. Letter to: 43–44
Fardel, L., 75, 314n
FitzGerald, Edward, 4, 140, 328n
Fitzroy, Admiral Robert, 139, 328n
Flore. *See* Colmache family
Ford, Ford Madox, 267
Forster, John, 134, 327n
Frank, Maude, 354n. Letters to: 278, 278–79
Fraser, Thomas, 46, 306n
Freak(e), Mr. and Mrs. Charles, 90, 319n
Freshwater, Isle of Wight, 84, 111, 154, 172, 176, 262, 264, 277

Garden, Mr. and Mrs. (Virginia), 132, 327n
Gardener (servant), 135, 147, 150
Garrick Club, 134, 136
Garrick Club Affair. *See* Yates, Edmund
Gaskell, Mrs. (Elizabeth?), 42, 349n
Gérin, Winifred, 171–72, 188, 269, 270
Gloyn(e), Mrs. (servant), 12, 14, 17, 297n
Gosse, Edmund, 266
Graham, Mary, 197, 336n
Gray, Sarah (servant), 40, 55, 57, 90, 147, 304n
Greathed, Colonel, 91, 319n
Grenfell, Bernard, 350n
Grey. *See* Gray, Sarah
Guizot, François, 207, 339n
Gurney, Mrs. Russell, 89, 318n

Hamerton, Bess, 11, 13, 16, 18, 19, 201, 297n, 337n
Hamerton, Maria, 12, 15, 16, 52, 297n

Hamley, Edward, 74, 91, 313–14n
Hankey, Frank, 198, 336n
Hannay, James, 131, 326n
Hennell, Sara, 273, 352n
Herbert, Lady, of Lea, 176, 332n
Hill, Octavia, 344n. Letter to: 234–35
Holland, Lord and Lady, 19, 74, 299n
Holmes, Mary, 43, 305n
House of Lords, 21, 300n
Hughes, Thomas, 175, 332n
Hunt, William Holman, 90, 319n

Irvine family, 16, 23, 129, 298n

Jackson, Rev. and Mrs. John, 129, 326n
James, Henry, 221–23, 258–59; *Guy Domville*, 246, 347n. Letters to: 229, 272, 277. Letters from: 246, 254–55, 274–75
James, Samuel (servant), 203, 338n
John (servant), 13, 297n
Johnson, C. P., 251–52, 349n

Kemble, Fanny, 83–84, 225, 316n, 332n
Kilmarlock, Lord, 82, 315n
Kingsley, Charles, 205, 338n
Knighton, Sir William, 123, 324, 326n
Kruger, Stephanus, 251, 349n
Kurzon, Robert (Curzon), 124, 324n

Lambert, William, 273, 352n
Laura. *See* Colmache family
Leech, John, 129, 148–49, 320n, 325n
Leslie, Charles, 124, 276, 324n, 353n
Leslie, George, 333n. Letter to: 178
Lewes, George, 68–69, 157, 334n
Lind, Jenny, 94, 321n
Locker-Lampson, Frederick, 232, 343n
Lockhart, John, 206, 258, 339n
Longfellow, Henry Wadsworth, 175, 332n
Longman, Thomas (?), 113, 126, 323n, 324n
Louise, Princess, 235, 344n
Low family, 16, 91, 298n, 341n
Lucas, Samuel, 94, 321n

Macbean, Alexander, 206, 339n
MacCarthy, Sir Charles Desmond, 253, 349n
MacKay, Carol Hanbery, 261
Macready, William, 201, 337n
Madame Tussauds, 13–14
Mansfield, Mrs. (friend of WMT's), 129, 326n
Maria. *See* Hamerton, Maria
Marochetti, Baron Carlo, 57, 91, 310n
Marsden, Dr. James. *See* Doudet, Célestine
Martineau, Harriet, 36, 43–44, 305–6n
Mennecy, France, 29, 303n
Merivale, Herman, 93, 125, 129, 320n
Merivale, Herman, Jr., 122–23, 174, 210, 324n
Midsummer-Night's Dream, A, 49
Mildmay, Henry, 176, 332n
Millais, John, 89–90, 96, 319n, 322n
Milnes, Richard Monckton, 91, 319n, 324n
Milsand, J. A., 181, 334n
Minny (or Mini). *See* Thackeray, Harriet Marian
Molyneux, Mr., 56, 121
Monod, Adolphe, 207, 339n
Montefiore, Claude, 256, 350n
Mt. Felix. *See* Sturgis, Mr. and Mrs. Russell
Murchison, Sir Roderick, 127, 325n

Napoleon, 37
Neate, Charles, 129, 325n
Nicholas I, 41, 304n

O'Connell, Daniel, 201, 337n
O'Connell, Morgan, 89, 92, 318n
Oliphant, Mrs. (reviewer), 95, 321n
Onslow Square, Brompton, 114, 138, 144, 148, 209, 304n
Owen, Richard, 129, 325n

Palace Green, 59–60, 84, 117, 195, 210–11, 311n, 316n
Paris, France: ATR in, 29, 38, 43, 48, 200, 209–10, 226; —, with Mrs. C-S, 3, 4, 68, 73, 144, 197, 202, 207; —, with WMT, 123; WMT in, 128
Parker, Mrs. (Parisian friend of Mrs. C-S's), 19, 23, 299n
Payne, James, 343n. Letter to: 231
Pearman, Charles (servant), 40, 55, 125, 126, 147, 206, 304n, 310n
Perry, Kate, 129, 326n
Perry, Sir Thomas, 38, 303n
Pollen, John, 92, 320n
Pollock, Lady Georgina, 349n, 354n. Letter to: 280–81
Prescott, William, 85, 139, 317n, 328n
Prime, Jane, 13, 297n
Prince of Wales, 144, 329n
Prinsep family, 74, 89, 130, 314n, 318n, 326n
Procters, 91, 129, 133–34, 303n, 326n

Quinn, Dr. Frederick, 18, 299n

Rashdale, Mr. (friend of the Thackerays'), 41, 304n
Ray, Gordon, 8, 27, 267
Ritchie, Anne Thackeray (Anny, Mrs. Richmond Ritchie, Lady Ritchie) (ATR), 98–99, 191; birth of, 2; childhood of, 190; critics on, 264–70; death of, 264; and drawing sketches, 9; and guilt, feelings of, 101–2, 107; and Henry James, 221–23, 258–59; and jealousy of HMT, 103–4, 190–91, 192; and journey to Paris in 1840, 4, 104, 130, 189, 197; and profession as a writer, 32, 36, 43; religion of, 30, 43, 68, 139–40, 189, 144–45, 207–8, 305n, 339n; travels of, 77–80, 111–12; and WMT, 10, 31, 227; WMT on, 3, 5–7, 35–36, 119–20, 302n, 311n, 312n; writing style of, 8, 33, 65, 172, 193. Works: *Across the Peat-Fields,* 195, 337n; *Blackstick,* 262; *Chapters,* 224–27; *Elizabeth,* 66–69, 207, 211; *Friend,* 262–63; Introductions to Thackeray's *Works,* 227–28, 248,

260–61, 273–74; *Island*, 171–72; *Jane Austen*, 333n; "Little Scholars," 65–66; *Miss Angel*, 163–64; *Mrs. Dymond*, 102, 214–16; *Old Kensington*, 10, 160, 178, 160–62, 202, 333n; "Out of the World," 69; *Porch*, 262; *Records*, 154–55, 158–59; *Toilers and Spinsters*, 167–69, 331n; *Village*, 155–56, 159–60, 165–66, 180, 194, 214. Letters to: 11–12 (to ATR and HMT from Mrs. C-S); 41–42 (from Mrs. C-S); 83–84, 95–96, 97 (from HMT); 181–82 (from Leslie Stephen); 183 (from Robert Browning); 254–55, 274–75 (from Henry James)

Ritchie, Anne Thackeray, reading of: *L'Ami des enfans*, 201; Bewick, 249; Carlyle, 91, 169–70; Dickens, *Dombey and Son*, 5, 18, 23; —, *Martin Chuzzlewit*, 204; *Journal des desmoiselles*, 200; Lamb, *Letters*, 249; Leslie, *Life*, 276; Martineau, *Deerbrook*, 43; *Monthly Packet*, 242; Oliphant, 242; Schmidt, 200; Scott, *Diary*, 242; —, *The Lay of the Last Minstrel*, 5; Tautphoeus, *At Odds*, 91; Smith, *The Adventures of Mr. Ledbury*, 51–52; Summerly, 200; Wyss, *Swiss Family Robinson*, 14; Yonge, *Daisy Chain*, 242; —, *That Stick*, 242

Ritchie, Anne Thackeray, writing of: 1864–65 Journal, description of, 116, 322n, 323n; —, structure of, 107–9; 1878 Journal, compared with 1864–65 Journal, 187–90, 192–93, 196; —, description of, 335n; notes on Jane Austen, 164–65, 333n; prayer, 118, 330n

Ritchie, Catherine, 335n. Letter to: 283
Ritchie, Charlotte and Jane, 49, 50, 58, 308n
Ritchie, Hester (Codge), 229, 233, 238, 251, 253, 255
Ritchie, Sir Richmond (Wizz), 235, 341n; and ATR, 210, 216–18, 340n; marriage to ATR, 170–71, 185, 192, 208, 259–60; travels of, 253, 255; youth of, 247
Ritchie, William (son of ATR), 213, 219, 243. Letters to: 246–47, 247–48, 249, 250, 250–51, 251–52, 253–54, 255, 256–57
Ritchie, William (cousin of WMT), 53, 309n
Ritchie family, 210, 325n, 328n, 340n
Robertson, Frederick, 144, 329n
Robins, Elizabeth, 220, 345n. Letters to: 237, 279–80
Rome, Italy, 28, 74, 87, 158, 174, 176, 194, 206, 210, 225, 301n
Rose and the Ring, The (WMT), 241, 345n
Ruskin, John, 96, 234, 322n
Russell, Lord John, 144, 329n
Russell, Katie, 74, 81, 313n

Sarah. *See* Gray, Sarah
Sargent, John Singer, 261–62
Sartoris, Adelaide Kemble, 111, 206, 209–10, 229, 318n
Scott, Susan, 15. Letter to: 40–41
Scott family, 25, 40, 299n, 304n
Senior, Mrs. Nassau William, 96, 175, 322n
Shawe, Arthur, 22, 145–46, 150, 314n
Shawe, Isabella. *See* Thackeray, Isabella
Shawe, Jane, 329n. Letter to: 144–46
Siddons, Sarah Kemble, 42, 305n
Sidgwick, Henry, 347n
Sims (servant), 55, 80, 125, 133–34, 137, 139, 147, 310n
Skeffington, Mr. Letter to: 244–45
Smith, George, 86, 265, 317n
Smith, Mrs., 17, 299n
Spencer, Herbert, 249, 348n
Spring-Rice, Stephen, 139, 140, 328n
Stanhope, Philip-Henry, 144, 329n
Stanley, Lady, 328n. Letter to: 141
Stephen, Laura (Memee), 179, 180, 181–82, 184, 186, 187–89, 330n

Stephen, Sir Leslie, 180, 185, 254; ATR on, 174, 177, 184, 186; and *Dictionary of National Biography,* 223–24, 232, 266; marriage of, to Minny, 156–57; *Mausoleum Book,* 188, 223, 266, 331n, 335n. Letters from: 173, 181–82
Stephenson, Mrs., 129, 326n
Stoddart, Mrs. (William?), 310n. Letter to: 54–55
Story, Edy, 46, 301n
Sturgis, Mr. and Mrs. Russell, 73, 74, 75, 76, 81, 313n, 315n
Swinburne, Algernon, 260, 311n
Synge, Henrietta. Letter to: 186
Synge, Robert, 40, 149–50, 304n, 330n
Synge, W. W. F., 53, 64, 304n. Letters to: 73–75, 75–76, 92–94, 146–48, 173, 185, 230–31
Synge, Mrs. W. W. F. Letters to: 81–82, 85–87, 146–48, 149–50

Tennyson, Alfred, Lord, 78, 83, 154–55, 172, 176, 204, 301n, 314n, 316n
Tennyson family, 216, 233, 262, 279–80, 351n
Thackeray, Anne Isabella (Anny). *See* Ritchie, Anne Thackeray
Thackeray, Edward, 23, 53, 84, 147, 247, 300n, 347n
Thackeray, Harriet Marian (Minny, later Mrs. Leslie Stephen) (HMT), 138, 173, 211; appearance of, 205–6, 211–12; ATR on, 50, 90, 142, 151; birth of, 2; as a child, 16–17, 18, 21, 37, 40, 197, 212; death of, 169, 183–84, 209; marriage of, 155, 174. Letter to: 11–12 (to HMT and ATR from Mrs. C-S). Letters from: 49–50, 82–83, 83–84, 94–95, 95–96, 97
Thackeray, Isabella: and ATR, 106–7, 218–19; insanity of, 2–3, 132, 188–89, 196, 200–201, 296n; and WMT, 1, 124. Letters to: 235, 243, 244
Thackeray, Jane, 2, 130, 326n
Thackeray, Margie and Anny, 151, 175, 177, 185, 186, 330n, 336n

Thackeray, Mary, 343–44n. Letter to: 233–34
Thackeray, Richmond, 325n, 328n
Thackeray, William Makepeace (WMT), 72; ATR on, 100–103; on ATR, 3, 5–7, 35–36, 119–20, 132, 302n, 311n, 312n; as a boy, 123, 128; at Cambridge, 115, 140; and *Cornhill Magazine,* 64, 82; death of, 113–14, 126, 146, 183, 301n; description of, by Carlyle, 296n; health of, 27, 29, 59, 73, 75–76, 83, 206; on HMT, 6, 7, 132, 312n; manuscripts of, 244–45, 272, 276, 278, 281; marriage of, 1; at Oxford, 55, 310n; reading Milton's *Epitaph on Shakespeare,* 125; religion of, 121–22; travels of, 37, 41, 202–3, 208; on women, 3, 6, 129. Works: *Boudin,* 245, 347n; *Denis Duval,* 69–70, 92, 131–32, 326–27n; *Henry Esmond,* 131, 179, 199, 335n; lectures, 27–28, 34, 51, 209; *Newcomes,* 33; *Pendennis,* 27, 131; *Philip,* 64, 84, 244–45; *Rose and the Ring,* 206, 347n; *Vanity Fair,* 9, 18, 24, 27, 161–62, 201, 215–16, 300n, 304n, 337–38n; *Virginians,* 33–34, 54, 61–62, 76, 314n, 335n. Letters to: (from HMT) 38–39, 94–95
Thackerays at Bagshot, 44, 306n
Thompson, Henry, 256, 350n
Titmarsh, A. I. (ATR's initials to WMT's nom de plume), 10, 301n
Titmarsh, Mr. (WMT's nom de plume), 19, 299n
Trevelyan, Lady, 93, 320n
Trimmer, Augusta, 48, 307n
Trollope, Anthony, 69, 82, 90, 93–94, 127, 144, 147, 164–66, 315n
Troubridge, Colonel and Mrs., 91, 127, 319n, 325n
Trufitt, Frances, 207, 339n

Vaughan, Virginia, 230, 342n
Vivian, Mrs. (friend of WMT's), 129, 326n

Von Tauchnitz, Baron, 343n. Letter to: 231

Waddell, Mrs. (Wadelle) (acquaintance of the Thackerays'), 16, 298n
Walker, Frederick, 90, 319n, 346n
Walter, John, 127, 325n. Letter to: 230
Watts, George Frederic, 130, 326n
Webb, Colonel Richmond, 248, 348n
West, Sir Algernon, 354n. Letter to: 281–82
Whately, Richard, 178, 333n
Whewell, William, 140, 328n
Whitmore, Mrs. (friend of the Thackerays'), 129, 325–26n

Williams, W. J., 352n. Letter to: 273, 273–74, 274, 276
Windsor, 45
Woolf, Leonard, 259, 353n. Letters to: 276, 277
Woolf, Virginia Stephen, 168–69, 259, 266–69, 276, 277, 351n, 353n; *Night and Day,* 165, 266–67
World War I, 263, 264, 278–79, 354n
Wynne, Eugenie (formerly Crowe), 84–85, 316n

Yates, Edmund, 34, 58, 63–64, 73, 103, 125, 302n, 310–11n, 312n
Yonge, Charlotte, 346n. Letter to: 242

STUDIES IN VICTORIAN LIFE AND LITERATURE
Richard D. Altick, Editor

The Presence of the Present: Topics of the Day in the Victorian Novel
Richard D. Altick

George Eliot's Serial Fiction
Carol A. Martin

Toward a Working-Class Canon: Literary Criticism in British
Working-Class Periodicals, 1816–1858
Paul Thomas Murphy

The Imagined World of Charles Dickens
Mildred Newcomb

The Lion and the Cross: Early Christianity in Victorian Novels
Royal Rhodes

A World of Possibilities: Romantic Irony in Victorian Literature
Clyde de L. Ryals

The Night Side of Dickens: Cannibalism, Passion, Necessity
Harry Stone

Carlyle and the Search for Authority
Chris R. Vanden Bossche